DEVON AND CORNWALL RECORD SOCIETY

New Series, Volume 44

DEVON AND CORNWALL RECORD SOCIETY

New Series, Volume 44

THE HAVENER'S ACCOUNTS OF THE EARLDOM AND DUCHY OF CORNWALL, 1287–1356

Edited by

Maryanne Kowaleski

Exeter
2001

ISBN 0 901853 44 5

Typeset by Mike Dobson, Quince Typesetting
Sabon 10.5/13

Printed and bound in Great Britain
by Short Run Press Ltd, Exeter

Contents

Map

Tables 65

Abbreviations

BPR	*Register of the Black Prince*, 4 vols. London,1930–33
C47	PRO, Chancery Miscellanea
C133	PRO, Chancery Inquisitions Post Mortem
C258	PRO, Chancery Files, Tower and Rolls Chapel Series, Certiorari Cum Causa
C260	PRO, Chancery, Tower and Rolls Chapel Series, Recorda
CChR	*Calendar of Charter Rolls, Henry III–Henry VIII*, 6 vols. London, 1903–27
CCR	*Calendar of Close Rolls, Edward I–Henry VII*, 47 vols. London, 1892–1963
CFF	*Cornish Feet of Fines*, ed. J. Hambley Rowe, 2 vols. Exeter, 1914–50
CFR	*Calendar of Fine Rolls, Edward I–Henry VII*, 22 vols. London, 1911–63
CIM	*Calendar of Inquisitions Miscellaneous*, 7 vols. London, 1916–69
CIPM	*Calendar of Inquisitions Post Mortem, Henry III–Henry IV*, 18 vols. London, 1904–89
CPR	*Calendar of Patent Rolls, Edward I–Henry VII*, 48 vols. London, 1894–1916
CRO	Cornwall Record Office, Truro
CUL	Cambridge University Library
DCO	Duchy of Cornwall Office, London
DCRS	Devon and Cornwall Record Society
DRO	Devon Record Office, Exeter
E36	PRO, Exchequer Treasury of the Receipt, Miscellaneous Books
E101	PRO, Exchequer K. R. Accounts Various

E119	PRO, Exchequer K. R. Accounts of the Revenue of the Earldom of Cornwall
E122	PRO, Exchequer K. R. Customs Accounts
E146	PRO, Exchequer Inquisitions Post Mortem
E152	PRO, Exchequer K. R. Enrolments of Escheators' Inquisitions
E163	PRO, Exchequer K. R. Miscellanea
E306	PRO, Exchequer Augmentation Office, Duchy of Cornwall Records
E356	PRO, Exchequer Enrolled Customs Accounts
E370	PRO, Exchequer L. T. R. Pipe Office, Miscellaneous Rolls
E372	PRO, Exchequer Pipe Rolls
E389	PRO, Exchequer L.T.R. Pipe Office, Miscellanea, New Series
JRIC	*Journal of the Royal Institution of Cornwall*
JUST1	PRO, Justices in Eyre, of Assize, of Oyer and Terminer, and of the Peace, Rolls and Files
LR2	PRO, Miscellaneous Books, Office of the Auditors of Land Revenue and Predecessors
Pipe Roll	Publications of the Pipe Roll Society, 96 vols. London, 1884–2000
PRO	Public Record Office, London
SC6	PRO, Ministers' Accounts
SC11	PRO, Rentals and Surveys, Rolls

Preface and Acknowledgements

From at least the mid-thirteenth century, the earl of Cornwall, the wealthiest and most politically powerful lord in the county, employed a special official—called the havener—to supervise the administration of his maritime profits in the county. When the duchy of Cornwall was created in 1337, the havener's duties were expanded, and he was made a permanent, salaried official. The office of havener, for which there was no parallel in medieval Britain, allowed the duchy to manage and exploit its maritime properties and prerogatives in a particularly efficient manner. The accounts of the havener record this management, and survive in summary form from the late thirteenth century, but in more detailed, separate accounts from the early fourteenth century. In focusing on the seventy years from 1287 to 1356, this edition allows readers to trace the impact on Cornwall of such major events as the Hundred Years War (begun in 1337) and the devastating plague of the Black Death in 1348–9. The annual accounts of the havener also offer a wealth of information on the development and prosperity of individual ports (including Plymouth in Devon), on fishing and the fish trade, on piracy and privateering, on shipwrecks and 'royal' fish such as whale and porpoise, and on the overseas trade in wine, tin, hides and other goods. Particularly fascinating are the glimpses we can see of the Spanish, French, Irish, and English traders, shipmasters, and fishers who visited Cornish shores, and the insights we gain about the people of medieval Cornwall—merchants, fishers, mariners, wreckers, pirates, and even peasants—who made their living from the sea.

Crown copyright material in the Public Record Office is reproduced by permission of the Controller of Her Majesty's Stationary Office. Seven of the havener's accounts, parts of three assession rolls, and the copy of the extent of 1345 are reproduced by kind permission of the Duchy of Cornwall Office. I am grateful to Joanna Mattingly for providing the photograph for the book cover, which is reproduced with the permission of St Neot PCC.

I am deeply grateful to Oliver Padel for helping to identify many of the Cornish place-names and for offering useful comments and suggestions on translating difficult passages in the text. I also acknowledge with thanks the advice of my colleague at Fordham University, Jocelyn Wogan-Browne, on my translations from Anglo-Norman French. Stuart Jenks kindly made available, in advance of publication, his calendar of the enrolled customs accounts (PRO, E356), so that I could include a full range of data in Tables 1 and 2. I also thank Todd Gray, John Brunton of the Devon Record Office, Angela Broome of the Courtney Library of the Royal Institution of Cornwall, Harold Fox, Stuart Jenks, Christine North of the Cornwall Record Office, Mark Page, David Postles, and Richard Unger for answering queries that came up during the course of writing this volume. Finally, I acknowledge with deep gratitude the long-standing guidance and support of Margery Rowe, who located a suitable illustration for the cover and guided the book through the press as editor of the Devon and Cornwall Record Society. Her sound advice and expertise—always delivered with good cheer, generosity, and undue modesty—for this project, as well as my earlier work on Devon, make her the model archivist-scholar, to whom I and all researchers of south-western England owe much.

Maryanne Kowaleski
New York City
December 2001

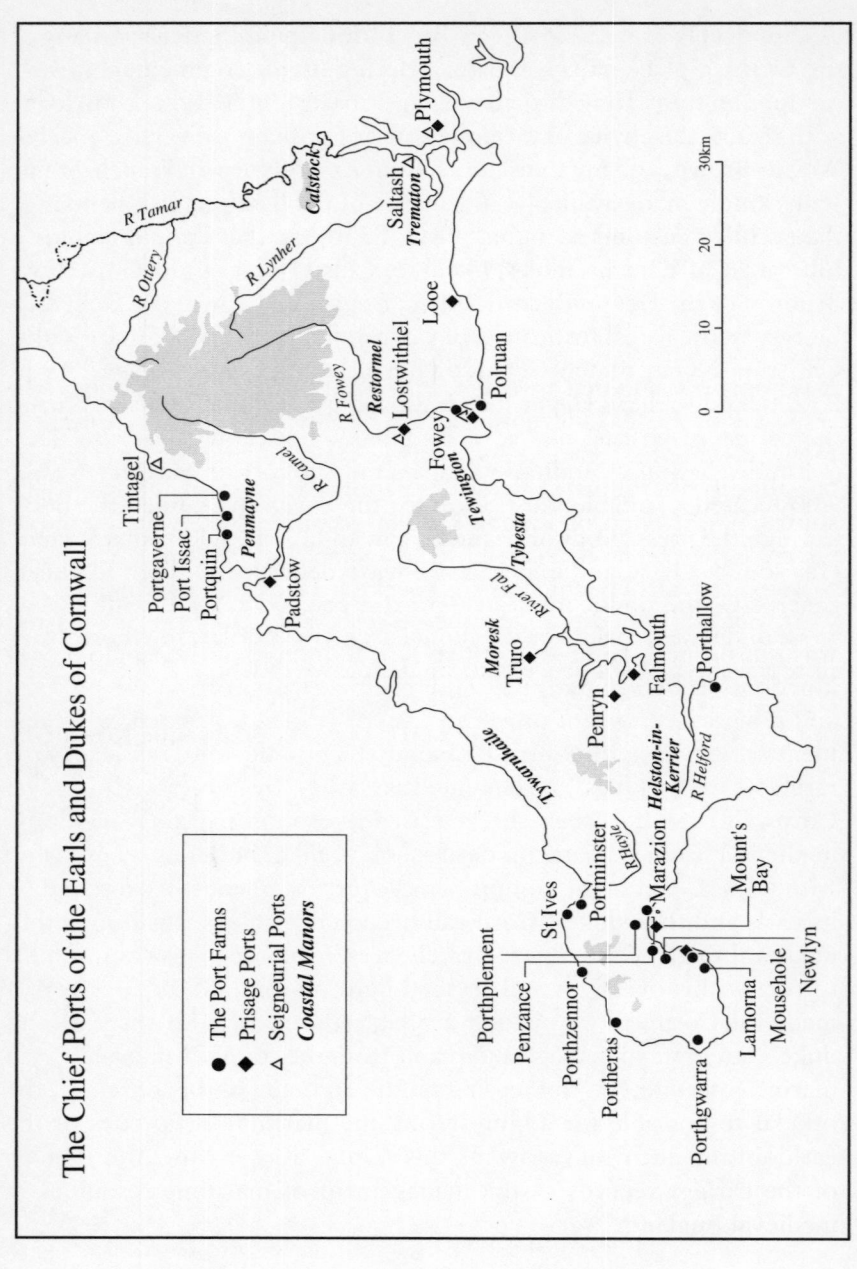

The Chief Ports of the Earls and Dukes of Cornwall

Introduction

It is not surprising that special officials and institutions to manage the resources of the sea evolved so early in Cornwall, the most maritime of England's counties. Surrounded on three sides by water, with the longest coastline in the country, Cornwall's peninsular location at the extreme southwestern edge of England made communication by sea more effective than by land. Visited by the ancient Romans (and, according to some, by the Phoenicians too) seeking to export its valuable tin, Cornwall was nonetheless conquered relatively late by the Saxons and was not brought firmly into the political control of the Anglo-Saxon kingdom of Wessex until the tenth century. Distant from the political and religious centres of power in eastern England, isolated by its residents' reliance on the Cornish tongue well into the fourteenth century, rarely visited by kings, and lamented as 'savage' by its bishops, medieval Cornwall has often been characterised as a poor, marginal region by medieval chroniclers and modern scholars alike. But in its relationship with the sea, and in the comprehensive territorial control exercised by its earls and then dukes, Cornwall occupied a unique position within medieval England that has too rarely been explored. This volume aims to rectify this oversight and to shed light on the maritime history of medieval Cornwall by making available the records of the earl and duke's attempts to manage and profit from the county's unusually rich marine environment. In focusing on the accounts of the 'havener', the official responsible for administering the maritime properties of the earldom and duchy of Cornwall, this volume also provides translations of the earliest records of the management of maritime resources in medieval England.

Maritime Administration under the Earldom of Cornwall

Although no charter specifically granting custody of the ports of

1

Cornwall survives until 1333,[1] earlier references imply that a range of maritime rights were vested in the earls of Cornwall by virtue of their tenure of the earldom. Earl Reginald de Dunstanville (*c.* 1141–75), for example, granted the right to wreck in the Scillies to a cell of Tavistock Abbey in the islands, reserving for himself stranded whales and whole ships.[2] And when the earldom was in the hands of the king, as it was during the reign of John (1199–1216), profits from wreck and royal fish (stranded whale, sturgeon, or porpoise) in Cornwall were recorded in the pipe rolls, the Exchequer's annual accounts of each county's revenues and expenses.[3] From at least 1199, the kings periodically appointed keepers of the sea to guard their maritime interests in coastal regions, particularly in Cornwall and Devon, where sheriffs were required to report to the keeper in all things pertaining to the seacoast,

---

[1] A grant of further lands to John de Eltham in 1333 (*CChR 1327–41*, pp. 302–3) is the first charter to single out custody of the ports ('all the profits of the king's harbours in Cornwall, with wreck of sea and the prise and customs of wines in the said county and in the water of Sutton, co. Devon'); earlier grants to John de Eltham do not note specific maritime revenues (*ibid*, p. 233), nor do grants of the earldom to Earl Richard (*CPR 1216–25*, p. 507; *CPR 1225–32*, p. 3; *CChR, 1226–57*, p. 139) and Piers de Gaveston (*CChR 1300–26*, pp. 108, 131), although the inquisition post mortem of Edmund does refer to specific maritime revenues (below, n. 10) and the second charter to Gaveston notes wreck of sea. There is no extant charter granting the earldom to Edmund, who inherited the title from his father ("Chronicon vulgo dictum Chronicon Thomae Wykes", in *Annales Monastici*, vol. IV, ed. H. R. Luard (London, Rolls Series, 1869), p. 251). The 1337 charter creating the duchy of Cornwall for the Black Prince singles out 'prisages and customs of wine in the same county of Cornwall; also all profits of our ports within the same county of Cornwall belonging to us, together with wreck of sea, as well as of whale and sturgeon, and of other fishes which belong to us, by reason of our prerogative, as other things whatsoever to such wreck of the sea, in anywise pertaining, in all the aforesaid county of Cornwall…and prisages and customs of wine in Cornwall in the water of Sutton, in the same county of Devon….' For the text of this charter, see *The Trial at Bar, Rowe v. Brenton,* ed. George Concanen (London, 1831), Appendix, pp. 38–9.

[2] *Monasticon Anglicanum*, ed. W. Dugdale (London, 6 vols., 1817–30), II, p. 501.

[3] For example, *Pipe Roll, 1177–78*, p. 17; *Pipe Roll 1181–82*, p. 83; *Pipe Roll 1184–85*, p. 202; *Pipe Roll 1185–86*, p. 148; *Pipe Roll 1186–87*, p. 155; *Pipe Roll 1202*, p. 168. The pipe rolls omit any section on Cornwall from 1158 to 1175, when Earl Reginald held the county, and from about 1213 to 1221, when it was farmed to Henry, son of Earl Reginald (and, for a brief period, to Robert de Cardinam, the sheriff). Nor do details about Cornish revenues appear in the pipe rolls during the tenure of Earl Richard (1227–72) or his son, Earl Edmund (1272–1300).

including investigations of those seizing wreck illegally.[4] These duties paralleled those of the haveners, who were first named as such during the tenure of Earl Richard (1225–72) when they were recorded levying customs from those drying fish on shore, taking tolls from fish sellers arriving with boats, and collecting profits from wrecks.[5] During the time of Earl Edmund (1272–1300), the haveners also collected wreck profits and carried out judgements on indicted mariners. Earl Edmund himself claimed that his rights to shipswrecks, prisage of wine, customs on drying fish on shore, and customs on fish sellers arriving by boat all dated back to the time of his father, Earl Richard.[6]

The annexation of specific maritime rights to the earldom probably stemmed from royal grants of the whole of the county of Cornwall to the earliest earls. King John, for example, granted 'the county of Cornwall, with its demesnes and appurtenances' to Henry Fitz Count, son of Earl Reginald, in 1215; this grant was most likely the one cited by Earl Edmund in his claim to the custody of ports and other rights during the *quo warranto* proceedings of 1284.[7] But confirmations of this grant indicate that the right to hold the *comitatus Cornubiae* (which can be translated as either the 'county' or 'earldom' of Cornwall) can be traced back to at least the mid-twelfth century (during the time of Earl Reginald) and into the early and mid-thirteenth century, during the tenure of Earl Richard.[8] No extant charter enumerates the full range of maritime revenues collected by Earl Richard in Cornwall,[9] but the accounts of Earl Edmund for 1287–8 and 1296/7 refer to profits from wreck, prisage of wine, and 'marine issues', while surveys

4. *Pipe Roll 1199*, p. 242; *CPR 1216–25*, p. 468; *Rotuli litterarum clausarum in Turri Londinensi asservati*, ed. T. D. Hardy (London, 1833–44), II, p. 12; *Rotuli litterarum patentium in Turri Londinensi asservati, 1201–1216*, ed. T. D. Hardy (London, 1835), I, pp. 83; *Pipe Roll 1211*, pp. 186–7. Keepers of the sea were also appointed for other coastal regions.
5. For references to the early haveners, see Appendix II.
6. PRO, JUST1/112, mm. 2d, 3d; JUST1/116, m. 1. See also *Rotuli hundredorum*, ed. W. Illingworth and J. Caley (London, 1812–18), I, pp. 56–7.
7. *Rotuli litterarum patentium*, p. 155. For Earl Edmund's claim, see PRO, JUST1/112, m. 3d.
8. *CPR 1216–25*, pp. 30, 266–7, 507; *CChR, 1226–57*, p. 139.
9. For the little that is known of the administration of the estates of Earl Richard, see N. Denholm-Young, *Richard of Cornwall* (New York, 1947), pp. 162–70.

summarising Edmund's holdings when he died in 1300 specify customs on boats, wreck of sea, and prisage of wine.[10]

This proliferation of references to different types of maritime revenues during the second half of the thirteenth century reflects the greater control the earls were beginning to exert over their Cornish estates.[11] Although their motives for tightening their grip on these estates were probably similar to those of other landlords seeking to profit from the commercialisation of agriculture at this time, the opportunities for maritime profits in Cornwall, with its long stretch of coastline and abundant fisheries, were significantly greater than elsewhere in the kingdom, as the earls and their chief ministers clearly recognised. Nowhere else in England did maritime management develop as fully, nor did special officials to manage marine profits emerge as early. The palatinates of Chester and Durham, the only comparable estates to the earldom and duchy of Cornwall in size and jurisdiction, kept track of their profits of wreck, wine prisage, and port customs, but their maritime management was less precocious and was never as centralised as it was in Cornwall.[12]

---

[10] PRO, C133/95, mm. 3d–4 (abstract printed in *CIPM*, vol. 3, p. 457); PRO, E146/6, m. 2. The custom of boats was worth £13 6s 8d per year, the issues of the sea with wreck were worth £40, and the prisage of wine £20. The phrase 'and with the fee farms underwritten in the county aforesaid' added after one list of these rights in his inquisition post mortem may refer to the port farms enrolled at the beginning of the havener's accounts. For the accounts of 1287–8 and 1296/7, see below, Part I.

[11] Since the documentation for Earl Richard's administration is so scarce, and that for Earl Edmund relatively sparse, the main evidence for changes in their exploitation of the estates comes from complaints against 'new' tolls or the earl's failure to honour 'old' liberties, as voiced in the eyre rolls, hundred rolls, and *quo warranto* rolls, as cited below (n. 18, 20). It is significant that over half of these complaints centre on maritime issues. Administrative re-organization, such as combining the offices of steward and sheriff, was perhaps another sign of the earls' increasing attention to their Cornish estates; see Denholm-Young, *Richard*, p. 164; L. Margaret Midgley, ed., *Ministers' Accounts of the Earldom of Cornwall 1296–1297* (Camden Society, 3rd series, vols. 66, 67, 1942 –45), I, pp. xxix–xxx.

[12] See, for example, G. H. Lapsley, *The County Palatine of Durham: A Study in Constitutional History* (Cambridge, MA, 1900), pp. 275–6, 310–11, 317–26; *Accounts of the Chamberlain and Other Officers of the County of Chester 1301–1360*, ed. Ronald Stewart-Brown (Lancashire and Cheshire Record Society, vol. 59, 1910).

The earls' growing interest in maritime management was also influenced by mounting awareness of the strategic value of the maritime location of Cornwall. The English kings certainly understood the strategic importance of the county's proximity and seawards access to Flanders, France, and Spain, as well as to Wales and Ireland, where the English were trying to consolidate their political interests. Henry III specifically called upon Earl Richard to guard the Cornish coasts against invasion from France,[13] while Edward II was supposedly prompted by concern about the ease with which an invading fleet could land in remote Cornwall when he took back the county from Queen Isabella in 1324 for the security of the realm.[14] Cornwall's long stretches of isolated coastline also raised anxieties about the ease of smuggling there, while its distance from English centres of power helped promote the idea of Cornwall—like Wales, Scotland, and Ireland—as somehow 'outside the realm'.[15] As for the earls, their appreciation of the strategic value of Cornish maritime properties is evident in Earl Richard's acquisition of the important castles of Restormel in 1268, and Trematon in 1270, both of which appear to have been 'forced purchases', made to strengthen his position in the county after the Barons' War, during which he had temporarily lost control of his Cornish possessions.[16] These acquisitions included authority over the lower reaches of the Fowey and Tamar rivers, Plymouth harbour (then called 'Sutton Water'), and the boroughs and ports of Saltash and Lostwithiel, along with other coastal properties.[17]

[13.] *CCR 1259–61*, p. 285.

[14.] Although Edward's reason was probably a pretext, it is significant that he highlighted this concern as a justification; *CFR 1319–1327*, p. 300.

[15.] *CFR 1337–1347*, p. 414. On the point of Cornwall's 'otherness' and distinctive 'national' identity, see also Mark Stoyle, "The Dissidence of Despair: Rebellion and Identity in Early Modern Cornwall", *Journal of British Studies*, 38 (1999), pp. 423–44.

[16.] Mark Page, "Cornwall, Earl Richard, and the Barons' War", *English Historical Review*, 115 (2000), pp. 32–5; N. J. G. Pounds, "The Duchy Palace at Lostwithiel", *Archaeological Journal*, 136 (1979), pp. 203–5. See also L. E. Elliott-Binns, *Medieval Cornwall* (London, 1955), pp. 160–1. The Trematon properties had once belonged to the earldom, but had been granted away to the Valletorts by Robert de Mortain.

[17.] PRO, E36/57, ff. 15v, 33–33v, 52v; *A Descriptive Catalogue of Ancient Deeds in the Public Record Office* (London, 1906), V, p. 54. Richard had acquired or recovered other coastal properties in earlier decades, including Tintagel and part of Tywarnhaile; see O. J. Padel, "Tintagel in the Twelfth and Thirteenth Centuries', *Cornish Studies*, 16 (1988), pp. 61–6; Page, 'Cornwall', pp. 23–4.

Other signs of the earls' increasing interest in their maritime resources included the appointment of special officials to supervise maritime revenues and expenses, the imposition of new charges on fishermen and the fisheries, and more vigorous enforcement of the earls' rights to wreck. The first official termed 'havener' appeared around the early 1270s, when Richard of Cornwall was earl.[18] By 1287, during the tenure of Richard's son, Earl Edmund, an additional official, responsible for keeping the seashore and coastal manors in northern Cornwall, was also active.[19] At around the same time complaints about the harsher administration of maritime revenues began to surface, which continued into the tenure of Earl Edmund. Cornish residents objected to 'new customs' imposed on those drying fish on shore or bringing fish to shore for sale, to 'new customs' assessed on dealers in fish, 'new fees' on sand barges and passenger ferries, and to the way the earl's bailiffs ignored long-standing liberties to force undue exactions on the fisheries of Cornwall.[20] Representatives of the king himself objected to the widening powers of the earl in collecting the profits of wreck throughout the county, as well as restrictions the earls' bailiffs placed on royal escheators and coroners.[21] Their objections had little effect, however, since the earl suffered no diminution of his rights. Indeed, it was during Earl Edmund's tenure that the specific sources of maritime revenue were spelled out more clearly in surviving accounts, in the eyre courts, and in his own inquisition post mortem.[22]

The first extant account of the maritime revenues of the earldom to offer full details appears in the pipe roll of 1300/1.[23] In this and subsequent accounts, revenues from several different marine prerogatives are recorded: 1) the port 'farms' (the rent paid for the right to collect the earl's revenues in a specific place) for fifteen seaports; 2) fines on pillagers of wrecks and profits from items of wreck sold (including royal fishes); 3) 'trantery', a toll paid by dealers in fish; 4)

---

18. PRO, JUST1/112, m. 2d; *Rotuli hundredorum*, I, p. 56. See also Appendix II, below, for references to the early haveners.
19. Wages for the 'serjeant' or 'bailiff to keep the sea-shore' and manors of Tybesta, Moresk, Tewington, and neighbouring manors were usually entered under the manor of Tybesta; see Part I, below, passim.
20. PRO, JUST1/112, m. 2d, 3d; JUST1/116, m. 1; JUST1/118, mm. 53, 56d, 68, 68d, 69; PRO, E370/9/1; *Rotuli hundredorum*, I, pp. 56, 76–7. 81.
21. PRO, JUST1/112, m. 3d; PRO E370/9/1.
22. See above, n. 10.
23. Below, Part I.

fines assessed on those forestalling fish (that is, retailing fish they had not caught themselves); 5) maritime courts; and 6) miscellaneous fines and perquisites, including forfeited goods and tolls charged on those drying fish on the earl's shore.[24] A seventh item, profits from prisage of wine, was noted in the account of 1287–8, but does not appear again until 1336, when the earldom became a duchy and the collection of prisage wines was centralised in the hands of the duchy's havener.[25] In several years, there were also small fines collected from mariners for salvage of items found from shipwrecks.[26]

Besides the marine revenues attached to the lordship of Cornwall, the earls also enjoyed a variety of maritime profits stemming from their seigneurial lordship of individual estates.[27] The most valuable of these were attached to the honour of Trematon (acquired from the Valletorts in 1270) and included the Saltash ferry; tolls on the collection of oysters, seine fishing, barges carrying sand, and boats in Tamar Water; Lynher fishery; and the issues (from maritime courts and customs on fishers) of Sutton Pool, the medieval harbour of Plymouth. Also profitable were the prerogatives associated with the castle of Restormel, which Earl Richard purchased in 1268; these included customs on ships in Fowey Water, the fishery in Fowey Water, and the maritime courts at Lostwithiel, which became the administrative capital of the earldom and duchy.[28] Trantery and wreck profits also occasionally appear under individual manors or, in one case, in the section on hundreds.[29]

[24.] These fines disappear from the accounts by 1307, a development perhaps linked to the acquisition of the earldom by Piers de Gaveston that year, and the succession of short-term lords until the creation of the duchy in 1337.

[25.] Prisage is mentioned in the account for September 1336 (printed below in Part I), but nothing was collected from it during the short time of the account. It is also noted as a prerogative of the duchy in *The Caption of Seisin of the Duchy of Cornwall (1337)*, ed. P. L. Hull (DCRS, n.s., vol. 17, 1971), p. 138, and below, Appendix I. Butlerage is recorded in the royal customs accounts for 1322–24 (below, Appendix III).

[26.] Fines 'for having aid' were noted in the accounts for 1301/2 and 1302/3 (below, Part I).

[27.] In addition to the honours of Restormel and Trematon (which included very profitable fisheries and weirs at Calstock, and a ferry across the Tamar), the earldom also held the custom on boats at Tintagel, and fisheries at Tybesta and Tewington.

[28.] For the acquisition of Restormel and Trematon, see above, p. 5. For the full extent of the fees and other properties attached to these honours, see Hull, ed., *Caption of Seisin*, pp. xi–xvii, xxiixxiii.

[29.] See below, pp. 47, n. 161, 173, 184, 201.

After the death of Earl Edmund in 1300, lordship of the earldom passed through several different hands, remaining with no one person for long and undergoing no fundamental changes in administration. The earldom at first reverted to King Edward I because Edmund had no heirs, but its management altered little since the same steward, Thomas de la Hyde, continued to account to the Exchequer from at least 1297, when Earl Edmund was still alive, to 1312, during which time the earldom passed through the hands of Edward I, Edward II, and Piers de Gaveston.[30] During this period, other individuals called 'havener' and 'bailiff of the ports' accounted for the issues of the ports to the steward. They included William Talcarn and Alan Wolwayn, both of whom seem to have had connections to Cornwall.[31] Even during the tumultuous tenure of Peter de Gaveston—who was granted the earldom by Edward II in 1307 soon after the death of Edward I, lost it when forced into exile by Parliament, and regained it from 1309 to 1312, when he was executed—there was no apparent alteration in the administration of the county.[32] In the period after Gaveston's death, however, there was a rapid succession of haveners and stewards (only

---

[30] *CIPM*, vol. III, p. 456. Seven accounts survive from this period, printed below, Part I. De la Hyde died around 1312 himself, since his son and heir accounted for him for a six-week period in 1312 (PRO, E372/158, m. 46) after which the king granted the stewardship to John de Bedowynde.

[31] Talcarn is noted in the eyre roll of 1302, but in a context that makes it unclear exactly when he was active; see PRO JUST1/118, mm. 53, 69; his name suggests he was a Cornishman. Wolwayn was also probably a local man, and the first for whom an official appointment survives; for references to both haveners, see below, Appendix II.

[32] *CChR 1300–26*, p. 108; *CCR 1307–13*, p. 225; *CPR 1307–13*, p. 187. For further details on these grants and Gaveston's fortunes, see Pierre Chaplais, *Piers Gaveston, Edward II's Adoptive Brother* (Oxford, 1994), especially pp. 27–34, 45–8, 68, 80. For Gaveston's benign administration of Cornwall, see J. S. Hamilton, *Piers Gaveston Earl of Cornwall 1307–1312: Politics and Patronage in the Reign of Edward II* (Detroit, 1988), pp. 39–43. Although the initial grants make no mention of maritime revenues, the second grant (*CChR 1300–26*, p. 131) does single out wreck of sea. Gaveston was also granted prisage of wine at Dartmouth and other Devon ports (*CPR 1307–13*, p. 200; *Foedera, conventiones, literae, et cuiuscumque generis Acta Publica inter Reges Angliae*, ed. T. Rymer (London, 4 vol. in 7, 1816–69), II, i, p. 98). Gaveston's widow, Margaret, retained the title of 'countess of Cornwall' (see, for example, *CFR 1327–37*, p. 214) and petitioned for the return of the county to her and her second husband (*Rotuli parliamentorum* (London, 6 vols., 1783), I, p. 453; *CPR 1317–21*, p. 251; *CCR 1318–23*, p. 143) although Parliament had revoked all grants to her first husband in 1318.

a few of who enjoyed custody of the ports). Edward II granted the shrievalty and stewardship of Cornwall to five different men from 1312 to 1317,[33] and during this same period farmed out the custody of the ports, for relatively short periods, to several others, including Thomas Algar, styled 'havener' and 'keeper of the waters of the king's ports in Cornwall;' Wynand Tyrel jr, who was obliged to pay an extra 30s beyond the normal amount rendered to the Exchequer for the ports; and Thomas Leygrave.[34] This rapid succession of stewards and haveners, few of whom had any connection to Cornwall, reflects quick profit-taking on the part of Edward II, as well as an appreciation of the separate source of income and administration now associated with custody of the ports.

In 1317, Edward II granted his wife, Isabella of France, the shrievalty, manors, hundreds, and other issues of Cornwall as recompense for another part of her dower that she had surrendered.[35] Only one account of the issues of the ports survives for the period of her lordship, which also includes her appointment of Henry de Guldeford as 'keeper of the havens in Cornwall'.[36] Edward II withdrew the Cornish lands from her

---

[33.] To John de Bedewynde in July 1312–Jan. 1313 (*CFR 1307–19*, pp. 139, 160–1); Thomas le Ercedekne in Jan. 1313 to November 1314 (*ibid.*, pp. 161, 221); Richard de Polhampton in Nov. 1314–Nov. 1315 (*ibid*, pp. 221, 262); Richard de Hewish in September 1315–May 1316 (*ibid*, pp. 262, 275, 278–9); Henry de Wylington in May 1316–July 1317 (*ibid.*, pp. 278–9). Although all accounted to the Exchequer for the profits of the county (below, Part I), only the grants for Hewish and Wylington specifically noted custody of the ports. Three other individuals received separate grants of the custody of the ports, one of whom, Thomas Algar, was called 'havener' (see below, Appendix II, for further details). Some of the other coastal properties were farmed separately as this time (PRO, E372/158, m. 46d, printed below, Part I; and PRO, SC6/811/11, 15).

[34.] Tyrel was probably a Cornishman, but the others were not. For references, see below, Appendix II.

[35.] *CPR 1317–21*, pp. 5, 8–9, 233, 268. The revenues were surrendered to her attorneys, William de Polleborne and John Thweyt, on 5 July 1317 (PRO, SC6/811/7, m. 1, printed below, Part I).

[36.] PRO, E389/62 (printed below, Part I); most of the documents in this holding class, formed only in 1995, were once part of E370. It is possible that other details of the issues of Cornwall are in one of her other surviving accounts, but a spot check of the ministers' accounts most likely to yield such information (PRO, SC6/1090/ 12, 13, and 14, and E389/54–65) provide no details beyond sums collected and this one account for 1322/3. For Guldeford, see Appendix II, below. For problems connected with her collection of prisage and butlerage, see below, n. 98.

in 1324, on the pretext that the king needed to control a region subject
to invasion by sea, but her son, Edward III, re-granted these lands to
her in 1327. She held Cornwall until 1330, when she fell out of favour
again and Edward III took the county back into his own hands.[37] In the
ten months that Edward III held the earldom, he treated the maritime
prerogatives much as his father had when the earldom was in his hands
by appointing, during pleasure, three different stewards and two
different haveners. One of the haveners, William de London, king's
sergeant and tailor to Queen Philippa, wife of Edward III, sub-farmed
the profits of the ports to another man, another indication of the
commercialisation of this maritime prerogative.[38]

In 1331, Edward III granted the estates associated with the earldom
to his brother, John de Eltham, upon whom he had conferred the title
of earl of Cornwall in 1328.[39] John did not receive the maritime
properties until 1333, however, in a charter that was the first to include
a specific reference to custody of the ports, in itself a significant
acknowledgement of the income-generating capacity of the Cornish
ports.[40] The first extant assessment roll for the earldom (1333), which
describes some but not all of the maritime properties, also dates from
this period.[41] The earldom was in the hands of John (d. 1336) for only

---

[37.] Her surrender is in: *CFR 1319–27*, pp. 300, 302–3, 308. For the re-grant, see
Anc. Deeds, I, p. 23; *CPR 1322–7*, p. 346. For her loss of Cornwall in 1330, see
CFR 1327–37, pp. 48, 204; *CPR 1330–4*, pp. 22, 23. For general background
on her changing financial arrangements, see also Hilda Johnstone, "The Queen's
Household", in T. F. Tout, ed., *Chapters in the Administrative History of
Mediaeval England* (Manchester, 1930), V, pp. 241–9, 274–8; and idem, "The
Queen's Household", in James F. Willard and William A. Morris, eds. *The English
Government at Work, 1327–1336* (Cambridge, MA, 1940), I, pp. 250–99.

[38.] William de Beauchamp was steward and sheriff (*CFR 1327–37*, p. 223) from
Dec. 1330 to Jan. 1331. Robert de Bilkemore was keeper of Cornwall for only
a few months (*ibid.*, pp. 223, 247–8) before William de Botreaux took over as
steward (*ibid.*, p. 200). For their accounts, see below, Part I. For references to
the haveners, see below, Appendix II. John Croth', the sub-farmer, accounted
to the steward of Cornwall, William de Botreaux in 1331–33 (below, Part I).

[39.] *CChR 1327–41*, p. 233.

[40.] *CChR 1327–41*, pp. 233, 302–3; and see above, n. 1. There are four very short
accounts for September 1331 to October 1333 when Cornwall was in the hands
of the king (printed below, Part I) and only two accounts date from the tenure
(covering 1333–4) of Earl John (below, Part I).

[41.] See below, Appendix I, for more on assessment rolls and extracts from them
relating to the maritime properties.

a few years, whereupon it reverted to Edward III for lack of heirs.[42] Edward used the estates to endow the newly-created duchy of Cornwall, which he bestowed upon his oldest son, Edward Woodstock, better known as the Black Prince. The charter of creation included specific references to the profits from prisage and custom of wines, the ports in Cornwall, wreck of sea and royal fish, and prisage and customs of wines in Plymouth and Dartmouth harbours.[43] These maritime prerogatives were further enumerated in the Caption of Seisin, a detailed survey of the duchy's Cornish holdings that was compiled a few months later.[44] Although modelled after the assession roll of 1333, the Caption of Seisin offered a far more nuanced assessment of the maritime properties, laying out not only the types of revenues that could be expected, but also the valuation of each type of profit, including the farms rendered by each port. It also recited the charter of Edward III appointing Thomas Fitz Henry as havener for good service to Earl John and in fulfilment of the earl's promise.[45] This appointment of a salaried manager in 1337, along with the fully articulated description and valuation of the maritime 'estate' of the duchy of Cornwall, represents the culmination of the development of the maritime administration of the earldom. Indeed, the scope and administration of the maritime revenues remained in much the same form for the rest of the middle ages, undergoing no fundamental changes even into the early modern period.[46]

The Haveners and Their Duties

The earldom's early haveners were often Cornish men. Most appear to have been prominent freeholders, although only one, John de Lambrun,

---

[42.] After Earl John's death, Edward III briefly granted custody of Cornwall to John Hamely, at his pleasure (*CFR 1337–47*, p. 2). The last account of the earldom covers about two weeks in 1336 (below in Part I).

[43.] *CChR 1327–41*, pp. 399–401; *Rowe v. Brenton*, pp. 36–44.

[44.] *Caption of Seisin*, especially pp. ix–x, lvi–lvii, 136–40. For a translation of the sections dealing with maritime properties, see below, Appendix I.

[45.] The original appointment is in *CFR 1337–47*, p. 4. For more details on Fitz Henry and his tenure as havener, see Campbell, 'Haveners', pp. 113–15.

[46.] Campbell, "Haveners". See also Tony Carne, "Foreshore and Fundus", in *The Duchy of Cornwall*, ed. Crispin Gill (Newton Abbot, 1987), pp. 178–93. For the later history of the duchy, albeit with few references to the haveners or maritime properties, see Mary Coate, "The Duchy of Cornwall: Its History and Administration 1640 to 1660", *Transactions of the Royal Historical Society*, 4th series, 10 (1927), pp. 135– 69.

was from a knightly family.[47] Starting in 1313, however, the men appointed as haveners were usually outsiders, who served at the pleasure of the king and usually had some connection to the royal court. There is no evidence that these early fourteenth-century haveners ever did more than collect the profits of the office. Presumably they farmed out the duties attached to the bailiwick to local men in Cornwall and operated with the help of deputies, such as the bailiff who watched over the coastal manors and collected the farms of the ports in northern Cornwall, in exchange for an annual stipend.[48] This change in the type of men who served as haveners probably reflects the more distant lordship of the Crown during much of this period, as well as the Crown's interest in using the maritime prerogatives as a source of royal patronage.[49]

When Edward III appointed the first havener of the duchy, Thomas Fitz Henry, he did so in fulfilment of a promise that Earl John de Eltham had made to Fitz Henry. The first duke, Edward, the Black Prince, honoured the appointment, which actually came a month before the estates of the earldom were attached to the duchy. Fitz Henry loyally served the prince as havener for some 35 years, until his death around 1373. Although probably not a Cornishman, he resided in Cornwall during this period, most likely at Fowey, where a tenement called 'Havener's Place' was located in the fifteenth century.[50] Well over half of Fitz Henry's successors had Cornish connections, but a fair

---

[47.] For this and the following, see the evidence presented in Appendix II.

[48.] The annual stipend was 53s 4d, but by around 1308/9 (account printed below, Part I), it seems to have dropped to 40s. See also Appendix II, below. For the accounts of deputy haveners at Mount's Bay, Falmouth, and Fowey in 1402/3, see PRO, SC6/819/13, m. 12. In 1405/6, the havener's account also included wages paid to bailiffs at Mount's Bay, St Ives, and *Terartu* (PRO, SC6/820/1).

[49.] This change may also be in part a result in the types of sources used to identify the haveners; see Appendix II, below, for a discussion of this point.

[50.] There were several Fitz Henry families active in early and mid thirteenth-century Cornwall (*CFF*, pp. 25–6, 93, 145–6, 151–2), but none in the fourteenth century. It is possible that Thomas Fitz Henry had connections in Cheshire where the lands of Sir Henry Filz Henri (Thomas Fitz Henry's surname was often spelled this way) were taken into the prince's hands in 1346 (*BPR*, I, p. 22). Thomas Fitz Henry was also sometimes called 'Thomas Havener' (for instance, the account of 1341/2, under 'Messengers'). In 1347, 'Thomas le Havener of Fowey' served as a customs collector (PRO, E356/5, m. 12), although there was also a custom collector at Mount's Bay called 'Thomas le Havener, bailiff of Mousehole', who was probably the same man. Campbell ("Haveners", pp. 114–15) also thinks Fitz Henry lived in Fowey. For 'Havener's Place', see CRO, CA/B46/6.

proportion were merely royal appointments to the highest bidder.[51] Like many of the early fourteenth-century haveners, these royal appointments were at the king's pleasure and made to men who fulfilled their duties with the use of deputies. In one long period, from 1415 to 1453, moreover, the office of havener was farmed to individuals who owed no accounting at all to the Exchequer.

Unlike his predecessors and most of his successors, Fitz Henry's appointment was for life, not during pleasure. And, unlike most of his predecessors, he did not farm the revenues but received a salary for managing them on behalf of the duke. His fee, 10 marks a year (£6 16s 4d) was the sum most of the medieval haveners received, except for a brief period when it was reduced to £4. Fitz Henry's original grant also gave him a robe each year, or one mark (13s 4d) in lieu of the robe, but the duke's auditors began disallowing the robe within a year, despite Thomas Fitz Henry's repeated claims to the contrary.[52] Only a few of the haveners who followed Fitz Henry were also granted life appointments, but most did collect a salary, and some also received the robe promised to Fitz Henry.[53] Other rewards did come his way, however, including a gift of venison in 1351 and, in 1361, after almost 25 years of service, the lucrative office of weigher of tin in Cornwall, as well as custody of the tinners' gaol, prerogatives that most of his successors also enjoyed.[54] Fitz Henry, like many medieval officeholders, also supplemented his salary with fees and, on occasion, with extortions which drew the attention of the duke when they began to cut into his profits.[55]

The surviving account rolls indicate that the responsibilities of the earldom's haveners were similar to those held by Thomas Fitz Henry and later haveners. Among the havener's most important duties, in

---

[51.] See Campbell, "Haveners", for this and the following.

[52.] In the account of 1338/9, the auditors claimed Fitz Henry had no warrant for the robe (even though the charter granting it was inserted into the Caption of Seisin of 1337). Thereafter the havener claimed it each year, and the auditors disallowed it. It made no difference that from 1348/9 on, the auditors noted that no robe was to be allowed per an order of the Black Prince's council made on 25 January 1349, or that in the accounts of 1353/4 and 1355/6, the auditors noted that the council's decision of 1349 stipulated that the havener should take his robe from the Prince's wardrobe rather than claiming it as an expense on his account, a provision that had first been mentioned in the account of 1344/5.

[53.] See Campbell, "Haveners", pp. 115–20 for this and the following.

[54.] *BPR*, II, pp. 15, 185.

[55.] See below, notes 59 and 61.

terms of profits, was supervising the collection of the earl or duke's
share of wrecks in Cornwall, including fines levied on wreckers—local
pillagers who carried away the cargo or parts of the ship that washed
ashore. Up until the early fourteenth century, chief tithing men usually
reported wreck profits when they appeared before the justices of the
eyre, while the sheriff, steward, or coroner carried out inquisitions
when disputes arose.[56] With the decline of the eyre courts, the tithing
men appear to have accounted more directly to their local reeve or to
the bailiff of the hundred, who in turn reported to the havener, who in
turn recorded the sums in his account.[57] Another change was the
temporary disappearance of fines on wreckers from the accounts of
1305 to about 1350, perhaps due to the rapid turnover of haveners
during much of this time; most of these haveners appear to have farmed
out the office and lacked the authority to enforce fines on wreckers, a
particularly recalcitrant group of profiteers.[58] Indeed, the earnings from
wreck even proved a temptation to the officials in charge of investigating
shipwrecks, including sheriffs, bailiffs of the hundreds, and haveners.
In the late thirteenth century, the havener, Elias de Bray, was accused
of taking and disposing of herring from wrecks before the coroner

[56] See, for example, *Rotuli litterarum clausarum*, II, p. 12; PRO, JUST1/112, 116,
118 passim; the account of 1287–8 under 'Wreck' and 'Memoranda' (below,
Part I). In several of the early accounts, moreover, the bailiffs of the hundreds
report on wreck arising in individual tithings; see, for example, the account for
1297/8 under 'Kerrier' and 'Pydar'. For the early jurisdiction of hundred bailiffs
and sheriffs (and, later, escheators) over wreck, see also R. F. Hunnisett, *The
Medieval Coroner* (Cambridge, 1961), pp. 6–7, 81, 149, 198.

[57] This chain of reporting can be seen in the 'Wreck' section of the account for
1302/3 (below, Part I), and in the 'Wreck' section of the accounts for 1339/40,
1344/5, and 1352/3 (below, Part II), where the amounts from wreck were first
recorded in the court rolls of the locality.

[58] Given the large amounts collected from fines on wreckers, it is unlikely that
they were merely subsumed under the general heading of 'fines' that occasionally
appears in subsequent accounts because the latter were relatively low amounts.
It is significant that sums collected from wreck were nil or very low when the
office of havener was farmed out to royal appointees; see especially the accounts
for Easter Term 1307, 1308–9, 1313, 1313–14, 1315/16, 1316–17, and 1331
(Part I, below). Fines on wreckers reappear at the end of the havener's account
of 1350/1, but they were made before two auditors, suggesting problems with
their collection. The need to collect such fines is also noted in the 'Wreck'
account of 1351/2.

arrived to value it.[59] To address this problem, controllers were appointed to check the accounts of the duchy haveners; they seem to have been especially active when it came to appraising the value of wrecks and royal fish.[60] The temptation to profit from their office was ever-present, however, as evidenced by the accusations of extortion and felonies faced by Thomas Fitz Henry in the early 1350s. He was cleared of most charges, but briefly gaoled for keeping for himself money paid by Spanish mariners for aid in salvaging goods when their ship was wrecked at Tywardreath.[61]

The havener's duties in regard to wreck were mainly supervisory. The tasks of actually collecting fines from wreckers or the bits and pieces of wrecked cargo appear to have been left to local officials, although the havener was in charge of selling the wrecked cargoes that came his way. Normally there were buyers readily available near the site of the wreck willing to pay for the timbers, masts, wine, and other goods cast up on shore, but on occasion it took the havener some time to find a suitable buyer, as was the case for a mast at Falmouth and silk vestments at St Goran.[62] It was also up to the havener to deal with problems that arose, such as the refusal of fishermen of Golant to turn over 11 tuns of wine because they had found it out at sea, rather than on the shore.[63] Some five years after the incident, the duke's auditors were still charging the havener for eight of the tuns (three were lost at sea) that the fishermen had sold. Haveners also had a hand in appraising the value of wrecked goods and handing over one-half of this fee as 'salvage' to those who first found the goods. Beached whales demanded their attention because of their value and status as 'royal fish'. Viewed as a delicacy and prized for their meat as well as their by-products (oil, blubber, and teeth), whales were usually earmarked for the lord's household. In 1353, for example, Sir William de Northwell, keeper of the duke's wardrobe, ordered the havener to deliver a whale taken in Mount's Bay directly to the duke's household.[64]

[59.] PRO, JUST1/112, m. 2d; *Rotuli hundredorum*, p. 56. For sheriffs and other officials accused of siphoning off the profits of wreck, see PRO, JUST1/118, mm. 56, 68d.

[60.] See the accounts of 1341/2, 1346/7 and 1348/9 under 'Wreck'.

[61.] PRO, C260/76/31.

[62.] See the accounts of 1348/9, 1349/50, 1350/1, and 1351/2 under 'Wreck'.

[63.] See the accounts of 1341/2 (under 'Wreck' and 'Sum of Expenses') and 1346/7 (under 'Sum of Expenses').

[64.] *BPR*, II, p. 66 and account of 1353/4, under 'Wreck'.

The haveners faced a variety of difficulties in carrying out their duties. Particularly time consuming was supervising the collection, storage, and transport of wines from prisage, which was the right of the lord to take one or two tuns of wine from each wine ship docking at port, in exchange for a nominal fee. Disposing of these wines, either by sale, gift, or transfer to the duke, was not only demanding in terms of time and expense, but also in terms of the constant attention these activities attracted from the duke and his council. [65] Because the business associated with prisage was so complex and was conducted at ports scattered over the entire south-western peninsula, the havener had to rely heavily on deputies to help him administer prisage. The size of the territory the havener had to cover in collecting the annual port farms must have also made him depend on deputies, although it is possible that bailiffs brought the farm payments to the havener.[66] The collection of trantery and fishing fines was also probably done by local bailiffs or deputies who then accounted to the havener who recorded the sums in his account. Nor did the havener have direct involvement with the collection of royal port customs. He recorded them in his accounts, but the work of collection and initial accounting were handled by specially-appointed officials, while local port customs were collected by local reeves and bailiffs, with usually only the sums accounted for by the havener.

The accounts of the havener and the letters recorded in the Register of the Black Prince (the first duke of Cornwall) reveal other miscellaneous tasks the havener was assigned. These included orders to seize a ship of Fowey and its shipmaster for piracy against the prince's Flemish allies and to sell a ship arrested at Plymouth for the prince's profit.[67] Periodically the havener also had to hire ships and pay freightage to transport wine and other victuals to the prince in London or elsewhere.[68] The prince's central role in leading expeditions to France also meant he occasionally required the havener to help out with purveyance, as in 1359 when he shipped fish, arrows, and other items to Sandwich.[69] But the havener had no role in arresting ships or men for naval service,

---

[65.] For more on the havener's duties with prisage, see the section below on 'The Prisage, Custody, Custom, and Sale of Wines'.

[66.] Unfortunately, the accounts offer no information on how the port farms, trantery, or fishing fines were paid.

[67.] *BPR*, II, 75, 77–8.

[68.] For example, the account of 1344/5, under 'Foreign Expenses' and 'Sum of Expenses'. See also *BPR*, II, p. 69.

[69.] *BPR*, II, 77, 98, 160–1, 207.

tasks that the duke generally assigned to the steward or receiver. Most problems that cropped up during war-time were left to other officials, even if they involved areas over which the havener normally had supervision. In 1347, for instance, the prince ordered his yeoman and sheriff to keep track of wine ships in order to deter the wine trade from enemy territories.[70] Given the wide range of duties the havener took on, however, it is unlikely that the duke or his council thought him incapable of handling these tasks. Indeed, the administrative responsibilities of the havener, which required financial acumen, supervision of deputies, knowledge of commercial freightage and commodity rates, and considerable travel, probably made him a valuable asset in the duke's administration, as evidenced both by Fitz Henry's long service and by the rewards that the duke gave him over the years. The havener's skills in managing people should also not go unnoticed. Serving as the intermediary between the duke and his council on one side, and the local populace on the other required considerable tact, while his involvement with shipmasters, merchants, mariners and even pirates brought him into contact with seamen from all over the British Isles and Europe.

The Profits of the Ports

During the earldom, the profits of the ports consisted of six main items: the port farms; wreck of sea (along with fines on pillagers, and salvage, waif, and royal fish); trantery; fines paid by forestallers of fish; the maritime courts; and a miscellaneous category of fines and perquisites that included forfeited goods, ships and goods captured from enemies of the realm, and fines on merchants accused of wrongdoing. With the creation of the duchy of Cornwall and the appointment for life of Thomas Fitz Henry as havener, the duchy administration seized the opportunity to centralise the collection of additional maritime profits in the hands of the havener. These perquisites included wine prisage and custom, which had only appeared irregularly in the earlier havener's accounts, and the collection of ancient and new custom (often called 'cocket' and 'maltot' in the accounts). These new items, particularly wine prisage, considerably bolstered the revenues handled by the havener, although his expenses, in terms of payments for prisage wines, the care of these wines, and his own salary, also rose (Table 1). Nonetheless, the appointment of a salaried havener capable of consistently

---

70. *BPR*, II, p. 45.

representing the duchy's maritime interests clearly allowed the duchy to exploit its maritime revenues more successfully.

The revenues reported by the havener could fluctuate sharply in response to the crises of war and plague. Many of the port farms had to be reduced, or remained uncollectable after the start of the Hundred Years War in 1337 and the Black Death in 1348–9. Revenues from Plymouth harbour were hit hard in 1338/9 when the town was nearly burned by the French. The effects of these disasters are evident in the reduction of the farms of the ports over the course of the fourteenth century (Table 1). Profits from the port farms, trantery and forestalling fish, and the maritime courts hit all-time lows in the year of the Black Death, while the profits of prisage wine was at its lowest in 1338/9, which coincided with the enemy attack on Plymouth and the start of the Hundred Years War. Yet these fluctuations were relatively minor in terms of overall profits. Although the percentage of profits coming from the port farms dropped from 63 per cent in 1301–6 to only 7 per cent in 1351–6, this decline was due primarily to the rising importance of prisage wine, which accounted for an astonishing 89 per cent of the havener's profits in the 1350s (Table 1). The actual drop in the value of the port farms was far less, only 13 per cent, while the declines registered for trantery and the maritime courts were even smaller.[71]

Government policy could also influence the sums collected for ancient and new custom, as in 1353 when the cocket accounts disappeared from the havener's accounts because of the Ordinance and Statute of the Staple, which required all exports to go through one of the staple ports. The harsh sea and dangerous coasts of Cornwall also affected maritime revenues. Sudden storms could force fleets of ships into the nearest port, thus augmenting the profits of prisage if the ships were carrying wine and Cornwall was their first land-fall in England.[72] Storms and coastal hazards also affected the frequency with which wrecks and royal fish washed ashore in Cornwall, making for substantial profits in some years, such as 1341/2, but no income at all in other years. It is likely, however, that nil profits were due not to the absence of wrecks, but to the havener's failure to pursue the earl and duke's prerogatives. The self-interests of local wreckers, who often pillaged wrecks with

---

[71.] Trantery profits, however, declined severely in the following decades, with nil returns for many years, due in large part to the difficulties that foreign fish dealers had in travelling to Cornwall during the war-torn decades of the Hundred Years War.

[72.] See below, the section on 'The Prisage, Custom, Custody, and Sale of Wine'.

impunity, must also have reduced the wreck profits due to the estate, as did the custom of paying salvage as a type of reward for reporting and harbouring the finds. Yet—as the following discussion of the different revenues collected by the havener indicates—the careful attention of an official willing to enforce his lord's perquisites did yield greater profits for the estate.

The Port Farms

Under the earldom, the annual 'farms' or rents paid by some seventeen fishing ports in Cornwall accounted for well over half of the havener's revenues (Table 1). Although the ports' share of overall profits fell considerably with the addition of prisage wines and customs under the duchy, their drop in actual revenues was only about 13 per cent. This decline was still significant, however, and was due largely to interruptions in trade caused by war, plague, or silting harbours. The Black Death of 1348–9 was the most frequently cited reason for declining port farms, but wartime hostilities also interfered with the peaceful conduct of fishing, on which the farms seem to have been based. In 1348/9, the year of the plague, for instance, the auditors explained that the amounts collected from the port farms were reduced 'because fishermen were dead from pestilence and also from war'. Such explanations continued to be offered for decades. Indeed, the port farms section of the havener's accounts provide a guide to subsequent outbreaks of plague, as in 1364–6 when a 'second pestilence' was singled out as the reason that revenues were reduced, an explanation cited well into the 1370s.[73]

Although the havener's accounts do not specify how the port farms were assessed, the explanations offered when revenues declined indicate that the port farms were based on tolls levied on fishing boats and fishers at each port. In the account of 1350/1, for instance, the havener claimed he was unable to collect the farms of several ports 'because no men or boats are there by which the said farm can be raised', while St Ives' farm was low 'because there are not many boats in the same port and there are accustomed to be 28 boats which render £6 per year' and 'for lack of fishers dead from the pestilence'. If the 28 boats each paid the same flat fee, each boat would have been liable for around 4s 4d to make up the annual farm of £6. In the earliest extant accounts of the

---

[73] DCO Ministers' Account 17 (1365/6), 20 (1374/5); PRO, SC6/818/8, m. 6 (1378/9).

port farms, moreover, several places were labelled 'fisheries' instead of 'ports', including the fisheries of Kerrier Hundred in the Lizard peninsula, the fisheries of Trigg Hundred in north Cornwall, and Fowey and Polruan.

The origin of these annual rents or port farms is harder to explain. They were never mentioned in early grants of the earldom, but must have been around for some time before the first extant accounts of the earldom in the 1280s and 1290s, when they already represented a major portion of the maritime revenues. Indeed, the earls had probably realised the taxation possibilities of the fishing industry by the late twelfth or early thirteenth century when there are signs that the Cornish fisheries had become a thriving commercial enterprise, as indicated by the large payments several Gascon merchants began making in 1202 to secure purchase rights to Cornish fish.[74] It is likely, in fact, that the cash lease recorded in the port farms merely replaced the earls' rights to a share of the fish landed (usually the best fish of every catch) on their foreshore, a well-known prerogative in medieval and early modern Cornwall that was often referred to as the right to 'head' fish.[75] The complaints raised in the 1270s about 'new' customs levied on those drying their fish onshore and tolls of 2s on every boat arriving with fish to sell may also refer to how these port farms were raised, although Earl Edmund's response to these complaints was to claim they dated back to the time of Earl Richard (1225–72).[76] Perhaps more relevant was Edmund's defence that 'the ports of the county belong to the same earl' and that

---

[74.] See below, the section on 'Sea Fisheries', and n. 149. Note also that David Harvey ("The Tithing Framework of West Cornwall: A Proposed Pattern and an Interpretation of Territorial Origins", *Cornish Studies*, 2nd series, 5 (1997), p. 42) argues that early acreage assessments for tithings in coastal regions probably took fishing rights into account.

[75.] In a suit at the Exchequer in 1684 about tithe fish, an interrogatory for the plaintiff (the rector of Paul) noted the port farm of Mousehole was paid annually to the duke of Cornwall 'in lieu of the best fish or cape [head] fish that they have taken or might take or bring on shore at any time within the said village of Mousehole". See *The Tidal Estuaries, Foreshores, and Under-Sea Minerals, Within and Around the Coast of Cornwall. Duke of Cornwall v. The Crown* (London, 1856–7), p. 145 (there is a copy in the DCO and a photocopy in the CRO under FS/3/1182). For other references to head fish in Cornwall, see CRO, ME 1543–44 (at Gorran and Mevagissey), Charles Henderson, "St Ives", in *Essays in Cornish History* (Oxford, 1935), p. 91, and idem, *A History of the Parish of Constantine in Cornwall*, ed. G. H. Doble (Long Compton, 1937), pp. 111, 112 (at Gweek and other ports in Merthen)

[76.] PRO, JUST1/112, m. 2d.

the fishermen freely paid these sums in order to sell their catch where they wanted. In other words, the earls' lordship of all Cornish ports was the basis of their right to collect what were really usage charges from fishermen.

But not all Cornish fishing ports were included in the farms (Table 2). Excluded were such well-known fishing ports as Looe and Mevagissey, as well as the ports of the Fal and Tamar estuaries (Map 1). Duchy officials were aware that many substantial fishing ports were missing from their list, but they went no farther than suggesting an inquisition look into why no annual rents were due from Plymouth, Saltash, St Germans, Truro, Penryn, Merthen, Lelant and Padstow in the Caption of Seisin in 1337, a directive that was not followed since it was repeated verbatim in the Extent of 1345. The geographic range of the ports paying the annual farms was also limited, heavily concentrated in westernmost Cornwall, with only Fowey and Polruan on the south coast and the three small Triggshire ports on the north coast located outside this region. No fewer than eleven of the seventeen ports lay in Penwith Hundred, with only three in Trigg, one in Kerrier, one in Powder, and one in West Hundreds. And none of the ports were coterminous with a Domesday manor or parish; indeed, only Polruan and Fowey were even manors in their own right. The list of ports also included some very tiny harbours, one of which, 'Porthplement', cannot be precisely located.[77] The answer to the regional concentration of the ports may have something to do with older tenurial arrangements and the earldom's firmer control over the foreshore of western Cornwall. Saltash, St Germans, and Plymouth, for instance, as well as West Looe (as part of Liskeard) were part of the honour of Trematon, which was separated from the earldom in 1227 and not reacquired until 1270, while Padstow was early on held by Bodmin Priory and East Looe by the Duchy of Lancaster.

The port farms can be divided into five groups based on the amounts paid. The most productive fisheries included Mousehole, whose farm of 100s per year remained unchanged during the fourteenth century, and St Ives, which paid the largest farm of 120s per year, but which fell

---

[77.] It was located probably near Mount's Bay, up the river inlet just east of Long Rock, where a farm called 'Plemun' is noted on the Old Series Ordnance Survey Map. See also Campbell, "Haveners", p. 125 for this attribution. It had difficulty paying its farm even before the plague (Appendix I, below, Extent of 1345), while the entrance to its harbour (and those of three other small ports) was said to have been blocked by sand in the account of 1428/9 (PRO, E122/180/4).

on some hard times after the Black Death and temporarily had to have its farm reduced (Table 2). Ranking second were Marazion on Mount's Bay, which normally paid 46s 8d per year, and Fowey, at 40s. The third group included fisheries owing 20s per year: Polruan at the mouth of Fowey River, Porthallow (the chief fishing port of the Meneage in Kerrier Hundred)[78] and Newlyn, also on Mount's Bay. The three ports of north Cornwall, Portgaverne, Port Isaac, and Portquin were together responsible for a 20s annual farm and thus should be grouped with Penzance, Porthgwarra and Land's End since each fishery yielded under 20s per year. The least profitable fisheries were the now lost 'Porthplement', Lamorna and Portminster, and Porthzennor and Portheras, all located on the western coast of Cornwall.[79] The ports in this last group were particularly hard hit by war, a lack of traffic as population decreased after the plague, and a build-up of sand that restricted access to their harbours.[80] In the late fourteenth century and

---

[78.] Beaulieu Abbey (Hampshire) owned the fish tithes of the large parish of St Keverne, wherein Porthallow was located. The abbey's account book for c. 1269–70 shows a seine fishery there, as well as a large hake fishery and profits from herring, conger, mulwell, and ling; see *The Account Book of Beaulieu Abbey*, ed. S. F. Hockey (Camden 4th series, vol. 16, 1975), pp. 103–4.

[79.] Porthgwarra was usually singled out by itself, but in 1336 its entry read 'Porthgwarra, namely Land's End' (Part I, below); in the Caption of Seisin it was simply termed 'Land's End', and in the Extent of 1345 it was recorded as 'Land's End Porthgwarra' (Appendix I, below). In the accounts of 1344/5 and 1346/7 it was called 'Porthgwarra and Land's End' (below, Part II). It continued to be recorded as only 'Porthgwarra' until 1428/9 when 'Penberth' and 'Killwethan' were added for three years (see PRO, E122/180/4, 216/19, and 180/5). The entry for Lamorna usually named only that port, but in 1336 it was called 'Lamorna namely Porthminster', in the Caption of 1337 it was called only 'Porthminster', and in the Extent of 1345 the entry read 'Porthminster and Lamorna' (Appendix I, below), the same terminology used in the account of 1344/5 and 1346/7 (Part II, below). Thereafter it was only referred to as 'Lamorna' although in an account of deputy haveners for 1404/5 (PRO, SC6/ 823/16) 'Porthminster' was listed separately, albeit with a nil return. Why the havener grouped Lamorna, located on Mount's Bay, with Porthminster, near St Ives, is not clear. The Triggshire ports were usually subsumed under a single heading, until the Caption of 1337 when the three ports were named, a practice that became increasingly common thereafter. Porthzennor was often named by itself in five of the eight earliest accounts (Part I, below), but thereafter it was almost always grouped with Portheras. For more details on the location and history of all of these ports, see Richard Pearse, *The Ports and Harbours of Cornwall* (St Austell, 1963).

[80.] The problem of sand for the ports of Porthzennor, Portheras, Porthgwarra/Land's End was noted in the account of 1428/9 (PRO, E122/180/4).

even into the fifteenth century, the havener often had to report that no farm could be levied from these ports because there were no boats there. As the low farms of these ports indicate, they had never been as productive as the other fisheries, so their ability to recover from the difficulties occasioned by war and population loss was commensurately weaker.

Wreck, Royal Fish, and Waif

More ships have come to harm off the bleak and treacherous coasts of Cornwall than any other county in England.[81] Storms can blow up suddenly and drive ships into the rocks that dot the Cornish coastline, particularly in north Cornwall. The weather or neglect that caused these accidents, however, were highly unpredictable, so the amounts collected from the profits of wreck varied more dramatically than any other prerogative of the havenery. As the survey of duchy profits in 1337 put it, 'Regarding the annual value of wreck of the sea, nothing can be estimated because the profit arising from it falls fortuitously by chance, sometimes more, sometimes less...'[82] The havener's accounts bear out this assessment. Nil accounts were returned in many years, particularly when the havenry was farmed out to a non-resident royal appointee. But, in other years, the returns could be quite stunning. When big ships were lost, the profits could be spectacular, as was the case around 1320, when a wreck off the Lizard was reputedly worth £400.[83] But such profits were more often anticipated than realised. In 1341/2, for example, the havener initially reported wreck profits of over £45 from wrecks near Golant, Mousehole, the Meneage, and Falmouth. This sum was eventually reduced because the Golant fishermen who found 11 tuns of red wine refused to turn the wine over, claiming they had found it out at sea, not on or near the shore. The auditors did not acknowledge their claim and continued to hold the havener accountable for several years, although they reduced the sum

---

[81.] See, for example, Richard and Bridget Larn, *Shipwreck Index of the British Isles. Vol. 1-South West England* (London, 1995).

[82.] *Caption,* p. 138, and below, Appendix I. Note that profits from wreck could sometimes be reported in the accounts or court rolls of the local manors; see, for example, the Wreck accounts of 1339/40 and 1344/5, printed below in Part II.

[83.] *CPR 1317–21*, pp. 605–6 (where the Spanish merchants claim their losses amounted to £6000); *Ancient Deeds*, V, p. 49.

owed when they discovered that the fishermen had only retrieved eight tuns in good enough condition to sell.

As one of the oldest maritime prerogatives in England, wreck of sea was the first maritime privilege to be singled out in royal grants of the earldom.[84] Given the regalian privileges attached to the earldom from an early date, it is likely that the right to wreck of sea was considered part of the grant of the county of Cornwall. There were some challenges to the earl's rights to wreck, of course, but the earls and dukes managed to enforce their right to wreck throughout Cornwall well into the late middle ages.[85] The regalian right, as defined by common law, dictated that any ship cast ashore was forfeited to the king (or, in the case of Cornwall, to the earl or duke), but by royal ordinances dating from the twelfth century, such ships could be judged wreck only if no man, dog, or cat escaped alive. The havener was well-aware of these technicalities, but the auditors and councillors usually interpreted the duke's right to wreck as liberally as possible, with little regard for how difficult it was for the havener to enforce the letter of the law. [86]

Reaching a shipwreck before too much was carried off by wreckers was the major obstacle in the collection of revenues from this maritime prerogative. As coastal residents, wreckers were first on the scene and felt it their right to claim the flotsam and jetsam that the sea cast up on their shores. There is no reason to believe that the Cornish were any more predatory than their counterparts elsewhere in England when

---

[84.] See above, notes 1 and 2. For a history of the right to wreck in England, see Stuart A. Moore, *A History of the Foreshore and the Law Thereto* (London, 3rd edn., 1888).

[85.] The king or even the earl could grant their privileges of wreck to others, which is how Tavistock abbey acquired rights to wreck in the Scillies (above, n. 2). For the crown's (losing) challenge of the earl's right to wreck in 1284, see PRO, JUST1/112, m. 3d. For Queen Isabella's efforts to preserve her right of wreck while she held Cornwall, see *CPR 1317–21*, pp. 170, 171, 172. Rights to wreck in Penwith hundred were claimed by the Arundells in right of their manor of Connerton, with one-third of the profits reserved to the duke; see P. A. S. Pool, "The Penheleg Manuscript", *JRIC*, n.s., 3 (1959), pp. 163–77.

[86.] See the account of 1338/9, where the escheator and havener (the 'keeper of the ports') justified declaring an enemy ship captured at sea as wreck because 'no man, dog or cat could be found then living in the same ship'. Note also the auditors' continued insistence on the earl's rights to the 11 tuns of wine taken at sea by the Golant fishermen, despite their claims that the law was on their side and despite the havener's inability to make the fishermen pay up. See also *BPR*, II, pp. 6–7 for the duke's request for a special investigation into a wreck he believed belonged to him.

faced with the unexpected bounty from shipwrecks, but the people of Cornwall clearly had more opportunities to enjoy the profits of wreck than most because of the appalling storms and rockiness of their coasts. To counteract such pillaging, maritime law allowed the finder of goods to claim one-half their value as 'salvage'. [87] Needless to say, full value was better than half, so the custom of salvage only deterred some of the wreckers. Those who were caught pillaging wrecks (or, as is more likely, those few whose deeds were reported to the authorities) were liable to substantial fines for failing to report what they found or for selling it. These fines are laid out in some detail in the havener's accounts of the early fourteenth century, when they annually brought in four times what the sale of wrecked goods garnered for the earl (Table 1). Most of the fines were in the range of 2s to 4s, but on occasion could rise to over 20s, presumably reflecting the value of the goods the pillager had taken. More problematic were those wreckers who hastened the demise of troubled ships by sailing out to rob them or by harming their crew in order to claim goods for themselves.[88] These more serious cases were handled not by the havener, but by the sheriff or by special commissions of oyer and terminer.[89] The enthusiastic participation of local lords in many of these wrecking ventures also made it particularly difficult for merchants to recoup their investments, especially when these same lords were appointed to the panel of inquiry.[90] Forced 'sales' of wrecked ships and their goods to local lords, at bargain prices, were also not unusual.[91]

[87.] See the account of 1344/5 for an explicit statement to this effect. Salvage payments are usually noted in the 'Wreck' section of the havener's accounts, and the earlier accounts give a particularly full picture of the custom.

[88.] See, for example, the charge in the eyre roll of 1284 that local Cornish residents killed the surviving sailors of a Shoreham ship and carried away the cargo: PRO, JUST1/112, m. 3.

[89.] See, for example, *CPR 1307–13*, pp. 255–6; *CPR 1317–21*, pp. 169, 604–5.

[90.] There are numerous examples, but for a particularly detailed case, see John Chynoweth, 'The Wreck of the St Anthony', *JRIC*, n.s., 5 (1968), 385–406. For the claims of the lords of coastal manors to a portion of the profits of wreck, including 'sales' of wrecked items to them, see the accounts of 1344/5, 1348/9, 1353/4, and 1354/5 under 'Wreck'. An investigation of the plunder of a Spanish shipwreck revealed that 32 men, including the steward of the earldom's estates in Cornwall, Thomas de la Hide, and William de Talcarn (havener in c. 1302), illegally carried away goods and also hindered the efforts of the shipowner to recoup his ship and cargo (*CPR 1307–13*, pp. 255–6).

[91.] For example, CRO, ARB 209/6 (sale and quitclaim of a wrecked ship of Barfleur to Sir John Arundell).

The havener's accounts printed here refer to well over 50 different wrecks in numerous locations along the Cornish coast. The wreckage that came to the attention of the havener included many items from the ship's gear, such as anchors, cords, beams, masts, sails, and boats. Some of the masts in particular were valuable, although the havener generally reported only half their value because the finders took the other half as salvage. Wine was the most frequently recovered cargo, and also the most lucrative, although most of it was too spoiled by salt water to fetch any great price. On occasion, more unusual items were also discovered, such as the embroidered silk vestments that the havener had difficulty selling in 1351/2. Given the activity of coastal pillagers, it is likely that much of the smaller cargo that came ashore was never recorded in the havener's accounts.

Closely associated with the earl and duke's right to wreck of sea was the regalian right to 'royal' fish, which included whales, grampuses, porpoises, and sturgeon.[92] Profits from the sale of these fish were usually included under the section on Wreck in the havener's accounts because they were more often discovered when stranded or washed up on shore than caught at sea. The meat, bones, and blubber from whales were especially valued, which made it difficult for the havener to enforce the duke's claims before the local populace carried off what they could. Intrusions by local lords were also a problem, as evident in 1341/2 when only sixteen small pieces of whale of no value were left to the havener by William de Aumarle, who had taken custody of the whale. Aumarle also had to be pardoned a few years later for spiriting away a porpoise that belonged by right to the duke.[93] In another case, the havener was obliged to pay 20s to local men for their aid in helping to bring in a little whale (*ceticulus*) at Mount's Bay, which he was then ordered to deliver to the keeper of the household who sent it on to the duke's household at Sonning (Berkshire).[94] As with wreck, it was customary to reward first finders of royal fish, as when several Tewington fishers were given half the value of two porpoises they

---

[92.] For the history of this right, see Moore, *History of the Foreshore*; C. H. Karraker, "Royal Fish", *Quarterly Review*, 267 (1936), pp. 129–36; and J. H. Baker, ed., *John Spelman's Reading or Quo Warranto Delivered in Gray's Inn (Lent 1519)* (Selden Society, vol. 113, 1997), pp. 26–7, 34, 40–2.

[93.] *BPR*, I, pp. 46–7.

[94.] Account of 1353/4, under 'Wreck of Sea' and 'Sum of All Expenses' (below, in Part II) and *BPR*, II, p. 66.

[95.] *Rowe v. Brenton*, Appendix, p. 107 (manorial account of 1341/2).

found.[95]

Another item frequently included in the section on Wreck was profits from the sale of items coming to the havener as waif, that is, goods forfeited because they were abandoned by their owners or because their owners were thieves fleeing justice. Like wreck and royal fish, waif was a royal prerogative that devolved to the earls and dukes. Although profits from waif were infrequent, they could be substantial. In 1341/2, a ship and a cargo of 100 quarters of coarse salt from waif at Falmouth were worth over £13, while waif generated 6s 4d from 152 pounds of onions at Mount's Bay and £13 6s 8d for a ship and 100 quarters of salt at Penryn in 1346/7. These profits were often more anticipated than real, however, since the havener's confiscation or valuation of these valuable goods were often protested. Thus the salt cargo in 1341/2 was placed in the hands of the bishop of Exeter because the duke's steward intervened in response to a parliamentary petition, while an inquisition showed the ship and salt arrested at Penryn had been significantly over-valued.

The Prisage, Custom, Custody, and Sale of Wines

The prise of wine was a regalian right that allowed the king to take one tun of wine from before the mast and another from behind from all ships arriving in England with wine, although small ships carrying less than 20 tuns of wine were obliged to hand over only one tun, while ships carrying less than 9 tuns were probably exempt from the custom.[96] The king paid 20s for each tun taken as prisage, significantly below the market price for wine. Although prisage was not specifically mentioned among the earl's prerogatives until the late 1260s, the earls were collecting it by the early thirteenth century and perhaps earlier, enjoying this right by virtue of their tenure of the earldom.[97] In 1302, the prisage on wine merchants from Gascony was commuted in exchange for a

---

[96.] For the history of royal prisage and butlerage, see N.S.B. Gras, *The Early English Customs System* (Cambridge, MA, 1918), pp. 35–47.

[97.] For prisage of wine taken by Earl Richard around 1268, see *CPR 1266–72*, p. 241. Earl Edmund claimed prisage of wines in the quo warranto proceedings of c. 1284 (PRO, JUST1/112, m. 3d). In the first extant account of the earldom in 1287/8 (below, Part I), £46 was collected from the sale of prise-wines. Note also that in c. 1275 the jurors of Powder Hundred (*Rotuli hundredrorum*, I, pp. 56–7) accused Henry de Bodrigan of first raising the prisage of wine in Cornwall in the time of Earl Richard (1225–72), but it is unclear from the context whether Bodrigan was acting on behalf of the earl or himself.

toll of 2s on each tun of wine they imported. With the passage of the
Carta Mercatoria the following year, the toll in place of prisage was
extended to all alien merchants and became known as the 'new custom
on wine' or 'butlerage'. The earls' rights to prisage also gave them the
authority to collect butlerage, the wine custom on aliens. In other words,
from 1303, the earls and dukes profited from the wine trade at Cornish
ports in two ways: by collecting cash from all alien wine merchants in
the form of a 2s per tun toll, and by taking actual tuns of wine for a
very small price from incoming cargoes of wine owned by denizen
(native) merchants. Their profits were significantly bolstered by the
fact that wine ships owed prisage and butlerage at their first port of
call, regardless if they disembarked the wine or not. Although the
sparsely-populated hinterlands of Cornwall generated little demand
for wine imports, the favourable location of the Cornish ports (and
Plymouth) on the sea route from Gascony ensured that the wine traffic
passing through these ports was considerable.

The earldom's accounts contain entries for prise wines in the late
thirteenth century, but prisage is not recorded in the accounts from
1300 (when Earl Edmund died and the earldom reverted to the Crown)
to the start of the duchy accounts in 1338.[98] Accounts of prisage and
butlerage in Cornwall occasionally surface in the pipe rolls or royal
butlerage accounts when they were in the king's hands, but the rapid
turnover of earls and haveners during this period appears to have

---

[98.] Peter de Gaveston and his wife were granted prisage in ports of Devon and
Cornwall in November 1309 (*CPR 1307–13*, pp. 200, 358), but no accounts
survive from this period to 1312, when he lost the earldom. In October 1312,
the king appointed a deputy butler to receive prisage in the Cornish ports on his
behalf (*CPR 1307–13*, p. 501). During her tenure of the earldom (1317–24 and
1327–30), Queen Isabella collected prisage in Cornwall, although her claims
were challenged after April 1327, when the king appointed a butler to collect
prisage in Cornwall on his behalf (*CCR 1327–30*, p. 370). The refusal of the
queen's ministers to allow the king's butler to take prisage in Cornwall is noted
as a cause of the king's reduced profits from prisage in 1330; see PRO E101/78/
4A (printed in Gras, *English Custom*, pp. 211–12).

hindered the regular and efficient collection of prisage and butlerage in early fourteenth-century Cornwall.[99] This situation changed with the establishment of the duchy, however, and the appointment of a salaried havener, Thomas Fitz Henry. From 1338 on, detailed accounts of prisage take up a significant portion of the havener's accounts, noting not only the amount (and frequently the type) of wine taken from each ship at each port, but also the ship, shipmaster, and the date of arrival. In contrast, the butlerage accounts are cursory and frequently record nil profits because the Hundred Years War so severely reduced the activity of French wine merchants in England.

Although the havener was aided by deputies and the duke's butler,[100] the administration of prisage could be complicated. For example, the duke could take the first tun of prise wine without paying 20s, a practice recorded by writing 'quit' next to ship entries in the accounts. For the

---

[99.] For the turnover in earls and haveners, see above, pp. 8–10 and Appendix II, below. There are no extant accounts of prisage or butlerage during the tenure of Gaveston and Queen Isabella, nor any mention of the Cornish ports in the butlerage accounts of 1300–2 (PRO, E101/77/10), 1314–15 (E101/77/18), 1320–22 (PRO, E372/166, E101/77/25), 1327–30 (E101/78/3, 78/5, although prisage was noted for Plymouth in 1329–30), and 1332–40 (PRO, E372/177, m. 22d, E372/179, m. 33; E101/78/13, 78/16, 78/18, 79/1, 79/3). The lone extant account for the queen's tenure (in 1322/3, printed below in Part I) records only that 15 tuns of wine were collected from prisage that year. A royal butler's account of 1331/2 (PRO, E372/178, m. 46) notes 14 tuns from prisage at Plymouth, 12 tuns at Fowey, and 2 tuns at Truro. These amounts seem low, however, in light of the tunnage collected from prisage in the early years of the duchy and in light of the prosperity of the wine trade as a whole during this period; see Margery K. James, *Studies in the Medieval Wine Trade* (Oxford, 1971).

[100.] For the butler's activity, see the account for 1348/9 under 'Custody of Wines;' for the deputy at Plymouth, see the account for 1351/2, under the prisage entry for Plymouth (both printed below, Part II). For the accounts of deputy haveners at Mount's Bay, Falmouth, and Fowey in 1402/3, see PRO, SC6/819/13, m. 12.

second tun of prise wine, however, the duke owed 40s, a sum referred to as the 'assize of wine' in the havener's accounts.[101] Presumably the second tun was taken only when the ship carried more than twenty tuns of wine. On occasion the havener departed from these rules, as in 1353/4, when he paid as much for a pipe (one-half of a tun) of Cretan wine as a whole tun of Gascon wine, probably because of the higher value of this sweet wine. In 1356, the havener was ordered to reduce the prisage for several ships that the duke as Black Prince wished to reward for transporting him and his retinue to Gascony.[102] Other problems arose over how to deal with small wine ships that were avoiding the Cornish ports because of the prisage and whether prisage could be collected on wines captured from the enemy and brought to south-western ports.[103] The havener also had to improvise when faced with protests from merchants forced to pay prisage when they stopped for water or victuals at St Nicholas Island (now called 'Drake's Island') outside the port of Plymouth, negotiating a deal that allowed them to depart without proffering prisage.[104] But if the ships moored at Plymouth or any of the other ports, they owed prisage (and butlerage), even if they did not unload any wines. To avoid paying these customs again when they docked elsewhere, the havener gave them a receipt, called a

---

[101.] There are only a few explicit references to how prisage should be assessed in the Cornish ports. The 1309 grant of prisage to Peter de Gaveston and his wife (above, n. 98) defines it as 2 tuns from each shipload of wine, paying 20s per tun to the merchants. The 1337 Caption of Seisin (below, Appendix I) comments that the annual value of prisage cannot be determined until peace is restored because of the disruption to the wine trade caused by the war. The section on prisage in the Extent of 1345 (below, Appendix I) notes that the havener should take 1 tun of wine from each ship arriving with wine, paying nothing for it. A later insertion adds that two tuns may be taken for the same assize, if 40s is paid for the second tun; a careful examination of the havener's accounts indicates that this was the practice followed by the duchy. Londoners were exempt from paying prisage; see the account for 1353/4 under "Falmouth" and Gras, *English Customs*, p. 46.

[102.] PRO, SC6/817/6, m. 10d (account of 1357/8); *BPR*, II, p. 141.

[103.] *BPR*, II, pp. 163, 186.

[104.] For example, see the prisage accounts for Plymouth of 1351/2 and 1352/3 (below, Part II). The burgesses of Plymouth sought to make all merchants stopping there free from any customs because they claimed such customs deterred merchants from visiting their port, thereby reducing their profits; see *CCR 1392–6*, p. 68; *1396–9*, p. 33. Protests by Spanish ships that refused to pay prisage at Falmouth in 1358/9 (PRO, SC6/817/7, m. 10) were resolved with the help of a mob of local sailors, merchants, and townsmen who convinced then otherwise.

'charter', that they could show to other port officials; these entries are sometimes marked '*cum carta*' in the accounts.[105] Ships that unloaded their wines in Cornwall did not receive this receipt, a practice the havener could record by writing '*sine carta*' next to these entries. To ensure their authenticity, these charter receipts had to carry a cocket seal. Since the seal was in the custody of the duke's keeper of the privy seal, he sent blank sealed charters to the havener from time to time, which the havener carefully recorded in his account. Unfortunately, the havener or his deputies occasionally failed to give merchants such receipts, or gave them charters in so torn and defective that merchants complained they were useless.[106]

The prisage and butlerage accounts offer intriguing glimpses into the wine trade at the ports of Cornwall and Plymouth. The trade was most vibrant at Plymouth, where 92 wine ships are recorded in the thirteen extant accounts for 1338–56. Fowey was close behind with 87 ships, followed by Falmouth (which included Penryn and Truro) with 75. Lagging considerably were the ports of Padstow with only 6 wine ships, and Looe and Mousehole with 3 each. St Ives, Lelant, and Mount's Bay were usually entered in the prisage accounts, but with nil returns. These figures need to be treated with caution, however, because other factors besides the market for wine could influence the size of the ship traffic. The recorded wine trade at Padstow, for instance, may have been small partly because of the men of Padstow and their lord, the prior of Bodmin, hindered the duke's collection of prisage in their port.[107] The totals recorded for some ports could also be artificially inflated in some years when storms compelled wine ships to seek safe haven, as seems to have occurred at Plymouth in November 1352, and at Falmouth in December 1344 and early January 1354. These visits, like those to St Nicholas Island in Plymouth Sound, were brief— primarily for shelter and victuals—as the ships soon left to discharge their valuable cargoes of wine in other English ports, but since they first touched the shores of England at the duke's ports, they were

---

[105]. This practice is spelled out in the accounts for 1355/6 (under the prisage accounts of Plymouth, Fowey, and Falmouth, printed below, Part II) and 1357/8 (PRO, SC6/817/4, m. 10d). The duke also ordered the havener not to take prisage from wine ships bound for his port of Chester, where he preferred that they pay; *BPR*, II, pp. 146–7.

[106]. *BPR*, II, pp. 43, 127–8, 149. For references to blank charters, see also the accounts of 1355/6 where there are separate sections for 'Receipt of Charters' and 'Delivery of Charters'.

[107]. See the account of 1339/40, under 'Prisage' (below, Part II).

required to pay prisage or butlerage there, rather than at their final destination. The amount of prisage wine was also severely affected by the Hundred Years War, which adversely influenced the timing and strength of the wine fleet arriving in some years, as remarked upon in the accounts on several occasions.[108]

The prisage accounts for 1338–56 record just over 300 denizen wine cargoes, about 75 per cent of which were red wine, mostly from Gascony. Roughly 70 per cent of the red wine was vintage, that is, arriving in England from about October through January from the first pressings of grapes. The remaining 30 per cent of Gascon wine was racked or 'reek' wines, drawn off the lees (the dregs) in January and February and normally arriving in England in the early spring. More mature and clearer than vintage wine, it was also more expensive. Red wine also arrived from Spain, as did a good proportion of the white wine, although red Spanish wine that arrived in August 1353 was considered of such poor quality that the havener voluntarily gave up his right to the second tun of prisage wine. Other imports included small amounts of sweet wine from Greece (called Cretan wine), *buret*, which appears to have been a cheaper red wine, rape wine and distilled wine.[109]

The custom of prisage also made the havener responsible for the custody, disposal, and sale of sometimes very large amounts of wine— almost 100 tuns in 1353/4 alone when the profit from prisage wines was about £360. Caring, storing, and transporting the wine represented by far the largest expense in the havener's accounts (Table 1) and must have kept the havener and his deputies very busy, as spelled out in some detail in the accounts. Once the wine was handed over to the havener, he had to have it towed in a small boat from the ship to land, which usually cost 2d–6d per tun, depending on the distance travelled. Sometimes he hired a boat at ports like Falmouth where the expense of transporting wine over two leagues warranted the 12d per day cost. The tuns then had to be rolled from the shore to the cellar for storage, a cost that rose from 2d to 3d in the early 1350s. Cellars then had to be

---

[108.] For example, the account of 1339/40 under 'Falmouth' (below, Part II). See also the remarks under 'Prisage of Wine' in the Caption of Seisin (below, Appendix I). For the influence of the War on the wine trade, see also James, *Wine Trade*, pp. 15–31, 41–6.

[109.] See the account for 1339/40 under 'Sale of Wines from Prisage' and the account for 1341/2 (both in Part II, below) where the havener paid to have 30 tuns of wine distilled.

leased at each port for weeks at a time to store the wine, which ran about 4d per tun per week, and men hired to guard the wines until they could be sold or sent to the duke. Long storage brought its own problems, such as evaporation and leakage, which had to be addressed by replacing the wine lost (called 'ullage' if from evaporation and 'leakage' if from a faulty barrel), for which the havener had to pay the going market rate, which was around 4d per gallon in the 1330s, but rising to 6d in the early 1350s and occasionally reaching as high as 8d in mid 1350s.[110] He also had to buy hoops and staves to repair barrels, hire coopers, and pay porters for lifting the wine. Supervising the disposal of the wine was also time-consuming. Some was sent to the duke's wine cellars at Lostwithiel, a process that involved further costs for rollage, towage, windage (hoisting the barrels into a ship) and unloading, with the boats sailing first to Fowey and then (often on another boat) upriver to Lostwithiel. Unforeseen accidents, such as broken tow-ropes or stormy weather conditions also raised costs. Even higher transport costs were incurred when the havener was ordered to send wine to the duke (the Black Prince) in London, Calais, and elsewhere.[111]

Further complicating the situation were the oft-changing instructions from the duke about what to do with the prisage wines. Indeed, despite Thomas Fitz Henry's long years of faithful service, the disposal of prisage wines provoked more orders and irritation from the duke than any of the havener's other duties. In 1347, for example, the havener got into trouble because he sold all the prisage wines without warrant to do so. The duke's butler was then instructed to purchase wines from local merchants at market rates, which he charged to the havener's account.[112] In November 1352, the havener was ordered to ignore recent letters to sell wines and instead to keep the wines and certify to the prince how many tuns he had. Various reforms in accounting were ordered the following month that further restricted the hand of the havener in disposing of prisage wines. By July 1353, however, the havener was being ordered to sell wines for as much profit as he could. In 1355 the

---

[110.] The havener paid 8d at Plymouth, Fowey and Falmouth in 1354/5 and at Fowey in 1355/6. The changing wine prices for gallons and whole tuns of wine in the havener's accounts could bear further study as a reflection of the pressures on the wine market at this time.

[111.] For example, *BPR*, II, pp. 6, 22.

[112.] See also *BPR*, I, pp. 82–3, 85, 87–8 and the account for 1348/9 under 'Custody of Wines' (below, Part II).

duke wrote the havener to sell the wines right away because he had heard they were reaching prices as high as 10 marks a tun, but the havener quickly replied that wine was selling much more cheaply than that in Cornwall. The orders to sell prisage wines as profitably as possible became more persistent in the following years, when the duke was in debt for his expeditions to France and was probably in need of the ready cash the sale of prisage wines could bring.[113]

The duke also used prisage wines as a form of patronage to reward faithful followers or to curry favour. Beneficiaries of his largesse included many of his own officials, such as Sir Robert Beaupel and Sir John Dabernoun (stewards of Cornwall), Sir Nicholas Pynnok and Sir William Spridlington (auditors of his accounts), and Sir Richard de Wolveston and William Daubeney (members of his household).[114] He was particularly generous to Sir Peter Gildesburgh, treasurer of his wardrobe (1341–44), receiver-general (1344–46), and keeper of the privy seal. For several years in a row, Gildesburgh was allowed to purchase two tuns of prisage wine at the same below-market price the duke paid (40s a tun), a perquisite that caused several accounting problems for the havener.[115] Other gifts of prisage wine went to the clergy, such as the Carmelites of Plymouth, and local nobles, such as Hugh Courtenay, son of the earl of Devon.[116] Even those further down the social ladder benefited, including a Dartmouth shipmaster who had his two tuns of prisage wine at Falmouth returned to him in recognition of the aid he

---

113. Earl Edmund was also concerned about the sale of prisage wine, as indicated in the memoranda to the steward on the terms that buyers should be offered in the account of 1297/8. The orders on prisage wines of the duke are recorded in *BPR*, II, 39, 41, 52, 59, 75, 76, 77, 87, 127, 150, 185. For the Black Prince's involvement in Gascony and the state of his finances, see H. J. Hewitt, *The Black Prince's Expedition of 1355–1357* (Manchester, 1958).

114. See the accounts of 1338/9, 1348/9, 1350/1, 1353/4, 1354/5 (below, Part II), and *BPR*, II, pp. 5, 7, 53, 124–5, 133, 165. For further details on these and other officials of the duke, see Margaret Sharp, "The Central Administrative System of Edward, the Black Prince", and "The Diplomatic of the Black Prince's Central Secretarial Departments", in T. F. Tout, ed., *Chapters in the Administrative History of Medieval England*, vol. 5 (Manchester, 1930), pp. 289–440, and 400–40, and John Hatcher, *Rural Economy and Society in the Duchy of Cornwall 1300–1500* (Cambridge, 1970).

115. See the accounts of 1351/2 and 1352/3 (below, Part II), and *BPR*, II, pp. 15, 31, 38. For problems this perquisite caused in the havener's accounts, see also *BPR*, II, p. 67 and the account of 1353/4 (below, Part II).

116. *BPR*, II, pp. 120, 138. For Courtenay, see the account of 1348/9 (below, Part II).

had offered the duke in transporting his messenger from Gascony to England.[117] In dispensing these gifts, however, the havener was usually instructed to save the best wines for the duke. Indeed, in one year the duke went so far as to send a messenger to procure samples from the prisage wines, presumably so that he could choose the best to be sent to him.[118]

Trade, Merchants, and Ships

Our earliest reference to the scale of overseas trade in Cornwall comes from a royal tax on port trade in 1203–4 in which the only Cornish ports mentioned were Fowey (taxed £48 15s 11d) and Saltash (taxed £7 4s 8d), which ranked 13th and 29th of 35 ports.[119] This tax was based largely on wool exports, but Fowey's relatively high ranking was almost certainly due to tin exports from its region. Fish was also exported from Cornwall at an early date, although the value of this trade could not compare to the export of tin.[120] As the records of prisage witness, imports of wine were also an early part of overseas trade in Cornwall. It is, however, difficult to determine the size of overseas trade in Cornwall much before the fourteenth century, because its foreign trade, along with that of most of western England, was so irregularly tracked in the royal customs accounts, in part because of its distance from London and the more active ports of eastern England.[121]

Given the paucity of data on the overseas trade of medieval Cornwall, the customs accounts enrolled in the havener's accounts represent a particularly welcome source of information. In addition to the accounts of prisage wines, three other customs accounts are often included in the havener's accounts. The earliest is the 'ancient custom' (though it was called 'new custom' up until *c*. 1303), authorised in 1275 by Parliament as a custom on exports of hides and wool. By tabulating the returns from this custom, it is possible to track fluctuations in the export

---

117. Account of 1355/56 under 'Sum' (below, Part II).
118. *BPR*, II, p. 59.
119. *Pipe Roll 1204*, pp. xliii–xlv, 218. For this tax, see also T. H. Lloyd, *The English Wool Trade in the Middle Ages* (Cambridge, 1977), pp. 9–13.
120. For the early licences over the Cornish fish trade secured by French merchants, see the section below on 'Sea Fisheries'.
121. T. H. Lloyd, *Alien Merchants in England in the High Middle Ages* (New York, 1982), p. 36.

of wool and hides (the first exports to be regularly customed by the Crown) from 1284 to 1354 (Table 3).[122] These figures indicate that Cornwall would have ranked below most northern counties in the value of its export trade in these goods. Cornish ports exported very little wool and even its exports of hides paled in comparison to the hide exports of Newcastle, which averaged over 1400 dickers a year in 1279–1307.[123] Within southern England, however, Cornwall would have been the chief exporter of hides, a reflection of the county's reliance on livestock husbandry. These figures also indicate the severe fluctuations from year to year in the number of hides exported. The peak years of hide exports were the 1280s when numerous cargoes of hides were leaving the Cornish ports for markets overseas. Thereafter exports fell, although the nil returns in the 1320s may have had as much to do with changes in the lordship of the earldom as with problems in the production of hides following the cattle murrain of 1319–21.[124] Hide exports never recovered their previous strength in the following years, although they did reach 370 dickers in 1350/1. In interpreting the seeming decline in Cornish hide exports over this period, it is important to recognise that other factors, such as the transport of hides by coastal craft to ports outside the county, from whence they would be exported overseas, could also explain the 'decline' since exports were recorded only when on their way overseas, not if 'exported' along the coast to another English port.

[122.] In Table 3, details on ancient custom come from three sources: 1) the particular customs accounts (PRO, E122) as printed below in Part III (for most of the period before 1324); 2) accounts of ancient custom enrolled in the havener's accounts (for most of 1324–54); and 3) the enrolled customs accounts (PRO, E356), which gives only sums (items in square brackets are for periods when data from the particular or havener's accounts are not available). Note that in the particular and havener's accounts, ancient custom is usually called 'cocket', a reference to the receipt (sealed with the cocket seal) certifying the merchant had paid custom on a particular cargo of wool or hides exported.

[123.] For the Newcastle figures and those of other ports, see J. Conway Davies, "Wool Customs Accounts for Newcastle Upon Tyne for the Reign of Edward I", *Archaeologia Aeliana*, 4th series, 32 (1954), pp. 237–8, 266–71. Note that Davies' list of ports does not include any Cornish ports.

[124.] For the changes in lordship, see the section above on "The Maritime Administration Under the Earldom". For the cattle murrain, see Ian Kershaw, "The Great Famine and Agrarian Crisis in England 1315–1322", *in Peasants, Knights and Heretics: Studies in Medieval English Social History*, ed. R. H. Hilton (Cambridge, 1976), pp. 106–8 [first printed in *Past and Present*, 59 (1973)]. Cornwall was not as affected by the grain famine as most counties; see Hatcher, *Rural Economy*, p.85.

The second type of custom recorded in the havener's account is 'new custom', a port tax authorised by Parliament in 1303 on the imports and exports of alien merchants, but not English merchants.[125] It first appears in the havener's account in 1339 where it is usually associated with the 'ancient custom' or 'cocket' on wool and hide exports. The only extant account of new custom before 1339 is a particular customs account of the Crown dated 1322–24 (below, Part III). The third type of custom was called 'maltot', a term meaning 'evil tax' that was used to describe any arbitrary imposition.[126] The duchy's maltot was an *ad valorem* tax of 3d on every £ value of imports or exports by alien merchants that first appeared in the havener's accounts in 1346/7 and was regularly enrolled thereafter. Although maltot accounts only record the trade of non-English merchants, the details they offer on the type, size, and direction of overseas trade make them a valuable source of information for the foreign trade of medieval Cornwall.

Taken together, these three sets of accounts yield some insights into the size, content, and fluctuations in overseas trade to and from Cornwall, albeit largely for the trade carried on by alien merchants (Table 4). Not surprisingly, tin was by far the most valuable export; in the seven years that recorded tin exports, almost £2700 worth of tin was exported by foreigners alone, most of it from Fowey, but some also from Lostwithiel, Falmouth, and Padstow. These accounts show only the tip of the iceberg, however, since much tin was either shipped by coast to other English ports, or exported overseas by denizens. In 1336/7, for instance, two Lostwithiel ships brought 26 M of tin to the port of Exeter, which would have been valued at over £100 in the royal customs accounts.[127] In 1344, two Cornish merchants laded tin worth £240 at Fowey, along with hides, cheese, bacon, butter, cloth, beds, armour, and feathers, but the ship was attacked at sea on its way

---

[125.] The tax was suspended in 1311–22 and appears at first to have been only occasionally collected in the south-western ports; see T. H. Lloyd, *Alien Merchants in England*, pp. 27–34, 59, and Gras, *English Customs*, pp. 66–71. Butlerage, the 2s per tun tax on alien wine imports that replaced prisage on aliens was a sub-set of new custom.

[126.] For maltots generally, see Gras, *English Customs*, 89–94. The best known maltots are the extra subsidies assessed on wool exports. In the Cornish havener's accounts, maltot appears to be the same as the new custom of 1303.

[127.] DRO, Exeter Port Customs Accounts, 1336/7. This shipment would have not been recorded in any of the royal customs accounts (including maltot) because it was a coastal, not overseas export.

to Flanders.[128] Because Cornwall and Devon were the sole source of tin in medieval Europe, the value of the tin trade was high and a matter of personal concern to the earls and dukes, who frequently used their lordship of the stannaries in Cornwall and Dartmoor as collateral for loans.[129] Other Cornish exports included hides, the most frequent and valuable export after tin, and fish.[130] The remaining exports were of minuscule value and included such items as cheese, cloth, and horses (Table 4 and Part III).

These customs accounts also reveal details about the trade in imports to Cornwall. Wine was undoubtedly the chief import and can be traced to some extent in the prisage and butlerage accounts that survive for the county.[131] Some idea of the relative size of the wine trade at each port can be derived from the number of wine ships that visited each port (Table 4); Fowey and the Falmouth ports (Penryn and Truro) ranked well above the other Cornish ports in vessels carrying wine. After wine, the second leading import was salt, which Cornish fishermen used in considerable quantity to help preserve their catch, some of which was then exported overseas. Salt imports were particularly high at Fowey, Falmouth, and the ports of Mount's Bay, including Mousehole (Table 4). Merchants from Guerande and Spain were prominent in the salt trade during this period since the huge influx of salt from Bourgneuf Bay in Brittany and Poitou was only beginning in the mid-fourteenth century.[132] There were also occasional overseas imports of grain; iron, figs and raisins from Spain; and garlic and onions (probably from the Channel Islands or Brittany).

The havener's accounts also record the names and activities of merchants and shipmasters, particularly those from Cornwall. We catch glimpses of trading families, such as Richard and William Carburra;

[128.] *CCR 1343–6*, pp. 334–5. These shipments would not have been recorded in the havener's maltot accounts because they were exported by English merchants.

[129.] For the tin industry and trade, see John Hatcher, *English Tin Production and Trade before 1550* (Oxford, 1973); for the earl's use of the stannaries for loans, see *ibid*, pp. 22, 93. The Black Prince gave his right of pre-emption to Tydman de Lymbergh, a Hanseatic merchant, in exchange for cash advances; see *BPR*, I, 23, 33, 121; II, 12. The Prince also exported tin to Flanders to help finance his war expeditions; see *BPR*, I, pp. 66, 92.

[130.] For fish, see the section below on 'Sea Fisheries'.

[131.] See the section above on the prisage of wine.

[132.] For the salt trade, see A. R. Bridbury, *England and the Salt Trade in the Later Middle Ages* (Oxford, 1955). For problems between Spanish salt importers and Plymouth merchants in 1352, see PRO, JUST1/195, m. 5.

the Coulyings (Ralph, John sr and John jr), and the Maynhers of Tregony, all of them engaged in the export of hides and most active in the wine and tin trades as well.[133] These overseas merchants came primarily from port towns such as Looe, Polruan, Fowey, Truro, Mousehole, and Plymouth, but many also resided in more inland settlements such as Helston, Lostwithiel, Bodmin, Tregony, Liskeard, and Ashburton in Devon. Duchy officials, including the havener, Thomas Fitz Henry, and the collector of royal customs, Benedict Noght, were also involved in overseas trade. One of the more prominent merchants was Gerard de Villers, who may have been originally from Gascony but was a resident of Lostwithiel by the late 1280s. He traded in a wide variety of goods, including tin, hides, wine, and salt, and owned a cog called *St Edmund* of Fowey. For many years he was the county's biggest dealer in tin, although his involvement in money exchange also led to his indictment in the 1302 eyre for exchanging sterling for pollards, a type of base money.[134]

By tabulating the home ports of ships (primarily those carrying wine) and where they docked, we can also get an idea of the geographic range of the carrying trade at Cornish ports (Table 5). The largest contingent of ships came from neighbouring Devon, particularly from Plymouth and Dartmouth, both prominent centres of overseas transhipment and shipping.[135] But, while Plymouth ships stuck to trade at Plymouth, Dartmouth ships ranged much further, being particularly prominent at Falmouth. After Devon, Cornish shipping ranked second, with Fowey providing the largest fleet. Polruan, across the estuary from Fowey, also furnished a sizeable number, with Lostwithiel, a good way up the Fowey River, also responsible for six ships. Together these three Fowey Estuary ports provided an astonishing 77 per cent of the Cornish ships plying overseas routes in the early fourteenth century. This shipping concentration reflected Fowey's position as the chief port in

---

133. For their trade in wine, see PRO, JUST1/112, mm. 9, 18; JUST1/118, mm. 54d, 60d. For the involvement of William and Adam Carburra; William and Walter Maynher; and Michael, Robert, Stephen, and William Coulying in the tin trade, see PRO, E101/261/2.

134. For his trade recorded in this edition, see the accounts for 1289–92 in Part III, below, and the accounts of 1297/8 and 1313–14 in Part I, below. For his other activities, see *CCR 1302–7*, pp. 38–9; PRO, E101/261/1; PRO, JUST1/118, mm. 58, 58d, 65; and James Whetter, *Cornwall in the Thirteenth Century: A Study in Social and Economic History* (Gorran, 1998), pp. 89, 90.

135. M. Kowaleski, *Local Markets and Regional Trade in Medieval Exeter* (Cambridge, 1995), pp. 27–31, 255–7.

Cornwall. Falmouth's seeming strength—it ranked first in the number of ships calling there—is a bit of an illusion since its total includes large numbers of wine ships who merely first touched English territory there, but then continued on to unload their cargoes elsewhere in England. Ships from smaller Cornish ports, which primarily travelled coastal routes, such as those from Saltash, Looe, Mousehole, and Penzance at Exeter, do not appear in the havener's accounts because the royal customs enrolled there focused exclusively on overseas trade.[136]

Ships and merchants also visited from further afield, from as far north as Yorkshire and as far west as Wales and Ireland (Table 5). Vessels from the European continent also arrived, particularly at Plymouth and Falmouth as their first English ports of call after leaving Gascony with wine. Norman and Spanish ships were the best represented of this group. Not surprisingly the frequent visits of these foreign shipmasters, sailors, and merchants also caused problems including disputes over customs exemptions for the Channel Islanders and an alien who claimed to be a burgess of Liskeard, confiscation of goods owned by Waterford merchants in retaliation for their refusal to honour letters of cocket issued by the havener, and frequently tense relations with Spanish traders at the port of Plymouth.[137] Relations with foreign visitors to Cornwall were aggravated by England's uncertain and shifting foreign alliances during the Hundred Years War. The capture of several Flemish cogs by Cornish shipmasters, for instance, created considerable anxiety among Cornish merchants afraid of retaliation by the Flemish. To allay their fears, the duke wrote letters to the civic elite of Bruges and Ghent asking them to not interfere with Cornish merchants trading tin there.[138] When retaliation was licensed by the king, it was called privateering, but when unlicensed it became outright piracy. West Country mariners were enthusiastic participants in this game, but the rules shifted so often that the line between privateering and piracy was not distinct. The havener's accounts generally ignore ships and goods captured through piracy, which were dealt with by the king or the duke's

---

[136.] For Cornish ships bringing goods by coast to Exeter, see *Local Customs Accounts of the Port of Exeter 1266–1321*, ed. M. Kowaleski (DCRS, vol. 36, 1993), p. 15 and passim; DRO, Exeter Port Customs Accounts, passim.

[137.] Customs exemptions: *BPR*, II, p. 127; account of 1351/2, under 'Maltot' (printed below, Part II). Waterford merchants: *BPR*, II, pp. 115, 128, 131,135, 141 and account of 1352/3 under "Fines of Merchants' (below, Part II). Spanish at Plymouth: *CCR 1348–50*, p. 25; *CPR 1348–50*, pp. 78, 282, 319.

[138.] *BPR*, II, pp. 162–3, 165. See also I, p. 98 for Polruan mariners worried about their role in taking a ship of Brabant.

council,[139] but they do record four ships seized as prizes of privateering. Two Norman ships were taken in 1354/5; the havener sold one brought into Plymouth, reaping a profit of £22 10s, but in the same year he was ordered to return another Norman ship and its cargo of herring to its owner because it was supposedly taken during a truce, vividly illustrating the uncertain and confusing conditions under which trade was conducted in this period.

Maritime Courts

The earls and dukes also profited from their rights to adjudicate disputes arising at sea or between mariners and merchants. In medieval England, such disputes were resolved via maritime law, which originated as local customs in maritime boroughs, was codified in the fourteenth century in an international body of law called the Laws of Oleron, and eventually became the basis of the admiralty courts in the late medieval and early modern periods.[140] In Cornwall, the earl and then the duke enjoyed the profits of maritime courts held at Newlyn, Mousehole, Lostwithiel, and Plymouth.[141] The maritime courts at Lostwithiel were usually included in the farm of Fowey Water leased to the mayor and commonalty of Fowey, while those at Plymouth were part of the farm of Sutton Water, which was normally leased to a member of the local elite. It is likely that maritime courts were also held at other Cornish ports, since later references note such courts at Port Isaac, Padstow, St

---

[139.] See, for example, *BPR*, I, pp. 4–5, 77–8; PRO, E163/2/4; PRO, C258/10/5.

[140.] For the early maritime courts, see T. Twiss, ed., *The Black Book of the Admiralty* (Rolls Series, 4 vols., 1871–76) and R. G. Marsden, ed., *Select Pleas in the Court of Admiralty*, vol. I (Selden Society, vol. 6, 1894), pp. xiii–xiv, xxiv, xlix. For the Laws of Oleron (Oleron was an island off the coast of Brittany), see *Black Book*, I, 88–131; P. Studer, ed., *The Oak Book of Southampton*, vol. II (Southampton Record Society, vol. 11, 1911), pp. xxix–lxxi, 54–103; and T. J. Runyan, "The Rolls of Oleron and the Admiralty Court in Fourteenth-Century England", *American Journal of Legal History*, 19 (1975), pp. 95–111.

[141.] For Mousehole and Newlyn, see the accounts of 1338/9 and 1339/40. The Fowey courts were usually mentioned in the entries for Fowey Water under 'Lostwithiel' and the Plymouth courts in the entries for Sutton Water under 'Trematon'.

Ives, Mount's Bay, Treath, and Looe.[142] The profits collected from the
fines assessed at the maritime courts were modest, annually averaging
about 30s to 40s except at the beginning of the Hundred Years War
when they fell to only 7s per year because commercial traffic decreased
as mariners entered naval service and war hostilities stymied trade (Table
1).[143] The value of the court perquisites could also fluctuate sharply,
amounting to only 9d in the year of the plague, 1348/9. The maritime
court at Plymouth (recorded separately as a seigneurial profit attached
to the honour of Trematon) seems to have been the busiest and most
profitable of the duchy's maritime courts; in 1338/9, for instance, the
'water courts' for Plymouth Water yielded 68s from pleas and perquisites, while the courts at Mousehole reported 7s 1d and those of Newlyn
only 4s 2d that year.

Maritime law, like law merchant, offered speedy justice to plaintiffs
and defendants whose business required that they settle problems and
be on their way as quickly as possible. Under the earldom, the bailiff
hired to keep the coasts of the north Devon manors was also expected
to hold maritime courts there.[144] In Plymouth, the water bailiff presided
over the proceedings, which in 1386 was held at the first hour of the
first tide at '*Foxhole*'.[145] The administrative machinery to enforce the
courts' decisions, however, was often lacking, particularly in cases
involving parties from different jurisdictions. In 1346, for example,
the duke had to intervene when the mayor of Lostwithiel failed to
enforce a judgement of the maritime court in favour of two of the
duke's tenants to recoup £20 against the mayor and commonalty of
Bristol for trespasses against them at sea by Bristol men.[146] Some of the
cases involved major debts, such as the failure of a Plymouth merchant
to deliver 500 marks he had received at Bruges from the sale of a ship

---

[142.] For Padstow (which was not under the jurisdiction of the earl or duke), see
Marsden, ed., *Court of Admiralty*, I, xlix–l and G. O. Sayles, ed., *Select Cases
in the Court of King's Bench* (Selden Society, vol. 88, 1971), p. 35. For maritime
courts held in the other ports, see the havener's accounts of 1429 (Campbell,
"Haveners", pp. 127–8) and 1506/7 (PRO, SC6/HenVII/1083). In 1393/4 (DCO,
Ministers' Account Roll 31) 6s 1d was collected 'for twelve courts'.

[143.] For the explanation about naval service, see the section on 'Maritime Courts'
in the accounts of 1338/9 and 1346/7 (below, Part I). In the account of September
1336 (below, Part I) the nil return for the maritime courts of Lostwithiel were
blamed on the lack of ships docking at the port. In 1339/40, court profits were
low because of the withdrawal of mariners and fishers in the face of hostile
challenges by Spanish ships and fishers.

[144.] See the final section of the account for 1301/2, printed below in Part I.

[145.] PRO, C260/98/10.

[146.] *BPR*, I, pp. 24, 25.

called the *Christopher* to the ship's owner, while others covered more petty matters, such as fishing out of season or with the wrong kind of nets.[147] Although the types of cases adjudicated by the Cornish maritime courts changed little over the centuries, the number of cases and profits collected for the duchy began to diminish as early as the 1380s in response to the growing power of the admiralty courts. Despite laws granting exclusive judicial rights to the Lord High Admiral in maritime matters, the duchy stubbornly insisted on its right to hold maritime courts well into the sixteenth century, although its profits from the courts had by then dwindled to virtually nothing.[148]

Sea Fisheries

Cornwall's maritime economy was heavily dependent on the bountiful harvest of fish from the seas surrounding the peninsula. As early as 1202, merchants from southern France farmed the county's fisheries from the king, claiming purchase rights on whales, hake, and conger, and paying for licenses to salt and dry fish for export on a large scale.[149] By the thirteenth and fourteenth centuries, the region was regularly exporting fresh, salted, and dried fish (particularly hake) to Spain and France, and to Gascony in particular.[150] Cornish hake and other fish also found its way to the markets of other English towns, including Exeter and London.[151] The duke recognised Cornwall's value as a source

---

147. For examples of the types of cases tried in the Cornish maritime courts before 1400, see PRO C260/98/10, 110/16; *BPR*, I, 25; *Court of Admiralty*, I, 1–17.

148. In 1382/3 (PRO, SC6/818/11) only 10s was collected from the maritime courts 'because the Admiral of the king held courts and took profits'. For admiralty courts held at Lostwithiel and Fowey in the late 14th century, see *Court of Admiralty*, I, pp. 1–17. In 1523/4, the duchy collected over £4 from maritime courts, but by 1541/2 the Admiral's intrusions were not allowing the havener to account for any profits from the courts; see *Tidal Estuaries*, p. 146. For the expanding power of the admiralty courts, see also Marsden, "Introduction", *Court of Admiralty*, I.

149. *Rotuli chartarum in turri Londinensi asservati, 1199–1216*, ed. T. D. Hardy (London, 1837), p. 191; *Rotuli de oblatis et finibus in turri Londinensi asservati, 1200–1205*, ed. T. D. Hardy (London, 1835), p. 194; *Pipe Roll 1212*, p. 68; *Pipe Roll 1222*, p. 128.

150. PRO, E101/555/1 (1297); *CPR 1313–18*, p. 488; *1361–4*, p. 496; *1364–7*, pp. 7, 11, 32, 50; *1370–4*, p. 181; *Caption*, pp. lvii, 136–7; and below, Part II, passim.

151. DRO, Exeter Mayor's Court Roll, 1323/4, m. 15d; M. Kowaleski, "The Expansion of the South-Western Fisheries in Late Medieval England", *Economic History Review*, 2nd series 53:3 (2000), pp.431–42; and the havener's accounts in DCO Ministers' Accounts, 17 (1365/6), 19 (1373/4) and 20 (1374/5).

of fish by ordering his steward to purvey a wide variety of fish there—
cod, salted conger, salted salmon, dried hake, salted ling and cod, and
dried whiting—to be sent him in London and Gascony, the latter
destination 'by some sure mariner of Cornwall'. [152] The duke was also
receptive to petitions from local fishermen and defended their interests
against the claims of other lords. [153]

The earldom and duchy's revenues from port farms, trantery,
merchant fines, and maritime courts all rested largely on the strength
of the fishing trade. In the first years of the Hundred Years War, for
instance, the havener explained falling revenues from these perquisites
as due to the harassment of Spanish ships that deliberately 'came to do
harm to the fishers in the time of fishing' and to the fact that no foreign
merchants came to buy fish, nor did boats venture out because of the
war at sea. [154] The fluctuating sums collected from trantery and fish
merchant fines were particularly sensitive to periods of truce (when
revenues rose). The diversion of fishers to naval service, as occurred in
1346/7, was also responsible for less than hoped-for revenues from the
maritime courts and trantery in some years.

One of the more unusual revenues connected to the sea fisheries
was trantery, explained in the accounts of 1300/1 and 1336 as a toll
levied on those who came to one of the earl or duke's ports to purchase
fish for re-sale elsewhere. [155] That they carried away horse-loads of fish
indicates they were fish dealers serving as middlemen between the
fishermen and consumers. Although returns from trantery first surface
in the havener's accounts in 1300, the toll had already been around for
several decades, part of Earl Richard's more intense exploitation of his
maritime prerogatives. Residents of settlements around Plymouth
objected to paying this toll in the 1270s, while men of Cornwall
complained in 1302 that trantery was a new custom that was harming
both the county and the tranters (a general term for chapmen). [156] The

---

[152.] *BPR*, II, pp. 98, 151, 207.

[153.] *BPR*, II, p. 129; PRO, E370/9/1.

[154.] See these sections for the accounts of 1338/9 and 1339/40, below, Part II, and
the section on 'Port Farms' in the account of 1336, Part I, below.

[155.] In the account of the farmers of Porthwyn in 1436–39 (PRO, SC6/825/20), it
was called 'a fine for purchasing fish'. In 1454/5 (DCO Ministers' Account 54,
m. 14) the account refers to 'fines of other tranters called *Jutes*' which is probably
a reference to 'jutors' or fish drivers.

[156.] *Rotuli hundredorum*, I, pp. 76, 81 (complaints from Tavistock and Plympton
residents about a 'new' annual charge of 3d to 4d on purchases of fish); PRO,
JUST1/118, m. 53.

havener in 1302, William Talcarn, defended the new imposition by saying that he took only 3d to 4d a year from each tranter for the privilege of fetching fish. This low rate of assessment meant that the toll never brought in large amounts. In the Caption of Seisin of 1337, the surveyors pegged the annual profits from trantery at 6s 8d per year, an amount that would have represented 20–26 dealers in fish if paying at the rate of 3d–4d each, but only 13 dealers if they were paying 6d apiece, the rate most often mentioned in the late fifteenth century. Trantery virtually disappears from the accounts in the third quarter of the fourteenth century, but enjoyed a period of recovery in the 1490s and first decade of the 1500s when about 20s and more per year was collected from trantery at Sutton Pool, and additional sums at Fowey.[157]

Trantery was usually linked to 'fines on merchants' (also called a fine for 'forestalling') which was a kind of licensing fee paid by 'foreign' (i.e., non local) fishmongers to purchase fish before it reached the market, probably at the seashore, straight from the fishermen, after which they would export it elsewhere. Although it is a normal retailing practice today, national and local statutes legislated against 'forestalling' the market because such practices could raise prices and lead to shortages; the fish trade in particular was the subject of considerable attention in this regard.[158] The forestalling 'fines' paid in the havener's accounts represented the earldom and duchy's pragmatic handling of a situation that was going to occur anyway; by making forestallers pay a fine, they derived some profit. The toll seems to have been levied mainly on dealers who were taking fish out of the county; in later accounts men from such places as Polruan, Dartmouth, Kingswear, and Poole were named; hake, pilchard and fish oil were the items they exported.[159] The complaints voiced in the eyre of 1302 against trantery also singled out the forestalling fines on overseas merchants as another new

---

[157.] See the sections on 'Sutton Pool' in the havener's accounts in DCO Ministers' Accounts 83, 85, and 89, as well as the section on 'Fowey' for DCO Ministers' Account 82 (account for 1498).

[158.] See M. Kowaleski, "The Internal Fish Trade", in *England's Sea Fisheries: The Commercial Sea Fisheries of England and Wales since 1300*, ed. D. J. Starkey, C. Reid and N. Ashcroft (London, 2000), pp. 29–30.

[159.] See the havener's accounts under 'Trantery' in DCO Ministers' Accounts 17, 19, and 20; PRO, SC6/817/9, m. 9. Hull (*Caption*, p. 137) defines tranters as 'stall-holders selling fish there', but the explicit references to dealers coming to horses and the identification of others paying the custom in the late 14th century suggest this was not the case.

imposition; the havener claimed that merchants were being amerced according to the taxation of the fishermen and the quantity of their transgressions, as had been the custom throughout the tenure of Earl Edmund (1272–1300). The fines first surface in the accounts in 1302/3 when six men paid fines for forestalling fish; one paid 3s, two paid 2s (including a clerk of Trungle), and three paid 12d, for a total of 10s. These fines were much larger than those paid by tranters because the forestalling merchants were exporters of fish on a larger scale, while tranters were primarily retailers. In the following year, the sum collected from merchants rose to 25s, but at the start of the Hundred Years War the fines fell rapidly. There was some recovery in the years of truce in the late fourteenth century, as in 1363/4 when six men (one associated with his 'fellows') paid sums ranging from 8s to 3s, but in general the War depressed revenues from this maritime prerogative because hostilities at sea discouraged merchants from travelling.

The havener's accounts offer occasional hints as to the relative size of the fish trade at individual ports. The port farms (Table 2) indicate that St Ives and Mousehole were in a league by themselves since their annual farms—directly dependent on the profitability of the local fishing industry—were more than twice that of their closest rivals, Marazion and Fowey. Mousehole is also singled out in the havener's account of 1354/5, when revenues from trantery and fishing fines were not as large as expected because the local fishers were coerced to fish for the duke's household.[160] The fisheries attached to Kerrier Hundred (only Porthallow is singled out by name) came next, followed by Polruan and Newlyn, all of which brought in about 20s per year. Fisheries at Land's End and Penzance came next, with far smaller sums accruing from the fisheries at Porthzennor, Portheras, and Lamorna. The fisheries at ports held by other lords, such as Looe and Padstow must also have been profitable, as was that of Plymouth, whose revenues were usually subsumed into a lump sum paid annually by the farmer of Plymouth Water.

Estuarine fisheries were also noted in the havener's accounts. One was attached to Tewington manor, which with trantery was supposedly worth 15s, but by 1349/50 had had reverted to the lord for lack of

---

160. For a glimpse at the growing commercialisation of fishing at Mousehole, see also BPR, II, pp. 93–4 for objections to a local merchant's cornering of the market.

tenants after the plague.[161] There was a small fishery at Tybesta, and another in the Lynher River attached to Trematon which usually rented for 5s per year, although its income, like that of Tewington, declined after the Black Death for lack of tenants. Profits from the Fowey River fishery fluctuated more widely, from as little as 2s in 1336 to over 53s in 1352/3. The rising profits were most like due to manorial investment in the fishery, as indicated by the nets, cords and other rigging the manor purchased and maintained from 1338/9 on.[162] The most lucrative of the estuarine fisheries, however, were those of the Tamar River. They included oyster fisheries attached to Saltash (which brought in less than 3d per year) and to Trematon borough, where tenants were obliged to pay the lord an annual toll of 1½d per year at Michaelmas.[163] Considerably more lucrative were the freshwater fish weirs attached to the manor of Calstock, most of which were for salmon; the chief fishery was farmed out to Tavistock Abbey for the princely sum of £10 a year.[164] Additional salt water marine fisheries were in Saltash Water and Sutton Water, both of which were frequently the subject of complaints and litigation. In the hundred rolls of 1274, burgesses of both Tavistock and Plympton complained that the bailiffs of Earl Richard were raising new tolls on river traffic, including 3d to 4d on every load of fish sold at Sutton Pool.[165] In the late fourteenth century there were efforts to

---

[161.] Trantery at Tewington was farmed for 2s in 1301/2. See also the references to trantery in the section on Tewington in the Assession Rolls of 1333 and 1356, printed below in Appendix I. The fishery at Tewington brought in 4s in 1338/9 (PRO, SC6/816/11, m. 7), but in the accounts of 1349/50 and 1350/1 (SC6/817/1, m. 6; DCO Ministers' Account 5, m. 5), both the fishery and trantery had reverted to the lord for lack of tenants 'in the time of the pestilence'.

[162.] See the Lostwithiel sections in the accounts of 1338/9, 1353/4, 1354/5, and 1355/6 (below, Part II).

[163.] For Saltash, see its entries in the havener's accounts printed in Parts I and II, below, and relevant sections in Appendix I. For Trematon, see Hull, *Caption*, p. 119 (printed below in Appendix I).

[164.] See Appendix I, below, for Calstock entries in the Assession Rolls of 1333, 1347, and 1356. Nets were also used to take fish in Calstock; see DRO, W1258/D77/4–5. For the Calstock fisheries, see also *BPR*, II, pp. 27, 31–2, 71, 74, 90; *Caption*, pp. 100, 105–6, and H.P.R. Finberg, *Tavistock Abbey: A Study in the Social and Economic History of Devon* (Newton Abbot, 1969), pp. 161–3; Hatcher, *Rural Economy*, pp. 66, 191 205.

[165.] *Rotuli hundredorum*, I, pp. 76–7, 81. The amounts of the toll suggest it probably referred to trantery, which was also the subject of complaints in the eyre of 1302 (above, n. 156).

compel fishermen to sell fish they caught within the bounds of the Tamar only at Saltash and Plymouth, because of the loss of custom when fishermen sold their catch at Snappedon, Stonehouse, and Landulph.[166] A similar dispute about fishermen's rights to sell their catch where they wanted without paying toll was at the heart of the defence of John de Montacute, another local lord, of his fishermen-tenants' right to be free of the duchy's fish tolls at Sutton Water in 1355/6.

The accounts also provide some information about fishing methods in medieval Cornwall. Seine nets were commonly used, especially in Tamar Water where as many as five fishing boats were taxed each year, along with four to eight seines, each of which owed 12d a year. The dues owed by these fishing boats and seines were often included in the farm of the borough of Saltash. Nets of an unspecified type were also used in the Fowey River fisheries, while the Caption of Seisin of 1337 refers to seines and nets 'dragging' for fish at Trematon. We also know that seine nets were used at Marazion and Goran Haven in this period.[167] Part of the revenues at Sutton Pool consisted of a 12d toll on each fishing boat for the right to dry its sails and nets on the foreshore.[168] The ability to lay out fishing nets to dry was an important part of the fishing industry and one that occasioned the murder of the Penryn keeper of pigs by a local fisherman furious that the pigs had trampled the nets he had laid out to dry.[169] There are no references to long line fishing in the accounts, but this method was the one employed to catch larger fish such as hake and cod.

The types of fish being caught in this period are mainly recorded in references to exports and purveyance, where hake figures most prominently, but cod, whiting, ling, conger and salmon are also noted.[170] Herring are strangely missing from this list, even though it probably represented the chief catch of the inshore fisheries of medieval Cornwall; its ubiquity on local tables may account for its omission from lists of Cornish exports. Pilchard, the fish most often associated with Cornwall, was first mentioned in the havener's accounts only in the 1360s, when

---

166. *CIM*, IV, p. 148; CRO, ME961/31. For the bounds of the earl and duke's lordship over Tamar Water, see *Caption*, p. 124 (printed below, Appendix I).
167. G.D.G. Hall, ed., "Three Courts of the Hundred of Penwith, 1333", in *Medieval Legal Records Edited in Memory of C.A.F. Meeking* (London, 1978), pp. 183, 188.
168. *CIM*, II, p. 81.
169. PRO, JUST1/112, m. 13.
170. See above, notes 150 and 151.

it was noted among the types of fish on which 'foreign' merchants paid forestalling fines. Pilchards crop up as a coastal import to Exeter as early as 1341, however, as well as in a list of purchases for the local lord's household at South Pool in 1342.[171] Several factors may be responsible for the infrequent references to pilchards before the late fifteenth and sixteenth century. Most importantly, the special curing process that encouraged the development of a large export trade in pilchards (especially to the Mediterranean) was not really adopted until the sixteenth century.[172] It is also possible that pilchard's similarity to herring, a point driven home by the Cornish word *hern*, which can be translated either as 'herring' or 'pilchard', meant that pilchard was rarely distinguished from the local herring catch. The tendency to conflate pilchards with herring is also evident in some of the early references to pilchards: 'herring pilchards' or 'herring called pilchard'.[173] These types of references dwindle by the later fifteenth century and sixteenth century when the new 'fumadoe' curing process had raised the commercial value of pilchards, thus making it worthwhile to distinguish them from herring.

The Seigneurial Ports

The havener's accounts did not record revenues from such ports as Tintagel, Fowey, Saltash, and Plymouth because the earl and duke's tenure of the manors to which these ports belonged was seigneurial. Profits from these ports are thus to be found enrolled in the accounts of the reeve or bailiff for these places in the ministers' accounts, relevant extracts of which are printed here in order to illustrate the full range of maritime revenues enjoyed by the earldom and havener. Although most revenues from seigneurial ports—covering such prerogatives as local port customs, estuarine fisheries, and shore-side rights—were not included in the havener's accounts, profits from prisage and royal port

---

[171.] DRO, Exeter Port Customs Accounts, 1340/1; CRO, AR12/25, m. 3v.

[172.] John Scantlebury, "The Development of the Export Trade in Pilchards from Cornwall during the Sixteenth Century", *JRIC*, n.s., 10 (1989), pp. 330–59. See also Kowaleski, "Expansion of South-Western Fishing", and idem, "The Western Fisheries", in *England's Sea Fisheries*, pp. 23–8 for this and the following.

[173.] CRO, ART2/2/8/5, m. 5 (1429): *allec' de pilchard*; PRO, E122/114/1 (1462): *allec' vocat' pylchard'*. For the Cornish terms, see R. Morton Nance, "The Celtic Names of Fish in Cornwall", *JRIC*, n.s., 2 (1954), pp. 74–5.

customs for Fowey and Plymouth were recorded there because the earl
and duke's title to these prerogatives grew out of their tenure of the
earldom and duchy, not their position as manorial lords of these ports.
Profits arising from the sea fisheries of Fowey were also included among
the port farms of the havener's accounts because they too were attached
to the tenure of the earldom and duchy. Another seigneurial port of
the duchy was Dartmouth, but this prerogative was early on granted
away, so revenues from the port of Dartmouth were not enrolled in the
havener's or the ministers' accounts.[174] On occasion, the ministers'
accounts of the duchy also contain stray records regarding the maritime
profits of other manors that temporarily escheated to the duke as chief
lord. In 1348/9, for instance, part of the Scillies came into the duke's
hands because its heir was underage, including 10s from two-thirds of
the rent of boats docking there, although this amount was noted as
considerably below the normal level because 'the greater part of the
fishers were killed by pestilence'.[175] The duke also acquired the fishery
at Looe because of the minority of its heir and leased it out in 1353 for
one mark per year.[176]

The jurisdiction over Plymouth was the most profitable of the
seigneurial ports, although it was restricted to lordship of Sutton Water
(also called Sutton Pool), the medieval harbour of Plymouth, which
was attached to the honour of Trematon. The profits from the harbour
grew markedly over the period covered by these accounts, although
they suffered temporary set-backs because of the War and plague. In
the last two decades of the thirteenth century, the earl's annual profits
from Sutton Water hovered around 45s, but they doubled in the first

---

[174.] In 1337, the value of Dartmouth Water to the duchy of Cornwall was listed as
£4 13s 4d (*Caption*, p. 140, n. 1). The history of Dartmouth harbour is
complicated by the convoluted history of the different manors and lordships
that made up Dartmouth (which in the middle ages, was often known as
Dartmouth-Hardness-Clifton); see Percy Russell, *Dartmouth: A History of the
Port and Town* (London, 1950), pp. 29–33, and Ray Freeman, *Dartmouth and
Its Neighbours* (Chichester, 1990), pp. 23–6. For the maritime development of
Dartmouth, see also M. Kowaleski, "The Port Towns of Fourteenth-Century
Devon", in *The New Maritime History of Devon*, vol. I, ed. M. Duffy et al.,
(London and Exeter, 1992), pp. 62–72.

[175.] DCO Ministers' Account 4, m. 11. See also *BPR*, II, p. 45.

[176.] *BPR*, II, pp. 50–1, 54 .

two decades of the fourteenth century.[177] These revenues stemmed largely from Plymouth's maritime courts and charges on fishermen for use of the foreshore for drying nets and selling fish. The more secure tenure the crown and earldom established over its prerogatives there in 1318 may have been partly responsible for these rising profits, but increased revenues probably arose largely from expanding business at the port, much of it because of the mounting use of Plymouth as an embarkation point for royal expeditions and voyages to Gascony.[178] By the Assession Roll of 1333 (Appendix I), the earldom was able to lease Sutton Water for £17 10s per year to Thomas de Spekenton; the increment of 30s and entry fine of 110s that he paid were further indications of the value of this prerogative. Spekenton, however, was unable to pay this sum for long so by the time of the Caption of Seisin in 1337 the harbour had been taken back into the duke's hands. Further problems occurred in 1338/9 when the farm had to be reduced because 'the whole town of Sutton was nearly burned by the enemy', a reference to a war-time raid by the French.[179] The financial difficulties of the farmers of Sutton Water continued into the next decade as John de Teuerton, who leased the farm in 1339/40, was in arrears by 1341/2. The patience of the auditors was obviously wearing a bit thin since they sharply rebuked the past steward of Cornwall for leasing Sutton Water to Teuerton without taking proper security. Around 1343, the farm of the Pool was handed over to John Hawley of Dartmouth (father of the infamous mayor, merchant, and privateer), who appears to have received title as a kind of reward for services rendered to the current duke, the Black Prince.[180] He too quickly fell into arrears, although

---

[177.] The £4 per year was identical to the profits claimed by the king (to whose hands the earldom had reverted) in Sutton in an inquisition in 1318 (*CIM*, II, p. 81; see *also Plymouth Municipal Records*, ed. R. N. Worth (Plymouth, 1893), pp. 10–11, 35–36). Note also that along with the port, the king on behalf of the earldom also successfully established his right in 1318 over a vacant plot of land near the port, one perch long and 5 perches wide, and another piece of land reclaimed from the sea containing six acres of land. This was where maritime courts were held and fishing boats landed, dried their sails and nets, and sold their fish.

[178.] Kowaleski, "Port Towns;" Crispin Gill, *Plymouth: A New History* (Newton Abbot, 2nd edn., 1979), pp. 64–88. For the 1318 inquisition, see above, n. 177.

[179.] See the account of 1338/9 under 'Trematon'. See also *CPR, 1338–40*, p. 279.

[180.] See the account of 1344/5 under 'Trematon'. For Hawley and his son, see H. R. Watkin, ed., *Dartmouth*, vol. I, *Pre-Reformation* (Parochial Histories of Devonshire, no. 5, 1935), passim.

probably not for want of cash. Within a few years the Pool changed hands again, being leased in the Assession Roll of 1347 to Richard de Brounmore for seven years for only £10 a year and no entry fine, clearly an acknowledgement of the reduced revenues resulting from the difficulties of the Hundred Years War. Plague further diminished its value, so that by 1350/1 Sutton Pool had been handed over to John Dabernoun (steward and sheriff of Cornwall) for the term of his life for only £6 13s 4d a year. Dabernoun was still holding it in the Assession of 1356.

We get a better idea of the items producing revenue at Sutton Water from a stray membrane attached to the havener's account of 1338/9 that records profits of about £10 10s over a four-month period: 68s came from Plymouth's maritime courts (by far the most lucrative maritime courts in the duchy and surely a reflection of the considerable activity occurring in the port), 58s from rents on boats, 53s from the sale of rushes, 14s from local customs on certain imports and exports, and a bit over 7s from tolls on the ferry over Plymouth Water. If the boat rents were the same charged in 1318 (12d per year), it meant there were at least 58 fishing boats working out of Plymouth in 1338/9.[181] The rents were also collected with the help of a local water bailiff or 'keeper of the water' as he was sometimes called, who was appointed by the duke as lord of Sutton Water.[182] This bailiff may have helped the havener collect prisage at Plymouth, which hosted more wine ships than any of the Cornish ships, including those that only stopped at St Nicholas Island to take on water and victuals. And unlike the Cornish ports, the national port customs (called 'cocket' and 'maltot' here) in Plymouth were generally not included in the havener's accounts.

The other seigneurial ports attached to the honour of Trematon were the boroughs of Saltash and Trematon, although Saltash was by far the more prominent of the two.[183] Its revenues were often farmed by a group of local burgesses (under the same conventionary tenure to which other manorial properties were subject), so it is difficult to tell the

---

[181]. For the 1318 inquiry, see *CIM*, II, p. 81; the annual charge included the right to dry their sails and nets and expose their fish for sale.

[182]. For examples of such appointments, see Watkin, ed., *Dartmouth*, pp. 45, 373.

[183]. See also M. Beresford, *New Towns of the Middle Ages: Town Plantation in England, Wales and Gascony* (Gloucester, 2nd edn., 1988), pp. 411–12 on the distinction between the two neighbouring boroughs.

exact value of each maritime prerogative, particularly during the tenure of the duchy. The most valuable perquisite was Saltash Water, the chief component of which was the Saltash ferry (referred to as 'the passage'), which was leased for £8 10s at the beginning of the fourteenth century, and for about £10 per year by the 1330s. As with most of the duke's other prerogatives, the havener often found it difficult to collect the full amount because of the difficulties caused by the Hundred Years War and depopulation following the Black Death; immediately after the plague, in fact, the prerogative was abandoned to the duke who leased it to the steward for a short term. Also included in the lease of Saltash Water were rents of four oars belonging to the ferry, customs on barges bringing sand down the Tamar, and tolls on seine fishing. Tolls on oysters, which brought in only a few pence each year, were usually part of the farm of Saltash borough.

The Caption of Seisin also refers to 'Tamar Water' as another prerogative attached to the honour of Trematon, but offers no valuation, nor does it ever appear as a separate item in the accounts. Its inclusion in the Caption seems to have been primarily to lay out the boundaries of the maritime jurisdiction claimed by the duke in the region. The grandly-named 'Lynher Water' also attached to Trematon actually referred to the relatively small fishery in the Lynher River between Saltash and St Germans, another duchy property.

Worth considerably more was Fowey Water, which stretched from Polruan to Respryn in Lanhydrock.[184] It was attached to the honour of Restormel and borough of Lostwithiel, the duke's capital in Cornwall that lay some miles up the Fowey River. Fowey was the county's most important port; the early customs accounts (cocket and maltot) indicate that it handled the lion's share of Cornwall's overseas trade, while ranking a close second to Plymouth in the amount of prisage wine arriving at its harbour. These wine imports were augmented by the prisage wines from elsewhere in the duke's jurisdiction, which were usually brought to Fowey to be sold or disbursed according to the duke's instructions. These prerogatives, however, were part of the earl and duke's maritime revenues anyway by virtue of their lordship of the Cornish ports. In contrast, their rights to local port customs at Fowey, such as keelage, measurage, and maritime courts, stemmed from their seigneurial lordship of Lostwithiel, which had long enjoyed control over the lower reaches of the Fowey River. As a result, the reeve of

---

[184.] PRO, E152/8 (abstracted in *CIPM*, vol. 3, p. 457, the IPM of Earl Edmund).

Lostwithiel, not the havener, handled the collection of port dues at Fowey and accounted for them.[185] Profits from the sea fishery of Fowey, however, were included in the farms of ports in the accounts of the havener.

The content of the Fowey local port customs were laid out in a series of disputes over the course of the early fourteenth century. A disagreement between Lostwithiel and Bodmin, whose burgesses claimed freedom from the local port customs at Fowey, outlined the rates for keelage, a charge on each 'keel' or ship arriving with goods at the port, that varied according to the size of the vessel.[186] Ships were required to pay 16d in keelage if they unloaded over 30 tuns worth of goods (wine was probably the chief import); 8d if unloading 10–30 tuns and 4d for additional trips; barges also paid 4d apiece. In contrast to keelage, measurage (also called 'bushelage') was a tax in kind on imports of dried goods such as salt and corn; in 1337, Lostwithiel claimed this toll was a fief pertaining to the office of mayor that dated back to the time of Earl Richard.[187] Those arriving with 20 quarters of salt or more owed the lord 1 bushel of salt (which had to be measured out, hence the name of the toll) and 2–4 bushels if more than 20 quarters was imported. In 1352/3, eleven ships brought salt to Fowey, but none carrying wheat or other grains subject to the toll; the bushels of salt were sold and the profit (as well as the price per bushel) was enrolled in the Lostwithiel accounts for Fowey Water. In 1355/6, measurage was charged on salt and *stonecol*, as well as wheat, barley, rye, and beans; the unusually large amounts of imported grain brought in this year may have reflected local shortages. It is important to note, however, that while these local customs are useful for indicating the type of

---

[185.] See also the account of 1355/6 under 'Fowey Water' for 8s 6d paid (presumably to the reeve of Lostwithiel) for collecting the customs at Fowey and bringing them to Lostwithiel, and for doing the measures at Fowey.

[186.] PRO, JUST1/118, m. 62. The 'barges' noted in the 1302 eyre probably referred to small river-boats since in 1351/2 (below, Part II) barges arriving with imported salt were paying 16d apiece, the amount assessed on ships carrying the largest loads. In the Caption of Seisin of 1337, the top rate was due from ships carrying over 40 tons, with 8d from ships with less than 40 tuns of goods but possessing a boat, and 4d from vessels without boats, rates which were also spelled out in the account of 1355/6.

[187.] See, for instance, the accounts for Fowey Water in 1351/2, 1352/3 and 1353/4 (below, Part II). Note that the Caption of Seisin (Appendix I, below) stated the toll a bit differently; a bushel was due from ships unloading but less than 40 tuns in size, while ships over 40 tuns owed 2 bushels.

trade that passed through Fowey, they do not directly measure the size of this trade since so many merchants were exempt from paying these tolls, including not only the Lostwithiel burgesses, but also, it appears, the burgesses of Bodmin. Indeed, references to keelage often specify it was imposed on 'foreign' ships, by which was meant non-local ships, but not necessarily 'foreign' in the sense of 'from overseas'.

Besides keelage and measurage, the prerogatives of Fowey Water included revenues from the maritime courts at Lostwithiel and the fishery of Fowey Water (most likely the estuarine fishery since the sea fishery was included in the annual port farms). The Lostwithiel burgesses normally leased Fowey Water from the duke as part of the farm of their borough, but accounted for the prerogatives separately. In 1354/5, the courts, which were held by the mayor of Lostwithiel, brought in 13s 4d. The fishery was a source of some anxiety since people were evading paying for the right to fish in Fowey Water, thus lowering the income from this seigneurial perquisite.[188] Income from the fishery (and Lostwithiel mills) was further reduced by damage from tinworks further upstream, a perennial problem in many Cornish rivers. And, as with other properties, income also fell after the Black Death, compelling the auditors to forgive the Lostwithiel burgesses a large part of the farm in 1353.[189]

Other coastal manors also included maritime revenues that accrued to the earl and duke by virtue of their seigneurial lordship. At Tintagel, 2s per year was collected from each boat beaching at the tiny port beneath the cliffs that was also called 'the port of Bossiney', the name of the borough within the manor.[190] In the first half of the fourteenth century, four to seven fishing boats paid this fee each year (with a high of eight boats in 1346/7), but plague reduced that number to three or four a year in the 1350s 'because the fishers died in the pestilence'. There were also estuarine fisheries attached to the manors of Trematon (in the Lynher), Liskeard (at East Looe), Tewington (probably around Par Sands), and Tybesta (in the Fal). The most profitable fishery, at Calstock, was primarily a freshwater fishery because it was so far up the Tamar River. In other cases, maritime revenues were subsumed into the farm of a borough and were thus not specifically delineated in

---

[188.] *BPR*, II, p. 25. For the following, see *ibid*, pp. 27, 121.

[189.] See also *BPR*, II, p. 52 on this point.

[190.] Beresford, *New Towns*, p. 414 does not believe it was a proper borough, but see Hull, *Caption*, p. xlvi. See also A. C. Canner, *The Parish of Tintagel: Some Historical Notes* (Enfield, Middlesex, 1982), pp. 12–13, 98.

the ministers' accounts. This was the case for Helston-in-Kerrier, whose burgesses claimed keelage from ships at Gweek (about three miles south) and maritime courts as part of the prerogatives they had been granted in their borough charter by the earl of Cornwall.[191]

At times the earls and dukes came into conflict with other lords when they tried to extend their seigneurial claims, attempting in some instances to expand their regalian prerogatives by infringing on the lordship of others in Cornwall. The most acrimonious and long-standing of these conflicts involved Earl Richard and Earl Edmund's struggles against Walter Bronescombe, bishop of Exeter (1258–80). The main point of contention seems to have been over-reaching on the part of the earls' stewards and other officials in locations where the manors of the bishop abutted those of the earls.[192] In several instances these disputes touched upon maritime prerogatives, most notably access to sand at Mylor and charges on the earls' ferry at Saltash. Although the bishop's officials were beaten and imprisoned, the bishop used his power of excommunication to prevail in the end. Yet other conflicts between the two powerful magnates arose later. In the Caption of 1337, for instance, the havener complained that the bishop of Exeter was usurping pleas and perquisites in the port of Falmouth, but in fact these would have belonged to the bishop by virtue of his lordship of the manor of Penryn.[193] The havener also cited lord William de Botreaux for the same offence in the port of Lelant, even though the duke's rights over this port only included prisage and overseas customs, not local customs or other maritime profits.

Ferries and Sand Ways

The ministers' accounts also record a variety of miscellaneous profits arising from maritime prerogatives. One of the most important was the Saltash ferry, attached to the honour of Trematon. Its revenues

---

[191.] PRO, JUST1/118, m. 61d. See also H. Spencer Toy, *The History of Helston* (Oxford, 1936), pp. 120, 392, 476–81.

[192.] See *The Register of Walter Bronescombe, Bishop of Exeter*, ed. O. F. Robinson (Canterbury and York Society, 2 vols., 1995–99), I, pp. xliii–xlv, 159; II, pp. 71–88 passim, 110, 124–6 passim, 137–8; *CPR 1272–81*, pp. 123, 293, 406; and below, notes 195 and 205.

[193.] See *Caption*, pp. 137, 139–40 for this and the following. Note that Lelant was in the list of non-farmed ports to be investigated in the Caption of 1337, but not in a similar list in the Extent of 1345; see below, Appendix I.

arose from the fees charged to row passengers and horses across the Tamar from Saltash, at sums that seem to have ranged from ¼d to ½d for each passenger, and ½d for a horse.[194] Disputes frequently surfaced about these rates, leading in one instance to the excommunication of several of the earl's men by the bishop of Exeter who objected to charges on his tenants using the crossing.[195] Exemptions from passage toll or reduced rates granted to the tenants of other lords further confused the matter of who should pay and how much.[196] The tendency for the ferry boat to break down was also a problem; the lessor of the Cremyll ferry in the 1350s complained that his ferry boat was co-opted by the farmers of the Saltash ferry whenever it was out of service in need of repair.[197] The third ferry under the overlordship of the earl and duke was the Tamar ferry by Calstock weir, which was leased for 4s 6d per year and a 12s entry fine in the Assessions of 1347 and 1356. There was also another ferry at Tewington which was frequently leased out with the fishery there. At the Assession of 1333 it was taken on a seven-year conventionary lease for 7s per year (which included an increase of 3s), with an entry fine of 3s 4d.[198] Another ferry, which connected Padstow with Penmayne on the other side of the Camel estuary, was farmed by the tenants of Penmayne for 13s per year in the early fourteenth century.[199]

The constant wear and tear on the Saltash ferry boat meant that the accounts contain fairly full details about repairs and the construction

---

194. These rates were noted in complaints about new customs raised by the former steward of the earl of Cornwall around the 1270s; see CRO, ME961/4 and *Rotuli hundredorum*, I, pp. 76, 77.

195. The bishop's action was taken in response to complaints about a variety of impositions newly made by the earl's men on the bishop's tenants, among others (above, n. 192). The bishop also excommunicated Saltash men who took money from the bishop's tenants for using the ferry; see PRO, JUST1/110. For other complaints about the rates, see also *Rotuli hundredorum*, I, pp. 76, 77; *BPR*, II, pp. 107, 122–3.

196. See the section on the free tenants of Trematon in the Caption of Seisin (below, Appendix I).

197. *BPR*, II, p. 87. See also P. L. Hull, "The History of the Cremyll Ferry", *Annual Report of the Royal Cornwall Polytechnic Society*, 130 (1963), pp. 22–49.

198. See below, Appendix I. In the Assession Rolls of 1364 and 1371, however, the passage was said to be worth 4s and the fishery 7s; *Rowe v. Breton*, pp. 134, 143.

199. *Caption*, p. 25. For the Cornish ferries, see also Charles Henderson, "Cornish Ferries", in *Essays in Cornish History* pp. 163–7; Whetter, *Cornwall in the Thirteenth Century*, pp. 257–8.

of new boats because the earl and duke were responsible for providing the boat to lessors of the passage. In 1297/8, a new ferry boat was made at the cost of a bit over 49s, but another boat had to be made by 1305/6 because the old one was so debilitated it could not be used. A boat was also purchased in 1350/1, at a cost of 66s 8d, plus another 5s for taking the boat from Looe, where it was purchased, to Saltash. It is likely that this boat was already several years old because within four years it too was insufficient. This time they decided to build a new boat from the ground up. The account of 1354/5 contains a very detailed record of the construction of the new boat, which cost £4 11¼d and took about two and a half weeks to build. Besides bringing in timber felled in Calstock Wood, the builders also purchased boards 7 and 12 feet in length, as well as 12 *sheverbords*. Pitch, bitumen, and a variety of nails were also procured. Master carpenters were hired to fell the wood and make the boat, including 'throwing down' the keel. The hire of clinchers and holders indicate that the boat was clinker-built (the external planks overlapped and were fastened with nails). The boat was actually an oared barge, probably without sails since they were never mentioned in any account. The four oars of the boat were often recorded in the accounts, however, because they had to be rented with the barge when the passage was farmed out to other lessors.[200]

The earls usually farmed out the Saltash ferry, which fetched £8 10s in 1301, but £10 a year by the second decade of the fourteenth century, the same value placed on it in Caption of 1337 and the Assession of 1347, although an entry fine of 40s was added to the latter lease. The burgesses of Saltash usually leased the ferry, but by 1348/9 the plague had so reduced passenger traffic that the ferry reverted to the duke, who leased it to the duchy steward along with the farm of Saltash borough in 1351. By 1355/6, it was being leased for £10 again as part of the farm of Saltash borough by a group of local burgesses, who were presumably attracted by the investment made the year before in constructing a new ferry barge. The ferry seems to have remained part of the borough farm in the following years, although from 1356 on the duke usually granted its profits to one of his loyal retainers.[201]

[200.] Note, however, that in the eyre of 1302 (PRO, JUST1/118, m. 51d), the king was said to hold the passage from Trematon, worth £8 10s per year, but Reginald de Ferrers held a sergeantry tenure in which he had to find four oars [*avyrones*] for the passage boat. A similar requirement was noted in the 1337 Caption of Seisin, as indicated in the section on free tenants of Tramaton (below, Appendix I).

[201.] *BPR*, II, pp. 98–9, 107; Hatcher, *Rural Economy*, p. 193.

The sandy beaches and estuaries of Cornwall also brought profits to the earl and duke because sand was widely used to aerate heavy soils in Devon and Cornwall.[202] The manor of Plympton (Devon), for example, employed two sand-men and paid for 31 barges to haul sand in one year.[203] Sand was also used in building masonry, as indicated by the collection of sand made in Tamar Water for work on Launceston castle in 1343/4.[204] As a result, access to sand was a valuable prerogative, and one that occasioned vociferous outcries when too much was charged for access. In the late thirteenth century, for instance, the earl's villeins in the manors of Brannel, Tybesta, St Ewe, Moresk, and other places complained that the bishop of Exeter had fined them enormous sums for taking sand 'to repair their land where the sea rises and withdraws near Mylor, which is common to all men'.[205] In 1357, the tenants of Helston-in-Kerrier complained to the duke that the bailiffs of Sir Henry de la Pomeray at his manor of Winniaton were demanding a toll of 3d per horse-load of sand, so 'their lands lie untilled'.[206] The earl's bailiffs were themselves the focus of attack for a new toll of 12d they had begun imposing in the late 1260s on each barge and boat carrying sand in Tamar Water.[207] Burgesses of Tavistock and Plympton in Devon led the outcry, claiming that in the past they had always taken sand in the Tamar for free. Their claims may have been successful, since in the Caption of 1337 the custom on sand barges attached to Saltash was only worth 8s a year, equivalent to only eight sand barges.

[202.] For the practice of sanding fields in south-western England, see H.S.A. Fox, "Devon and Cornwall", in *The Agrarian History of England and Wales*, vol. IV, ed. E. Miller (Cambridge, 1991), pp. 311–12.

[203.] K. Ugawa, "The Economic Development of Some Devon Manors in the Thirteenth Century", *Transactions of the Devonshire Association*, 94 (1962), p. 635. For sanding at Tavistock, see Finberg, *Tavistock Abbey*, pp. 88–94.

[204.] PRO, E101/461/11. The account noted 25s 7d paid for 102 quarters of sand, at 3d per quarter collected and carried; there were additional expenditures on sand for the great hall at Launceston.

[205.] These complaints and many others were voiced in an inquisition under quo warranto proceedings in 1278 to settle long–standing disputes between the Earl Edmund and Bishop Walter de Bronescombe; for the inquisition, see PRO, JUST1/110. The dispute led to the bishop excommunicating those who had carried sand away. For the bishop's complaints against the earl's bailiffs and stewards, see n. 192, above. The place described as near Mylor where the sea rises probably refers to the bishop's manor of Penryn and his claims over the Fal, on which Penryn was situated.

[206.] *BPR*, II, pp. 129–30.

[207.] *Rotuli hundredorum*, I, pp. 76, 77, 81.

The outcries against excessive charges for sea-sand probably stemmed in part to the long-standing access Cornish residents had enjoyed to supplies of sand. As early as 1261, Earl Richard had granted all Cornish inhabitants the right to take sea sand without payment and to carry it to their lands 'by a proper road assigned, ' as long as they offer 'reasonable compensation' to lords on whose lands the sand was taken or carried.[208] As a result, several duchy manors charged tenants for using a local sand way to fetch horse-loads of sand for their fields. In Tywarnhaile manor, tenants were obliged to pay ½d for each horseload of sand they brought up the sand way; in 1344/5, 60 horses used the sand way for a profit of 12s, the equivalent of 288 horse-loads of sand.[209] There was also a sand way in the manor of Tewington at Duporth, but it usually brought in nothing because the violence of the sea prevented tenants from using it.[210] Indeed, blowing sand caused immense problems at Tewington, illustrating that maritime resources were not always easy to exploit.[211]

The Maritime Economy of Medieval Cornwall

The preceding discussion offers only an over-view of the development and management of the maritime revenues attached to the earldom and duchy of Cornwall. Little has been said here, for example, about the many other estate officials mentioned in the accounts: in their financial capacity as auditors or receivers; in their managerial position as stewards or customs collectors; or in their role as tenants, lessors, landlords, merchants, or favoured retainers receiving special gifts of wine or venison. Ordinary men (and some women) of medieval Cornwall also surface in various capacities, as pillagers of wreck, mariners, shipmasters, traders, local reeves, felons, and lessors of land and other prerogatives. The accounts also contain much information about the place-names and maritime settlements of medieval Cornwall, including ports such as Truro and Lostwithiel which have long since

---

208. *CChR, 1257–1300*, p. 36. For the early history of sanding in Cornwall, see also Whetter, *Cornwall in the Thirteenth Century*, pp. 31–2.

209. DCO Ministers' Account 2, m. 5. In 1346/7, it brought in only 2s 6d; see DCO Ministers' Account 3, m. 4d.

210. See, for example, the accounts for 1338/9 (PRO, SC6/816/11, m. 7) and those for the 1340s (DCO Ministers' Accounts 4, m. 5, Ministers' Account 5, m. 5. Similar entries were made in the accounts for the 1350s through 1370s).

211. Hatcher, *Rural Economy*, pp. 150–1; *Caption*, pp. 81–2.

silted up. Fishing pools, sand-ways, ferries, and the location of shipwrecks are all singled out in the accounts, offering much detail about the coastal landscape of this most maritime of counties. Further study of these accounts and those of later decades should also reveal much about not only the evolution of managerial strategies to exploit the profits of the sea, but also the relationship of medieval Cornish people to the sea.

Some of the more valuable insights offered by the havener's accounts regard marine fishing, which emerges as a cornerstone of the maritime economy of medieval Cornwall. The majority of the earldom's maritime revenues—from the port farms, trantery, forestalling fines, and maritime courts—rested largely on the prosperity of the fishing industry. Indeed, when Earl Richard and Earl Edmund tried to increase their revenues in the late thirteenth century, they targeted this industry by imposing tolls for drying fish on their foreshore, for buying fish and carrying it inland for re-sale, for selling fish from boats, and for fishing in their waters. Fishing also affected such ancillary trades as the import of salt for preserving fish, the export of cured fish overseas, the production of fish oil, and the manufacture of boats, nets, and ropes. The dukes also recognised the value of this sector of the maritime economy in their frequent purveyance of the abundant varieties available in Cornish waters and in their sympthetic responses to petitions from local fishermen.

The long stretch of coastline around the south-western peninsula meant that opportunities to earn a living from the sea were many and varied. Fishing was but one of these options; others included serving on a vessel plying coastal routes or sailing overseas, building ships, manufacturing naval supplies (such as ropes, sails, barrels, and nets) and working shore-side at one of the quays where wine, wool, tin and other goods were hauled, loaded, and stored. As the havener's accounts spell out in some detail, residents of coastal communities also enjoyed windfall profits from wreck. There is no reason to believe that the Cornish were any more predatory than their maritime counterparts elsewhere, but they clearly had many more opportunities to enjoy the profits of wreck because of the dangers of their coastline and their central location on busy sailing routes from southern France and Iberia. The havener's accounts plainly indicate that the tales of wreckers so popular in later Cornwall can be traced back to the enthusiastic pillaging of their medieval ancestors.[212]

The accounts are particularly useful for the data they provide on the relative size of the shipping and trade at individual ports, whether in wine, fish, or tin. The seemingly dull recitation of sums paid out and taken in also reveals much about fluctuations in the maritime economy, whether in the profits of fishing ports, the leases of ferries, or the traffic in wine ships. The Black Death levelled a severe blow to the maritime economy because labour became scarce and expensive (as witnessed by the higher rates charged for shore-side rollage and haulage of wine), good tenants became harder to find, and the number of visiting traders and mariners dwindled. The Hundred Years War had an equally negative effect, evident in the attacks on Cornish fishers by the Spanish and other French allies, local raids on such ports as Plymouth, and the rising incidence of privateering and piracy, both of which made sea-going ventures more dangerous and costly. The same coastline that gave Cornwall such advantageous access to a variety of overseas markets also made it vulnerable to attack when the enemy lay across the sea. Royal and ecclesiastical authorities recognised the severity of the threat and tried to rouse the locals to ready themselves to resist such attacks. In so doing, they noted in particular the need to protect fishermen, an indication of the high importance attached to fishing even at this early date.[213]

The pressures of war-time hostilities also placed heavy burdens on Cornwall and other maritime counties to provide men and ships to transport troops and patrol the seas. But up until the 1330s, Cornwall was never been able to provide many ships when called upon, despite its long length of coastline. In 1303, for instance, the admiral in charge of impressing western ships for the war effort in Scotland complained that the three ports he visited, East Looe, West Looe (*Porthpighan*), and Saltash all claimed to be too poor to furnish ships unless aided by

---

[212.] A. K. Hamilton Jenkin's book on *Cornish Seafarers*, reprinted in *Cornwall and Its People* (Newton Abbot, 1945), pp. 2–122, does an especially good job of capturing the role of wrecking (as well as smuggling and fishing) in Cornish history.

[213.] See in particular the letter sent to the archdeacon of Cornwall on this matter in *The Register of John de Grandisson, Bishop of Exeter (A.D. 1327–1369)*, ed. F. C. Hingeston-Randolph, 3 vols. (London, 1894–99), III, 1547–8; see also *BPR*, II, p. 5. Other war-time problems included ships lost in naval service (*BPR*, I, p. 84) and the potential damage when troops assembled in ports such as Fowey (*BPR*, II, p. 32).

their inland neighbours, all of whom responded that they were not accustomed to give such aid.[214] The establishment of the duchy in 1337, however, and the appointment of a salaried havener helped to place new emphasis on the naval capacity of Cornish ports, due in no small measure to the leading military role of the first duke—Edward, the Black Prince—in the early stages of the Hundred Years War. In granting the three finest harbours in south-western England—Fowey, Plymouth, and Dartmouth—to the newly formed duchy of Cornwall, King Edward III may well have had strategic concerns in mind. Large-scale military and royal expeditions from Plymouth increased markedly, for instance, most notably the Black Prince's expedition to Gascony in 1355–7, which brought about 2600 men and hundreds of ships to Plymouth for a period of six weeks and more at a time when the population of the port barely exceeded 2000.[215] But it was to Fowey that the Prince turned in particular for individual ships and men to serve him at sea. He regularly hired local shipmasters, pilots, and mariners to transport supplies and troops to Gascony and elsewhere, and often rewarded them with exemptions from prisage and other perquisites.[216]

This regular patronage, as well as the advantages of embarking from ports that were not only well situated on the route to France and Iberia, but also under the duke's lordship, did much to stimulate the maritime economy of Plymouth, Fowey, and other Cornish ports. The rising demand for shipping, for instance, may have fostered ship-building

---

[214.] PRO, C47/22/9/135 (for a translation, see *Calendar of Documents Relating to Scotland AD 1108–1516*, ed. J. Bain, 4 vols. (Edinburgh, 1881–88), II, p. 349). Fowey, Polruan, Lostwithiel and Bodmin were jointly to furnish one ship (*CPR 1301–07*, p. 75) although Bodmin later objected strongly to this obligation (see *CCR 1339–41*, p. 196). In 13th-century impressments, the Cornish ports were not prominent; no galleys were ever built at Cornish ports and Fowey and Falmouth were the only two Cornish ports regularly mentioned; see, for example, *Pipe Roll 1205*, pp. xiii–xiv; *Rotuli litterarum clausarum*, II, pp. 146, 205; *CPR 1292–1301*, p. 584. See also British Library, Additional MS 26,891, ff. 50–69 where impressment for transport from Plymouth to Gascony in 1324 shows 5 ships from Fowey as the sum total of the Cornish contribution to the fleet, made up of about 80 ships, most from west coast ports.

[215.] See Hewitt, *Black Prince's Expedition* for a full discussion. For other expeditions from Plymouth at this time, see also *CCR 1350–4*, pp. 184–5, 486.

[216.] For example, *BPR*, I, p. 84; II, pp. 98, 141; IV, pp. 18, 253–4, 296, 283. See also the havener's account of 1357/8 (PRO, SC6/817/6), and John Keast, *The Story of Fowey* (Redruth, 1950), pp. 11–14.

and the commercial exchange of ships in the duchy's ports.[217] One
indication of an increased supply of ocean-going vessels in the region
was the growing presence of Cornish ships in naval ship calls from the
1340s on. In the vast fleet assembled for the siege of Calais in 1347,
for instance, Cornish ports provided 72 ships and almost 1200 mariners,
thus ranking behind only Devon and Kent in its naval contribution.[218]
The Hundred Years War may have reduced seigneurial revenues and
added uncertainty and hardship to the lives of many coastal residents,
but it also stimulated investment in ships, mariners, naval supplies,
and administrative expertise in the port towns controlled by the duke
of Cornwall, who as the Black Prince played a leading role in England's
war effort. When war abated, the supply of shipping and experienced
mariners it had created bolstered the region's efforts to compete
successfully in marine fishing, overseas and coastal trade, and pilgrim
transport, all sectors which prospered in late medieval Cornwall.[219] In
detailing the maritime revenues and expenses of the late thirteenth
and early fourteenth century, the havener's accounts printed in this
volume reveal the basis for this late medieval expansion, while also
providing crucial insights into the evolving administration of the
maritime assets of the county's largest landowner and lord.

[217.] For shipbuilding, see *BPR*, II, pp. 116–17, 150. For ship sales, see the havener's
accounts of 1338/9 (on m. 11d, printed below, Part II), and 1352/3 (under
'Maltot', below, Part II).

[218.] The figures are from the so-called 'Calais Roll' which survives only in 16th-
century copies. I used the collated version printed in N. H. Nicolas, *A History
of the Royal Navy* (London, 1847), II, pp. 507–10, emended in places by
comparison with versions in J. Charnock, *A History of Marine Architecture*
(London, 1800–2), I, pp. xxxviii–xliii; British Library, Cotton MS Titus E. III.,
f. 262; Harleian MS 78, ff. 16–17; Harleian MS 246, ff. 15v–16v; and Harleian
MS 3968, ff. 131v–3. See also N. A. M. Rodger, *The Safeguard of the Sea: A
Naval History of Britain 660–1649* (New York, 1997), p. 496 for the growing
naval contribution of Cornish ports.

[219.] For the maritime prosperity of late medieval Cornwall, see Kowaleski,
"Expansion of the South-Western Fisheries". The growth of the maritime
economy can also be seen in the expansion of piracy and privateering in 15th-
century Cornwall; see C. J. Kingsford, *Prejudice and Promise in Fifteenth Century
England* (Oxford, 1925), pp. 78–106, 177–203 and *A Calendar of Early
Chancery Proceedings Relating to West Country Shipping 1388–1493*, ed. D.
Gardiner (DCRS, vol. 21, 1976).

Tables

TABLE 1

Annual Revenues and Expenses in the Havener's Accounts, (in pence) 1301–1356

	Ann. Aver. 1301–06	Caption of 1337	Ann. Aver. 1338–47
Wreck	36.8	varies	212.1
Fines on Pillagers	146.1		0
Salvage	18.3		0
Port Farms	430.7	418.0	373.0
Trantery & Forestalling Fish	21.7	36.7	5.9
Maritime Courts	31.7	40.0	7.1
Fines and Perquisites			
Wine Prisage & Custom		varies	854.6
Total Revenues	687.5	N/A	1452.6
Wages	53.3	146.7	133.3
Payment for Prisage Wines			352.0
Care of Wines			81.3
Other			26.6
Total Expenses	53.4		593.3
Average Annual Profit	634.1		859.3
Cocket & Maltot (Ancient & New Custom)			208.6

Sources and Notes

Five havener's accounts (below, Parts I and II) are included in each of the three periods in which annual averages have been computed. The highest and lowest sums refer to the highest and lowest amounts paid in each category during the period from 1287 to 1356. The Maritime Courts do not include maritime courts in seigneurial jurisdictions such as Plymouth and Fowey. Note that there was no

Extent of 1345	Ann. Aver. 1351–56	Highest Sum	Lowest Sum
1400.0	64.6	903.4 (1341/2)	0 (several)
	0	284.6 (1300/1)	0 (several)
	0	81.0 (1301/2)	
403.4	376.5	439.3 (1334)	311.0 (1350/1)
	21.5	34.0 (1303/4)	0 (1348/9)
13.3	39.6	68.6 (1304/5)	0.8 (1348/9)
	97.4	933.7 (1350/1)	0 (many)
varies	4806.9	7196.7 (1353/4)	180.0 (1338/9)
N/A	5406.2		
	133.3	146.7	53.3 (1300s)
	992.0	1800.0 (1353/4)	120.0 (1339/40)
	150.3	255.3 (1352/3)	17.3 (1339/40)
	10.0	132.8 (1338/9)	0 (many)
	1285.7		
	4120.5		
133.3	139.1	470.0 (Jan. 1338– Mich. 1339)	0 (1348/9)

wine prisage or customs recorded in the accounts of the early 1300s. Starting in 1353/4, moreover, no cocket or ancient custom (on hide and wool exports) from denizens was collected because all were required to use the staple ports. For the cocket and maltot customs, see also Part III. For the Caption of 1337 and Extent of 1345, see below, Appendix I.

TABLE 2

Changes in the Farms Paid by the Cornish Ports to the Earldom and Duchy (in shillings)

Port	Farm Paid 1301	Farm Owed 1337 Caption	Farm Owed 1345 Extent	Farm Paid 1350/1	Farm Paid 1355/6
Polruan	20.0	20.0	20.0	20.0	20.0
Fowey	40.0	40.0	40.0	40.0	40.0
Ports of Kerrier	23.0			25.0	25.0
Porthallow		22.0	25.0		
Marazion	46.6	60.0	46.7	46.7	46.7
'Porthplement'	8.0		[8.0]	0.0	2.0
Penzance	12.0	12.0	12.0	12.0	12.0
Newlyn	20.0	10.0	20.0	20.0	20.0
Mousehole	100.0	100.0	100.0	100.0	100.0
Lamorna	2.0		1.0	1.0	0
Porthgwarra/ Land's End	12.0	12.0	12.0	0.0	2.0
Porthzennor & Portheras	6.0		6.7	0.0	0.0
'Portminster'		2.0			
St Ives	120.0	120.0	120.0	60.0	120.0
Ports of Trigg	20.00			20.0	20.0
Portgaverne					
Port Isaac		20.0	20.0		
Portquin					

Sources
The havener's accounts of 1301 (printed below, Part I), 1350/1, and 1355/6 (below, Part II); the Caption of Seisin and the Extent of 1345 (below, Appendix I).

TABLE 3

Hide and Wool Exports from Cornwall, by Year 1284–1354

Year (months)	Hides		Wool Sacks	Year (months)	Hides		Wool Sacks
	Dickers	Cargoes	(Cargoes)		Dickers	Cargoes	(Cargoes)
1284/85	292	22	0	1323/24			
1285/86	459	28	0	1324–25 (10)	[0]		[0]
1286/87	403	27	0	1325–26 (10)	[0]		[0]
1289/90	121	13	4 (1)	1326–27 (14)	[0]		[0]
1290/91	172	13	0	1327–28 (10)	[0]		[0]
1291/92	172	8	0	1328–29 (10)	[0]		[0]
1292/93	195	6	0	1329–30 (14)	[0]		[0]
1301 (5)	[91]		[0]	1330/31	[0]		[0]
1301/02	[84]		[0]	1331/32	[30]		[0]
1302/03	[102]		[0]	1332–33 (7)	[18]		[0]
1303/04	[120]		[0]	1333–34 (17)	[0]		[0]
1305/06	[175]		[0]	1334–35 (9)	[0]		[0]
1306/07	[110]		[0]	1335–37 (27)	[0]		[7]
1307/08	[85]		[0]	1337–38 (3)			
1308/09	17	7	0	1339 (6)			
1309/10	32	10	0	1339/40	208	12	0
1310/11	35	8	0	1341/42	a152	15	0
1311/12	20	5	0	b1345 (3)			
1312/13	36	9	0	1346/47	162	12	7(1)
1313/14	43	12	0	1347–48 (13)			[0]
1314/15	19	11	0	1349/50	34	3	
1315/16	33	9	0	1350/51	c370	13	11 (3)
1316/17	20	4	0	1351/52	43	5	d4 (3)
1317/18	15	6	0	1352/53	22	2	18 (4)
1322/23	280		0	1353/54			

Sources and Notes
See page 74.

TABLE 4

The Value (in £) of Overseas Trade at the Cornish Ports, with the Number of Wine Ships at Each Port

Type of Trade	Years	Looe	Lost-withiel	Fowey	Falmouth, Penryn & Truro
Grain Imports by Aliens	1322–4, 1338–56		34	65	92
Salt Imports by Aliens	1322–4, 1338–56		184	595	425
Other Imports by Aliens	1322–4		90	19	19
Imports & Exports by Aliens	1324–1338				
Imports and Exports	1347/8	46	1583		668
Imports and Exports	1350/1				
Hide Exports	1284–1353		1187		
	1341/2 1346/7	10	79	46	22
Wool Exports	1284–1354				
Tin Exports by Aliens	1322–4, 1338–53		241	399	31
Fish Exports by Aliens	1322–4			108	
Other Exports by Aliens	1322–4, 1338–53			17	5
(No.) of Wine Ships	1338–56	(3)		(87)	(75)
Total Value in £		56	628	1249	1262
			2770		

Sources

For hide and wool exports, see Table 1; the figures for 1341/2 and 1346/7 are noted separately because these accounts specified the port of export for hides. Figures for 1322–24 are from the account of new custom in PRO, E122/39/6 (below, Part III). Figures for imports and exports of aliens in 1324–38 come from transcripts of the enrolled accounts in PRO, E356/2, m. 42 (1324–6) and E356/9, m. 4 (1326–38); figures for imports and exports in 1347/8 are from poundage and wool subsidies noted in the enrolled accounts in E356/5, m. 11d; those from 1350/1 are on m. 14d. I am grateful to Stuart Jenks for providing me with transcripts of these enrolled accounts. All other figures are from the Havener's Accounts in Part II, below.

Marazion	Newlyn	Mousehole & Mount's Bay	Padstow	Unspeci-fied	Total Value
46	52				289
69	5	385		16	1679
		10			138
				5816	5816
		382	299		2978
				187	187
				2983	4170
		8			165
				344	344
			93	1935	2699
		73		49	230
					22
		(3)	(6)		(174)
115	57	858	392	11,330	18,717

Notes
The years noted represent the chronological range of the data, which are only available for some of the years within the range. Note that this table offers only an approximation of the relative value and type of overseas trade in each port because it records primarily trade by alien merchants and omits wine, the most valuable import into the county. The value for hides was calculated as £1 per dicker, for wool as £6 5s per sack (from E. Miller and J. Hatcher, *Medieval England: Towns, Commerce and Crafts 1086–1348* (Cambridge, 1995), p. 213, note). The other values are customs valuations stated in the accounts; note that these are considerably
(cont'd on page 74)

TABLE 5

Home Ports of Ships Carrying Wine Imports and Hide Exports at the Cornish Ports and Plymouth, 1322–4 and 1338–56

Home Port (No. of Different Home Ports)	Total Ships	Ports of Call								
		Plymouth	Looe	Fowey	Lostwithiel	Truro	Falmouth	Mousehole	Padstow	Unknown
Cornwall (9)										
Millbrook	1									1
Looe	9		3							6
Polruan	19			18						1
Fowey	35			27	1	1	1	1	2	2
Lostwithiel	6			4					1	1
Bodennick	4			4						
Truro	1					1				
Penryn	1						1			
Falmouth	2						2			
Devon (5)										
Plymouth	47	40		6						1
Dartmouth	33	6		7			18		1	1
Teignmouth	2						2			
Lympstone	1	1								
Sidmouth	2			1			1			
Dorset (4)	9	2		2			5			
Hampshire (2)	5			1	1		3			
Gloucestershire (3)	13	1					8	2	1	1
Wales (2)	2						2			
Sussex & Kent (4)	5				1		4			
London & Essex (4)	12	3		2	1		3			3
Suffolk & Norfolk (4)	17	7		1			9			
Lincs. & Yorkshire (5)	13	3	1	2			7			

Home Port (No. of Different Home Ports)	Total Ships	Ports of Call								
		Plymouth	Looe	Fowey	Lostwithiel	Truro	Falmouth	Mousehole	Padstow	Unknown
Ireland (4)	5	2		1			1		1	
Guernsey (1)	2			1	1					
Flanders & Picardy (5)	7						7			
Normandy (10)	29						29			
Brittany (4)	4		1				3			
S. France (2)	12	3		3			5			1
Iberia (8)	14	8					4	1	1	
Unidentified (4)	4			2			2			
Not Given	9	6		2						1
Total (80)	325	82	5	84	5	2	117	4	7	19

Sources

1322–24: PRO, E122/39/6 (below, Part III); 1338–56: the Havener's Accounts (below, Part II).

Notes

Since the accounts do not record shipping details for any imports but wine, and since only 33 of the ships involved in the export trade are recorded (32 exported hides, 1 exported tin), this table primarily reflects the shipping involved in the transit of wine to the ports of Cornwall and Plymouth. Dartmouth includes one ship of Kingswear. Normandy includes ships from *Ance*, *Baudeville*, and *Bonevyle* which, though the exact locations are unidentified, were clearly located in Normandy.

Sources and Notes for Table 3

Sources

Figures up to 1324 are from the particular accounts in PRO, E122, as in Part III, below, except for items in square brackets, which are from the enrolled accounts in PRO, E356/1, m. 18d (1301–8), and E356/2, m. 5A (1308–1318), m. 14d (1324–6); and except for 1322/3 which are in PRO, E389/62, m. 2 (printed below, Part I). Figures for the remaining years are from the havener's accounts, as in Part II, below, except for items in square brackets, which are from the transcripts of enrolled accounts in PRO, E356/8, m. 34 (1326–38) and E356/5, m. 14d (1347–48), that were kindly supplied by Stuart Jenks.

Notes

A blank space means that no information is available for that item (in most cases, the value would be 0).

a. Includes 19 dickers tanned hides and 102 dickers salted hides.
b. The account ran from 19 June to 29 September 1345 (below, Part II), but a note at the bottom of the account records that nothing was received during the period from 20 March to 19 June 1345.
c. Includes 75 dickers of kips (hides of young animals); the account reckons 2 hides equals one kip, so strictly speaking the total hides exported came to 335.5 dickers.
d. 3.5 sacks, 16 cloves, 17 pounds of wool. The wording of the account implies this sum could be for the preceding year, but the amounts exported and names of the exporters suggest otherwise.

Notes for Table 4 cont'd

below market values. **Falmouth**: Other Imports include tables and onions (valued at £19); Other Exports include horses and cheese (£5). The hide exports were all through Truro. **Fowey**: Salt Imports include one cargo of salt and honey (£8). An export of tin, cod, cloth, and horses valued at £57 was assumed to include £40 of tin, £7 of cloth, and £5 each of cod and horses (included in Other Exports). Other Imports include figs and raisons (£3), garlic and onions (£16). **Lostwithiel**: Other Imports includes iron (£90). **Mousehole**: Fish exports include fish and cheese (£46); Other Imports includes wine and honey (£10).

Editorial Conventions

This edition includes passages from the accounts of the earldom and duchy of Cornwall that concern maritime revenues and expenses. Up to 1336, these passages were usually in sections labeled 'Sea-Shore' [*Marina*] or 'Issues of the Ports' [*Exitus Portuum*] and could be found in a wide variety of accounts, such as those of the steward, receiver, and ministers' accounts of the earldom, or in the sheriff's account in the pipe rolls, or steward's account in the foreign accounts. After the foundation of the duchy, these passages were usually placed in sections called the 'Havener's Account,' although maritime-related items continued to be enrolled under other sections of the duchy's ministers' accounts as well. In order to provide a comprehensive picture of the maritime revenue associated with the earldom and duchy of Cornwall, this edition comprises not only the separate havener's accounts, but also passages from the ministers' accounts that touch on the profits of the ports of Saltash and Plymouth (entered under the manor of Trematon) and Fowey (entered under the manor of Lostwithiel) since they were an important part of the estate's maritime properties. Also included are stray references to port revenues in other sections of the ministers' accounts of the earldom to illustrate how and when the havener consolidated control over different types of revenues and expenses in the ports of the earldom and duchy.[1]

[1.] These include stray accounts of wreck or trantery enrolled under individual manors rather than the havener's account, or the wage paid to the bailiff in charge of the sea-shore of manors in north Cornwall, which was sometimes entered under the manor of Tybesta and sometimes under Issues of the Ports. For the responsibilities of the early haveners under the earldom, see Appendix II, below.

Because of this selection process, this edition often incorporates isolated passages from different sections of the accounts surveyed, a practice that may offend editorial purists who believe that all parts of the document under consideration should be transcribed and included. To do so, however, would have meant restricting this edition to only two or three years' worth of accounts and to covering a very wide range of non-maritime revenues and expenses.[2] Because the sea ports represented a discrete, separate form of revenue and expense, and because the vast majority of these port revenues and expenses were eventually consolidated under one account—that of the havener—the practice followed here of printing only selected portions of the various accounts seems justified. The havener's accounts and associated material, moreover, offer us an unusual opportunity to focus on medieval maritime sources, few of which have appeared in print.

The context of these isolated passages is made clear by recording the location and marginal heading of the sub-account heading in which they appear. Those parts of the sub-accounts that have been omitted (ranging from several words to many lines) are indicated by placing [...] at the beginning of a section—to indicate text skipped before the lines printed here—or at the end of a section—to indicate text was skipped after the lines printed here. When [...] appears by itself on one line, it indicates that a longer portion (ranging from one line to several membranes) of the manuscript has been omitted. Membrane numbers are only given when text from these specific membranes is printed here. [3]

Account and marginal headings are in small capitals; sub-headings are also in small capitals but indented. When parts of the original were underlined or struck through, this text is so indicated in the transcription. Interlineations or suprascripts are enclosed in round brackets; when a caret has been inserted in the original text to indicate where the suprascript text is to be inserted, a ^ is added at the

---

2. The ministers' accounts also include the accounts of the Devon and Cornish stannaries, Dartmoor forest, the receiver, keeper of the fees, the bailiffs of the hundreds, and the reeves or bailiffs of about twenty different manors. The immense holdings of the earldom and duchy of Cornwall could make even the account for one year very long, as indicated in *Ministers' Accounts of the Earldom of Cornwall, 1296–1297*, ed. L. Margaret Midgley (Camden 3rd series, vols. 66 and 67, 1942-45), II, pp. 212–77.

3. The membranes lack contemporary numbering, and some have not been given modern numbering either.

appropriate place. Words or lines that were clearly added later are enclosed in curly brackets; almost all of these insertions are suprascripts. Empty square brackets ([ ]) indicate places where the scribe deliberately left a blank space in the manuscript. Modern punctuation (mainly commas) has been inserted to ease comprehension. For the most part, spacing and the form of paragraphs reflects the layout in the original text.[4]

Uncertain transcriptions or translations are followed by a question mark. Illegible sections are indicated by three dots (…). Editorial insertions are placed within square brackets. When warranted, specific words or lines are also given in the original Latin, italicized, and placed within square brackets. Sums of money given in pounds [*libra*] are printed as £; half-pence [*obolus*] is printed as ½d; the farthing or quarter-pence [*quarta*] appears as ¼d, and a half-pence and quarter-pence together as ¾d. Numerals in the original text appear in Roman but are here rendered in Arabic. The feast of St Michael is translated as Michaelmas. Fiscal years, running from Michaelmas to Michaelmas are indicated by a slash, as in '1301/02'. Dates stated in the form 1301–02 imply a period from some time in 1301 to some time in 1302. Note also that footnote references are generally not given in the Introduction when the date of the account is given and the account is printed in Part I or II.

Place-names have been rendered in their modern version whenever possible. The first time they appear in the text they are also given in their original spelling, italicized, and placed in square brackets;

[4.] There are two exceptions. One is the placement of the 'summa' that appears at the end of each marginally-headed section of the accounts. In the original, these were normally inserted after the section, on a separate line, and situated near the right margin. In this edition, these sums appear at the end of the section, but as part of the same paragraph. The second exception is in the long sections containing lists of ships customed for maltot, cocket, or prisage, and the long sections on sums spent for care of wines. To ease comprehension, these long sections have been divided into paragraphs reflecting individual entries, rather than the run-on paragraphs they normally appear in.

thereafter, only variant spellings are noted.[5] Place-names of locations now lost appear within quotation marks. The parish of each place in Cornwall has been noted in the index, while the county has been given for other places in England, and the département or region for places located abroad. Surnames have been left in their original spelling. First names have been Anglicized except when the name is unusual or foreign, when it has been italicized. Names of ships are preserved in their original Latin spelling and italicized; standardized English forms of these ship names may be found in the index. The Glossary in Appendix III provides definitions for many specialized terms, particularly weights and measures, and the different payments and customs associated with maritime trade.

In 1336 King Edward III created the duchy of Cornwall out of the earldom and appointed his oldest son, Edward of Woodstock, as duke. Edward is more commonly known as the Black Prince, but in this edition he is referred to primarily as duke since it is that aspect of his lordship with which this volume is concerned.

---

5. The complexity of Cornish place names means I have been unable to identify several places recorded in these accounts. The following sources were employed to identify the modern equivalents of medieval place names: J. E. Gover, *The Place Names of Cornwall* (typescript in 5 volumes at the Royal Institution of Cornwall in Truro); Cornwall Record Office, *A List of Cornish Manors* (Truro, 1990); O. J. Padel, *Cornish Place-Name Elements* (Nottingham: English Place-Name Society, 1985); idem, *A Popular Dictionary of Cornish Place-Names* (Penzance, 1988); Charles Henderson, *The 109 Ancient Parishes of the Four Western Hundreds of Cornwall* (Truro, 1962). I am extremely grateful to Oliver Padel for answering my many queries on place-names and for correcting errors I made in my initial identification of several places.

Part I

The Accounts of the Earldom of Cornwall, 1287–1336

[1287–88]

PRO, SC6/816/9

[16 Edward I]. 4 membranes. Account of Roger de Ingepenne, steward and sheriff of Cornwall. The dating clause is missing, but L. Margaret Midgley dates the account to 1287–8.[1] A considerable portion of the left side of the manuscript containing the marginal headings is missing, but internal evidence makes it possible to supply most of the missing headings. Well written with ruled lines both horizontal and vertical, and with large elaborate marginal headings.

(m.1d)

[...]

[TREMATON]
The same renders account for [...] 108s 10½d from the passage of Saltash Water [*passagio aque de Esse*] this year [...] ... from the customs of oysters this year. For 5s from the seines [*sagenis*] this year. For 14s 4d from the barges [*Bargiis*] this year. For 42s 10d from Sutton Pool [*Pola de Sutton*] this year [...]

[LOSTWITHIEL]
The same renders account for [...] 14s? 4d from Fowey Water [*aqua de Fowe*] this year. [...]
[...]

[CARE OF WINES?]
... for buying and selling and seizing wines for the earl of Cornwall and for holding [them] for the earl of Cornwall within the same house and for administering other merchandise in the same [house] by the order of the lord earl of Cornwall... [...]

---

[1] L. Margaret Midgley, ed., *Ministers' Accounts of the Earldom of Cornwall 1296–1297* (Camden 3rd series, vol. 66, 1942), I, p. xxxviii.

(m. 2)

[...]

FOREIGN PERQUISITES

The same renders account for £30 10s 4d from marine issues this year.
[...]

[...]

WRECK

The same renders account for £63 11s 4½d for wreck of sea from the
last eyre of the Justices in Cornwall and no more because William de ...

WINES

The same renders account for £46 for 23 tuns of wine sold, taken for
prisage this year. For £13 6s 8d of profit on 80 tuns of wine ...
[...]

NECESSARY EXPENSES

The same accounts for 53s 4d per year for the stipend of one serjeant
keeping [*servient' custod'*] the manor of Moresk [*Moresk*] and other
neighbouring manors and the sea-shore [*marinam*]. [...]

NON-NECESSARY EXPENSES

The same accounts for £24 for 24 tuns of wine taken from prisage. For
13s 4d per year for the stipend of one vintner who took prisage ... [...]
[...]

WINES

The same renders account for 24 tuns of wine taken from prisage this
year. From which, 1 tun for the drink of the steward. For 23 tuns sold,
as above. Sum, 24 tuns.
[...]

[MEMORANDA [ORDERS TO THE STEWARD]]
[...]
Also the steward is to respond in the future for wreck of sea presented
in the (^ last) eyre of the Justices in Cornwall [...]
[...]

1296/97

PRO, E119/1

25 Edward I. 25 membranes. Account of Thomas de Ocham, receiver in the time of Thomas de la Hide, steward and sheriff of Cornwall; mm. 22–23d in the ministers' accounts of the earldom of Cornwall. The Latin account is printed in L. Margaret Midgley, *Ministers' Accounts of the Earldom of Cornwall 1296–1297* (Camden 3rd series, vol. 67, 1945), pp. 237–8, 241, 248.

(m. 22d)

TREMATON
  RENTS
The same renders account for [...]. And for £6 18s 10d from the passage of Saltash Water this year. [...] And 3s from custom on boats in Tamar Water [*aqua de Tamere*] this year. [...] And 3d from the custom of oysters this year. And for 4s from seines this year. And for 11s 4d from barges this year. And for 49s 6d from Sutton Pool this year. [...] And for 5s from the fishery of Lynher this year. [...]
[...]

(m. 23)

LOSTWITHIEL
  ISSUES OF THE MANOR
The same renders account for [...] And for 4s 4d from custom of ships in Fowey Water. [...]
[...]

FOREIGN PERQUISITES
The same renders account for £40 7½d from marine issues this year with wreck. [...] Nothing from wreck of sea because included above in marine perquisites. [...]
[...]

NECESSARY EXPENSES
53s 4d for the stipend of one serjeant to keep the manor of Moresk and other neighbouring [manors] and the sea-shore for one year [...].
[...]

(m. 23d)
[...]

[MEMORANDA, ORDERS TO THE STEWARD]
[...] Also remember that 2 great cords and 2 anchors remain that came this year from wreck, for which he should respond in the future [...]

1297/98

PRO, SC6/811/1

26 Edward I. 3 membranes. Account of Thomas de Ocham, receiver in the time of Thomas de la Hyde, steward and sheriff of Cornwall. Membrane 3 is torn and illegible in parts, particularly on the dorse which was used as the outside wrapping for the roll.

(m. 1d)

TREMATON
The same renders account for [...] £6 18s 10d from the passage of Saltash Water per year. [...] and 6s from custom of boats in Tamar Water this year. [...] 1¼d from custom of oysters this year. 6s from six seines this year. 11s 4d from barges this year. 49s 6d from Sutton Pool this year. [...]
    ALLOWANCES
[...] 49s 3¾d for the ferry boat [*batillo ad passag'*] newly made this year. [...]

(m. 2)

LOSTWITHIEL
    ISSUES OF THE MANOR
The same renders account for [...] 9s from the custom of ships in Fowey Water this year [...]
[...]

FOREIGN PERQUISITES
The same renders account for £44 16s 8d from marine issues this year, with wreck. And for £189 8s 2¼d from perquisites of the county and hundred with fines this year. And for 5s 1½d from one-half of the fines of the Prior of Launceston for breaking the assize of bread and ale. Nothing from wreck because [noted] above. Sum, £234 9s 11¾d. And he owes all.
[...]

(m. 2d)

WINES

The same renders account for 10 tuns of wine bought from Gerard de Villar' by order of the earl. And for 16 tuns arising from prisage this year. Sum, 26 tuns. Then 1 tun for the drink of the steward. And 25 tuns remain.

Sum of all debts [...]

NECESSARY EXPENSES

ALLOWANCES

[...] Also £38 for delivery of 16 tuns of prisage wine which are accounted for above and also for 22 tuns of the same which are not likewise accounted for. For 15s 1d for carriage of the said 16 tuns from Fowey to Restormel [*Rostormel*] with barrel hoops [*circul'*] for fixing the same [...]

RESPITED DEBTS

[...] Reginald de Thunderle owes £10 13s 4d for his obligation which is in the Wardrobe for mainprise of a certain boat arising from wreck in Cornwall.

[MEMORANDA ORDERS TO THE STEWARD]

[...]

It is ordered that he should sell all wine coming from prisage in his bailiwick and that for goods to be had by sale he grants to purchasers long terms [of payment] provided that they meet the next account? [*et quod bona vendicione habenda concedit emptor' longos? terminos dum tamen proximum comp' preveniant*].

(m. 3)

[PERQUISITES OF THE HUNDRED COURT]

[...]

KERRIER

The same renders account for [...] 10s 3¼d from the price of one cord arising from wreck in the tithing of Winianton [*Wynineton*] [...]

[...]

PYDAR

The same renders account for [...] 26s 10d from 5 ... from a wreck arising in the tithings of Tywarnhaile [*Tiwarnail*] , Connerton [*Con'*], Perranzabuloe [*Sancti Pirani*], Ellenglaze [*Elilglas*], Gluvia [*Glivion*],

and Carnanton [*Carnaton*]. And for 3s from the tithing of Tywarnhaile
for concealment. And for 3s from the tithing of Tywarnhaile similarly
for false presentment. And for 3s from the tithing of Tywarnhaile ...
And for 2s from the same for concealment.[2] [...]
[...]

1300/01

PRO, E372/146

28–29 Edward I. Pipe roll containing the account of Thomas de la
Hyde of the issues of the stewardship of the county of Cornwall and
the lands and tenements and other appurtenances which Edmund, earl
of Cornwall, the king's cousin deceased, held in the said county and
which after the death of the said earl came to the king as his next heir,
from 1 October 1300 to 29 September 1301. A similar account (though
missing several details, including the port farms) is in PRO, SC6/811/2.
This is the first surviving account that offers a specific list of the farms
of the ports.

(m.31)

[...]

TYBESTA

[...]

WAGES AND EXPENSES

The same renders account for [...] 20s for the wages and stipend of one
serjeant per year to keep the manors of Tybesta, Tewington and Moresk
and other neighbouring manors, as allowed there.

[...]

TREMATON

The same renders account for [...]. And for £8 10s per year from the
common passage of the same [Saltash] Water leased at farm.[3] [...] And
for 6s from the custom of 6 boats fishing in Tamar Water this year, as

---

2. Fines for concealment follow for six other tithings. It is not clear whether these
   fines or those above were for concealing wreckage or not.
3. The account in PRO, SC6/811/2 reads 'for Saltash passage with toll [*cum dote*]'.
   All the sums in this part of account are, moreover, underlined.

contained there. And for 20s from fair tolls this year. And for 4s from fishing of 4 seines this year. And for ¾d for the custom of fishers of oysters [*piscatorum ostriorum*] this year. And for 12s from the custom of 12 barges taking [*ducent'*] sand in Tamar Water this year, namely 12d from each barge as contained there. And for 5s from the fishery of Lynher Water this year. And for £4 from pleas and perquisites and other customs of mariners landing in the port of Sutton as leased at farm this year. [...]
[...]

LOSTWITHIEL

The same renders account for [...] And for 8s 8d from the custom of ships mooring this year. [...]
[...]

ISSUES OF THE SEA PORTS WITH WRECK

The same renders account for 46s 8d from the farm of the port of Marazion [*Marcaisiou*] this year. And for 12s from the farm of the port of Penzance [*Pensans*] this year. And for 20s from the port of Newlyn [*Lulin*] this year. And for 100s from the farm of the port of Mousehole [*Mousehole*] this year. And for 2s from the farm of the port of Lamorna [*Nansmorno*] this year. And for 12s from the farm of the port of Porthgwarra [*Porgortwethu*] this year. And for 8s from the farm of the port of 'Porthplement' [*Porthpleming*] this year. And for 2s from the farm of the port of *Porthseres* this year. And for 12s from the farm of the port of Portheras and Porthzennor [*Porthrest et Portsenar*] this year. And for £6 from the farm of the port of St Ives [*Porthre*] this year. And for 40s from the farm of the port of Fowey [*Fawe*] this year. And for 20s from the farm of the port of Polruan [*Polruan*] this year. And for 20s from the fisheries of Triggshire [*piscar' de Triggeshire*] this year. And for 22s from the fisheries of Kerrier [*piscar' de Kerrier*] this year. And for 44s 5d from the pleas and perquisites of the courts this year, as contained in the roll of particulars. And of 9s 3d from a certain custom called trantery [*Tranentria*], received of diverse persons passing through the parts of Cornwall with horses to buy fish this year, as is contained there. And for £14 4s 7d from 5 tuns, 4 pipes, 2 rundlets, and four small remnants [*parvis remantibus*] of 4 tuns of wine spoiled by salt water, a certain piece of a mast, 3 empty tuns, certain small pieces of wood, and the hide of a bullock [*boviculi*], coming from a wreck of sea and sold, as contained there. And for £28 6s 2d from the fines of diverse persons for carrying away or disposing of things landed and thrown up to land [*pro discaria vel distractione facta de rebus applicatis et proiectis ad terram*] from wreck of sea this year, as is contained there. The sum of receipts, £67 13d.

The same accounts for 53s 4d for the stipend of one serjeant keeping the manor of Moresk and other neighbouring manors, and the sea shore this year, as was allowed in the time of the said earl.

The sum of the expenses, 53s 4d, as was allowed in the time of the said earl. And he owes £64 7s. And he answers within on the dorse of the roll.
[...]

(m. 31d)

[...]
EXPENSES
[...] And for £64 7s 9d remaining from his account for issues of the sea ports with wreck, as contained there.[4] [...]
[...]

1301/02

PRO, SC6/811/3

30 Edward I. 2 membranes. Account of Thomas de la Hyde, steward and sheriff of Cornwall. 2 membranes. A vertical line is drawn through most of the account, but not the account of the sea-shore. A similar, but less full, enrolled account is in PRO, E372/148, m. 27.

(m. 2)

[...]
TYBESTE
[EXPENSES]
[...] 20s for the stipend of one serjeant to keep the manors of Tybesta, Tewington, Moresk, and other neighbouring manors.

[4.] In PRO, SC6/811/2, this item appears under 'FOREIGN PERQUISITES' as 'The same renders account for £67 19d from marine issues this year'.

[...]
TREMATON

The same renders account for [...]. And for £8 10s from the Saltash passage this year with toll [*cum dote*]. [...] And for 6s from the custom of boats in Tamar Water this year. And for 20s from fair tolls this year. And for 1d from the custom of oysters this year. And for 5s from 5 seines this year. And for 12s from 12 barges there this year. [...] And for £4 from Sutton Pool this year.[5] And for 5s from Lynher Water this year. [...]

[...]

m. 2d

LOSTWITHIEL

ISSUES OF THE MANOR

The same renders account for [...] 13s 4d from the custom of ships this year. And 2s 1½d from fair tolls. [...]

m. 3

[...]

THE SEA-SHORE [*MARINA*]

FARMS

The same renders account for 46s 8d from the farm of boats at Marazion [*Marcasou*].[6] And 12s from the farm of Penzance [*Pensans*]. And 20s from the farm of Newlyn [*Lulyn*]. And 100s from the farm of Mousehole [*Mosehole*]. And 2s from Lamorna [*Nansmorno*]. And 12s from Porthgwarra [*Porthgorwythou*].[7] And 8s from 'Porthplement' [*Porthplenym*][8]. And 6s from Porthzennor [*Porthsinard*].[9] And £6 from St Ives [*Porthy*]. And 40s from Fowey [*Fauwe*]. And 20s from Polruan. And 20s from the fisheries of Triggshire [*Triggeschyr'*]. And 23s from the fisheries of Kerrier. Sum, £21 9s 8d.

[5.] The enrolled account in E372/148 adds "And for £4 from pleas and perquisites and other customs of mariners landing in the port of Sutton, leased at farm".

[6.] E372/148 reads *Marcadyou*.

[7.] E372/148 adds 'Nothing from the farm of the port of Portheras [*Porthrest*] this year because the boats there were submerged'.

[8.] E 372/148 reads *Porthplenyt*.

[9.] E372/148 reads 'Nothing from the farm of the port of *Portheres* because boats [blank]'. At the end of the entry on Kerrier is 'And for 6s from the farm of Porthzennor [*Porthynsinnard*]. And for £6 8s from pleas and perquisites of the marine court this year'. Then follow entries on wreckage values that appear in the section on WRECK, below.

PERQUISITES

The same renders account for 24s from petty marine perquisites this year. And for 26s 8d from William de Castro and his fellow sailors for having aid in salvage of their things [*auxilio hab' ad res suas salvand'*]. And for 40s from the master of the ship *St Bartholomew* for the same. And for 9s 6d from trantery [*Tranentria*] this year. And for 14s 6d from John Bonone and his fellows for trantery [*tr'*]. And for 13s 4d from Abraham Whyte and his fellows for having aid. Sum, £6 8s.

WRECK

The same renders account for 10s for the price of a certain anchor next to Padstow [*Oldestou*][10]. And for 17s for the price of another anchor there. And for 3s (^ 8d) for 9 hides sold there. And for 2s from the price of a certain cord sold there. And for 8s from a beam [*tigno*] of a certain ship thrown up as wreck there. And for 8d from the price of a certain timber [*ligni*] landing at Lanherne [*Lanhernon*] that was sold. And for 3d from the price of a certain piece of a timber [*pec' ligni*] there. And for 13d from part of one cord and a small beam [*parvo tigno*] landing in the hundred of Kerrier (^ in the tithing of Trelan [*Trelanni*]).[11] And for 26s 8d from the price of a certain mast landing at Tregear [*Tregayr*]. And for 3s 4d from the price of another mast landing at Pentewan [*Bentewyn*]. And for 12d from the price of a certain beam there. And for 15d from a small beam sold at Talland and *Bodcote* [*Tallan et Bodcote*]. And for 4s from a certain mast at Rame [*Rame*]. {And for 12s 4d from wreck landing in *Hydrath*, next to the bridge? [*Hyrdrayth iuxta pouton*].}[12] Sum, £4 10s 3d.

PROFITS OF WRECK

The same responds for 20s from a certain fish from a wreck landing in the port of Fowey that was sold this year. Sum, 20s.

FINES FROM PILLAGING [*DISCARD'*] WRECKS

The same responds for 2s from John Le Tenur for fine for removing

---

10. E372/148 reads *Oldestowe*.
11. In E372/148, this reads *Treloma*.
12. This could also read *Hydrath* next to Pawton [*Pouton*]'. E372/148 adds 'And for 20s from a certain fish landed in the port of Fowey [*Sawe*]. And for £9 19s 8d from fines of diverse people for pillaging and waste made on things landing on land and in the sea this year as contained there'. The sum received is recorded as £43 7s 7d.

goods from a wreck. And for 4s from Richard Sampson and Michael his brother for the same. And for 4s from Richard and John Cornwaleys for the same. And for 2s from John Yarker for the same. And for 4s from Ralph de Trevelves and John Kydel for the same. And for 2s from John Nansreson for the same. And for 2s from Walter Kilben and Richard Blendyn for the same. And for 2s from William de Trefunnans for the same. And for 2s from Reginald and Henry of the same place for the same. And for 4s from John and *Amideus* de Trenelles for the same. And for 8s from Hervey Ennals and six of his fellows for the same. And for 2s from Richard Le Rous for the same. And for 5s from *Poly* de Mythian and four of his fellows for the same. And for 8s from Martin Carucator for the same. And for 6s from Ralph Poulari for the same. And for 3s 6d from Martin Pyngin and Eustace son of Ralph for the same. And for 3s from Nicholas and Martin his sons for the same. And for 4s from Edmund son of Paul and Richard Le Eyr for the same. And for 3s from Richard de Treuorra for the same. And for 6s from John son of Margaret and three of his fellows for the same. And for 4s from John Pescha and Thomas Molend' for the same. And for 26s 8d from *Pascas'* de Trenans for the same. And for 5s 6d from John Tounon and three of his fellows for the same. And 5s from Gervase de Tregayhou and two of his fellows for the same. And for 2s from Roger Skyn for the same. And for 6s from William Le Rous for the same. And for 5s from John Pykard and two of his fellows for the same. And for 2s from Henry de Sancto Cadoco for the same. And for 8s from Thomas Pastore and Richard Neel for the same. And for 11s from Matthew le Rous and four of his fellows for the same. And for 6s from Hervey de Treuemeder for the same. And for 18s from Henry Polda and John Philip, Henry de Halesworthy, Richard son of Jocelin, Peter Le Foulur, Henry de Westcote and Robert Vacy for the same. And for 5s from Robert Cleric of Rame and John Stobel for the same. And for 4s from John Blouwa for the same. And for 3s from Reginald Sacha for the same. And for 4s from William Bastard for the same. And for 6s from Robert Offord and John Brusia for the same. Sum, £9 19s 8d.

SUM TOTAL OF SEA-SHORE, £43 7s 7d

FROM WHICH: For the stipend of a bailiff to watch the sea-shore and hold the court of the same, 53s 4d per year. Sum, 53s 4d. And he owes £40 14s 4d.

m. 3d [blank]

1302/03

PRO, SC6/811/4

31 Edward I. 3 membranes. Account of Thomas de la Hyde, steward and sheriff of Cornwall. A vertical line is drawn through the middle of the account. A similar account is in the pipe roll, PRO, E372/148, mm. 56–56d.

(m. 2d)

[...]

TREMATON

The same renders account for [...] £8 10s for the passage of Saltash [*passag' de Asshe*] this year [...] and for 4s from the customs of boats in the Tamar and no more because the steward was prevented from taking anything from the men of Exeter during the eyre. And for 15s from fair tolls and no more because the eyre began on the same day. And for 1d from the custom of oysters this year. And for 4s from 4 seines this year. And for 16s from 16 barges there. And for £4 from Sutton Pool this year. [...]

[...]

LOSTWITHIEL

ISSUES OF THE MANOR

The same renders account for [...] 10s from the custom of ships this year. [...]

[...]

(m. 3d)

THE SEA-SHORE

The same renders account for 46s 8d from the farm of the port of Marazion [*Marcadiou*].[13] And for 12s from the farm of the port of Penzance. And 20s from the farm of the port of Newlyn [*Lulin*].[14] And for 100s from the farm of the port of Mousehole. And for 2s from the farm of the port of Lamorna. And 12s for the farm of the port of Porthgwarra [*Porthcorwetheu*]. And for 8s from the farm of the port of 'Porthplement' [*Porthplemmyng*]. And for 6s 8d from the farm of the ports of Porthzennor [*Porthsenar*] and Portheras [*Porthrest*]. And for

---

[13.] E372/148, m. 56 reads '*Marcadyou*'.
[14.] E372/148, m. 56 reads '*Lulyn*'.

£6 from the farm of the port of St Ives [*Porthie*]. And 22s 6d from the fisheries of Kerrier. And for 40s from the farm of the port of Fowey. And for 20s from the farm of Polruan. And for 20s from the fisheries of Triggshire. Sum, £21 9s 10d.

PERQUISITES

The same renders account for 17s 6d for perquisites of diverse marine courts this year. And for 9s 7d from trantery this year. And for 6s 8d from a certain mariner at Portheras [*Porseres*] for having aid [*pro auxil' habend'*]. And for 4s from other mariners at Porthoustock [*Portheustek*] for the same. And for 2s from Richard, clerk of Trungle [*Treuunglorth*] for forestalling fish. And for 12d from Ralph Fol for the same. And for 2s from Ailward Wennon for the same. And for 12d from John le Saer for the same. And for 3s from William Stabba for the same. And for 12d from Gregory Wrau for the same. Sum, 47s 9d.

WRECK

The same renders account for 49s 7d from wreck of sea in the hundreds of Penwith [*Pen'*] and Kerrier as appears in the particulars. And for 6s 1d from the particulars of wreck in the hundred of Pyder [*Pidr'*]. And for 5s from wreck in the hundred of Trigg. And for 3s 3d of profit [*approwamento*] of the same wreck beyond its price made before the coroner. Sum, 63s 11d.

PILLAGING OF WRECK
PERQUISITES

The same renders account for 12d from Thomas le Seu' for pillaging wreck in the hundred of Kerrier. And for 12d from John Julis for the same. And for 12d from William his brother for the same. And for 12d from Richard le Mareis junior for the same. And for 12d from Andrew his brother for the same. And for 2s from Reginald le Du for the same. And for 18d from Richard Gorges for the same. And for 2s from Robert Wymark for the same. And for 2s from Geoffrey de Penros for the same. And for 2s from Richard son of Ralph for the same. And 2s from John de Rettalek for the same. And for 2s from Benedict de Tnoukian for the same. Sum, 18s 6d.

Sum total, £28.

ALLOWANCES

From which 53s 4d per year is delivered to a servant for watching

manors in the district [*per loca*] and the sea-shore. Sum, 53s 4d. And
he owes £25 6s 8d. And he responds below.

[end of manuscript]

1303/04

PRO, SC6/811/6

32 Edward I. 2 membranes. Account of Thomas de la Hide, steward of
Cornwall. A vertical line is drawn through the middle of mm. 2–2d.
Parts of the account are very faded or darkened. More summary versions
of this account can be found in PRO, SC6/811/5, m. 3, and in the pipe
roll, PRO, E372/150, m. 46.

(m. 2)

TREMATON
The same renders account for [...] £8 10s for the Saltash passage this
year [...] 4s from the custom of boats in Tamar Water this year. And for
15s of fair tolls. [...] And for ½d from the custom of oysters this year.
And for 6s from 6 seines this year. And for 17s from 17 barges there.
And for £4 from Sutton Pool this year. And for 5s from Lynher Water
this year. [...]
[...]

LOSTWITHIEL
    ISSUES OF THE MANOR
The same renders account for [...] 10s from the custom of ships this
year and 2s from fair tolls. [...]
[...]

(m. 2d)

ACCOUNT OF THE CORNISH SEA-SHORE IN THE 32ND REGNAL YEAR OF KING
EDWARD
The same renders account for 46s 8d from the port of Marazion
[*Marcadyou*]. And for 12s from the port of Penzance. And 20s from
the port of Newlyn. And 100s from the port of Mousehole. And 2s
from the port of Lamorna [*Nosmorou*]. And 12s from the port of
Porthgwarra [*Porthgorwydham*]. And 8s from the port of 'Porthplement'
[*Porthplumig*]. And 6s 8d from the ports of Porthzennor [*Porthsinard*]
and Portheras [*Porthrest*]. And £6 from the port of St Ives [*Porthloe?*].

And 23s 6d from the fisheries of Kerrier [*Kerr'*] this year. And £4 from the fisheries of Fowey, Polruan [*Polrowan*] and Trigg. Sum, £21 10s 10d.

PERQUISITES

The same renders account for 26s 7d from court perquisites this year. And for 25s from forestallers this year. And for 9s for trantery this year. Sum, 60s 7d

WRECK

The same renders account for 5s from timber of a certain boat docking in the port of Rosenithon [*Rosneython*]. And 3s from a certain small anchor in the tithing of Pengersick [*Pengersek*]. And for 12d from timber of a certain little boat of Lanisly [*Lanoscly*] Sum, 9s.

FINES OF WRECK

The same renders account for 6s 8d from Andrew Mochayne and 4 companions [*soc'*] for pillaging [*dissacar'*]. And for 20s fine from Martin de Trewof and 11 companions for the same. And for 5s from John de Trewranec for the same. And for 10s from Stephen de Treskon and 5 companions for the same. And for 4s from John le Frank for the same. And for 10s from *Yonene* de Hoskeles and 5 companions for the same. And for 6s 8d from Thomas Hargansaus and 4 companions for fine for the same. And for 6s 8d from Jocelin le F... for the same. And for 3s 4d from John Cleric for the same. And for 23s from Luke de Trewyn for the same and 14 companions. And for 3s from Henry Ponytz for the same. And for 13s 4d from Richard Poer and 5 companions for the same. And for 6s 8d from Roger Treman? and John de Trebruer for the same. And for 2s from Robert Jon and 2 companions for the same. And for 6s 8d from John Eyt? for the same. And 3s from William son of Michael for the same. And for 26s from Richard Stifore and 20 companions for the same. And for 3s from Richard ... and Thomas ... for the same. And for 6s 8d from William Wyntere and 4 companions for the same. And for 10s from William de Frang... and 12 companions for the same. And for 10s from Edmund de Germas? and 4 companions for the same. And for 25s from William Dovere and 16 companions for the same. And for 18s from Osbert de Kenegy and 6 companions for the same. And for 7s from Brian de Trenals and 2 companions for the same. And for 8s from Oliver Resugyon and 2 companions for the same. And for 2s from Silvester de Kenegy for the same. Sum, £12 6s 8d.

Sum total, £37 7s 1d

From which is allowed 53s 4d to one of the servants of the keeper of the lord for holding the court in the absence of the steward. Sum, 53s 4d. And the sea-shore [account] clears [*de claro*] £34 13s 9d.

[end of membrane and account]

1304/05

PRO, SC6 811/5

32 and 33 Edward II. 7 membranes, sewn end to end, with blank dorses. Account of Thomas de la Hide, steward, of issues and lands of Edmund, once earl of Cornwall, from 30 September 1303 to 30 September 1305. The account reads as a short, summary receiver's account. A line is drawn vertically through the middle of the entire account. On m. 3, this roll contains a summary version of the account for 1303/04 in SC6 811/6 (above). Below is the part of the account covering 1304/05; a similar enrolled account for 1304/05 is in the pipe roll, PRO, E372/ 150, m. 47.

(m. 5)

[...]

TREMATON

The same accounts for [...] £8 10s for the common passage of the same Water as leased at farm this year. And 4s from the custom of 4 fishing boats in Tamar Water this year. [...] And for 7s 7d from rents of the boroughs [*censer' Burgorum*] of Trematon and Saltash, namely from foreign men to have licences to trade in the same boroughs quit of toll this year. And for 17s from tolls of the fairs of Saltash this year. And for 4s from 4 fishing seines in Tamar Water this year. And ½d from the custom of fishers of oysters this year. And for 17s from the custom of 17 barges taking sand in Tamar Water [*ducent sabulon' in aqua de Tamer*] this year, namely 12d from each barge. And for 5s from the fishery in Lynher Water this year. And for £4 from pleas and perquisites and other customs of mariners landing in the port of Sutton as leased at farm this year. [...]

[...]

(m. 6)

LOSTWITHIEL
The same accounts for [...] 14s from the custom of ships docking there this year. [...]
[...]

(m. 7)

ISSUES OF THE SEA PORTS WITH WRECK
The same renders account for 46s 8d from the farm of the port of Marazion [*M'cadyou*] this year. And for 12s from the farm of the port of Penzance (^ this year). And for 20s from the farm of the port of Newlyn this year. And for 100s from the farm of the port of Mousehole this year. And for 2s from the farm of the port of Lamorna [*Nansmorno*] this year. And for 12s from the farm of the port of Porthgwarra [*Porthgorweythou*] this year. And from the farm of the port of Portheras [*Porthrest*] nothing this year because the boats there were submerged [*sumersi fuerunt*]. And for 8s from the farm of the port of 'Porthplement' [*Porthplenynt*] this year. And for £6 from the farm of the port of St Ives [*Porthy*] this year. And for 40s from the farm of the port of Fowey this year. And for 20s from the farm of the port of Polruan [*Polrouan*] this year. And for 20s from the fisheries in Triggshire as leased at farm this year. And for 23s 6d from issues of the fisheries of Kerrier this year. And for 6s 8d from the farm of the port of Porthzennor [*Porthsynnard*] this year. And 68s 7d from pleas and perquisites of the marine court this year as contained in a roll of particulars. And for 2s from the price of a certain timber [*ligni*] from wreck thrown up on land in the tithing of Carminow [*Carminou*] as contained in the same place. And for £9 3s 6d from fines of diverse people for pillaging and waste made on things thrown to land from wreck of sea this year as contained in the same place. Sum received, £34 4s 11d.

EXPENSES: The same accounts for a stipend of 53s 4d for one bailiff keeping the sea-shore and manor of Moresk and other neighbouring manors as allowed in the time of the said earl. Sum of expenses, 53s 4d. And he owes £31 11s 7d. And he responds below.

1305/06

PRO, SC6/811/7

34 Edward I. 4 membranes. Account of Thomas de la Hyde for the
stewardship of the county of Cornwall that was of Edmund, once earl
of Cornwall, from 30 September 1305 to 29 September 1305. The
heading is missing, but 'the 34th year' [*Annus 34*] is written at the top
of m. 1 and a similar account in the roll of foreign accounts, PRO,
E372/152B, mm. 9–9d, provides the missing heading. A vertical line is
drawn down the centre of the account.

(m. 2)

TYBESTA

EXPENSES

The same renders account for [...]. And 20s in wages and stipend for a
serjeant keeping the manors of Tybesta, Tewington, and Moresk and
other neighbouring manors this year as contained in the roll of
particulars.[15]

[...]

(m. 2d)

[...]

TREMATON

[ISSUES]

The same renders account for [...] £8 10s for the common passage of
the same Water as leased at farm this year. And for 4s from the custom
of four boats fishing in Tamar Water this year. [...] And for 4s from
four fishing seines in Tamar Water this year. And for ½d for the custom
of oyster fishing this year. And for 15s for the custom of 15 barges
taking sand in Tamar Water this year, namely <u>12d</u> from each barge.
And for 5s from the fishery of Lynher Water this year. And for £4 from
pleas and perquisites and other customs of fishers[16] landing in the port
of Sutton and leased at farm this year. [...]

EXPENSES

The same renders account for [...] and 1 boat newly made for the Saltash
ferry because the other was so debilitated that men could not pass over
[...]

[15.] The same expense is noted at the end of the account under SEA SHORE, EXPENSES.

[16.] PRO, E372/152B reads 'mariners'.

(m. 3)

[...]

Lostwithiel

The same renders account for [...]. And for 7s 6d from custom of ships landing there this year. [...]

[...]

(m. 3d)

Tewington

[...]

   [Fines and Perquisites]

The same renders account for [...]. And for 2s from John Jacony for having trantery this year. [...]

[...]

(m. 4)

Issues of the Sea ports with Wreck

The same renders account for 46s 8(^ ½)d from the farm of the port of Marazion [Marcadyo] this year. And for 12s from the farm of the port of Penzance [Pensans] this year. And for 20s from the farm of the port of Newlyn this year. And for 100s from the farm of the port of Mousehole this year. And for 2s from the farm of the port of Lamorna [Nansmerno] this year. And for 12s from the farm of the port of Porthgwarra [Porthgorweythou] this year. Nothing from the farm of the port of Portheras [Porthrest][17] this year because the boats were submerged. And for 8s from the farm of the port of 'Porthplement' [Porthplenit][18] this year. And for 6s 8d from the farm of Porthzennor [Porthsynard] and Portheras [Porost].[19] And for £6 from the farm of

---

[17.] Since Portheras is also noted a few lines down in its usual place with Porthzennor, this port was probably the same as the Porthseres that appeared in the account of 1300/01, above.

[18.] PRO, E372/152B reads 'Porthpleynton'.

[19.] PRO, E372/152B omits this sentence and includes after the entry on the fisheries of Kerrier: 'And for 6s 8d from the farm of the port of Porthzennor this year. And for 54s 9d from pleas and perquisites of the marine court this year as contained in the roll of particulars. And for 9s from the price of one coffer, one runlet of wine and certain other timbers thrown to land in the tithings of Pentewan [Bendevy], Pentire [Pentir], Trelan [Trelan] and Widemouth [Wydemwe] as contained there. And for £4 2s from the fines of diverse persons for unloading and wasting [diversorum discaria et distractionem] things thrown up to land from wreck of sea this year as contained there. Sum received, £28 1½d'.

the port of St Ives [*Porthye*] this year. And for 40s from the farm of the port of Fowey this year. And for 20s from the farm of the port of Polruan [*Polrowan*] this year. And for 20s from the farm of the fisheries [*piscarie*] of Triggshire [*Trigerschire*] as leased at farm this year. And for 25s from the fisheries [*piscaria*] of Kerrier this year. Sum, £21 12s 4d.

PERQUISITES

The same renders account for 15s 2d from petty amercements of the court this year. And for 22s 10d from forestallers. And for 10s 4d from trantery. And for 6s 5d from perquisites of the marine court at Lostwithiel [*Lostwythiel*]. Sum, 54s 9d.

WRECK

The same renders account for 12d from the price of a beam landing in the tithing of Trelan [*Trelan*]. And for 2s from the price of four boards [*bord'*] landed at Widemouth [*Wydemuwe*]. And for 3s from the price of one coffer landed in the tithing of Pentewan [*Bendeuy*]. And for 3s from the price of one runlet of wine in the tithing of Pentire [*Pentyr*]. Sum, 9s.

£24 16s 1d[20]

FINES OF WRECK

The same renders account for 50s from John Russo and thirty-two fellows from the tenants of Roger of Carminou for fines for unloading? [*pro discaria?*]. And for 2s from John Contor for fine for the same. And for 30s from Matthew Sterra and 15 of his fellows for fines for the same. Sum, £4 2s.

EXPENSES

The same accounts for 53s 4d for the stipend of one bailiff to keep the sea-shore and manor of Moresk and other neighbouring manors per year as allowed in the time of the earl. Sum, 53s 4d. And he owes £26 4s 9d.

[...]

---

[20]. Scribbled in the left-hand margin just before the next marginal heading.

30 September 1306–6 August 1307

PRO, E372/152B

33–34 Edward I. Roll of foreign accounts containing the steward's account of Thomas de la Hyde, for the profits of the county of Cornwall, from 30 September 1306 to 7 July 1307 when his son and heir, Edward, succeeded to the reign, and from that day to 6 August next, when Peter de Gaveston, knight, was granted the county of Cornwall by the king. For the period of this account covering Easter term 1307, see also the account below, PRO, SC6/811/8.

(m. 10)

[...]

TREMATON

The same accounts for [...]...3s from the custom of 4 boats fishing in Tamar Water [...] and for 3s 9d from the custom of 5 seines fishing in Tamar Water for the same time as contained there. And for 1d from the oyster fishery [*de piscar' ostr'*] for the same time. And for 12s from the custom of 6 barges taking sand in Tamar Water for the same time, namely 9d from each barge as contained there. And for 3s 9d from the fishery of Lynher Water for the same time as contained there. And for 60s from the pleas and perquisites and other customs of mariners landing in the port of Sutton, leased at farm for the same time as contained there [...].

[...]

LOSTWITHIEL

The same renders account for [...]. And for 5s from the custom of ships landing there during the same time. [...]

[...]

(m. 10d)

[...]

ISSUES OF THE SEA PORTS OF CORNWALL

The same renders account for 23s 4d from the port of Marazion this year. And 6s from the port of Penzance for the said term as contained there. And for 10s from the farm of the port of Newlyn [*LeWelen*] for the said term as contained there. And for 50s from the farm of the port of Mousehole [*Meschele*] for the said term. And for 12d from the port of Lamorna for the said term. And for 6s from the farm of the port of Porthgwarra [*Porghgorhwoyheu*] for the said term as contained there.

And for 4s from the farm of the port of 'Porthplement' [*Portpleynton*]
for the said term. And for 3s 4d from the farm of the ports of Portheras
and of Porthzennor [*Porthrost et de Porthsenare*] for the said term as
contained there. And for 60s from the farm of the port of St Ives for
the said term. And for 12s 3d from the farm of the ports of Kerrier
[*Kyrier*] for the said term. And for 20s from the fishery of Fowey as
leased at farm for the same time as contained there. And for 10s from
the farm of the port of Polruan for the said term. And for 10s from the
farm of the fisheries of Triggshire for the said term as contained there.
And for 16s 6d from the pleas and perquisites of the maritime court
for the same time. And for 10s from receipts of forestallers and trantery
for the said term as contained there. Sum received, £12 2s 5d.

EXPENSES
The same accounts for 40s for the stipend of one bailiff to keep the
sea-shore and manor of Moresk and other neighbouring manors from
the said Michaelmas to the said 6 August, as allowed in the time of the
said earl. Sum of expenses, 40s. And he owes £10 2s 5d. And he responds
below.
[...]

Easter Term 1307

PRO, SC6/811/8

35 Edward I.[21] 3 membranes. Account of Thomas de la Hyde, sheriff
and steward of Cornwall. The account for the sea-shore specifically
notes that it only covered revenues collected at Easter term, although
those for Tybesta, Trematon, and Lostwithiel seem to have covered
three terms: Christmas, Easter, and St John the Baptist. A vertical line
is drawn through the middle of the account.

(m. 2)

TYBESTA
[...]
ALLOWANCES
15s in wages and stipend of 1 serjeant keeping the manors of Tybesta,
Tewington, and Moresk and other neighbouring manors for the said
term. [...][22]

---

21. The manuscript mistakenly has the year as '25' instead of '35'.
22. This same expense also appears at the end of the account for the sea-ports.

[...]

TREMATON

And for £6 7s 6d from the passage of the same Water leased at farm for the said terms. And for 3s from the custom of 4 boats fishing in Tamar Water for the said terms. [...] Nothing from the toll of the Saltash fair because at Michaelmas. And for 3s 5d from the custom of 5 seines fishing in Tamar Water for the said terms. And for 1d from the custom of oyster fishing for the said terms. And for 12s from the custom of 16 barges taking sand in Tamar Water for the said term, namely 9d from each barge. And for 3s 9d for the fishery in Lynher Water for the said terms. And for 60s from pleas and perquisites and other customs of fishers landing in the port of Sutton as leased at farm for the said terms. [...]

[...]

(m. 2d)

[...]

LOSTWITHIEL

The same renders account for [...] 5s from the custom of ships for the said terms. [...]

[...]

(m. 3)

[...]

ISSUES OF THE SEA PORTS WITH WRECK

The same renders account for 23s 4d from the port of Marazion [*Marcasyou*] for Easter term. And for 6s from the port of Penzance for the said term. And for 10s from the port of Newlyn [*Luelyn*] for the said term. And for 50s from the port of Mousehole for the same term. And for 12d from the port of Lamorna [*Nansmorno*] for the said term. And for 6s from the port of Porthgwarra [*Porthgourwytheu*] for the same term. And for 4s from the port of ~~Plymouth~~ ~~[*Plummue*]~~ ('Porthplement' [*Porthpleynton*]) at the said term. And for 3s 4d from the port of Portheras [*Porthrest*] and Porthzennor [*Porth senare*] at the said term. And for 60s from the port of St Ives [*Porthie*] at the said term. And for 12s 3d from the ports of Kerrier at the said term. And for 20s from the fishery of Fowey at the said term. And for 10s from the farm of the port of Polruan at the said term. And for 10s from the farms of the fisheries of Triggshire [*Triggeschire*] for the said term. Sum, {£10 15s 11d}.

PERQUISITES

The same renders account for 16s 6d from petty court perquisites. And for 4s from forestallers. And for 6s from trantery this year. Sum, 26(s) 6d.

Sum total, £12 2s 5d.

EXPENSES

From which 53s 4d for the stipend of one of the bailiffs of the marine keeper [*balli' custod' marinam*] and the manor of Moresk and other neighbouring manors per year as allowed in the time of earl Edmund. Sum, 53s 4d. And he owes.

FROM WRECK

Nothing this year.

FROM FINES OF WRECK

Nothing.

24 June–29 Sept. 1308

PRO, SC6/811/9

1 Edward II. Account of Thomas de la Hyde, sheriff and steward of Cornwall, from 24 June [the feast of St John the Baptist[23]] 1308 to the following 29 September. 2 membranes. A vertical line is drawn through the middle of the account.

(m. 1d)

[...]

TYBESTA

ALLOWANCES

For 5s in wages and stipend of one serjeant to keep the manors of Tybesta and Tewington and Moresk and other neighbouring manors from the Nativity of St John the Baptist [24 June] to Michaelmas for the said term [...]

[...]

[23.] Although the specific feast is not noted in the heading of the account, it is noted in the section on Tybesta.

TREMATON

The same renders account for [...]. And for 42s 6d for the passage of the same Water leased at farm. And for 12d from the custom of 4 boats fishing in Tamar Water for the said term. [...] And for 18d from fishing of six seines in Tamar Water for the said term. ½d from the custom of oysters this year. And for 4s from 16 barges taking sand in Tamar Water for the said term. And for 15d from the Lynher fishery for the said term. And for 20s from pleas and perquisites and other customs of fishers landing in the port of Sutton leased at farm for the said term. [...]
[...]

m. 2

[...]

LOSTWITHIEL

The same renders account for [...]. And nothing from the custom of ships for the said term. [...].
[...]

(m. 2d)

ISSUES OF THE SEA PORTS WITH WRECK

The same renders account for 23s 4d from the port of Marazion [*Marcadiou*] for Michaelmas term. And for 6s from the port of Penzance for the said term. And for 10s from the port of Newlyn [*Lulyn*] for the said term. And for 50s from the port of Mousehole for the said term. And for 12d from the port of Lamorna [*Nansmurnou*] for the said term. And for 6s from the port of Porthgwarra [*Porthgurwitheu*] for the said term. And for 4s from the port of 'Porthplement' [*Plement*] for the said term. And for 3s 4d from the ports of Portheras [*Porthrest*] and Porthzennor [*Porthsenar*] for the said term. And for 60s from the port of St Ives [*Porthye*] for the said term. And for 12s 3d from the ports of Kerrier. And for 20s from the fishery of Fowey for the said term. And for 10s from Polruan for the said term. And for 10s from the ports of Trigg for the said term. Sum, {£ 10 15s 11d.[24]

For court perquisites and trantery, nothing because in escheat.

[24.] This sum and the following lines were added later in a different hand.

EXPENSES

13s 4d for the stipend of a serjeant to keep the sea-shore and manor of
Moresk and other neighbouring manors for one-quarter of one year.
Sum, 13s 4d. And he owes £10 2s 7d.}

[...]

29 September 1308–5 August 1309

PRO, SC6/811/10

2–3 Edward II. 5 membranes. Account of Thomas de la Hide, steward
and sheriff of Cornwall, from 29 September 1308 to 5 August 1309. A
vertical line is drawn through the middle of the account. The cocket
account for 1308–9 is in PRO, E122/39/5, printed below in Part III.

(m. 1d)

TYBESTA

[...]

ALLOWANCES

15s for wages and stipend of one serjeant to keep the manors of Tybesta,
Tewington, and Moresk and other neighbourning manors at the said
terms.

[...]

(m. 2)

[...]

TREMATON

The same renders account for [...]. And for £4 5s for the passage of the
same Water as leased at farm for the said terms. And for 2s from the
custom of 4 boats fishing in Tamar Water for the said terms. [..] And 2s
6d from fishermen of 5 seines fishing in Tamar Water for the said terms,
at 12d per seine. 2d from the custom of oysters. And for 8s from 16
barges taking sand in Tamar Water for one-half year at 12d per barge.
And for 2s 6d from the fishery of Lynher Water for one-half year. And
for 40s from the pleas and perquisites and other custom of fishermen
landing in the port of Sutton as leased at farm for the said terms. [...]

[...]

(m. 2d)

[...]

LOSTWITHIEL

The same renders account for [...]. And for 5s from the custom of ships landing there during the same time. [...]

FINES AND PERQUISITES

The same renders account for [...]. And for 14s 8d from John Rosshel and 20 of his fellows for trantery of men concealing forestalling and for trantery? [*pro tr' hmi' forstall' concell' et tr*ᵃ].

[...]

(m. 4)

~~ISSUES OF THE PORTS. None this year because the lord king conceded via his charter to Alan Wolwayn, havener, at Michaelmas.~~

ISSUES OF THE PORTS

The same renders account for 23s 4d from the farm of the port of Marazion for the said term as contained in the roll for three-quarters of the 35th year [of Edward I]. And for 6s from the farm of the port of the farm of the port of Penzance for the said term as contained in the same place. And for 10s from the farm of the port of Newlyn for the said term as contained in the same place. And for 50s from the farm of the port of Mousehole for the said term as contained in the same place. And for 12d from the farm of the port of Lamorna [*Nansmorus*] for the said term as contained in the same place. And for 6s from the farm of the port of Porthgwarra [*Portheweyu*] for the said term. And for 4s from the farm of the port of 'Porthplement' [*Porthplumewe*] for the said term. And for 3s 4d from the farm of the ports of Portheras [*Porthrest*] and Porthzennor [*Porthsanre*]. And for 60s from the farm of the port of St Ives [*Porthyes*]. And for 12s 3d from the farm of the ports of Kerrier. And for 20s from the fishery of Fowey. And for 10s from the fishery of Polruan. And for 10s from the fisheries of Trigg. And for 16s 6d from the pleas and perquisites of the maritime court during the same time. And for 10s from forestallers and trantery during the said time. Sum received, £12 2s 5d.

EXPENSES

40s for expense of one bailiff to keep the sea-shore and manor of Moresk and other neighbouring manors during the said term as contained in the account of the 35th year preceding. Sum of expenses, 40s. And he owes £10 2s 5d.

[...]

19 June–31 July 1312

PRO, SC6/811/11

5–6 Edward II. 2 membranes. Account of Thomas de la Hide, recently
steward of Cornwall, from 19 June [the Monday before the feast of the
Nativity of St John the Baptist in the 5th year [of Edward II]] to 31 July
1312 [Monday in the vigil of the Gules of August next] on which day
John de Bedowynde received custody of the whole county [*comitatus*]
of Cornwall by writ of the lord king. The account is very faded and
darkened by gall in parts. A vertical line is drawn through the middle
of the account. A similar account is in the pipe roll, PRO, E372/158,
m. 46, where Thomas de Hide accounts as son and heir of Thomas de
la Hide, deceased, recently steward of Cornwall for the issues of the
county which are in the hands of the king following the death of Peter
de Gaveston, recently earl, for 6 weeks, before being delivered to John
de Bedewynd by grant of the king. The cocket account for 1312–13 is
in PRO, E122/39/5, printed below in Part III.

(m. 1)

[...]

TYBESTA

ALLOWANCES

The same renders account for 5s from the wages and stipend of one
servant to watch the manors of Tybesta and Tewington and other
neighbouring manors for the said term [...]

[...]

TREMATON

The same renders account for £4 10s 9¾d of assize rents of the aforesaid
manor, for the term of the Nativity of St John the Baptist, as contained
in the roll of particulars [...]. And for 42s 2d from the passage of the
same Water thus leased at farm for the said term. And for 12d from the
custom of 4 boats fishing in Tamar Water for the said term. [...] 15d
from the custom of 5 seines fishing in Tamar Water for the said term.
Nothing from the custom of oysters because all [due] at Michaelmas.
And for 4s from the custom of 16 barges taking sand in Tamar Water
for the said term. And for 15d from the fishery in Lynher Water for the
said term. And for 20s from pleas and perquisites and other customs of
fishers[25] landing in the port of Sutton thus leased at farm for the said
term. [...]

---

25. PRO, E372/158, m. 46 reads 'mariners'.

[...]

LOSTWITHIEL
[...] Nothing from the custom of ships during the said time.[26][...]
[...]

(m. 2)

[...]
ISSUES OF THE PORTS
Nothing from issues of the ports because all at [other] said terms.[27]
[...]

27 July 1312–27 January 1313

PRO, E372/158

6 Edward II. Pipe roll containing the account of Eudo le Ercedekne for the issues of the castle and vill of Trematon from 27 July 1312 to 29 September next and from then to 27 January when he delivers custody of the castle and vill to Thomas le Ercedekne.

(m. 46d)

[...]
TREMATON: for 9 weeks and the last quarter of the 5th year
The same responds for [...]. And for 42s 6d from the passage of the same Water thus leased at farm for the same part of time as contained there. And for 12d received from the farm of 2 boats fishing in Tamar Water during the same time. And for 9d from 3 seines fishing in Tamar Water during the same time. And nothing from oysters because during the time of Lent [*tempore quadrages'*]. And for 14½d from the farm of

---

26. PRO, E372/158, m. 46 notes 'He does not respond for the custom of ships landing there nor for the parcel [of land] next to Fowey Water nor for the fair tolls because the farms arising from these should be paid at the terms of St Bartholomew and Michaelmas'.
27. PRO, E372/158, m. 46 records this as 'FEE FARMS. He does not respond for the fee farms of [...] nor the issues of the sea ports because said farms and issues should be paid at the terms of Michaelmas and Easter, which did not occur within the time of the aforesaid account as contained there. [...]'

the fishery of Lynher Water for the same time as contained there. And
for 20s from the pleas and perquisites of fishers landing in the port of
Sutton as leased at farm during the same time as contained there. [...]
And for 4s from the custom of 16 barges taking sand in Tamar Water
during the same time as contained there. [...]

TREMATON: for the first quarter of the year
And for 42s 6d from the passage of the same Water as leased at farm
during the same time as contained there. And for 12d from the farm of
2 boats fishing in Tamar Water during the said time. And for 9d from 3
seines fishing in Tamar Water during the same time. Nothing from
oysters because during the time of Lent. And for 14½d from the fishery
of Lynher Water during the same time as contained there. And for 20s
from the pleas and perquisites and other customs of fishers landing in
the port of Sutton as leased at farm for the same time as contained
there. And for 4s from the custom of 16 barges taking sand in Tamar
Water during the same time as contained there. And 8s 6d from fair
tolls of the borough of Saltash at the feast of St Denis. [...]
EXPENSES
[...] and 6s 8½d for fixing the boat of the passage of Tamar Water. [...]
[...]

1. 28 January–30 September 1313

2. 1313/14

PRO, SC6/811/12

3. Michaelmas Term 1314

PRO, E372/160

6–8 Edward II. PRO, SC6/811/12 has 6 membranes, placed in a leather
bag. It includes: 1) Account of Thomas le Ercedekne, sheriff and steward
of Cornwall (from 13 January) from 28 January [the Sunday after the
feast of the Conversion of Saint Paul, 6 Edward II] until 30 September
next. 6 membranes, placed in a leather bag; and 2) On m. 4 begins the
account of Thomas le Ercedekne, sheriff and steward of Cornwall from
29 September 1313 to 29 September 1314. On m. 6 begins the account
of Thomas le Ercedekne for the profits of the stewardship of the county
of Cornwall from 29 September 1314 to 16 December, for 11 weeks,
but the account must be incomplete since only the summary headings

are noted, with very few sums recorded. A vertical line is drawn through the middle of the account. 3) A similar account is also in the pipe roll, PRO, E372/160, that covers the period from 27 January 1313 to Michaelmas 1313 (m. 47); and from 29 September 1313 to 29 September 1314 (m. 47d); and from 29 September to 16 December 1314 (m. 47d) . The latter's account is abbreviated and incomplete, so it is not included here. Since the pipe roll account for 1313/14, however, does include the account of Thomas Alger as guardian of the ports for this time, it is printed below. The cocket account for 1313–14 is in PRO, E122/39/5, printed below in Part III.

1. 28 January–30 September 1313

(m. 2)

[...]

TYBESTA

ALLOWANCES

The same accounts for [...] 15s for the wages and stipend of one bailiff to keep the manors of Tybesta, Tewington, Moresk and other neighbouring manors for three terms. [...]

[...]

(m. 2d)

TREMATON

The same renders account for [...] £6 7s 6d from the passage of the same Water leased at farm for the said terms. And for 3s from the farm of 4 boats fishing in Tamar Water. [...] And for 3s from 3 seines fishing in Tamar Water. Nothing from oysters. And for 12s from custom of 16 barges taking sand in Tamar Water for the said terms. And for 3s 9d from the fishery in Lynher Water for the said terms. And for 60s from pleas and perquisites and other customs of fishers[28] landing in the port of Sutton leased at farm for the said terms. [...]

[...]

LOSTWITHIEL

The same renders account [...] for 13s from the cellar below the (great) hall this year and no more because after Gerard de Villors handed it over no merchants wanted to lease it except for the said [term] and

---

[28.] PRO, E372/160, m. 47 reads 'mariners' rather than 'fishers'.

because the burgesses of the said town have built themselves many new houses [*et non plus quia postquam Gerardus de de Villors illud dimisit nulli mercatores volver' ille conducere nisi per dict' et quia burg' dict' ville plur' de novo sibi construger' domos*].[29] Nothing from the custom of ships because Thomas Algor, havener [*havenar*],[30] received all by writ of the lord king [...]

[...]

(m. 3d)

[...]

WRECK: Nothing because all assigned to Thomas Algor, valet of the chamber [*valleto camere*] of the lord king by writ.[31]

[...]

2. 1313/14

(m. 4)

[...]

TYBESTA

ALLOWANCES

The same accounts for 20s per year for the wages and stipend of one serjeant to keep the manors of Tybesta, Tewington, Moresk and other neighbouring manors for three terms. [...]

[...]

(m. 4d)

[...]

TREMATON

The same renders account for [...]. And for £8 10s from the passage of the same Water leased at farm. And for 4s per year from the farm of 4

---

29. The cellar under the great hall was usually leased for 66s 8d per year.
30. In PRO, E372/160, m. 47 he is termed 'valet of the chamber of the king, keeper of the water and ports in the county of Cornwall as long as it pleases the king' instead of 'havener'.
31. In PRO, E372/160, m. 47 is noted 'He does not respond for issues of the seaports with wreck because the king committed custody of the waters of the ports in the county of Cornwall to Thomas Alger, valet of the chamber of the king, to have as long as it pleases the king. Rendering to the Exchequer of the king each year as much as the other guardians [...]. {for which custody Thomas Alger responds in roll 16 in Cornwall}.

boats fishing in Tamar Water. [...] And for 3s from 3 seines fishing in Tamar Water. Nothing from oysters. And for 16s per year from 16 barges taking sand in Tamar Water. And for 5s from the fishery of Lynher Water this year. And for 11s 6d from the tolls of Saltash fair. And for £4 from pleas and perquisites and other customs of fishers[32] landing in the port of Sutton this year. [...]
[...]

(m. 5)

[...]

LOSTWITHIEL

The same renders account for [...]. Nothing from the custom of ships because Thomas Alger (^ valet) of the chamber of the king receives all by writ of the king[33] [...]

[...]

3. Michaelmas Term 1314

(m. 47d)

[...]

SEA PORTS WITH WRECK

The same renders account for 23s 4d from the farm of the port of Marazion [*Marcadiou*] for Michaelmas term as contained in the roll of particulars. And for 6s from the farm of the port of Penzance for the same term as contained there. And for 10s from the farm of the port of Newlyn [*Luelyn*] for the same term as contained there. And for 50s from the farm of the port of Mousehole for the same term as contained there. And for 12d for the farm of the port of Lamorna for the same term as contained there. And for 6s from the farm of the port of Porthgwarra [*Porthgorweytheu*] for the same term as contained there. And for 4s from the farm of the port of 'Porthplement' [*Porthpleynton*] for the same term as contained there. And for 3s 4d from the farm of the port of Portheras and Porthzennor for the same term as contained

---

32. PRO, E372/160, m. 47d has 'mariners' instead.
33. PRO, E372/160, m. 47d reads "He does not respond for customs of the ships landing there because the king committed custody of the waters and issues of the sea-ports to Thomas Alger, for which he is to respond to the Exchequer of the king each year as contained in the account of three-quarters of the sixth year'.

there. And for 60s from the farm of the port of St Ives for the same term as contained there. And for 12s from the farm of the ports of Kerrier [*Kerreer*] from the same term as contained there. And for 20s from the farm of the fishery of Fowey for the same term as contained there And for 10s from the farm of the port of Polruan for the same term as contained there. And for 10s from the farm of the fisheries of Trigg for the same term as contained there. He does not respond for pleas and perquisites and for wreck because he received nothing as he said for the return of Easter term because Thomas Alger then had custody of the aforesaid ports by writ of the king, allowed above. Sum received: £10 16s 2d.

The same accounts for 26s 8d the stipend of 1 bailiff keeping the seashore, manor of Moresk and other neighbouring manors for the aforesaid term, as allowed in the preceding accounts.

16 December 1314–29 September 1315

PRO, SC6/811/13

8–9 Edward II. 9 membranes, placed in a bag; all dorses are blank. Account of Richard de Polampton, steward of Cornwall, of profits that came into king's hands at the death of Peter de Gaveston, once earl of Cornwall , from 16 December 1314 when he received custody from the preceding steward, Thomas Lercedekne, until 29 September 1315 when he delivered custody to Richard le Hywyssh. A similar enrolled account appears in the pipe roll, PRO E372/160, mm. 45–45d, except the ISSUES OF THE PORTS receives a separate section.[34] The cocket account for 1314–15 is in PRO, E122/39/5, printed below in Part III.

---

[34] It is on m. 45d: 'From the issues of the ports in the county of Cornwall from the aforesaid 16 December in the 8th year (1314) to 7 March next (1315) before which he should deliver custody of the aforesaid ports to Wynand Tyrel jr, to whom the king committed custody to have as long as it pleases the king. Rendering hence to the king each year at the Exchequer as much as the custodians of the same [ports] were accustomed to render and 30s beyond for each year, by writ of the king; he does not respond because there were no profits during the same time as he says (^ whence the same Wynand ought to respond. And he responds in rotulo 16 for Cornwall). The same Wynand responds ~~in rotulo 42 for Cornwall~~'.

(m. 5)

[...]

LOSTWITHIEL

He renders account for [...] and for 10s from custom [of ships] landing there this year. [...]

(m. 7)

[...]

TREMATON[35]

He renders account for £10 14s 5½d for assize rents of the manor of Trematon which was in his custody with its members of Lake [*Lake*], Saltash, Carkeel [*Karkil*] and Sutton Water from 16 December in the 8th (1314) year of Edward II to 27 July next when he delivered the manor with its members and all of its appurtenances and custody of the castle to (^Thomas de Govely) by writ of the king of an order directed to him which is dated at Canterbury 11 June in the 8th year, namely for the terms of St Thomas the Apostle, Easter, and the Nativity of St John the Baptist. [...] And £6 7s 6d from the ferry of the same water for the aforeseaid time. And 3s from the farm of 4 boats fishing in Tamar Water for the same time. [...] And for 2s 3d from 3 seines fishing in Tamar Water. And for 1½d from oysters during the same time. And 12s from 16 ~~seines~~ (barges) taking sand in Tamar Water by a certain custom. And for 3s 9d from the fishery of Lynher Water. And for 11s from fair tolls because all [collected] within the aforesaid time. And 60s from pleas and perquisites and other customs of fishers landing in the port of Sutton leased at farm for the said time. [...]

FINES AND PERQUISITES OF THE COURT OF TREMATON

[...] And 30s fine from a certain man of Sutton holding Sutton Water and also pleas and perquisites and other customs (^pertaining) to the port of Sutton at farm at the will of the king for having the said farm, owed when the farm first rendered.

---

35. The Trematon account in PRO E372/160, m. 45d, runs from 16 December 1314 to 27 July 1315, and includes £6 7s 6d from the ferry crossing, 3s from 4 boats fishing in Tamar Water, 2s from 3 seines fishing there, 1½d from the farm of oysters, 12s from 16 barges taking sand, 3s 9d from the Lynher fishery, 11s from fair tolls, and 60s from pleas and and other customs of mariners in the port of Sutton. The 10s repairs to the ferry boat are noted under Expenses. The fine for having the farm of the port of Sutton may be related to the extra 30s per year the custodian was expected to pay (above, n. 34).

Allowances

[...] 10s for repairing and fixing at task 1 boat for the passage of Saltash Water [*batello per passagio aque de Esse*] which was totally broken and so debilitated that it could not service the crossing [*passagio*].
[...]

1315/16

PRO, SC6/811/16

[9–10 Edward II]. 3 membranes. No heading, but in a leather bag marked 'from ... to next Michaelmas' and the paper tag reads 'Michaelmas 9–10 Edward II'. A vertical line is drawn through the middle of the account. Parts of this account (although not the section on Issues of the Ports) are also contained in PRO, SC6/811/14 (account of Richard de Hywyssh, steward of the earldom of Cornwall, after the death of Piers de Gaveston, once earl of Cornwall, when the earldom came into the hands of the king, from 29 September 1315 to 29 September 1316) and in PRO, SC6/811/15 (account of Richard de Hywysh of the issues of the stewardship of the earldom of Cornwall from the castle and manor of Trematon which was in the hands of Thoms de Goveyly by commission of the king after the death of Peter de Gaveston, once earl of Cornwall, from 29 September 1315, when he received custody from Richard de Polhampton, until 18 May when the king committed custody to Henry de Wylington, for as long as the king pleases). The portion of this account covering 15 May–29 September 1316 is also in the pipe roll, PRO, E372/161, m. 53, where Henry de Wylington and Henry de Kirkeby account for the issues of the stewardship of Cornwall, now in the hands of the king. The cocket account for 1315–16 is in PRO, E122/39/5, printed below in Part III.

(m. 2)

[...]

Lostwithiel

[...] And for 10s from custom of the ships and boats landing here. [...]
[...]

(m. 2d)

Trematon

The same renders account for [...]. And £4 5s from the common passage of the same water at the same terms. And for 2s from the fishing of 3 boats in Tamar Water as affirmed for the same terms. [...] And for 18d from 3 seines fishing in the said Tamar Water at the same terms. And for 1d from oysters sold during the same time. And for 8s from 16 barges taking sand in the said Water for the said terms. And for 2s 6d from the fishery in Lynher Water as affirmed for the aforesaid lands. Nothing from the fair tolls because it did not happen during this time, but at the feast of St Fides virgin [6 October]. And for 40s from pleas and perquisites and other customs of mariners landing in the port of Sutton for the aforesaid terms. [...]

EXPENSES

[...] 12s for repairing and fixing the boat for the passage of Saltash Water during the aforesaid time.[36] [...]

[...]

ISSUES OF THE PORTS

The same renders account of £21 11s from fixed rents of said ports of Cornwall for one whole year, because the total paid at Michaelmas. And 65s 11d from fines, pleas and perquisites of court from May 15 in the ninth regnal year of King Edward [1316] to Michaelmas. Sum, £24 17s 9d.

EXPENSES: The same accounts for 16s 8d for the stipend of one (bailiff) to watch the sea-shore, taking 2½ marks during the aforesaid time. Sum, 16s 8d. And he owes £24 13d.

(m. 3)

ISSUES OF THE PORTS: The same renders account for[37]

[...]

29 Sept. 1316–5 July 1317

PRO, SC6/811/17

10–11 Edward II. 2 thin membranes, sewn end to end, with 2 small riders attached. Account of Henry de Wylingtone, recently steward of Cornwall, of the issues of the castles and manors of the king within the

---

36. In PRO, E372/161, m. 53, 12s 12d was said to have been spent on repairs to the boat.
37. A large blank space about 7 inches long follows, as if account was to be put in later, rather than squeezed at bottom of m. 2d; the next section is on issues of the Cornish stannaries, but then another big blank space follows.

aforesaid county, from 29 September 1316 to 5 July 1317 when custody
was delivered to William de Polleborne and John Thweyt, attorneys of
Queen Isabella. A vertical line is drawn through the middle of the
account. A similar enrolled account is in the pipe roll, PRO, E372/162,
m. 35d.

(m. 1d)

[...]

ISSUES OF THE PORTS

The same renders account of 41s 10d from fines, pleas and perquisites
of courts of the ports during the same time. And he renders nothing
for rents of assize [*assesso nichil*][38] because all [due] at Michaelmas.
Sum, 41s 10d.

[...]

(m. 2)

[...]

TYBESTA

EXPENSES

[...] And 15s for the stipend of a keeper for the manors of Tybesta,
Tewington, Moresk, Tywarnhaile and Helson-in-Kerrier for the said
term.

[...]

LOSTWITHIEL

[...] Nothing from the cellar under the great hall, the custom of ships
and boats, and a certain meadow near Fowey Water and fair tolls because
all [collected] at Michaelmas. [...]

[...]

TREMATON

[...] £6 7s 6d from the common passage of Tamar Water at the same
terms. And for 3s from fishing of 4 boats in Tamar Water as affirmed at
the same terms. [...] And for 2s 4d from three seines fishing in Tamar
Water at the same terms. And for 1½d from oysters at the same terms.
And for 12s from a certain custom from 15 barges taking sand in Tamar
Water at the same terms. And for 3s 9d from the fishery of Lynher

---

[38]. In PRO, E372/162, m. 35d, this entry reads "he does not respond for rents of
assize of these ports because the term of payment for them is at Michaelmas".

Water as affirmed at the same terms (^and 60s from pleas and perquisites in the port of Sutton as affirmed). And for 11s from fair tolls. [...]
[...]

1322/23

PRO, E389/62

16–17 Edward II. 3 membranes, sewn end to end. Account of Thomas de la Hyde, sheriff and steward of Cornwall, of the issues of the castles and manors within the county of Cornwall due to Queen Isabella, from 29 September 1322 to 29 September 1323.

(m. 1)

[...]

LOSTWITHIEL

The same renders account for [...] 15s from a cellar under the great hall of pleas. And for £29 from two mills newly constructed with multure, the fishery of Fowey Water, ~~custom of boats mooring there~~, perquisites of the same Water, tolls of the Lostwithiel fair of St Bartholmew, and pleas and perquisites of the court of the same town, leased at farm to the burgesses of the same town by commission of the lady queen. [...]
[...]

(m. 2)

[...]

TREMATON

The same renders account for £86 from the same manor with members leased at farm to Sir Robert Bendyn by commission of the lady queen. Sum, £86.
[...]

ISSUES OF THE PORTS

The same renders account for £21 11s 10d from the rents per year of the ports of diverse towns [*villat'*] leased at term. Nothing from pleas and perquisites because Thomas de Leygrave has custody of the said ports by grant of the lady queen, so he answers for nothing in the aforesaid sum below.

PRISE OF WINE

The same renders account for £45 received from 15 tuns of wine arising from diverse ships mooring in diverse ports of Cornwall and sold for 60s per tun.

EXPENSES

The same renders account for £15 that he paid to the sailors [*nautis*] of the aforesaid ships for a certain custom, namely 20s per tun.. Also 5s 9¼d for carriage of the same 15 tuns to the wine cellar and hire of the same cellar and for rollage of them.

CHATTELS OF FELONS AND FUGITIVES (challenged because not shown in particulars)

The same renders account for 110s from the goods and chattels of David le Hurl, felon and fugitive. And for 38s from the goods and chattels of William Pegast, felon and fugitive. And for 8s 10d from the goods and chattels of Roger Sturhous, felon and fugitive. And for 15d from the goods and chattels of William Godrich, a hanged thief. And for 13s 10d from the goods and chattels of Thomas Achym, felon and fugitive. And for 4s 6d from the goods and chattels of the same felon and fugitive at Lelant [*Lananta*].

ISSUES OF CUSTOMS

The same renders account for £9 7s arising from cocket, received from 14 lasts and 5 hides, according to customs of those parts, namely 1 mark per last, as appears in the particulars.

FAWTON [*FAWYNTON*][39]

The same renders account for £20 5s 2d from the aforesaid manor leased at farm to Sir William de Monte Acuto, until the full age of Richard, son and heir of *Helye* Daubonee, by commission of the lady queen.

WRECK OF SEA (challenged because not shown in particulars)

The same renders account for 29s 4d for diverse things from a certain boat thrown up to land as wreck by a tempest of the sea to the port and next to the port of Looe. And for 20s from a certain boat indicated as

---

[39.] This entry, and perhaps the previous section on 'Chattels of Felons and Fugitives' do not seem to belong in the havener's account.

wreck at Mousehole. And for 6d from a timber [*ligno*] sold. And for 8s from a semi-filled tun of salty wine. And for 26s 8d from two semi-filled tuns of salty wine. And for 13s 4d from a 4th semi-filled tun of salty wine. And for 40 from wreck (^ of a certain boat) docking at the port of *Trelewych* next to St Keverne [*Sancti Keeranum*] in *Manek*. [...]

Isabella, by the grace of god, etc... Know all that we have granted to Sir [*Mons'*] Robert Bendyn our manor of Trematon with the appurtenances, that is the castle of Trematon, the borough of Saltash and the water passage from the same borough, the borough of Trematon castle and the manors of Carkeel [*Karkyl*], Lake [*Laak de Sutton*] and Tregartha [*Tregarth*] with the farm of Sutton Pool that Ralph de Whitelegh holds from us at farm for £10 per year, together with the mills, fines, pleas, and perquisites of courts, and all other appurtenances on water as well as on land. Sir Robert and his heirs are to have and hold the aforesaid from Michaelmas [29 September] next for the following seven years as is contained in an indenture made between our beloved and trusted Sir Henry Beaufitz, steward of our lands, and the said Sir Robert, except for woodland, game, heriots? in our control and well-made vineyards? [*Voies vert voneson postherios? en nos lays et viniers fetiz*], advowsons, wardships, marriages, reliefs, escheats, franchises and all manner of other foreign profits that do not at all fall into the extent [or value?] [*ne encourent mye en estente*] of the aforesaid manors, castle, and borough with appurtenances. Rendering for this to us £86 per year, that is, at the feasts of Easter and Michaelmas in equal portions. Notwithstanding [*Issuit nekedent*] he is to sustain and maintain during the aforesaid terms our said manors, castle, and borough, with their aforesaid appurtenances and return them in as good estate as when he leased them. By which we order and command to all those to whom it pertains that they should attend and respond to the said Sir Robert as our farmer of these same places. In testimony of which we have had made these letters patent. Given at Thorp on 7 August in the 13th regnal year [1319] of our dear lord the king.[40]
[...]

[40.] The preceding is in French, written in a small, neat hand at the bottom of the membrane. On m. 1d is a memorandum (also in French) from Isabella, dated at Tavistock on 30 June 1319, that also notes this lease.

(m. 2d)

[...]

{COMMISSION FOR HENRY DE GULDEFORD OF THE HAVENERY OF CORNWALL[41]
Isabel, by the grace of God, etc..., to all those, etc... know that we
have appointed our beloved valet, Henry de Guldeford, keeper of our
havens in Cornwall, to do and perform in all good ways those things
pertaining to this office and to respond to us by the hands of our receiver
of Cornwall for the time being for the issues of the same. By which we
order and command to all those to whom it pertains, that they should
attend and respond to the said Henry as our keeper of the aforesaid
havens. In testimony of which we have had made these letters patent
for him, to last during our pleasure. Given at Westminster on 10 March
in the 17th regnal year [1324] of our dear lord the king.}

29 September–10 October 1331

PRO, SC6/811/18

5 Edward III. 2 short membranes. View of account of William Botreaux,
steward of Cornwall, for [a long list of places in Cornwall], from 29
September 1331 to 10 October next, for 11 days. On m.2 is a particular
account of William Bordeaux, steward of the issues of coinage. The
pipe roll in PRO, E372/176, m. 45, contains an account of Robert de
Bilkmore, steward of Cornwall for 28 January to 24 February 1331,
but the steward collected nothing from the issues of the ports or prisage
of wine because the account covered only 26 days.

(m. 1)

[...]

ISSUES OF PORTS AND THE HAVENER
The same renders account for £24 10s 4d received from the issues of
sea ports during the aforesaid time, namely from John Croth', sub-
farmer of William, taillor of Philippa, queen of England [*cissoris Phe'*

[41.] The following is in French and is written in a darker ink than the other letters on
the dorse, suggesting it was added later, which the dating clause also indicates. It
is the second to last entry on the roll.

R'e Angl'], farmer of the said ports by writ of the king and as contained in the same place. He renders nothing from wreck of sea because nothing occurred during the said time as is declared [*ut dicitur*]. Sum received, £24 10s 4d.

1332–33

PRO, E372/177

6 Edward III. Pipe roll containing the account of William de Botreaux, steward of Cornwall, for issues belonging to the stewardship of Cornwall from 29 September 1332 to 10 October next [1333] when William delivered the aforesaid castles, boroughs, manors and fisheries with their appurtenances to John de Eltham, earl of Cornwall. Most of the entries are short and contain no details because no revenues were collected during the short time of the account.

(m. 22d)

[...]

SEA PORTS AND WRECK

And for £24 10s 4d received from the issues of sea-ports there, as contained there. He responds for nothing from wreck of sea because nothing occurred during the same time, as he declares.[42]

[...]

Easter Term 1333

PRO, E372/179

7 Edward III. Pipe roll containing issues of the sea ports in the (1) account of William de Botreaux, steward of Cornwall for Easter term,

---

42. Most of the port farms and some other rents were collected at Michaelmas, which explains why this section lists more revenue than most other earldom properties in this account.
43. For the problems of dating these accounting terms, see below, notes 45 and 47.

which appears to cover the period from Easter (4 April 1333) to the start of the next account at Michaelmas in 1333. [43] This pipe roll also contains summaries of the particular account in PRO, SC6/3479/8, printed below, in the next entry, including: (2) the account of Henry de Trethewy, sheriff of Cornwall, for Michaelmas term 1333; and (3) the account of the same for Easter and Michaelmas terms [1333/34], both of which are printed in the next section.

(m. 20d)

[...]

ISSUES OF THE SEA PORTS
The same renders account for £10 15s 11d for the farms of the ports of Marazion [*Markedeou*], Penzance, and other ports in the county of Cornwall at Easter term within the said time as contained in the roll of particulars which was delivered into the treasury. And for 5s received from forestalling and trantery at the said term as contained there. And for 10s 6d from pleas and perquisites of the said ports during the said time as contained there. Sum of receipts, £11 10s 11d. From which:
    EXPENSES
The same accounts for 30s for the stipend of one bailiff collecting farms and aforesaid issues in the abovesaid ports during the aforesaid time, as contained in the roll of particulars. Sum of expenses, 30s. And he responds above in the summa of the same William, sheriff.
[...]

(m. 32d)

THE REMAINDER FOR CORNWALL [*RESIDIUM CORNUB'*]
[...]
The same Henry, sheriff, owes £1138 16s 7½d for many debts as contained in the principal roll, of which £21 12s 8d are for issues of the sea ports in this county for the 8th year [1333/34] as contained in the pincipal roll in the account of the same Henry for these issues. But he does not owe for the sum nor is he charged for issues of these same ports by writ of the king enrolled in the memoranda [roll] of the 9th year of this king in the Easter term [1335]. In which it is contained that the king on 3 October in the 7th year ending, the 8th beginning [1333] by his charter grants and concedes among other lands and tenements to John, earl of Cornwall, brother of this same king, the town of Lostwithiel with appurtenances as well as all profits of the ports of the king in this county, to have under established form and through a certain writ of the king ordering that the said sheriff is to be exonerated for

the issues of the said town and profits of the ports from 3 October and to be made quit. [...]

[...]

Thomas Quenit and John Vivian, collectors of new custom in each port of the county of Cornwall, render account for £6 from issues of the same custom from 12 April in the 7th year [1333] to 28 June in the 9th year [1335], as contained in their account for the same time thereof as the roll of the account of customs. Delivered into the treasury.

The same Thomas and John render account for £9 10s for the remainder of their account for ancient custom in the said ports from 28 May in the 5th year [1331] to 12 April in the 7th year [1333] as contained in their account thereof for the same time there. Delivered into the treasury.

[...]

1. Michaelmas Term 1333

2. Easter and Michaelmas Terms 1334 [1333/34]

PRO, SC6/3479/8

[7–8 Edward III]. One parchment square, folded in half; the dorse is blank. No heading, but a similar though more summary account in the pipe roll, PRO, E372/179, m. 20d, notes both accounts as those of Henry de Trethewy, sheriff of Cornwall, for profits from 5 July to 29 September 1333 and from 1334/35 [the 8th year]. These two particular accounts are also summarized in PRO, SC6/812/1, m. 3.[44]

[44.] PRO, SC6/812/1, m. 3 contains a summary account [accountant not named] from 5 July in the 7th year to Michaelmas next [5 July 1333 to 29 September 1334] and for Easter and Michaelmas terms in the 8th year [27 March 1334 to 12 January 1335].

1. Michaelmas Term 1333 [45]

ISSUES OF SEA PORTS[46]

The same responds for 23s 4d from the farm of the port of Marazion [*Marcadiou*] for Michaelmas term at the end of the 7th regnal year of the aforesaid king. And for 6s from the farm of the port of Penzance for the same term. And for 10s for the farm of the port of Newlyn for the same term. And for 50s from the farm of the port of Mousehole for the same term. And for 12d from the farm of the port of Lamorna [*Nanmorno*] for the same term. And for 6s for the farm of the port of Porthgwarra [*Porthgurwytheu*] for the same term. And for 4s for the farm of the port of 'Porthplement' [*Plement*] for the same term. And for 3s 4d from the farm of the ports of Portheras and Porthzennor for the same term. And for 60s from the farm of the port of St Ives for the same term. And for 12s 3d for the farm of the ports of Kerrier for the same term. And for 20s from the (^ farm of the port and) the fishery of Fowey for the same term. And for 10s from the farm of the (^ fishery) of Polruan for the same term. And for 10s from the farm of the ports of Triggshire for the same term. And for 2s 8d for pleas and perquisites of the courts there from 5 July in the aforesaid year to Michaelmas; and no more here because William de Botriaux the predecessor of this Henry

---

[45]. Strictly speaking, Michaelmas term should start on 29 September and end just before the feast of St Hilary (12 January), but in two places (below, under Expenses, and in the parallel, though summary accounts in PRO, E372/179, m. 20d and PRO, SC6/812/1, m. 3 (above, n. 43)), the dates are specified as 'from 5 July in the 7th year to Michaelmas next' [5 July–29 September 1333] but the reference to 'at Michaelmas term for one-half year' in the opening line of the on the issues of the ports in PRO, SC6/812/1, m. 3 suggests the longer period of 5 July 1333 to 12 January 1334 is meant.

[46]. PRO, SC6/812/1, m. 3 and PRO, E372, m. 20d both summarize this account as: 'ISSUES OF THE PORTS. The same renders account for £10 15s 11d from the farms of the ports of Marazion [*Marcadion*], Penzance [*Pensanx*] and other ports in the county of Cornwall at Michaelmas term for one-half year as contained in the roll of particulars which he delivered to the treasurer. And for 2s 8d from pleas and perquisites of the courts of the said ports during the said time as contained in the same place. He responds for nothing from the customs levied on forestalling and trantery because nothing occurred there within the same time as is said. Sum, £10 18s 7d.

EXPENSES: The same accounts for 10s for the stipend of one bailiff collecting farms and issues of the aforesaid ports during the said time, as contained in the said roll of particulars. Sum of expenses, 10s. And he owes £10 8s 7d. And he responds below.

ought to respond for more and does not respond for forestalling and trantery because nothing occurred in that time. Sum, £10 18s 7d.

EXPENSES

The same accounts for 10s for allowance (^of a stipend) for one (^bailliff) ~~servant~~ to watch the aforesaid ports and sea-shore from 5 July in the 7th year [1333] to Michaelmas next following. And he owes £10 8s 7d.

2. Easter and Michaelmas Terms 1334 [1333/34][47]

[ISSUES OF THE PORTS][48]

The same responds for 46s 8d for the farm of the port of Marazion for the terms of Easter and Michaelmas in the 8th regnal year of the aforesaid king. And for 12s for the farm of the port of Penzance (^for the same terms). And for 20s for the farm of the port of Newlyn (^for the same terms). And for 100s for the farm of the port of Mousehole (^for the same terms). And for 2s for the farm of the port of Lamorna for the same terms. And for 12s for the farm of the port of Porthgwarra [*Porgorwetheu*] for the same terms. And for 8s for the farm of the port of 'Porthplement' [*Porthplemyng*] for the same terms. And for ½ mark for the farm of the ports of Portheras and Porthzennor for the same terms. And for £6 for the farm of the port of St Ives for the same terms. And for 22s for the fisheries of Kerrier for the same terms. And for 40s for the farm of the ~~fishery~~ (port) of Fowey for the same terms. And for 20s for the farm of the port of Polruan for the same terms. And for 20s

---

[47.] The dating clause at the bottom of this section, as well as dating evidence in PRO, E372/179, m. 20d suggests this account covers an entire year, 1334/35.

[48.] PRO, SC6/812/1, m. 3 and PRO, E372/179, m. 20d both summarize this account as follows: 'THE 8TH YEAR. The same renders account for £21 19s 4d from the farm of the ports of Marazion and Penzance and other ports in the aforesaid county at the terms of Easter and Michaelmas this year as contained in a roll of particulars. And for 10s from a custom called forestalling [*forstallar*] and trantery this year as contained there. And for 33s 4d from pleas and perquisites of the courts of the aforesaid ports during the same time as contained there. Sum, £23 12s 8d. From which [ ].
EXPENSES: The same accounts for the stipend of a bailiff collecting farms and issues of the said ports in the aforesaid time. Sum of stipend, 40s. And he owes £21 12s 8d. And £10 8s 7d remains on his account for issues of the said ports from 5 July to Michaelmas next [29 September 1334] as contained above'. Sum total, £32 15d. And he responds for issues of another part of the king to the Exchequer ... [illegible].

for the farm of the ports of Triggshire for the same terms. (^ Sum, £21
19s 4d). And for ~~2d~~ 10s for a certain custom called trantery and
forestalling [*forstallator'*] this year. And for 33s 4d for pleas and
perquisites of the marine court during the same time. He responds for
nothing here from wreck of sea ~~because in the hand of~~ from (^ the
aforesaid) Michaelmas in the 7th year until the third day of October
next following [29 September to 3 October 1333] because nothing
occurred during the same time nor does he respond for anything from
the said third of October to Michaelmas then following next [3 October
1333 to 29 September 1334] because in the hands of John de Eltham,
earl of Cornwall, by writ of the king. Sum, £23 12s 8d.

EXPENSES
The same accounts for 40s for allowance of a stipend for one servant
to watch the aforesaid sea-shore ports and also to levy the farms and
other above-mentioned profits during the same time. Sum, 40s. And
he owes £21 12s 8d.

13–29 September 1336

PRO, SC6/1094/13

10 Edward III. 17 membranes. Account of William de Cusancia cleric,
guardian of all lands and tenements that belonged to Lord John, recently
earl of Cornwall, from the day he died and they came into the hands of
the king, from 13 September 1336 to 29 September next. On m. 12
begins the account of the issues in the county of Cornwall, which include
six membranes sewn end to end. A line is drawn through the middle of
these accounts.

(m. 12, ii)

TREMATON
[...] The mill and Water and Pool of Sutton and Saltash borough with
the passage assessed at a term of 7 years, as above. [...] And for 15s
4¾d from the farm or conventionary rents [*redd' convent'*] etc., with
customs etc., and all pertinences etc., rated for the time of this account
for £17 10s from the farm called rent of the same conventionaries per
year etc., as assessed on them and for the said term of 7 years as above.
[...]

[...]

(m. 12, vi)

PROFITS OF THE PORTS [*PROFICUA PORT'*]

RECEIPTS

The same renders account for 23s 4d rent from the farm of Marazion for Michaelmas term. And for 6s rent from the farm of the port of Penzance at the same term. And for 10s rent from the farm of the port of Newlyn at the same term. And for 50s rent from the farm of the port of Mousehole at the same term. And for 12d from the farm of the port of Lamorna namely Porthminster [*Nansmornow vid' Porthmenstr'*][49] at the same term. And for 6s rent from the farm of the port of Porthgwarra namely Land's End [*Porgorwhathou vid' Loundeshende*] at the same term. And for 4s from the farm of the port of 'Porthplement' [*Porthplement*] at the same term. And nothing from the farm of the port of Portheras [*Portheret*] because no boats are in the said port from which the farm there can be raised. And for 60s rent from the farm of the port of St Ives at the same term. And for 12s 11d rent of the farm of the ports of Kerrier at the same term. And for 20s for the farm of the port of Fowey at the same term. And for 10s rent from the farm of the port of Polruan at the same term. And for 10s rent of the farm of the ports of Triggshire at the same term. Nothing from the fines of foreign merchants buying fish in the aforesaid ports nor from the custom called trantery in which diverse men pass through Cornish parts to buy and forstall fish [*qua exiit divers' hominibus transentibus per partes Cornubie ad emend' piss' et forstall'*] nor for court perquisites during the time of this account because no merchants came there to buy fish on account of the war at sea during the same time so that none passed through nor [had] pleas during the same time, etc... Sum (^ total received), £10 13s 3¼d. And all is owing. Which is charged on his account for issues of the same ports after Michaelmas.

WRECK OF SEA

Nothing from wreck of sea because nothing happened in his bailiwick during the time of this[50]

---

49. This must be a mistake since Porthminster is located near St Ives.
50. There is a blank space here and after this section and the following section on prisage as if more would be added later.

Prisage and Customs of Wine

Nothing from wines or custom of wines because no prisage of wine occurred in his bailiwick because no ships or boats with wine arrived in his bailiwick during the same time.

Lostwithiel Town

[...] And nothing from keelage [*cullag'*] or custom of corn and other things etc., of ships docking in Fowey Water during the same time. Nothing received from perquisites of the marine court held there during the same time for the aforesaid reason. And for 2s from the rent of the fishery there during the same time. [...]

[...]

Part II

Havener's Accounts of the Duchy of Cornwall, 1337–1356

10 March–29 September 1337

PRO, SC6/812/2

11–17 Edward III. 4 membranes; parts of the roll are damaged. The roll contains several different accounts; view of the account of coinage of John Hamely, steward and sheriff of Cornwall, from 10 March to 29 September 1337 (m. 1); account of Robert de Beaupel [*Bello Pello*], steward and sheriff of Cornwall, for the issues of the sheriff and coinage, fines, amercements, and forfeitures before the justices of the king and the treasurer and barons of the Exchequer and fines and amercements made before James de Wodestoke from 21 September 1338 to 29 September next and from then to 29 September 1340 for 2 years and 8 days (m. 2); account of Henry de Trethewy, sheriff of Cornwall after Robert de Beaupel, for issues of the shrievalty and fines, amercements and issues before the justices of the king, treasurer, and barons of the Exchequer, as well as fines and amercements, and issues before Hugh de Courtenay, earl of Devon, and his fellow justices in the county of Cornwall 29 September 1340, to 29 September 1342 for two whole years (m. 3).[1]

(m. 2)

[...]

[No heading]

And he responds for £10 fine of a certain ship coming with salt stolen at sea [*sale fur' in mar'*]. [...]

[...]

Sum

[...] {and afterwards, on 22 October in the 18th year [1344] comes Robert Beaupel and renders account [...] and he is charged with £12 which John de Teuerton, farmer of Sutton Water, owes from his farm

---

[1.] This section notes that issues from the ports, customs, cocket, wreck of sea, prisage of wines, and Sutton Water were accounted for before the auditors of the duke and delivered to the duke's receiver.

with custom from the last part of the 14th year and the first part of the 15th year [1340–41] as appears in the account of John Roger, reeve of Trematon, from Michaelmas in the 14th year [1340] to the same feast in the 15th year [1341] because the same Robert permitted the said John, farmer of the aforesaid, to pay the said farm without security against the tenor of the lord's writ, and he withdrew himself from rendering account. He is also charged with 52s ½d that Thomas de Gorleston, keeper [*custos*] of the said Water before John, charged by the same Robert, owed from the profits of the said Water with custom and for which the said Robert mainprised the same Thomas on his account [*et pro quo dictus Rob' sr' comp' ipsius Thom' manucepit*].}
[...]

[...]

1338/39

PRO, SC6/816/11

12–13 Edward III. 16 membranes. Ministers' account of the duchy of Cornwall (mm. 1–7d), with accounts of the stannaries (m. 8), hundreds (m. 9), havener, (mm. 10–10d), keeper of the fees (m. 11–11d), customs (m. 12), Plymouth Water (m. 13) and receiver (mm. 14–16). Many of the membranes are made up of two or more pieces of parchment sewn end to end.

(m. 2)

TREMATON
[...]
ISSUES OF THE MILLS AND WATER AND POOL OF SUTTON WITH CUSTOM
[...] And for £10 10½d received from issues of the Water and Pool of Sutton with custom from the feast of All Saints to Michaelmas as settled by particulars [*const' per parcell'*] delivered on account. And hence less than last year by £6 19s 1d because the whole town of Sutton was nearly burned by the enemy [*quia tota villa de Sutton fere erat combursta*]. And he responds for no issues from Michaelmas to All Saints [1 November] because none were gathered during this time as said and as was testified by Walter de Horton, lieutenant of the steward.
ISSUES OF THE MANOR
[...] And 3½d from toll of oysters this year. [...]
[...]

SUM
[...] He is allowed 40s for fixing part of one barge by letter of the lord dated 23 February in the 13th year [1339] (letters and indentures for this year) delivered on account. [...]
[...]
BARGE FOR THE PASSAGE
He renders account for 1 barge for Saltash passage newly repaired this year by the farmer of the said passage under the oversight of the lord by his letters, as above. There remains one barge for the Saltash passage. And he renders account for 4 oars received from the remainder of the preceding account. And for 4 oars received from rent owed for the said passage at Michaelmas. Sum, 8. Then he accounts for the farmer using up [*in perusitationem*] 4 of the same of the said passage per year. Sum, 4. And 4 oars remain in the custody of the said farmer.
[...]

(m. 2d)

LOSTWITHIEL
RENTS OF ASSIZE AND CUSTOMARY RENTS
[...] And for 80s 6d from the court of the town and portmoot court and fair tolls there and their pleas and perquisites as contained in the same roll [...] And 19s 11d rendered from the issues of Fowey Water with customs and pleas and perquisites of the marine court and fishery in the same Water as contained there.
[...]

NETS
Also remaining is 1 fishing net containing 17 *teysede* received from the remainder of the preceding account. And 1 fishing net remains.
[...]

(m. 10)

ACCOUNT OF THOMAS FITZ HENRI, KEEPER OF THE PORTS IN THE COUNTY OF CORNWALL FOR PRISAGE OF WINES IN THE SAME COUNTY AND IN SUTTON WATER IN THE COUNTY OF DEVON AND FOR PROFITS OF THE PORTS IN THE SAME COUNTY OF CORNWALL AND WRECK OF SEA IN THE SAME COUNTY, NAMELY FROM MICHAELMAS IN THE 12TH YEAR TO THE SAME FEAST FOLLOWING FOR ONE WHOLE YEAR.

ARREARS
From arrears, nothing here because at the foot of the preceding account.

SALE OF WINES FROM PRISAGE
The same renders account for £9 received from 3 tuns of vintage wine [*vini de vendag'*] sold to the lord. Sum, £9.

WINE CUSTOMS
Nothing from wine customs of aliens because no foreign ships arrived in my bailiwick during the said time.

WRECK OF SEA
Nothing from wreck of sea, whales or sturgeon [*Balena sive sturion'*] because none (^ occurred) this year.

ISSUES OF THE PORTS
The same renders account for ~~46s 8d~~ (60s per the preceding account) farm received annually from the farm of the port of Marazion equally at Easter and Michaelmas terms. And for 12s received annually from the farm of the port of Penzance equally at the same terms. And for 20s farm of the port ~~from the farm of the port~~ of Newlyn [*Niwelin*] annually at the same terms (equally). And for 100s from the farm of the port of Mousehole annually at the same terms equally. And for 2s received from the farm of the port of Lamorna annually at the same terms equally. And for 12s received from the farm of the port of Porthgwarra [*Porgorwetheu*] annually at the same terms (equally). And for 8s received annually from the farm of the port of 'Porthplement' [*Porthplement*] at the same terms equally. And for ~~25s~~ (32s per the preceding account) received annually from the farm of the ports of Kerrier [*Kyrr'*] at the same terms equally. And for 40s received annually from the farm of the port of Fowey at the same terms equally. And for 20s received annually from the farm of the port of Polruan at the same terms. And for 20s received annually from the farm of the ports of Trigg at the same terms equally. And for £6 received annually from the port of St Ives [*Porthia*] at the same terms equally. ~~Nothing from the farm of the ports of Porthzennor [Porthenor] and Portheras [Portherest] because no boats are customed there from which the said farm could be raised~~ (And for 6s 8d received from the farm of the aforesaid ports of Porthzennor [*Porthen'*] and Portheras per year at the same terms equally as in the preceding account). Sum, £22 12s 8d.

FINES OF MERCHANTS WITH TRANTERY
Shown in the particulars [*ostend' parcel'*]
The same renders account for 5s 2d received from fines of merchants

and of tranteries [*Tranentriarum*] during the same time. And no more because no foreign merchants came there to buy fish nor did the boats hardly dare to go to sea because of the war at sea [*batell' ausi fer' ire ad mar' propter guerram per mar'*]. Sum, 5s 2d.

PLEAS AND PERQUISITES OF THE COURT SHOWN IN THE COURT ROLLS
Shown in the court rolls [*Ostend' rotul' cur'*]
The same renders account for 7s 1d from pleas and perquisites of the court of the port of Mousehole during the aforesaid time. And for 4s 2d received from pleas and perquisites from the court of Newlyn. And no more from that port nor other ports because mariners and fishers were elected by the admiral of the sea [*admirallum mar'*] to the fleet of the lord king to keep the sea [*ad flot' domini Regis pro mare custod'*]. Sum, 11s 3d.

Sum total received with wine sold, £32 9s 1d, from which:

UNLOADING [*DISCARCAG'*], ROLLAGE [*ROLLAG'*], BOAT-HIRE [*BATELL'*], ETC.
The same accounts for 2s 4d for 4 tuns wine taken at Falmouth from ships there for unloading into boats, for boat-hire [*batellag'*] of the same to land, rollage of the same from the boat to the cellar at Penryn [*Penrin*] and for laying them down [*cuband'*] in the same cellar, namely for unloading each tun 2d; for boat-hire, 3d; and for rollage, 2d.

And 2s 6d for 6 tuns taken at Fowey from ships there unloading into boats, for boat-hire of the same to land, rollage of the same from boats to the cellar there and laying them down in the same cellar; for unloading each tun 2d; boat-hire, 1d; and rollage, 2d. And 2s 2d for 4 tuns from the aforesaid 6 tuns for rollage again from the aforesaid cellar to the sea and for boat-hire for the same from Fowey to Lostwithiel by sea because of fear of war [*pro timore guerre*] and for rollage of the same from the boat to the cellar and for laying them down, namely for rollage of each tun out of the cellar at Fowey, 2d; and at Lostwithiel, 1½d, for boat-hire, 3d.

And 3s 6d for 6 tuns taken at Sutton from a ship unloading there into a boat; for boat-hire of the same to land, for rollage of the same from the boat to the cellar there, and for laying them down in the same cellar, 3s 6d; namely for unloading each tun, 2d; boat-hire, 1d; rollage and laying down, 4d. Sum, 10s 6d.

CELLAR LEASE [*CONDUCTIO CELAR'*]
The same accounts for 10d for 1 cellar leased at Penryn for putting (1

138

The Havener's Accounts

tun) of wine from 17 November (^ on which day they were arrested, as on the other side,[2] [*quo die capt' fuer' ut extra*]) to Christmas for 5 weeks 2 days, at 2d per week. For 2s 10d for 1 cellar hired [conduct'] (leased) [*locat'*] there for storing [*imponend'*] (^ 2 tuns) from 26 March (^ on which day they were arrested, as on the other side) to 24 July accounting for 17 weeks and 4 days, at 2d per week.

For 10d for 1 cellar leased [locat'] hired [*conducend'*] at Lostwithiel for keeping 1 tun of wine from 18 November on which day they were taken at Fowey until Christmas for 5 weeks and 2 days, at 2d per week.

For 2s 4d for 1 cellar leased at Fowey for keeping (^ 4 tuns) wine from 25 March on which day they were taken out until 20 May on which day they were carried [*cariat' fuer'*] to Lostwithiel for fear of war, for 8 weeks, at 3½d per week.

And for 10d for 1 cellar leased at Sutton for storing 1 tun of wine from 19 November on which day they were taken (^ there) until Christmas for 5 weeks and 1 day, at 2d per week. For 2s for 1 cellar leased at Sutton for storing 4 tuns of wine from 22 March to 19 May, on which day the said tuns were lost by war [*perdita fuer' per guerram*], for 8 weeks and 2 days, at 3d per week. Sum, 9s 8d, approved [*prob'*].

ULLAGE

The same accounts for 3s for 9 gallons of wine purchased for ullage of 1 tun taken at Falmouth, kept in the cellar at Penryn from 17 November until Christmas for 5 weeks 2 days, priced at 4d per gallon. Also 5s for 17 gallons of wine purchased for ullage of 2 tuns kept in the same cellar from 27 March until 24 July for 17 weeks and 4 days, price per gallon as above.

Also 2s 4d for 7 gallons of wine purchased for ullage of 1 tun taken at Fowey, kept in the cellar at Lostwithiel from 18 November until Christmas for 5 weeks and 2 days, priced at 4d per gallon. Also 6s 4d for 20 (19) gallons purchased for ullage of 4 tuns kept in the cellar at Fowey from 25 March until 20 May on which day they were carried to Lostwithiel for fear of war (^ for 8 weeks), priced per gallon as above.

Also 2s 8d for 8 gallons of wine purchased for ullage of 1 tun kept in the cellar at Sutton from 19 November until Christmas for 5 weeks and 1 day, priced per gallon as above. Also 5s 4d for 16 gallons of wine purchased for ullage of 4 tuns kept in the cellar at Sutton from 22 March until 19 May for 8 weeks and 2 days, priced per gallon as above. Sum, 25s 4d, approved.

---

2. This refers to the prisage account on the dorse of this account.

EXPENSES MADE ON CARRIAGE TO BRISTOL OF WINES OF DIVERSE FELLOWS
OF THE LORD

He also accounts for 4s 6d for (^ rollage) and boat-hire of the aforesaid
2 tuns kept in the cellar at Penryn carried from there to Fowey by sea
(^ to the ship in which they were carried). For 12d for rollage and
boat-hire of 4 tuns kept in the cellar at Lostwithiel (^ for) carrying
(^ from there) to Fowey by the ship in which they were loaded. For
21d for windage [*windag'*] of the said 6 tuns from the boat to the ship
and for stillage of them in the ship, namely 2d for hoisting each tun,
and 1½d for stillage. For 13d for 26 barrel hoops [*circul'*] purchased
for binding [*ligand'*] the said 6 tuns, at ½d per hoop. For 32s for 1 pipe
of wine purchased for ullage of the same 6 tuns for filling when they
should have been removed [*implend' quando ammoveri debuissent*]
from the said cellar and likewise when they were stored [*stillat' fuer'*]
in the aforesaid ship and likewise when they left the same [ship] and
also in the cellar at Bristol until they were put in tuns [*quousque dolibat'
fuer*] there by William, gatekeeper [*Janitor*] of the lord's household
and Robert de Neville, valet of the Butlery [*vadlet Butill'*] of the same
household assigned to receive wines from the same. For 22s 3d for
freightage of the ship for carrying the aforesaid 6 tuns from Fowey to
Bristol. For 4s 8d for hoisting the same 6 tuns from the ship into boats
at Bristol, for boat-hire for the same to land, for hauling [*tractatione*]
of the same from the boat onto [*sr'*] the quay, for rollage from the quay
to the cellar, for lease of 1 cellar there for 3 weeks, namely 2d for
hoisting each tun, 1d for boat-hire, 2d for hauling, 3d for rollage, and
8d for the cellar, inclusive [*in grosso*]. Sum, 67s 3d.

MONEY PAID FOR ASSIZE OF PRISAGE OF 2 TUNS OF WINE FROM EACH SHIP

The same accounts for £16 that he paid to diverse merchants for assize
of 16 tuns of wine taken for prisage of 10 ships, as on the other side [*ut
extra*], from each ship 2 tuns each for 40s. Sum, £16.

Turn over and view the other side [*Verte et respice extra*]

(m. 10d)

CARE OF TUNS OF SPANISH WINE, GROCERY [*GROSSE*], HONEY, AND PELTRY
[*PELETERIA*]

The same accounts for 12s 6d for 150 barrel hoops for binding 5 tuns
of honey, 4 tuns of red wine of Spain, 1 tun of grocery, and 1 pipe of
the same, priced at ½d per barrel hoop. He also paid 12d for 2 tun-
staves put [*Tunstav' poit'*] on 2 tuns of the aforesaid honey. He also

paid 10d for 1 pipe in which grocery was placed arising from one-half of 1 tun shared [*partit'*] between the lord and the merchant. Also 30s 8d for the lease of 2 cellars at Lostwithiel for keeping said tuns of wine, grocery, honey, and aforesaid peltry from Sunday after the birth of Blessed Mary in the 12th year [13 September 1338] to 21 August in the 13th year [1339], namely for 46 weeks and 6 days, at 8d per week. Also 10½d for rollage of 10 tuns and 1 pipe of red wine of Spain, grocery, and honey from the cellar at Lostwithiel to the water. And 21d for boat-hire for the same from Lostwithiel to Fowey by water, at 2d per tun. Also 21d for hoisting the aforesaid 10 tuns and 1 pipe from the water into the ship, at 2d per tun. Also 15 ¾d for stillage of the aforesaid 10 tuns. Also 11d for porterage [*portag'*] and boat-hire for 7 bales [*ball'*] of skins from Lostwithiel to Fowey. Also 43s 3d for freightage of a ship from Fowey to Bristol for carrying Spanish wines, grocery, honey and peltry there, and no more because the aforesaid Thomas le Haveneor had 15d for carriage of 1 M of tin carried to Bristol in said ship. He also accounts for 16d for small pilotage [*petit loudmanag'*] and towage of the same ship from *la Hole Bakkes*[3] to Bristol. Also 21d for hoisting the said 10 tuns and 1 pipe from the ship into boats, at 2d per tun. Also 14d for hire of 1 boat for carrying the said tuns from the ship to the quay. Also 21d for hauling [*intractatione*] said tuns from the ship to land, at 2d per tun. Also 2s 7½d for rollage of the said tuns from the quay to cellar, at 3d per tun, and 12d for cellarage. 3d for repairing [*in emend'*] 2 tuns of honey. Also 26s 8d inclusive for 1 man hired to watch all the aforesaid goods and supervise for 4 weeks and 5 days and to go from Bristol to London to secure the advice of the lord [*propter ire de Bristowe usque Lond' ad certificat' consilium dm'*] on the arrival of the aforesaid goods and returning from London to Windsor where the household of the lord then was; and from there to Bristol, as by agreement. He also accounts for 1 pipe in ullage of 5 tuns of honey. He also accounts for 1 pipe in ullage of 4 tuns of red wine of Spain. Sum, £6 12s 8¾d.

Sum total of expenses, £28 5s 5¾d . And he owes £4 3s 7¼d. ~~Thus,~~ £29 4s 7d remains on his account by agreement from last year [*de rem' compoti' sui de cons' ex' anni prox' preterit'*]. Sum of these two debts

---

3. *Holowbakkes* was an anchorage near Blackstones off Clevedon in the Bristol Channel where ships waited at low water until the tide turned and they could sail up the Severn River to Bristol; see E. M. Carus-Wilson, ed., *The Overseas Trade of Bristol*, 2nd edition (London, 1967), pp. 156, 315.

joined, £33 8s 9¼d (2¼d). From which he accounts for money delivered to John de Moneroun, receiver of monies of the lord duke in the county of Cornwall, £17 18¾d by 1 sealed bill of the said receiver sealed here on the ~~account~~ shown (this seen [*istium vis'*]) and custody remains to him [*et penes ipsum custod' rem'*]. And thus he owes £16 6s 7½d. For which he puts himself in grace until, etc.. £13 6s 8d for his wages and robe for this year and next year are not allowed for want of warrant and here respited until the final accounting which follows in the meantime, etc... And £4 20d charged on the account from wreck of sea last year. And 66s 3d charged on the account for the farm of ports from the same year and this year and respited here because contained in his preceding account. Sum of respited debts, £20 14s 7d. And so he has a surplus (in this view) of £4 7s 11½d. {And then the aforesaid £16 6s 7½d was charged to his account for counsel extended in the next year following.}

Wines of Prisage

FALMOUTH WITH PORTS [*PORTICULI*] OF PENRYN AND TRURO
The same renders account for 4 tuns of red wine taken there from 3 ships docking at Penryn during the aforesaid time of which 2 tuns of wine are for assize.
From a ship called *la Goudbiyete* of Fowey, burthen [*port' oneris*] 10 tuns and more whose master [is] John Cogan, on 18 November, 2 tuns of wine for assize.
From a ship called *Cog John* from the same, burthen 10 tuns and more, whose master [is] Alan de Rosmaryn, on 27 March. Sum, 4 tuns

FOWEY, WITH NO MEMBER PORTS [*FOWEY NULL' PORTUS PARTIUM*][4]
The same renders account for 6 tuns of red wine taken there from 3 ships docking there during the aforesaid time of which:
2 tuns of wine [are] for assize from a ship called *le Pedorok*, burthen 10 tuns and more, whose master [is] Matthew Sabyn, on 17 November.
For 2 tuns of wine for assize from a ship called *Cog Seint Savour*, burthen 10 tuns and more, whose master [is] John Saundre, on 25 March.
For 2 tuns of wine for assize from a ship called *la Trinite*, whose master [is] John Oty, on the same day. Sum, 6 tuns.

---

4. In contrast with Falmouth, with which the ports of Penryn and Truro accounted.

SUTTON

The same renders account for 6 tuns of red wine taken there from 3 ships docking there of which:

2 tuns [are] for assize of a ship called *la Katerine* of Sutton, burthen 10 tuns and more, [master] John Langmon, on 19 November.

2 tuns of wine for assize from a ship called *Cog John* of Polruan, burthen 10 tuns and more, whose master [is] John Portalla, on 22 March.

2 tuns of wine for assize from a ship called *Jonette*, burthen 10 tuns and more, whose master [is] Thomas Lewen, on 22 March. Sum, 6 tuns

Sum total received, 16 tuns. Of which 3 tuns delivered to Sir R. Beaupel, knight, as gift of lord by letter of the same dated 16 August, and by quittance of the same Robert here delivered on account. For delivery of 6 tuns made to William, gatekeeper of the household of the lord and to Robert de Nevyll, namely etc..., at Bristol, by letter of Sir Robert de Beaupel, steward and sheriff of Cornwall, by indenture in which is included other wines and diverse goods that were taken from merchants of Portugal so that William and Robert familiars [*familiar'*] of the household of the lord were assigned to receive the said goods. ~~In capture and depredation of 4 tuns of red racked wines made by foreign enemies from galleys at S... [Sutton?]~~ (cancelled because they are owed ... in the remainder on account until ...)[5] 3 tuns sold for expenses of the lord's household. Sum, 12 ... And 4 tuns of wine remain which ...

GOODS REMAINING IN THE PREVIOUS HEADING

The same renders account for 5½ tuns of honey, 5 tuns of red wine, 1½ tun of lard [*pinguedinis*] debited [*port'*], 350 skins of Aragon [*Arragoun*] at 136 skins per hundredweight [*centena*], and 150 skins of Morocco [*Marrok*][6] accounted for in the same way, 3000 [*m^l m^l Dcccc v^{xx}*] *Cabrotyns* accounted for in the same way, 229 fox and cat [*mureleg'*] skins accounted for in the same way, 1600 rabbit skins of Spain accounted for in the same way, and 9 dozen and 11 sheep [*multon'*] skins remain from the preceding account. Sum, as shown. From which:

The same accounts for ½ tun of honey from the aforesaid 5 tuns of honey remaining in the cellar from Sunday after the birth of St Mary in

---

[5.] The remainder (about seven words) is illegible.

[6.] Lambskins imported from Aragon and Morocco; see E. Veale, *The English Fur Trade in the Later Middle Ages* (Oxford, 1966), pp. 216–17.

the 12th year [13 September 1338] until 1 August amounting to 46 weeks and 1 day, taken from the cellar for transport by sail to Bristol. And for carriage to Bristol per the aforesaid letter of said Robert and delivered there to the aforesaid William Porter [*Port'*] and Sir Robert Nevill assigned for this, etc... 5 tuns of honey per the aforesaid indenture (...). ~~Also ½ tun of wine in ullage of the aforesaid 5 tuns of wine remaining in the cellar per the same account~~ (because it was not charged above). For carriage and delivery to Bristol of 4 tuns made in the same way, to the aforesaid William and Robert by the said indenture. Account and delivery also made in the same way at Bristol to the aforesaid Robert and William by the aforesaid indenture for 350 skins of Aragon at <u>136</u> [skins] in each hundredweight, 150 skins of Morocco accounted for in the same way, 3000 *Cabrotins* skins accounted for in the same way, 200 fox and cat skins accounted for in the same way minus in total <u>7 skins</u>, 1600 rabbit skins of Spain accounted for in the same way, and 10 dozen sheep skins curried and white-tawed accounted for in the same way minus in total <u>1 skin</u>. And 1 tun and 1 pipe of Cretan wine charged [*port'*]. ~~For sale of 1 tun rape wine [*vini raspe*] wine made to Sir R. Beaupel~~ (because below). Sum, as appears. And nothing remains ...

And 1 tun rape wine remains, which is charged in the account of customs issues next year.

SEAL
He also renders account for 1 seal of latten remaining from the aforesaid account. And one seal of latten remains for the office of prisage of wines.

Keeper of the Ports[7]

(m. 11d)
[...]
The escheator and keeper of the ports responded for 1 ship, burthen 200 tuns of wine, captured at sea from enemies of the realm, in which ship no man, dog or cat could be found then (living) in the same ship when it arrived at Fowey and it was not judged as wreck because an Englishman of Fowey and a certain man of London [were?] in two

---

[7.] In large letters centred at the bottom of the membrane.

ships[8] [*in qua navi nullus homo canis vel mureligus de hiis qui prius erat (vivens) in eadem navi cum arrupuit apud Fowey inventus fuit et non videtur Wercc' non ob^te quod anglicus de Fowey et quid' de Londonis' in 2 navibus*]. Of which one [ship] of London was of William Haunsard and the other [was] of Dartmouth. And there was in the same ship Spanish salt of great value. And William Haunsard had for his part of the salt 3000 pounds of stamped tin and £15 in cash for the half of the ship he sold.

(m. 12)[9]

COCKET

ACCOUNT OF GERARD AVERAY, ONE OF THE COLLECTORS OF OLD CUSTOM AND NEW CUSTOM ON ALL ALIENS COMING INTO ANY PORT WITHIN THE COUNTY OF CORNWALL AND IMPORTING MERCHANDISE OR EXPORTING THE SAME OUTSIDE THE COUNTY FROM EASTER IN THE 13TH REGNAL YEAR OF KING EDWARD III TO THE NEXT MICHAELMAS FOLLOWING IN THE SAME YEAR [28 MARCH–29 SEPTEMBER 1339].

RECEIPTS

The same renders account for £6 10s received from John Boyllet, merchant of the Bardi Society exporting beyond the realm tin of the value of £700 during the time of this view, namely 3d on each £. Sum of receipts: £6 10s. From which:

~~The same accounts for 10s for his wages during the time of this view~~ {cancelled because without warrant and not agreed on what wages he ought to take or not [*non constat' de cuiusmodi vad' capere deb' vel si qua necne*]. And he owes £6 10s. And £17 from these revenues (^per the same G. and Benedict Nought') collected between 3 January in the 11th year [1338] and 28 March which was Easter in the 13th year [1339] when he accounted at London before Ambrose de Novo Burgo (as he says). Sum he owes together, £23 10s. Of which he delivered £17 to William de Hoo, keeper of the wardrobe of the lord duke by quittance (delivered on account) sealed by the seal of this same William, dated at London, 24 May in the 13th year [1339]. And he owes £6

---

8. The meaning of this last passage is unclear; it could imply that the two survivors, one from Fowey and one from London, were picked up by the London and Dartmouth ships that 'captured' the enemy ship.

9. This membrane is only a quarter of the size of the other membranes in the roll.

10s. For which he puts himself in respite until he received the 10s cancelled above. And he owes £6 net [*de claro*]. And afterwards the aforesaid £6 10s is charged to his account as an issue for the next year following.}

(m. 13)[10]

Memorandum of profits [*explect'*] of 53s 1d from rushes [*Joncare*] of Plymouth Water from Sunday in the feast of All Saints in the 12th regnal year of King Edward III [1 November 1338] after the conquest of England to the Sunday before the feast of St Matthew the apostle in the 13th regnal year of King Edward [21 February 1339]. Sum, 53s 1d.

Memorandum of 14s ½d profits of customs of (Plymouth) Water for the whole time of the aforesaid. Sum, 14s ½d.
Memorandum of 58s 3d profits of rents of boats for the whole year. Sum, 58s 3d.
Memorandum of 7s 6d profits from passage tolls [*de passagio*] on Plymouth Water. Sum, 7s 6d.
Memorandum of 68s from pleas and perquisites of water courts of the aforesaid. Sum, 68s.
Sum of sums: £10 10½d.

For fuit in h'ame fuit fuit in h [scribbled upside down at bottom of membrane]

(m. 14)

ACCOUNT OF JOHN DE MONEROUN, RECEIVER OF MONIES OF THE LORD [...]
[...]

KEEPER OF THE PORTS
The same renders account for £17 18¾d received from Thomas Fitz Henr', keeper of the ports, by bill.

COLLECTORS OF OLD AND NEW CUSTOM
Nothing from Gerard Avery because he owes all.
[...]

[10.] A very short and thin membrane, about 3 inches wide.

1339/40

PRO, SC6/816/12

13–14 Edward III. 13 membranes. Ministers' account of the duchy of Cornwall (mm. 1–7); accounts of the keeper of fees (mm. 8–); havener (mm. 9–10), and receiver (mm. 11–13).

(m. 2)

TREMATON

ASSIZE RENTS

The same renders account for [...] 8s received from rents of free tenants owed for the passage of Saltash [*Essh*] per year. 5s from the rent of Lynher fishery per year at Michaelmas term [...].

ISSUES OF MILLS AND WATER AND POOL OF SUTTON WITH CUSTOM

The same renders account for £4 3s 2d received from the issues of the Water and Pool [*pole*] of Sutton between the beginning [*princeps*] of this account and Sunday before the Annunciation of Blessed Mary (namely, 20 March) when they were leased to a certain John de Teuerton by commission of the lord duke at the rent of £12 per year. And for £6 8s charged for the farm of the said Water and Pool with custom, prorated for the aforesaid time, £12 from the aforesaid 19 March [sic] to Michaelmas.

ISSUES OF THE MANOR WITH CHEVAGE

The same renders account for [...] 3½d from the toll of oysters this year [...]
[...]

SUM

[...] £6 8s from John de Teuerton ~~keeper~~ (farmer) of Sutton Water for the farm as leased to him by the council of the lord. [...]
[...]

(m. 3)

LOSTWITHIEL

ISSUES OF FOWEY WATER WITH CUSTOMS, PLEAS, AND PERQUISITES OF MARITIME COURT, AND FISHERY IN THE SAME WATER

The same renders account for 8d received for the custom of one ship of Yarmouth [in the Isle of] Wight [*Yiernemuthe Wyth*] loaded with hurdles [*claia*], burthen 25 tuns, carrying a boat[11] [*portag' 25 dol' batell' ducent*]. And for 16d received from the custom of one ship of Hook [*Hoke*] loaded with hurdles, burthen 40 tuns, carrying a boat [*portag' oneris 40 dol' batell' ducent'*]. And for 8d received for the custom of one ship of Lymington [*Lymeton*] loaded with salt, burthen 20 tuns, carrying a boat. And for 4d received for custom from one boat of Lymington, loaded with salt. And for 8d received from one ship of Newport [*Nyweport*] loaded with hurdles, burthen 22 tuns, leading a boat. And for 16d received from the pleas and perquisites of the marine court. And for 7s 10d received from the fishery of the aforesaid Water during the time of this account. Sum, 12s 10d.

(m. 8)

[...]

BAILIFF OF EAST HUNDRED

[...]

   MEMORANDA

[...] He responds for nothing from a certain ship, burthen 200 tuns of wine, taken at sea from enemies of the realm (as contained the preceding account) because the said Robert Beaupel then sheriff and steward remitted the same ship with its goods etc... to the men who took it for a <u>fine of £10</u> hence the same said Robert is charged in his account for the issues of the county of Cornwall. [...]

[...]

(m. 9)

COCKET

ACCOUNT OF GERARD AVERAY AND BENEDICT NOGHT', COLLECTORS OF OLD AND NEW CUSTOM ON ALL MERCHANDISE OF ALL ALIENS IMPORTED IN WHATEVER PORTS WITHIN THE COUNTY OF CORNWALL AND MERCHANDISE EXPORTED BEYOND THE SAME COUNTY FROM MICHAELMAS IN THE 13TH REGNAL YEAR OF KING EDWARD III AFTER THE CONQUEST TO THE SAME FEAST FOLLOWING IN THE 14TH YEAR [1339/40].

CUSTOM OF TIN Received by G. Averay

The same renders account for 14s received by the same Gerard from John Boylet attorney of the merchants of the Bardi Society of Florence for tin exported out of the realm to the <u>value of £56</u> carried

---

[11.] Ships carrying a boat were usually customed at a higher rate.

in a ship called *la Johannette* of Winchelsea [*Wych'*] on 13 January this year[12] [1339] <u>at 3d per £</u>.

And for 35s received by the said G. from the aforesaid John for tin exported (^outside the realm) to the value of £140 carried in a ship called *La Gonnote* of Fowey, on 17 March this year [1339].

And for 30s received by said G. from the aforesaid John for tin exported (^outside the realm) to the value of £120 carried a ship called (^*le*) *Petre* of Southampton [*Hamme*], on 20 March this year.

And for 32s received by the said G. from the aforesaid John for tin exported outside the realm to the value of ~~£108~~ (£128) carried in a ship called *la Gracedieux* of Fowey, on 22 March this year.

And for 30s received by the same G. from the aforesaid John for exporting tin outside the realm to the value of £120 carried a ship called *Seynte Mariecog* of Fowey, on 8 April this year.

And for 25s 6d received from the same G. from the aforesaid John for tin exported outside the realm to the value of £102 carried in a ship called *la Trynite* of Winchelsea [*Wynchelse*] on 11 April (this year).

And for 14s 6d received by the said G. from the said John for tin exported outside the realm to the value of £58 carried in a ship called *la Johannete* of Fowey on 17 April this year.

And for 10s received by the same G. from the aforesaid merchants by the hand of Serlo Quoynte for tin exported outside the realm to the value of £40 carried in a ship called *la Petur* of Poole [*la Pole*] on 3 August this year.

And for 41s 6d received by the same G. from Peter de Permee attorney of the aforesaid merchants for tin exported outside the realm to the value of £166 carried in a ship called *la Katerine* of Portland on 9 August this year. Sum, £11 12s 6d.[13]

CUSTOM OF HIDES RECEIVED BY G. AVERAY

And for ~~20s~~ (30s) received by said G. from Thomas Goldsmyth (^of Bodmin) for 30 dickers of hides exported outside the realm carried in a ship called *Seynte Mariecog* of London on 3 January this year (^ ~~13s4d~~ (20s) for a last with 6s 8d of increment).

And for ~~13s 4d~~ (20s) received by the same G. from John Coterel for

---

12. Since the regnal year started on 25 January, this date would technically fall in 1340, but given the chronological order of the entries, the clerk must have meant 1339.

13. *£11 12s 6d* scribbled in small letters in the left-hand margin at the end of this section.

exporting 20 dickers of hides outside the realm in the aforesaid ship on the same day per dicker as above (per last as above).

And for ~~13s 4d~~ (20s) received by the same G. from John Monek for exporting 20 dickers outside the realm in the same ship on the same day (per last as above).

And for ~~13s 4d~~ (20s) received by the said G. from Stephen atte Pole for exporting 20 dickers outside the realm in the said ship on the same day.

And for ~~6s~~ (10s) received by the same G. from John Badyn of Truro for exporting 10 dickers of hides outside the realm in a ship called *Marie* of Winchelsea [*Wych'*] on Tuesday after the feast of St Lucy virgin this year [14 December 1339].

And for ~~6s~~ (10s) received by the same G. from Nicholas Piers for exporting 10 dickers of hides outside the realm in a ship called *Seynte Mariecog* of Winchelsea on the Thursday after the feast of St Hilary this year [20 January 1340].

And for 8s 4d (9s) received by the same G. from John Martyn of Bodmin for exporting 20 dickers of hides outside the realm in a ship called *la Wal* on the same day.

And for ~~6s 8d~~ (10s) received by the same G. from John Monek for exporting 10 dickers of hides outside the realm in a ship called *le Petur* of Plymouth on Friday after St Hilary this year [21 January 1340].

And for ~~26s 8d~~ (40s) received by the same G. from Roger Blaca and Stephen atte Pole for exporting 40 dickers of hides outside the realm carried in the aforesaid ship on the same day.

And for ~~6s 8d~~ (10s) received by the same G. from John Rogger for exporting 10 dickers of hides carried in the aforesaid ship on the same day.

And for ~~5s 4d~~ (8s) received by said G. from Adam Sulk for 8 dickers of hides exported by him outside the realm carried in a ship called *le Wal* of Fowey on the same day.

And for ~~6s 8d~~ (10s) received by the same G. from John Coterel for exporting 10 dickers of hides outside the realm carried in the same ship on the same day. Sum, ~~£6 18s 8d~~ (£10 8s).

CUSTOM ON FISH RECEIVED BY B. NOGHT'

And for 5s received by Benedict Noght' from Arnald Bydal for exporting fish outside the realm to the value of £20, at 3d per £.

And for 5s received by the same B. from Francisco de Bordelaco for exporting fish to the value of £20 per £ as above.

And for 2s 3d received by the same B. from Raymond de Laspar for exporting fish outside the realm to the value of £9 per £ as above.
And for 2s received by the same B. from Geoffrey de Bordelaco for exporting fish outside the realm to the value of £8. Sum, 14s 3d.

[CUSTOM ON WOOL, CLOTH, WAX, AND OTHER GOODS]
Nothing received from the custom of wool which is 6s 8d for every sack exported outside the realm for old custom and 40d for the increment; nor from custom on wool fells which is 6s 8d on every 300 wool fells exported outside the realm for old custom and 40s for the increment; and not for custom of cloths which is 2s for each scarlet cloth dyed in grain, 18d for each cloth partly colored with grain, and 12d for each other cloth without grain; nor from custom of wax which is 12d for each quintal; nor from custom of avoirdupois and delicate things such as silk cloth of Tars [*pann' tarsent' de serico*], muslin [*de sindat'*], cloth of silk [*de seta*] and other diverse merchandise and for horses and other animals, and he receives nothing from other mercantile goods that cannot be easily assigned a true custom so each £ silver of value of things and merchandise are estimated by whatever means judged fit at 3d per £ silver when entering or brought in and unloaded there or sold and 3d per £ for exports of all sorts of things and merchandise which were purchased in the realm and dominion of the lord king, because no alien merchants with their merchandise come to sell or buy there in the aforesaid time in accordance with the above-mentioned on which custom is charged.

Sum total received, £22 14s 9d, which is owed. And 2s 6d remains from the view of account of Benedict Noght' for the 12th year. And £6 10s remains from the account of Geoffrey Averay in the said last year. Sum of joined debts: £29 7s 3d, which he delivers to John de Montovyron, receiver of the lord. And 16s 9d to the duke of Cornwall in the county of Cornwall and Devon by the hand of Benedict Noght delivered on account in one bill under the seal of the said receiver. And £6 to the same receiver by the hand of the aforesaid Geoffrey Averay, delivered on account by his quittance dated at Lostwithiel on Tuesday before the Annunciation of the Blessed Mary in the 14th year [21 March 1340]. Sum of deliveries, £6 16s 9d. And he owes £22 10s 6d which is charged on his account for the subsequent year.

R̶E̶S̶P̶I̶T̶E̶D̶ (IN HIS ACCOUNT OF NEXT YEAR)
T̶h̶e̶ ̶a̶b̶o̶v̶e̶-̶m̶e̶n̶t̶i̶o̶n̶e̶d̶ ̶a̶r̶r̶e̶a̶r̶s̶ ̶a̶r̶e̶ ̶r̶e̶s̶p̶i̶t̶e̶d̶ ̶f̶o̶r̶ ̶G̶e̶r̶a̶r̶d̶ ̶A̶v̶e̶r̶a̶y̶ ̶f̶o̶r̶ ̶6̶2̶s̶

4d charged above on customs of hides, namely 20s charged for each last for alien merchants, are respited. And the aforesaid collectors say that merchants who are not alien but English only owe 13s 4d per last; to be investigated at the Exchequer of the King, etc... Also the same is respited 26s 8d for his labor and for collection of customs this year and last year because nothing allowed then. And he owes net [*de claro*] £18 18d.

[m. 9d is blank]

(m. 10)

ACCOUNT OF THOMAS FITZ HENRI, KEEPER OF THE PORTS IN THE COUNTY OF CORNWALL FOR PRISAGE OF WINES IN THE SAME COUNTY [AND] IN SUTTON WATER IN THE COUNTY OF DEVON AND FOR ISSUES OF THE PORTS IN THE SAME COUNTY OF CORNWALL AND WRECK OF SEA IN THE SAME COUNTY NAMELY FROM THE FEAST OF ST MICHAEL IN THE THIRTEENTH YEAR (^ OF KING EDWARD III AFTER THE CONQUEST) UNTIL MICHAELMAS NEXT FOLLOWING FOR ONE WHOLE YEAR.

ARREARS

He is respited at the foot of this account for the arrears of the preceding account.

SALE OF WINES FROM PRISAGE

The same accounts for £13 (^ 6s 8d) received from 5 tuns of wine sold and no more sold because wine tuns were delivered to the steward of the lord by letter of the said lord etc. (all after seizure of prisage). And for 40s received for the price of 1 tun of wine sold to Sir Robert de Beaupel, steward, by letter of the lord as on the other side [*ut extra*]. And for 10s received from 1 tun of rape wine of remaining from goods coming from a ship of Portugal as in the preceding account. Sum, £15 16s 8d.

WINE CUSTOMS

The same renders account for 10 shillings received from one merchant of Gascony for 5 tuns of wine landing in the port of Fowey, namely 2s per tun. Nothing from customs in the other ports because there were no alien merchants. Sum, 10s.

WRECK OF SEA

Nothing from wreck of sea, whales or sturgeon because none this year.

(And for 6s 8d from 1 boat coming from a wreck in the port of Plymouth, sold as contained in the court roll of the fee of Launceston.) And for 6s 8d received from 2 partly-full [*non dum plen'*] tuns of weak and salty wine from wreck of sea at Tywarnhaile [*Tywernail*], sold as contained in the court roll of the manor of Tywarnhaile. Sum, ~~6s 8d~~ 13s 4d.

ISSUES OF THE PORTS
The same renders account for ~~46s 8d~~ (60s per the preceding account) received from the farm of the port of Marazion per year at the terms of Easter and Michaelmas equally. And for 12s received from the farm of the port of Penzance per year at the same terms equally. And for 20s from the farm of the port of Newlyn [*Niwelyn*] per year at the same terms equally. And for 100s from the farm of the port of Mousehole [*Mouseholl*] per year at the same terms equally. And for 2s from the farm (^ of the port) of Lamorna per year at the same terms equally. And for 12s received from the farm of the port of Porthgwarra [*Porgorwethou*] per year at the same terms. And for 8s received from the farm of the port of 'Porthplement' [*Portplemont*] per year at the same terms equally. And for 40s received from the farm of the port of Fowey per year ~~at the same terms equally~~. And for ~~25s~~ (32s per the preceding account) received from the farm of the ports of Kerrier per year at the same terms equally. And for 20s received from the farm of the port of Polruan per year (^ at the same terms equally). And for 20s received from the farm of the ports of Trigg per year (^ at the same terms equally). And for £6 received from the farm of the port of St Ives (^ at the same terms equally). ~~Nothing from the farm of the port of Porthzennor [Porthener] and Portheras [Portherest] because no boats were there by which it could be raised.~~ (And for 6s 8d charged for the farm of the ports of Porthzennor and Portheras per year at the same terms equally as in the preceding account.) ~~Sum, £21 5s 8d.~~ (Sum, £22 12s 8d).

FINES OF MERCHANTS AND OF TRANENTRIES [*TRANENTRIARUM*]
The same renders account for 6s 2d received from the fines of merchants and of tranteries during the same time. And no more because no foreign merchants nor boats came there to buy fish nor were boats sent to sea on account of the war at sea. Sum, 6s 2d.

PLEAS AND PERQUISITES OF COURT
The same renders account for 5s 4d received from pleas and perquisites

of the court of Mousehole. And for 2s received from pleas and perquisites of the court of Newlyn and no more from these ports or others because the mariners and fishers withdrew from the aforesaid fishing because ships from Spain came there during the time of fishing to do harm to the aforesaid fishers. Sum, 7s 4d.

Sum total of receipts, £40 6s 2d

EXPENSES
UNLOADING, ROLLAGE AND BOAT-HIRE
The same accounts for 14d for unloading onto boats 2 tuns of wine taken at Falmouth from a ship there, for boat-hire of the same to land, for rollage of the same from the boat to the cellar at Penryn, and for laying down in the same cellar, namely 2d for unloading each tun, 3d for boat-hire, and 2d for rollage.

And 2s 4d for unloading 4 tuns taken at Fowey from a ship there into boats, for boat-hire of the same to ~~land~~ (Lostwithiel), rollage of the same ~~from land~~ (from the boat) to the cellar and laying down in the cellar, namely 2d for unloading each tun, 3d for boat-hire for each, ~~2 tuns~~ (2d) for rollage each, and ~~½d~~ for laying down into the cellar. Sum, 3s 6d.

CELLAR HIRE
The same accounts for 2s 6d for one cellar leased at Penryn for storing 2 tuns of wine from 12 April (^ on which day it was taken) until 21 June for 10 weeks, at 3d per week. Also 9 gallons of wine in ullage for the same tuns, priced at 4d per gallon which is 3s 4d.

Also ~~5s 4½d~~ (20d) for a cellar leased at Lostwithiel for storing 4 tuns taken at Fowey from 10 April until 8 September for ~~21~~ (10) weeks and 4 days, at ~~3d~~ (2d) per week. Also for ~~9s 4d~~ (6s) paid for ~~28~~ (18) gallons of wine bought for ullaging the aforesaid 4 tuns, priced at 4d per gallon. Also ~~21d~~ (8d) for ~~42~~ (16) barrel hoops for binding the aforesaid tuns, at ½d per barrel hoop. Sum, ~~22s 3½d~~ (13s 10d).

MONEY PAID FOR ASSIZE
He also accounts for £6 paid to diverse merchants for assize of 6 tuns of wine taken for prisage from 3 ships, as on the other side [*ut extra*]. Sum, £6.

EXPENSES FOR VENISON [*VENATIONE*]
~~The same accounts for 2s 8d paid for carrying venison [*venat'*] from~~

Restormel [*Rostormel*] to Pendavey [*Pendeuy*] by land. Also 18d for carrying the said venison by boat from Pendavey [*Bendceuy*] to Padstow [*Padyrstouwe*]. Also 2d for hoisting the said venison from the boat into the ship. Also 5s for carriage by sea from Padstow to Bristol Water [*aqua Brystollye*]. Also 2d for hoisting said venison from the ship into the boat. Also 10d for carriage of said venison from Pendavey [*Pen'*] by sea to Bristol by boat. Also 8d for unloading and rollage of said venison from the boat to the cellar. Also 6d for hire of a cellar for storing the aforesaid venison for one week. Also 6s 8d for hire of one valet for watching and safeguarding the aforesaid venison. Sum, 18s 2d. (because in the receiver's account for this year).

Venison

He also accounts for 12d for carrying venison from Restormel to Lostwithiel. Also 5d for carrying the aforesaid venison by water from Lostwithiel to Fowey. Also 2d for hoisting said venison from the boat into the ship. Also 4s 6d for carriage of said venison from Fowey to Southampton [*Hamptone*] by sea. Also 2d for hoisting said venison from the ship. Also 6d for carriage and rollage of said venison from the ship to the cellar. Also 8s for hire of a valet to watch and safeguard the aforesaid venison. Sum, 14s 9d. (because in the account of John de Mountvyroun, receiver for this year).[14]

Surplus

The same accounts for £4 7s 11½d paid in surplus from the preceding account, as shown.

Wages and Fees[15]

The same seeks allowance for £6 13s 4d for his wages per year (because not guaranteed nor ... allowed in preceding account). And he renders account for 13s 4d for his robe (cause as above).

[14.] On m. 12d is a section on CARE OF VENISON that is also crossed through with the note "because not charged for venison and it is allowed, etc... debt to be allocated to the wardrobe of the duke". The section notes sums spent on purchase, storage, and carriage of salt for 24 beasts [*best'*] from Restormel to Lostwithiel to Fowey to Southampton, as well as 30 roe-bucks [*best' de capre'*] carried from Pendavey to Padstow to Bristol.

[15.] This section is written on a short piece of parchment sewn on to the end of m. 10. A large piece of the parchment on the left side is torn away, and much of the rest of the membrane is faded and illegible. The last section appears to be a summary of allowances and delivery of monies subtracted from the sums owed by the havener.

[SUMMA]
... £6 17s 4d. And he owes £33 8s 10d/... ½d remaining from his account for similar things from the preceding year./... £49 15s 5½d. Then £19 15s 4d delivered to John de/ ... of Edward, duke of Cornwall in the county of Cornwall and Devon/... assigned and delivered on account by indenture. And he owes £30 1½d for .../... of Launceston by indenture, delaying there according .../... Monday, 19 August in the 16th year [1342] at Launceston for advice/... fee and Hugh de Berewyk assigned to [collect?] all unresolved things [*dubia*] pending in the accounts of diverse ministers/ ... familars ... per letters of the same duke to the same directed to D.../ July in the 16th year [1342] ... Richard/ White, reeve of Calstok, enrolled in the 15th year, allowed ... 20 .../... and his wages from this year ... and 2 years before, taking 10 marks each year, which he ought to take .../ ... Also for ... 40s for his robe, existing in arrears for the same .../... /.../3s ... taken ... for his robes for .../... ordered that aforesaid £20 for his fee and his wages and 40s for his robe/... And that the aforesaid Thomas also for custom of the ports and prisage of wines and .../ ... his account of the aforesaid office ... per year for his fee .../... for his robe according to the tenor of his charter ... except he has a robe from the wardrobe of the lord/ ... And he now owes £8 1½d.

(m. 10d)

RED WINE REMAINING
He also renders account for 4 tuns of red wine remaining from the preceding account, namely those that were counted in the same previous account for the enemies of the lord king at Sutton and not allowed.[16] Sum, 4 tuns red wine which remains [*r'*] below.

RAPE WINES REMAINING
The same renders account for 1 tun rape wine remaining from the preceding account. Sum, 1 tun which remains below.

FOWEY
The same renders account for 4 tuns of red wine taken from two ships landing there during the time of the aforesaid account of which:

[16.] These 4 tuns of wine were presumably those captured by foreign enemies during the raid on Plymouth noted in the account for 1338/39, above, under the prisage account for Sutton.

2 tuns for assize of a ship called *Seynte Maria Cogga* of Fowey, burthen 10 tuns and more, whose master is Roger Frencha, on 10 April.

And 2 tuns of wine for assize from a ship called *Cogg Johan* of Bayonne, burthen 10 tuns as above, whose master is John Gillemot, on 10 April.

And no more from tuns of wine because merchants withdrew from travelling by sea as they were accustomed because of war at sea. Sum, 4 tuns which remain below.

Falmouth [*Falemouthe*]

The same renders account for 2 tuns of red wine taken there (^ at Penryn) for 1 ship landing there during the time of the aforesaid account for assize of a certain ship called *la Katerine* of Falmouth whose master is John Beneyt, on 12 April and no more from tuns of wine because merchants withdrew from travelling by sea as they were accustomed because of war at sea, etc... Sum, 2 tuns, which remains below.

From Prisage in the Ports of Sutton, Looe, Truro [*Truru*], Bay of St Michael [*Baia Sancti Michaelis*] next to Mousehole, St Ives [*Porthia*], Lelant [*Lananta*] nothing remains because no ships carrying wine landed there this year.

From Prisage in the Port of Padstow [*Oldestowe*] which is called *Patrikestowe*, nothing because the men (^ of the said) town of Padstow and the bailiff of the prior of Bodmin do not permit the lord duke prince to take away any prisage or any profits in his ports of Cornwall there. And they say that that Water is thus free so they should take no prisage or any profits pertaining to the lord as it is proclaimed there [*Et dicunt ill' aquam esse ita lib' quod null' prisa seu al' profit' domino pertin' ut predictum est ibidem capere debent*] Sum of all tuns, 11 tuns of red wine of which 1 is rape.

Then he accounts for 1 tun of wine sold to Sir Robert Beaupel, steward of the lord, by letters of the lord dated 26 April in the 14th year [1340]. Also for a sale to the said Sir Robert of 1 tun of rape wine. Also for sale as below of 5 tuns of red wine. Sum, 7. And 4 tuns of red wine remain.

Seal

The same renders account for 1 seal of latten remaining from the preceding account. And 1 seal of latten remains for the office of prisage of wines.

(m. 11)

ACCOUNT OF JOHN DE MOUNTUYROUN, RECEIVER

[...]

(m. 11d)

[...]

COLLECTION OF CUSTOM

And for 16s 9d received from Benedict Noght' collector of new and ancient custom, by one bill. And for £6 received from Gerard Averay collector of the same customs by one quittance. Sum, £6 16s 9d.

KEEPER OF THE PORTS

And for £19 (^ 15s 4d) received from Thomas Fitz Henry keeper of the ports and prisage of wines in the county of Cornwall and Devon from issues of his bailiwick by 2 bills. Sum, £19 15s 4d.

[...]

(m. 12)

[...]

MINISTERS' ARREARS NOT SEIZED

[...] Nothing received here of the arrears of £16 6s 7½d of Thomas Fitz Henri, keeper for the ports and prisage of wines in the county of Cornwall for the same year, because the same Thomas is later charged in his account for this year. Nothing received here of the £6 10s arrears of Gerard Averay one of the collectors of ancient and new custom and of 2s 6d from arrears of Benedict Nogth' another collector of the same custom for the aforesaid year, because they were charged in their account for this year.

[...]

1341/42

DCO Ministers' Account Roll 1

15–16 Edward III. 13 membranes. Ministers' account of the duchy of Cornwall in Cornwall and Devon (mm. 1–7); accounts of the havener (mm. 7d–8d), keeper of the fees (mm. 9), and receiver (mm. 10–13). Membrane 8 has four pieces, three sewn end to end and the fourth sewn on to the side of m. 8iii and used as a wrapper for the entire roll.

(m. 2)

TREMATON

[...]

ISSUES OF THE MANOR

The same renders account for [...] £6 9s 11d received from diverse issues of the Water and Pool of Sutton with customs for the time of the account as appears in the particulars [*per parcell'*] delivered on account (^ by John Kene keeper of the same Water and Pool) and examined. Nothing from the pasture of the castle ditch which was accustomed to sell for <u>8d</u>, the oyster toll which valued <u>3d</u> each year, rents in Trematon borough which valued <u>12d</u> each year because they are leased above with the conventionary tenants and mills, as charged above. [...]

Sum of all expenses: 76s 3d. And he owes £82 20d. He also owes [...]. From which is allowed to him £12 that John de Teuerton, farmer of the Water, and John de Sutton owe for their farm with customs from the last part of the 14th year [1341] and for part of the 15th year [1341/42] as appears in the account of John Roger, reeve of this manor last year, because Robert de Beaupel [*Bello Pello*] recently sheriff of Cornwall was charged for it in his account ...[17] for <u>£1453 13s 5d</u> for which he remains in arrears at the end of his last account as sheriff for the aforesaid rent at Westminster at the exchequer of the prince on the 22nd of October in the 18th year [1344] because the same Robert leased to the aforesaid John the aforesaid farm without security against the tenor of the letters of the lord directed to the same Robert. He is also allowed 52s ½d that Thomas de Gerleston, keeper of the aforesaid Water and Pool after the aforesaid John, owed afterwards per the same Robert and the same Robert is hence charged on his aforesaid account. And he owes £11 19d {which is charged in the following account under issues of this manor}.

[17.] Several words are struck through (probably a sum of money), erased, and now illegible.

Respited, hence owing [*UNDE SUPER*][18]

[...] 53s 3d for John Kene, keeper of the Water and Pool of Sutton, for issues of his bailiwick for this year.

[...]

(m. 3)

[...]

Lostwithiel

[...]

Farm of Mills with the Farm of Fowey Water

The same renders account for £13 6s 8d received per year at the terms of Easter and Michaelmas from the farm of 3 water mills and the isues of the fishery of Fowey Water with the customs of the same Water and pleas and perquisites of the marine court of the same Water, leased to the mayor and commonalty of the town by Peter de Guldesburgh, treasurer of the lord duke, and Hugh de Berwyk, steward for all lands of the same lord duke, for the term of 10 years, this year being the first. [...]

[...]

(m. 7d)

Collector of Customs

Account of Thomas Dengel, clerk of the collector of the ancient and new custom in all the ports of the county of Cornwall, from Michaelmas in the 15th regnal year of King Edward III after the conquest to the same feast following in the 16th year for one whole year.

Receipts

The same renders account for ~~12d~~ (2s) received of William Olyver of Guernsey on the second day of October of this year [1341] for custom on 2 dickers of salted hides loaded at Lostwithiel in his ship called *la Cog Seynt Michel* of Guernsey, at ~~13s 4d~~ (20s) per last.

[18.] *Unde super* is probably for *unde superplusagium*, which means literally 'whence the balance due' or 'whence the remainder'. I thank Harold Fox and Dave Postles for their advice on translating this phrase. This section lists sums still owing and is thus like a section of 'arrears' since it appears henceforth at the end of the accounts of individual ministers and records sums owed but still uncollected year after year.

And for ~~10s 4d~~ (15s 6d) received from Adam Sulk of Bodmin [*Bodmyn*] on 27 October for custom on 15½ dickers of salted hides loaded at Lostwithiel in a ship called *Helewencog* of Fowey in which the master is John de Loo, customed at ~~13s 4d~~ (20s) per last.

And for ~~2s~~ (3s) received from John Greek of Fowey on 10 January [1342] for custom of 3 dickers of salted hides loaded at Fowey in a ship called *la Sauver* of Fowey, customed at ~~13s 4d~~ (20s) per last

And for ~~2s 4d~~ (3s 6d) received from John de Sully and Stephen Bullok of Lostwithiel on 25 January for custom on 3½ dickers salted hides loaded at Lostwithiel on a ship called *le Petur* of Lostwithiel, customed at ~~13s 4d~~ (20s) per last.

And for ~~2s 10d~~ (4s 3d) received from Richard Solunce of Polruan for custom on 4 dickers and 2 hides loaded at Fowey on 25 January in a ship called *la cog Seynte Mar'* of Polruan, customed at ~~13s 4d~~ (20s) per last.

And for ~~2s 4d~~ (3s 6d) received from Peter de Polstoth on 29 January for custom on 3½ dickers of hides loaded at Fowey on a ship called *la cog Seynt Sauveour* of Fowey, customed per last as above.

And for ~~5s 4d~~ (8s) received from Benedict Noughth of Mousehole on 17 March for custom on 8 dickers of salted hides loaded at Mousehole on a ship called *Cog Johan* of Bristol, customed per last as above.

And for ~~4s 4d~~ (6s 6d) received from John Cope of Sandwich [*Sandwico*] for custom on 6½ dickers of salted hides loaded on 17 [ ] at Lostwithiel on a ship called *Seyntemariebot* of Faversham, customed per last as above.

And for ~~21s 4d~~ (32s) received from Walter Stonhard of Lostwithiel for custom on 32 dickers of salted hides loaded in the same place on 18 March in a ship called *la Margarete* of Hook [*Hoke*], namely ~~13s 4d~~ (20s) per last.

And for ~~15s 4d~~ (23s) received from John de Dipham for custom on 23 dickers of salted hides loaded at Lostwithiel on 18 March in a ship called *la Seyntmariecog* of London, customed per last as above.

And for ~~8s~~ (12s) received from Urban de Insula and Ralph Colyng of Truro for custom on 12 dickers of salted hides loaded at Truro on 20 March in a ship called *la Katerine* of Truro.

And for ~~6s 8d~~ (10s) received from John Hereward for 10 dickers of tanned hides loaded at Looe on 22 March in a ship called le *Cog* of Looe, customed per last as above.

And for ~~6s 8d~~ (10s) received from John Badyn and Richard Mel for custom on 10 dickers of hides loaded at Truro on 23 March on a ship called *la Katerine* of Fowey.

And for 6s 8d (10s) from William Bidow of Guernsey for custom on 10 dickers of hides loaded at Fowey on 18 May in a ship called *la Anne* of Guernsey.

And for 6s (9s) from Robert Languiow of Plymouth for custom on 9 dickers of tanned hides loaded at Fowey on 11 June on a ship called *Seyntmariecoge* of Plymouth.

CUSTOM OF GRAIN

And for 8s 6d received from a certain alien merchant for custom on grain he imported and sold at Lostwithiel, namely to the value of £34, at 3d per £.

CUSTOM OF TIN

And for 20s (23s 4d) received from Peter de Parme, merchant of the Bardi company, for custom on 20M of stamped tin, price £4 13s 4d per M, carried to Padstow [*apud Paderstouwe*] on the last day of July in a ship called *Cog Thomas* of Bristol.

Sum total of receipts, £9 2s 10d. And all is owing. And 73s 3½d remains from the preceding account. Sum of debts together, £12 16s 1½d.

From which he restored to himself 55s from the surcharge on the custom of hides charged at 20s for each last and which he does not take, except for 13s 4d, nor does he owe except for the hides of alien merchants, as he declares. And so he owes £10 13½d.

(m. 8)

ACCOUNT OF THOMAS FITZ HENRY, KEEPER OF THE PORTS IN THE COUNTY OF CORNWALL FOR PRISAGE OF WINES IN THE SAME COUNTY AND IN SUTTON WATER IN THE COUNTY OF DEVON, FOR PROFITS OF THE PORTS IN THE SAME COUNTY OF CORNWALL AND WRECK OF SEA IN THE SAME COUNTY NAMELY FROM MICHAELMAS IN THE 15TH YEAR TO THE FOLLOWING MICHAELMAS IN THE 16TH YEAR.

SALE OF WINES FROM PRISAGE

The same renders account of £72 19s 2d received from 30 tuns of wine sold, at a price per tun for 8 tuns of racked wines [*viii dol' vini de Reek'*] of 58s 5d, with 5s 1d from ullage and custom placed on each tun; at a price per tun for 22 tuns of vintage wines of 45s 1d, with 5s 1d from similar customs placed on each of these tuns. Thus sold for the expenses of the lord's household and delivered to John de

Montvyroun, receiver of monies of the lord duke in Cornwall at Fowey, on the 26th day of April in the aforesaid year {and by the same John delivered to John de Waverchyn, valet of the butler of the lord}. Sum, £72 19s 2d.

CUSTOMS OF WINES
The same renders account of 40s received for customs on 20 tuns wine namely 2s per tun, from William de Conket, merchant of Brittany, docking at the port of Falmouth. Sum, 40s.

WRECK OF SEA WITH GOODS FROM WAIF [*CUM BON' WEYVIAT*] {Memorandum of charge in subsequent account for the price of 1 whale that William Daumarle had}
{The same is charged with £29 6s 8d for the price of 11 tuns of red wine coming from wreck and carried to land by fishermen of Golant [~~Golonand~~ Golonant], price of each tun 53s 4d and no more value by testimony of Thomas de Dyngel, controller and supervisor of the said office.} The same renders account for 10s received from ½ tun of { ^ salty} white wine coming from a wreck at Mousehole and no more because {the rest was given to diverse} men for salvage of the same. And for 4s 6d received from ½ pipe { ^ salty} red wine coming from a wreck at St Anthony { ^ and no more for cause aforesaid}. And for 9d received from 1 piece of wood [*1 pec' arborum*] coming from a wreck at Meneage [*Manayk*] and no more because the other half is given for salvage of the same to diverse men; and for 18d received from 3 pieces of one broken mast coming from a wreck at Meneage [*Manayk*]. And for 33s 4d from a mast coming from a wreck which is in the custody of John de Walesbrew and no more because the said John retains half the value of the said mast, namely 33s 4d, for salvage [*tenet penes se med' apprec' dicti masti quod est 33s 4d et hoc pro eius salvatione*]. {And he is charged with ~~10 marks~~ (£6 13s 4d) for a certain ship coming from waif [*Weyft*] in the port of Falmouth. And for ~~10 marks~~ (£6 13s 4d) from 100 quarters of coarse salt [*grossi sal'*] also coming from waif in the same port. Sum £45 3s 5d.

~~ISSUES~~ FARM OF PORTS
The same renders account for ~~46s 8d~~ (60s in the preceding account) for the farm of the port of Marazion [*Marcasiou*] at ~~the feast of St James~~ {(the feasts of Easter and Michaelmas)}. And for 12s from the farm of the port of Penzance [*Pensans*] ~~at the same term~~ {at the same terms in equally}. And for 20s from the farm of the port of Newlyn

(per year at the same terms). And for 100s farm of the port of Mousehole {per year at the same terms}. And for ~~12~~ {2s} from the farm of the port of Lamorna [*Nansmornou*] {per year at the same terms}. And 12s from the farm of Porthgwarra [*Porgorwecthan*] {per year at the same terms}. And for 8s from the farm of the port of 'Porthplement' [*Porthplement*] {per year at the same terms}. And for 40s from the farm of the port of Fowey [*Fawe*] {per year at the same terms}. And for ~~25s~~ {32s} from the farm of the ports of Kerrier [*Kerr'*] {per year at the same terms}. And for 20s from the farm of the port of Polruan [*Polruwan*] {per year at the same terms}. And for 20s from the farm of the ports of Trigg {per year at the same terms}. And for £6 from the farm of St Ives [*Porthia*] (per year at the same terms). ~~From the farm of the ports of Porthzennor and Portheras, nothing because no boats are there by which the farm can be raised~~ {and for 6s 8d for the farm of the same ports, charged in the preceding account}. Sum ~~£21 4s 8d~~ {£22 12s 8d}.

FINES OF MERCHANTS, WITH TRANTERY

The same renders account for 7s 2d received from fines of merchants with trantery during the time of the account. {Sum, 7s 2d.}

~~SOLD ON ACCOUNT~~[19]

~~The same is charged with £28 (£29 6s 8d) charged on the account for 11 tuns of wine sold on the account as appears on the other side [extra]. Sum, £28 (£29 6s 8d).~~

PLEAS AND PERQUISITES OF COURTS

The same renders account for 6s 6d received from pleas and perquisites of marine courts during the same time. {Sum, 6s 6d.}

{Sum total of receipts, ~~£148 8s 11d £150 2s 3d~~ (£143 8s 11d).}[20]

DISCHARGE OF ROLLAGE, BATELLAGE AND ULLAGE

The same renders account for payment of 5s for windage of 30 tuns from ships docking in the ports of Plymouth [*Plymouthe*], Fowey, Falmouth, Mousehole, Looe and Padstow [*Padrestowe*], at <u>2d</u> per tun.

[19.] An initial, that looks like a B., is placed over the marginal heading.

[20.] In the margin to the right of this line is scribbled 'for the court roll' [*pro rotulo cur'*].

Also 2s 8½d for batellage and rollage of 13 tuns to the head cellar at Fowey, namely ½d for batellage of each. And for rollage 2d. And 8s 8d for the lease of one cellar there from 30 October until 26 April for 25 weeks and 2 days, namely at 4d per week.

Also 15d for batellage and rollage of 5 tuns of wine taken at Falmouth, namely 1d for batellage of each and 2d for rollage of each. Also 6s 3d for the hire [*alloc'*] of one cellar there from 26 October until 26 April for 24 weeks and 5 days at 3d per week.

Also 5d for batellage [and] rollage of 1 tun of wine taken at Mousehole, namely 2d for batellage and 3d for rollage. Also 14d for ~~hire~~ {lease} of one cellar there from 21 January until 26 April for 13 weeks and 3 days at 1d per week.

Also 3d for batellage and rollage of 1 tun of wine taken at Looe, namely 1d for batellage and 2d for rollage. Also 2s for ~~hire~~ {lease} of one cellar there from 5 January until 26 April for 15 weeks and 5 days, namely at 1½d per week.

Also 2s 3d for batellage and rollage of 9 tuns taken at Sutton, namely 1d for batellage and 2d for rollage. Also 6s 6d for the lease of 1 cellar there from 23 October until 26 April for 25 weeks and 3 days, at 3d per week. Also 3s for rollage and windage of 9 tuns of wine taken at Sutton, namely rollage from the cellar to the sea and windage into the ship, 2d for rollage of each and 2d for windage of each. Also 10s 6d for carriage of said 9 tuns by sea from Sutton to Fowey. Also 3s 4½d for unloading them at Fowey, for their batellage and rollage, namely 2d each for unloading, ½d for batellage and 2d for rollage.

Also 20d for rollage of 5 tuns taken at Falmouth from the cellar to the boat, their windage into the boat, namely 2d for rollage of each, 2d for windage of each. Also 5s 5d for their carriage by sea from Falmouth to Fowey. Also 20d for unloading them and rollage at Fowey, namely 2d for unloading and 2d for rollage.

Also 5d for rollage of 1 tun taken at Mousehole and windage of it there into a ship, namely 3d for rollage and 2d for windage. Also 16d for their carriage then by sea to Fowey. Also 4d for unloading them and rollage at Fowey, 2d for unloading and 2d for rollage.

Also 4d for rollage and windage into a ship of 1 tun wine taken at Looe, namely 2d for rollage and 2d for windage. Also 14d for their carriage from Looe to Fowey by sea. Also 4d for unloading and rollage of said tuns at Fowey, 2d for unloading and 2d for rollage.

Also 10s for rollage of all aforesaid 30 tuns of wine and windage into a ship at Fowey, namely 2d for rollage and 2d for windage of each.

Also 18d for 48 { ^ small *sheueromnib'* called} *Reggis* purchased for distilling [*stillag'*] the said 30 tuns wine. Also 11d for 350 hacknails [*ccc et di' haychnayl*] for ~~distilling wine~~ {distilling the said tuns in fire [*dicta dol' stilland' in igne*]}. Also 2d for 1 quarter of spike-nails [*spyknayl*] bought for the same.

Also 3s 9d for one carpenter hired to bind said wine tuns, at <u>1½d</u> per tun. Also 7s 2d for 86 barrel-hoops [*circulis*] bought for binding the said ~~wine~~ {tuns}, at <u>1d</u> per hoop. Also 2s 6d for 5 tun-staves [*tunstavis*] put in 5 tuns of wine to fix the said tuns, at 6d per tun-stave.

Also in ullage of all tuns of red wine, priced at 40s for 1 tun. Also in ullage of all white and red wine, priced at 20s for 1 pipe of white wine. {£7 12s 1½d. And the sum of each tun <u>5s 1d</u>, ... in total 5d}[21]

Sum {£7 12s 1d}.

MONEY PAID FOR ASSIZE
The same accounts for payments of £8 to diverse merchants for assize on 4 tuns wine taken as prisage from 4 ships, as on the other side. Sum, £8.

WAGES AND FEES
The same accounts for payment of £6 13s 4d to himself { ^ keeper of the ports, prisage, wine custom and wreck of sea for his fee and} his wages per year {by charter of the king. Nothing here for the <u>13s 4d</u> allowed in the preceding account for his robe each year because he has a robe from the king's Wardrobe this year}. Sum, £6 13s 4d.

Sum of all expenses, £22 5s 5d. And he owes ~~£127 16s 10d~~ (21 3s 6d). And £70 12s 3½d remains from his account in the preceding year. Sum of these combined debts: ~~£196 9s 1½d~~ (£191 15s 9¼). From which is restored to him £40 5s 9d which he says he delivered to Sir Peter de Guldesbourgh, keeper of the wardrobe of the lord duke, for the price of 16 tuns wine sold to him for expenses of the lord's household and delivered to him, <u>namely 14 tuns</u> that John Parker received at Fowey on 25 July in the 15th year [1341] and 2 tuns by the hand of the receiver for certain expenses of the lord made at Restormel in the same year. And £72 19s 2d that he says he delivered to the aforesaid Sir Peter, keeper of the said wardrobe, for the price of 30 tuns wine from

---

[21.] Written in the left-hand margin opposite the last three lines of this section.

prisage sold to him for expenses of the household (of the lord) and delivered to him by the hand of John Waverchyn, valet of the lord's butler, which wine he received at Fowey on 26 April this year. And £7 4s 9d from the surcharge [*superon'*] of the farms of the ports of Marazion, Kerrier, Porthzennor and Portheras, namely 13s 11d from Michaelmas term in the 16th year [1342] and £6 10s 10d from the 12th, 13th, 14th and 15th years and this year, namely 26s 2d per year, which the said Thomas confirms [*op' se verificar' per quod' etc*] because no boats were hosted [*conversant' sunt*] in the said ports of Porthzennor and Portheras so that the annual farm of ½ mark charged could not be levied at any time, after which the said bailiff had it and so ... [nothing?] is owed from the port of Marazion for 46s 8d per year, though he is charged for 60s, nor for 25s 10d from the ports of Kerrier, though he is charged for 32s. And then it was agreed by John de Stouwford and Hugh de Berwyk, assigned to consider all dubious charges in the accounts of diverse ministers of the lord duke (in the county of Cornwall), that stewards should be diligently examined regarding such surcharges and that the council of the lord should henceforth certify [them], as is supported in the foot of the preceding account, and because nothing is then done, the said keeper is ordered that execution of this ordinance should be followed, by which he will be warned of the imminent danger [*quod sequatur executionem illius ordinacionis contra proxim' periculo quo monebit*]. And ~~20 marks~~ (£13 6s 8d) from the price of wine and 100 quarters of salt coming from waif [*Weyft*] that the bishop of Exeter holds [*ocupat*] because the keeper was forbidden by Hugh de Berwyk, steward of the lands of the lord, from levying these 20 marks against a fine of Parliament summoned to Westminster in the quinzaine of Easter next after the end [*finem*] of this account. And £29 6s 8d from the price of 11 tuns of wine taken by fishermen of Golant [*Golonta*] and by them carried to port of Fowey because the said fishermen say that they are not owed to the duke as wreck because they found them in the sea beyond the distance of human view from land [*ultra spacium human' visus a terra*] and led to land on board their boats and that things thus found and led to land on board ship or boat ought not to be judged as wreck acording to the custom of the sea. Sum respited, ~~£169 16s 4d~~ (£163 3s). And he owes ~~£21 19s 5d~~

{£28 12s 9½d which is charged in the view of his account in the following year.}[22]

(m. 8d)

{WINES REMAINING

The same renders account of 4 tuns red wine charged in the remainder of the preceding account. Sum 4 tuns.}

FOWEY [*Fawe*]

The same renders account of 13 tuns wine of which 2 tuns are white wine taken from ships docking there in the time of this account of which:

1 tun red wine quit [*q^iet*] on 30 October taken from a ship called *la Katerine* of Polruan of which Stephen Boioun is master.

1 tun red wine quit from a ship called *le Petre* of Polruan of which John Matheu is master on 2 November.

1 tun red wine quit from a ship called *le Petre* of Lostwithiel [*Lostwythiel*] of which Nicholas Denyas is master on 3 November.

1 tun red wine quit from a ship called *la Margarete* of Plymouth of which John Brousthaks is master, on 6 November.

2 tuns red wine for assize of a ship called *le Jorge* of Lostwithiel of which John Parker is master, on last day of November.

1 tun red wine quit of a ship called *le Rede cogge* of Grimsby [*Grymysby*] of which Simon of the same [place] is master, on 7 ~~November~~ (January).

1 tun white wine quit from a ship called *le Jamys* of Plymouth of which John Cryour is master, on 19 January.

1 tun white wine quit from a ship called *la Katerine* of Poole of which John de Wyndesore is master, on 19 January.

2 tuns red wine for assize from a ship called *Seint Saveriscogge* of which John Boucher is master, on 6 April.

---

22. There is another piece of parchment sewn onto the bottom of this membrane that contains part of the account of the receiver; the writing on this piece (m. 8iii) is perpendicular to the rest of the account and a big X is drawn through the whole membrane, probably because the entries here are repeated on m. 10 of the receiver's account. Another (blank) membrane has been sewn onto the side of m. 8iii at a later date; it was obviously meant to serve as a wrapper for the whole roll since it also contains a string for tying the roll. Indeed, m. 8, with its three pieces and fourth sewn on the side, is the longest membrane of the roll.

<u>2 tuns</u> red wine for assize from a ship called *la Margarete* of Lynn [*Lenne*] of which John Albon is master, on 6 April.
Sum, 13 tuns wine of which 2 white and 11 red.

FALMOUTH

The same renders account for 5 tuns wine of which <u>1 white</u> taken from ships docking there in time of account of which:
<u>1 tun</u> red quit [*quiet'*] from a ship called *la Katerine* of Penryn of which John Gaudera is master, on 26 October.
<u>1 tun</u> red quit from a ship called *la Cristiane* of Weymouth of which William Gilberd is master, on 23 November.
<u>1 tun</u> white wine quit from a ship called *le Blythe* of Weymouth of which William Groos is master, on 23 November.
<u>1 tun</u> red quit from a ship called *la Margarete* of Falmouth of which Roger Hastyng is master, on last day of December.
<u>1 tun</u> red wine quit from a ship called *le Godyer* of Lynn of which William Roy is master, on 18 February.
Sum, 5 tuns wine of which 1 white.

MOUSEHOLE

The same renders account of 1 tun white wine quit [*quieti*] from a ship called *la Nicolas* of Bristol of which William Dollyng is master, on 21 January.
Sum, 1 tun white wine.

TOWN OF LOOE

The same renders account of 1 tun white wine quit received from a ship called *la Margarete* of Looe of which William Poddyng is master, on 5 January.
Sum, 1 tun white wine.

PADSTOW

The same renders account of 1 tun white wine quit received from a ship called *le Jorge* of Lostwithiel of which Robert Parker is master, on 27 March.
Sum, 1 tun white wine.

PLYMOUTH

The same renders account of 9 tuns wine of which 3 white, taken from ships docking there during the time of account, of which:

1 tun red wine quit from a ship called *le Blythe* of Sutton of which Robert Langon is master on 23 October.

1 tun red wine quit from a ship called *Seinte Marie Cogge* of the same of which William Northecote is master, on 23 Octber.

1 tun red wine quit from a ship called *Seinte Marie Cogge* of the same of which John Bagge is master, on 4 January.

1 tun white wine quit from a ship called *le Laurens* of Weymouth of which John Solard is master, on 8 November.

1 tun white wine quit from a ship called *le Petre* of Sutton of which Robert Totewille is master, on 28 January.

2 tuns red wine quit for assize from a ship called *la Grace deu* of the same of which John Austyn is master, on 8 March.

2 tuns red wine quit (from a ship called) *Seinte Marie Cogge* of the same of which Adam Folleforde is master, on 13 March.

1 tun white wine quit from a ship called *le Jorge* of the same of which William Julyan is master, on 27 March.

Sum, 9 tuns wine of which 3 white.

Sum total of tuns received: ~~30 tuns of wine~~ {34 tuns of wine} of which ~~31~~ {25} tuns red wine and 9 tuns white wine. {Of which 4 tuns of red wine were taken for assize as below, and no more taken for assize because other wines were not valued for the assize, as he says, so inquire [*non valuer' assissam ut dicit Ideo inquir'*]}[23]

PROFITS OF WINES

From which he accounts for a sale below for expenses of the lord's household and delivered to John de Mountuyueroun, receiver of lord E., duke, at Fowey on 26 April this {year}; loaded into a ship and carried to London, {30 tuns} of which 8 tuns [are] racked wines, 14 tuns [are] vintage, and 8 tuns are vintage white wine as appears in a certain indenture made between the aforesaid John de Mountuyoun and John Waverchym, valet of the lord's butler. Sum, 30 tuns wine {and 4 tuns red wine remain from the surcharge of the preceding account}.

WHALES

And [ ] for 16 small pieces of whales remaining from the preceding account. And 16 pieces of whale remain {declared to be of no value}.

---

23. *Inquir'* is also scribbled in the right-hand margin opposite this section.

WRECK OF SEA

From wreck of the sea {occurring in the time of the account along the sea coast of the county of Cornwall, nothing here because all is charged below because it is not yet agreed whether they were imported or not and so it is permitted, etc., as accustomed, etc., by which he is charged for the price of the said 11 tuns of wine as profit of the wreck of sea} ~~for the price of 11 tuns of wine found at sea by fishermen of Golant and taken by them to the port of Fowey, from which nothing is received because the said fishermen say that they do not belong to the duke nor are they owed as his wreck because they found it beyond human view of land and carried it to land on board their boats and because things thus found and carried to land on board a boat or ship ought not to be judged as wreck according to the customary law of the sea.~~[24] ... 53s 4d. And no more because it was not worth more by the testimony of Thomas B... ... and supervisor of the office of the said keeper of the ports, etc...

(m. 10)

ACCOUNT OF JOHN DE MOUNTVYROUN, RECEIVER OF MONIES OF LORD EDWARD, DUKE OF CORNWALL IN THE COUNTY OF CORNWALL AND DEVON, RENDERED AT LAUNCESTON IN THE MONTH OF APRIL IN THE 17TH YEAR [1343] BEFORE SIR NICHOLAS PYNNOK AND THOMAS DE HOCKEL', AUDITORS OF THE ACCOUNTS OF ALL MINISTERS OF THE LORD DUKE [...].

[...]

COLLECTOR OF CUSTOMS

The same ~~rendered account~~ {nothing} received from Thomas Dyngel, clerk of the collector of customs and keeper of the cocket for issues of his bailiwick {because he received nothing from the issues of his bailiwick this year}.

KEEPER OF THE PORTS

The same ~~rendered account~~ {nothing} received from Thomas Filz Henri, keeper of the ports, for prisage and custom of wines in the county of Cornwall and in Sutton Water in the county of Devon and wreck of sea in the said county of Cornwall from issues of his bailiwick {because he received nothing form the issues of his bailiwick this year}.
[...]

[24.] A line has been erased after this section. The erasure also made illegible part of the following line and something that had been scribbled in the right-hand margin opposite these lines.

(m. 10d)

[...]

FOREIGN EXPENSES

The same accounts for [...]. For 10s 2½d for the expenses of Thomas le Havenour and Robert Clyve and Walter Prat riding and 10 walking [*x pedestr'*] going from Restormel, by decision of Hugh de Berwyk, steward, to distrain the manors of Helston-in-Kerrier and Moresk, staying 3 days to levy the money of the lord and returning, as warranted by letters (^directed to the said John delivered on account) of the lord.[25] [...]

[...]

(m. 11)

[...]

MESSENGERS [*MESSAG'*]

The same accounts for wages of 2s 6d and stipend of 6d for one boy [*garcon*] for 12 days going from Restormel on 2 April to London with letters of the receiver and Thomas Dyngel to certify to the treasurer for numerous tuns of wine in the custody of Thomas Havenator and for having warrant to deliver and carry them and for knowing to which place they ought to to be carried. Sum, 2s 6d.

[...]

1344/45

DCO Ministers' Account Roll 2

18–19 Edward III. 11 membranes. Ministers' account of the duchy of Cornwall in Cornwall and Devon (mm. 1–6d); accounts of the havener (mm. 7–8), keeper of fees (m. 9), and receiver (mm. 10–11). Membrane 7 is made up of two pieces of parchment sewn end to end.

(m. 1d)

[...]

TREMATON

[...]

ISSUES OF THE MANOR

The same responds for [...]. And £10 received from the farm of the

---

[25.] Similar parties were sent to levy money at several other manors, but this was the only trip that involved the havener.

Water and Pool of Sutton with customs at Easter and Michaelmas terms equally, as leased to John de Haudlegh by Hugh de Berewyk, steward, for a term of 8 years, this year the second, by indenture of the lord prince enrolled in the account of the 17th year [1343][26] [...]
[...]

Sum of all expenses, 7s 8d. And he owes £69 9s 11d. He also owes [...]. And 100s delivered to the same receiver by the hand of John de Haudle, farmer of the Water and Pool of Sutton, for Easter term, by his own recognizance. [...]

HENCE OWING [*UNDE SUPER*]
£4 5s of John Kene keeper of the Water and Pool of Sutton for the 16th year [1342] and for part of the 17th year [1343] ... John Walter now reeve of this manor 100s owed by John de Haulee, farmer of the Water and Pool of Sutton for Michaelmas term this 19th year [1345] as the same reeve said, for which he is arrested and committed to the keeper of the gaol of the lord king at Launceston ... [illegible]

(m. 2d)
[...]
LOSTWITHIEL
[...]
    FARMS
The same responds for £13 6s 8d received per year from the farm of three water mills and the issues of the fishery of Fowey Water with customs of the same water, pleas and perquisites of the marine courts there per year at the terms of Easter and Michaelmas equally as leased to the community of the aforesaid vill for a term of 10 years, this year the 5th [...].
[...]

Sum total received, £28 16s 1d which he owes with 75s 4d from the remainder of his account in the preceding year whence the mayor and community of the town of Lostwithiel owe <u>53s 4d</u> for the farm of the

---

26. A small parchment rider attached to the side of this membrane contains a much darkened agreement (in French) between the duke of Cornwall and John de Haudelegh of Dartmouth granting John the bailiwick of the Water(?) of 'Sutton Plymouth' in the county of Devon.

mills, water, and fishery of Fowey. Sum of joined debts, £32 11s 5d.
[...]
[...]

(m. 7)

ACCOUNT OF THOMAS FIL'HENRY, KEEPER OF THE PORTS IN THE COUNTY OF
CORNWALL AND OF PRISAGE OF WINES IN THE SAME COUNTY AND IN SUTTON
WATER IN THE COUNTY OF DEVON, FOR THE PROFITS OF PORTS IN THE SAME
COUNTY OF CORNWALL AND WRECK OF SEA IN THE SAME COUNTY, NAMELY
FROM MICHAELMAS IN THE 18TH YEAR TO THE SAME FEAST IN THE 19TH YEAR
FOR ONE WHOLE YEAR.

SALE OF WINES FROM PRISAGE
The same responds for £25 13s 4d received from 11 tuns of red wine
sold, as appears on the other side [*ut patet extra*], at <u>46s 8d</u> per tun.
Sum, £25 13s 4d.

CUSTOM OF WINES
Nothing this year from the custom of wines coming from aliens docking
at Cornish ports with wines from which the lord is owed <u>2s</u> per tun
because no aliens came or docked in said parts this year as is testified
on account [*super comp'*].

WRECK OF SEA
The same responds for 66s 8d received from one-half of <u>5 tuns</u> of salty
wine coming from a wreck at Carminow [*Carmynou*], and Oliver de
Carmynou and his men have the other half for salvage of the said tuns
according to the right [*jus*] and custom of maritime law [*legis maritane*]
used in the said county. And for 6s 8d from one-half tun of white salty
wine coming from wreck in Kerrier, and Alexander de Godolghan has
the other half for the aforesaid reason. And for 13s 4d coming from
one-half of 2 tuns white salty wine in Penwith [*Penewith*], and John
Darundel has the other half for the aforesaid reason. And for 6s 8d
from one-half of 1 tun of salty wine coming from wreck in the hundred
of Stratton, and Ralph de Blaunkmonst' has the other half for the
aforesaid reason. And for 8s from one-half of 1 tun of salty wine coming
from wreck, and John de Chuddelee has the other half for the abovesaid
reason. And for 5s 9d coming from trees and boards [*arboribus et bordis*]
from a wreck at Tintagel [*Tyntagel*] as appears in the court rolls of the
said manor. Sum, 107s 1d.

FARMS OF THE PORTS

The same responds for 46s 8d received from the farm of the port of Marazion [*Marcasyou*] each year at Easter and Michaelmas equally. And it is permitted, in the preceding account for the whole time of the prince and duke, for <u>13s 4d</u> beyond the aforesaid farm to be charged each year as a certain surcharge along with other monies surcharged in the same way, as appears below. They are respited to him in his preceding accounts, as contained at the bottom of these same accounts, when the cause of the same surcharge can be found. It is found [*compertum est*] by an extent made before Sir William de Cus[ancia] and Hugh de Berwyk, assigned by commission of the lord to survey, etc... that the aforesaid farm and subsequent farms or the rest of the farm [*sive cetere firme*] and they do not amount to more than is contained in this account, as appears in the extent they made. And for 12s from the farm of the port of Penzance at the same terms. Also for 20s received from the farm of the port of Newlyn per year at the same terms. And for 100s from the farm of the port of Mousehole each year. Also for 12d received from the farm of the port of Lamorna (^ and Porthminster [*Porthmonstr'*]) each year at the same terms. And for 12s from the farm of the ports of Porthgwarra [*Porgorwythu'*] and Land's End [*Londesende*] each year at the same terms. And for 8s from the farm of the port of 'Porthplement' each year at the same terms. And for 40s from the farm of the port of Fowey each year at the same terms. And for 25s from the farm of the port of Porthallow in Kerrier [*Porthaleu in Kerr'*] each year at the same terms (^ and no more for the aforesaid reason). And for 20s from the farm of the port of Polruan each year at the same terms. And for 20s from the farm of ports of Port Isaac, Portgaverne, and Portquin [*Portisek, Porteveran et Porthquyn*] in Trigg each year at the same terms. And for £6 from the farm of the port of St Ives [*Porthyau*] each year at the same terms. {And <u>6s 8d</u> charged in the preceding account} for the farm of the ports of Porthzennor [*Porthenar*] and Portheras [*Portherest*] each year at the same terms; {nothing received because} the havener said that no farm could be levied in any way because no boats docked there. Sum, £21 4s 8d.

FINES OF MERCHANTS WITH TRANTERY

The same responds for 4s 9d received from fines of merchants with trantery. Sum, 4s 9d.

PLEAS AND PERQUISITES OF COURTS

The same responds for 6s 8d received from pleas and perquisites of maritime courts this year. Sum, 6s 8d.

{Sum total of receipts £52 16s 6d.}

EXPENSES

WAGES AND FEES

£6 13s 4d for wages of the same Thomas, havener and keeper of the aforesaid ports, prisage of wines and wreck of sea for his fee and his wages for this year. And nothing for the 13s 4d that should be owed each year for his robe by charter, because he has livery in the wardrobe of the lord. Sum, £6 13s 4d.

MONEY PAID FOR ASSIZE

The same accounts for £22 in payment of assize of ~~11~~ (22) tuns of wine {^taken in 11 ships from} diverse merchants, namely ~~40s~~ (20s) per tun. Sum, £22.

Sum of all expenses, £28 13s 4d. And he owes £24 3s 2d. The same owes £132 16s 8¼d from the remainder of his account from custom issues of years past and future.

Sum of joined debts. £156 19s 10¼d. Then he accounted for delivery of £31 19s 11d to John de Montviroun, receiver of monies of the lord and prince of Wales, duke of Cornwall and earl of Chester, in the counties of Cornwall and Devon, by sealed bill of the said John signed and delivered on account. And he owes £124 19s 11¼d.

From which is allowed £9 16s 3d to the same Thomas by assent of the council of the lord at Westminster in the month of November in the 19th year of the present king [1345], from the surcharge of the farms of the ports of Marazion, Kerrier and the two ports of Porthzennor and Portheras, hence he is charged 26s 2d in his preceding account and this year for the (whole) time of the lord, namely from Michaelmas in the 11th regnal year of the present king to Michaelmas in the 18th year [1337–44] for 7 years with one-half of the first and last terms computed as a year: 13s 4d each year for the farm of the port of Marazion, 6s 2d for the ports of Kerrier, and 6s 8d each year for the (two) aforesaid ports of Porthzennor and Portheras, because it is found by a new extent made in the 19th year of the present king [1345] by Sir William de Cusance, clerk, and Hugh de Berewyk, steward of the duchy of Cornwall, that the said port of Marazion only responds for 46s 8d from which 32s is charged for it per year. And the said farm from the said ports of Portzennor and Portheras could not be levied because no boats were hosted [*nulli sunt batelli conversantes*] by which the said farm charged for the said ports could be levied.

Also £8 allowed to him by assent of the said council of the lord for the price of 4 tuns of red wine similarly sold on his account in the next year that was plundered at Sutton by enemies of the lord king who burned the said town in the 13th regnal year of the present king [1339], as was testified by Henry de Trethewy and John de Montviroun, present before the council of the lord. And 38s 6d of part of 40s that he was charged in his account of the 17th year [1343] for the price of one tun of white wine similarly sold on his account in the same year that was destroyed at night while stored in the cellar [*quod noctant' perdit' fuit in locagio in celar'*] at Plymouth, as is testified by the same Henry and John before the aforesaid council, and no more because the same Thomas remains charged for 18d for wastage? [*vase*] of the said tuns. And £4 12s 10d allowed to the same by assent of the same council in the aforesaid month for which he is charged in his account in the said 17th year [1343] for the price of 2 tuns 7½ sesters [*sextr'*] of wine lost from full gauging [*deficient' de plena gaugea*] in 57 tuns of wine sold for the expenses of the household of the lord in the 18th year [1344], at the price of 43s 4d per tun and 10d per sester. Sum of allowances, £24 7s 7d. And he owes £100 12s 4¼d for which he is charged at the foot of his account for the same office in the following year.

(m. 7d)

FALMOUTH

The same responds for 53 tuns of wine taken in ships docking there during the time of the account, namely:

From a ship called *Seynt Sampson* of Cherbourg? [*Cherebrok*] of which John Bounalet is master, on 5 November, 1 tun wine (^ white, quit).

From a ship called *le Barge* of St Valery [*Seynt Walry*], on 5 November, of which Henry de Godeford is master, 1 tun of white wine, quit

From a ship called *Seynt John* of Barfleur [*Barflet*], on 5 November, of which Nicholas Manges is master, 1 tun of white wine, quit

From a ship called *le Jowanet* of *Belavylet*, on the same day, of which William Roge is master, 1 tun of white wine, quit

Form a ship called *Seynt Jake* of *Bonevyle*, on 6 November, of which John Ran is master, 1 tun of white wine, quit

From a ship called *Nicholas* of Cherbourg, on 6 November, of which John [ ] is master, 1 tun of white wine, quit

From a ship called *James* of Boulogne [*Boleyne*], on 7 November, of which John Spert is master, 1 tun of white wine, quit

From a ship called *le Goion* of Loire? [*Lure*], on 8 November, of which William Stanbon? is master, 1 tun white wine, quit

From a ship called *le Gracedieu* of Dartmouth [*Tertemouth*], of which William Shipman is master, on 8 November, 1 tun of red wine, quit

From a ship called *le Jowanet* of Kingswear [*Kyngeswere*], on 10 November, of which Henry Suewery is master, 1 tun of red wine, quit

From a ship called *le Trinite* of Bristol, on 7 December, of which Richard Harle is master, 1 tun of red wine, quit

From a ship called *le Petre* of Bristol, on 7 December, of which Richard Harke is master, 1 tun of red wine, quit[27]

From a ship called *le Pylegrym* of Bristol, on 12 December, of which John Donfras is master, 1 tun of of red wine, quit

(From a ship called *le Mariot* of Chepstow [*Schipestowe*], on 12 December, of which John Donfras is master, 1 tun of red wine, quit)

From a ship called *le James* of Exmouth [*Exemouth*], on 14 December, of which Bartholomew Sopere is master, 1 tun of red wine, quit

From a ship called *cog Thomas* of Newport [*Neuport*], on 16 December, of which William Corder is master, 1 tun of white wine, quit

From a ship called *Nicholas* of Dartmouth, on 16 December, of which (John Bourne) is master, 1 tun white of wine, quit

From a ship called *Laurence* of Milton [*Milletoune*] on 17 December, of which Henry Flute is master, 1 tun of white wine, quit

From a ship called *Seynte Marie Cogge* of Harwich [*Herwych*] of which William Olyver is master on 21 December, 1 tun of white wine, quit

From a ship called *le Lawrence* of Hull [*Holle*], on 25 December, of which Henry de Notyngham is master, 1 tun of white wine

From a ship called *le James* of Dartmouth [*Tertemouthe*], on 25 December, of which John Bronde is master, 1 tun white of wine, quit

From a ship called *le Seynt Espirut* of Dartmouth, on 27 December, of which John Gyge is master, 1 tun of white wine, quit

From a ship called *Seynt Jake* of Cherbourg, on 27 December, of which Nicholas Hasse is master, 1 tun of white wine, quit

From a ship called *le Petit Nief* of St Malo [*Seynt Molou*], on the same day, of which Nicholas Lucas is master, 1 tun of white wine, quit

From a ship called *Notre Dame* of Sluys? [*Lestu*], on the same day, of which [ ] is master, 1 tun of white wine, quit

---

[27.] This entry was written perpendicular to the body of the text in the right-hand margin.

From a ship called *Trinite* of Cherbourg, on 28 December, of which
Richard Bostard is master, 1 tun of white wine, quit

From a ship called *Notre Dame* of Ance, of which Raymond de Baydevyle
is master, on the same day, 1 tun of white wine, quit

From a ship called *Seynt Johan* of *Baydeville*, on 28 December, of which
Thomas Cremolet is master, 1 tun of white wine, quit

From a ship called *Seynt Marye* of Caen? [*Cain*], on the same day, of
which Ralph Damatyn is master, 1 tun of white wine, quit

From a ship called *Nicholas* of Honfleur [*Honyflyte*], on the same day,
of which John Symond is master, 1 tun of white wine, quit

From a ship called *Seynt Julyane* of Honfleur [*Honyflyte*], on the same
day, of which Richard Berthlet is master, 1 tun of white wine, quit

Fron a ship called *Nicholas* of *Baudeville*, on the same day, of which
John Gutor is master, 1 tun of white wine

From a ship called *Seynt Marye Cogge* of Cherbourg, on the same day,
of which John Bordeaux is master, 1 tun of white wine, quit

From a ship called *Seynt Loys* of Dieppe [*Depe*], on the same day, of
which John Lovet is master, 1 tun of white wine, quit

From a ship called *cog Seynt Michel* of Harfleur [*Hareflete*], on the
same day, of which William Gardien is master, 1 tun of white wine,
quit

From a ship called *le Nicholas* of Abbeville [*Abbevyle*], of which John
Forke is master, on the same day, 1 tun of white wine, quit

From a ship called *Seynt Benet* of Sluys? [*Lescel*], on 29 December, of
which William Kerneret is master, 1 tun of white wine, quit

From a ship called *Notre Dame* of Barfleur [*Barflete*], on the same day,
of which Denis Lovel is master, 1 tun of white wine, quit

From a ship called *Seynt Loys* of Abbeville? [*Abbey de Vyre*], on the
same day, of which William Richard is master, 1 tun of white wine,
quit

From a ship called *Seynt Jounwe* of Barfleur, on the same 29th day, of
which John Vyncent is master, 1 tun of white wine, quit

From a ship called *Pelegrym* of Cherbourg, on the same day, of which
Thomas Gerueys is master, 1 tun of white wine, quit

From a ship called *Seynte Croice* of Cherbourg, on the same day, of
which John de la Mote is master, 1 tun of white wine, quit

From a ship called *Nostre Dame* of St Valery [*Seynt Wallerey*], {on the
same day, of which Nicholas Boneville is master}, 1 tun of white
wine, quit

From a ship called *Notre Dame* of Harfleur, on 30 December, of which
John Toten is master, 1 tun of white wine, quit

From a ship called *Michel* of Harfleur, on the same day of which Richard Fenereor is master, 1 tun of white wine, quit

From a ship called *Margaret* of Barfleur, on the same 30th day, of which Ralph Jane is master, 1 tun of white wine, quit

From a ship called *Notre Dame* of Cherbourg, on 5 January, of which William Barnevile is master, 1 tun of wine, (^ white quit)

From a ship called *la Trinite* of Cherbourg, on 5 January, of which Jordan Morel is master, 1 tun of white wine, quit

From a ship called *Seynt Johan* of Dieppe, on the same 5 January, of which Richard Debean is master, 1 tun of white wine, quit

From a ship called *Margeret* of Dieppe, on the same day, of which John Benfitz is master, 1 tun of white wine, quit

From a ship called *Seynt Martyn* of Caen? [*Caain*], on the same day, of which John Reweles is master, 1 tun of white wine, quit

From a ship called *Seynt Pere* of Cherbourg, on the same day, of which Richard Plaunke is master, 1 tun of white wine, quit

From a ship called *Messager Notre Dame* of Cherbourg, on 5 January, of which Nicholas Symond is master, 1 tun of white wine, quit

Sum 53 tuns wine of which <u>7 red and 46 white</u>.

FOWEY

The same responds for 16 tuns of wine taken in ships docking there during the same time, namely:

From a ship called *la Katherine* of Fowey, on 28 October, of which Robert de Parisham is master, 2 tuns of wine for assize

From a ship called *le Nicholas* of Fowey, on the same October day, of which Nicholas Denyas is master, 1 tun of white wine, quit

From a ship called le *Laurence* of Fowey, on the same October day, of which Simon Poges is master, 1 tun of red wine, quit

From a ship called *la Kateryne* of Lostwithiel [*Lostwyth'*], on 3 January, of which Robert Parker is master, 2 tuns of red wine for assize

From a ship called *la Margarete* of Bodinnick [*Bodenuᶜ*], on 8 January, of which Lawrence William is master, 2 tuns of red wine for assize

From a ship called *le Gracedieu* of Fowey, on 11 January, of which Thomas Lewyn is master, 2 tuns of red wine for assize

From a ship called *la Katerine* of Fowey on the same January day, of which Mark Saundre is master, for 2 tuns of red wine for assize

From a ship called *Seyntemarye Cog* of Bodinnick [*Bodenuc*], on 15 January, of which John atte Yette is master, 2 tuns of red wine for assize

From a ship called *Seynt Sauveor*, on 15th day of above, of which John le Carueour is master, 1 tun of white wine, quit

From a ship called *le Whal* of Polruan, on 19 January, of which Henry Carueour is master, 1 tun of white wine, quit

Sum 16 tuns of which 13 red from which 6 tuns for assize, and 3 tuns of white wine, quit.

PLYMOUTH SUTTON

The same responds for 15 tuns of wine taken in ships docking there during the same time, namely:

From a ship called *le Edward* of Plymouth, on 28 October, of which William Saunder is master, 2 tuns of red wine for assize

From a ship called *Seintemariecog* of Plymouth, on 2 November, of which Richard Bole is master, 2 tuns of red wine for assize

From a ship called *Seintemariecogge*, on 2 November, of which William Blerok is master, 2 tuns of red wine for assize

From a ship called *Seintemarie cog*, on 4 November, of which John Spert is master, 1 tun of white wine, quit

From a ship called *le Grace Dieu* of Plymouth, on 5 January, of which John Coule is master, 1 tun of white wine, quit

From a ship called *le Rode Cogge*, on 5 January, of which John Wystan is master, 1 tun of white wine, quit

From a ship called *le George*, on 13 January, of which Richard Steeda is master, 2 tuns of red wine for assize

From a ship called *Cog Thomas*, on 15 January, of which Simon Garston is master, 2 tuns of red wine for assize

From a ship called *le Rede Cog* of Plymouth, on 15 January, of which Robert Totewell is master, 1 tun of white wine, (^ quit)

From a ship called *Godebyete*, on 15 January, of which Robert Beste is master, 1 tun of red wine, quit

Sum, 15 tuns of which 11 red. From which 5 for assize, and 4 tuns white.

MOUSEHOLE, LOOE AND PADSTOW

From a prisage of wines in the port of Mousehole, nothing this year because no ships docked there as Thomas Havener asserts by his oath on account.

From prisage of wines in ports of Looe and Padstow, nothing this year because no ships docked there this year as the same Thomas asserts on account.

Sum received of all tuns, 84 tuns, of which <u>21 tuns</u> are red. And for
assize, <u>20</u> tuns of red wine. And <u>54</u> tuns of white wine, quit.

From which is delivered to John Skyrbek, butler of the lord prince and
duke, by letters of (the same) lord prince directed to the same Thomas
le Havener dated the first day in April in the 19th year [1345] at Byfleet
[*Biflet*], and by indenture under the seal of the said John dated at London
8 June in the same year, for 71 tuns. ~~Also from the sale, as below, of 11~~
~~tuns red wine~~ (because below). In ullage of the aforesaid 82 tuns wine
which were taken in the said ports, and afterwards 2 tuns white wine
remained in the custody of the said Thomas le Havener. Also from the
sale, as below, of 11 tuns of red [wine]. Sum, 84 tuns. And none remain.

The same renders account for 1 latten [*de latoun*] seal remaining which
belongs to the office of the havener. And 1 latten seal remains.

(m. 8)

ACCOUNT OF THOMAS FILZ HENRI, KEEPER OF THE CUSTOMS OF WOOLS, HIDES,
WOOL-FELLS, AND OTHER THINGS EXPORTED FROM CORNWALL AND IMPORTED
TO ALL PORTS OF THE SAME COUNTY, FROM 11 JUNE IN THE 19TH REGNAL YEAR
OF KING EDWARD III [1345] WHEN THE SAID THOMAS RECEIVED THE AFORESAID
OFFICE BY LETTERS PATENT OF THE LORD PRINCE AND DUKE TO HIM FOR
REMAINDER AFTER THOMAS DE DYNGELEE THE PREVIOUS KEEPER OF THE SAME
OFFICE RETIRED [*CESSANTEM*], UNTIL MICHAELMAS NEXT [1345].

The same responds for 5s received from John Martyn of Bermeo
  [*Vermeou*], alien merchant of Spain, docking at the port of
  Mousehole with £20 worth of salt [*xx libratis salis*] sold there, namely
  <u>3d</u> on each <u>20s</u> [worth] [*de singulis xx s', iiid*].
And 4s received from John Pierres, alien merchant of Spain, and his
  fellow in the same ship for £16 worth of salt sold there, at <u>3d</u> on
  each <u>20s</u>.
And 3s received from David Trembrathan, alien merchant of Gascony,
  docking at aforesaid port, for £12 worth of whiting fish [*pissis de*
  merlus] purchased there and exported overseas, at 3d on each 20s.
Sum, 12s, which was delivered to lord John de Pyrie, receiver of the
lord in Cornwall and Devon, by the hand of John de Portes, his clerk,
by one bill. And so he leaves this account quit.

He responds in this file [*filaco'*] for nothing from the issues of the same
custom from Michaelmas in this 18th year [1344] until the 11th June

above, namely in the 19th year, because Thomas de Dyngele, receiver of the same office, then accounted until 20 March in this 19th year [1345]. And from that day until the 11th June above, no profits occurred, etc... And the account of the same Thomas for the whole of his time was placed in one bag by him.

(m. 10)

VIEW OF CORNWALL. ACCOUNT OF JOHN DE MONTVIROUN, RECEIVER OF MONIES [...]

[...]

COLLECTOR OF NEW CUSTOM AND COCKET

Nothing received from the issues of new custom or cocket because Thomas de Dyngele, collector of them, has not yet rendered account nor has the same receiver received anything during the time of this account.

KEEPER OF THE PORTS

The same renders account for £31 19s 11d received from Thomas Fil' Henry, keeper of the ports, prisage, and customs of wine, per 1 bill as contained in the roll of particulars of the same.

[...]

FOREIGN EXPENSES

[...] £26 paid to John Parker of Lostwithiel for freightage of a ship for carrying 65 tuns of wine from Fowey in Cornwall to London, by virtue of order in letters of the lord which are dated at Tyneham [*Tenham*], 22 February in the 19th year [1345], at 8s per tun, remaining among necessary [expenses] for this year.

(m. 11)

ACCOUNT OF JOHN DE PYRYE, RECEIVER OF MONIES OF EDWARD, PRINCE OF WALES AND DUKE OF CORNWALL, IN CORNWALL AND DEVON [...]

[...]

ISSUES OF THE COCKET

And for 12s received from Thomas le Fiz Henry, keeper of the cocket, by bill during the time of the account.

ISSUES OF THE PORTS

Nothing here from the keeper of the ports because nothing received from him during the time of the account.

[...]

1346/47

DCO Ministers' Account Roll 3

20–21 Edward III. 12 membranes. Minister's accounts of the duchy of Cornwall in Cornwall and Devon (mm. 1–6d); accounts of the havener (mm. 7–7d); keeper of the fees (mm. 8–8d); and receiver (mm. 9–12d). Membrane 7 consists of three pieces of parchment sewn end to end and used as a wrapper for the roll.

(m. 1d)

TREMATON

[...]

ISSUES OF THE MANOR

The same renders account for [...]. And for £10 received from the farm of the Water and Pool of Sutton with customs at Easter and Michaelmas terms equally as leased to John de Hamerlegh[28] [*Ham'legh*] by Hugh de Berewik steward for the term of 8 years, this year the 4th, by indenture sealed with the seal of the lord prince in the 17th year, of copy of which is sewn on to the roll of the account for the 19th year [1344/45]. [...]

[...]

Sum of all expenses, 68s 4d. And he owes £67 7s 3d. And he is charged [...]. Also £22 to Tydman de Lymbergh, receiver of the lord in the same parts after the aforesaid John de Pirye, by 1 bill sealed with the seal of John Conyng attorney of the said Tydman, delivered on account. And 50s to the same [receiver] by the hand of Richard Bremmor, farmer of the Water and Pool of Sutton, for his aforesaid farm for the last part of the present year by recognizance of the lord receiver, and by a bill remaining to the bailiff. Sum of these deliveries, £69 8s 3d. And he owes £21 12s 6d.

HENCE OWING [*UNDE SUPER*]

£4 5s 3d of John Kene, farmer of the Water and Pool of Sutton from the 16th year and for the first part of the 17th year. £17 10s of John de Haudlegh, farmer of the aforesaid Water by commission of the lord prince and by mainprise of John de Montiviroun and John Dabernoun, namely from last year and 3 parts of this year.

[...]

---

28. This appears to be a mistake for 'Haudlegh'; see the section on HENCE OWING, below.

(m. 2d)

[...]

LOSTWITHIEL

[...]

FARMS

The same renders account for £13 6s 8d received each year for the farm of 3 water mills and issues of the fisheryof Fowey Water with the customs of the same Water, pleas and perquisites of the marine courts there, at the terms of Easter and Michaelmas equally each year, as leasted to the community of the aforesaid town for a term of 10 years, this year the 7th. [...]

[...]

(m. 3)

[...]

TEWINGTON

[...]

ISSUES OF THE MANOR

The same renders account for [...]. And for 4s charged on account for one porpoise [*porco maritimo*] taken in the port of Towan [*Tewyn*] plus [*ultra*] 2s paid to the fisherman for the capture of the same by concession [*ex concess'*], of which William Bodrian took a third part of the said porpoise etc... [...]

[...]

(m. 7)

KEEPER OF THE PORTS

ACCOUNT OF THOMAS FILZ HENRY, KEEPER OF THE PORTS IN THE COUNTY OF CORNWALL AND PRISAGE OF WINES IN THE SAME IN SUTTON WATER IN THE COUNTY OF DEVON, FOR PROFITS OF THE PORTS IN THE SAME COUNTY AND WRECK OF SEA IN THE SAME COUNTY, FROM MICHAELMAS IN THE 20TH REGNAL YEAR OF KING EDWARD III TO THE SAME FEAST FOLLOWING IN THE 21ST YEAR FOR ONE WHOLE YEAR.

SALE OF WINES

The same renders account for ~~£10~~ (£13 6s 8d) received from four tuns wine coming from prisage at Plymouth, priced ~~50s~~ (66s 8d) per tun, which the lord will buy [*pro ut dns' emebat*]. And for ~~£75~~ (£84 6s 8d) received from 25 tuns wine coming from prisage at Plymouth, Fowey, Falmouth, Mousehole and Padstow, each priced at ~~60s~~ (66s 8d) and no more in sales because ten tuns were delivered to John Skirbek by letters of the lord prince to be taken to London. Sum, £96 13s 4d

Custom of Wines
Nothing here from the custom of wines, namely from alien merchants docking there who will give 2s by custom for each tun, because none docked this year.

Wreck of Sea with Waif [*Wayf'*]
The same renders account for 6s 4d received from 152 pounds of onions [*cep'*] coming into Mount's Bay [*la Mountysbay*] in the month of August, priced at ½d per pound. And 5s from a grampus whale [*Graspeys*] coming into the port of Lansallos [*Nantsalutz*] on the land of Richard de Hewysch, appraised by J. Portes. And for 15s charged on account for three grampus whales [*Graspays*] taken in Falmouth next to the land of John Soor. And 3s 4d charged on account for 1 debilitated sail of a Spanish ship taken in Tamar Water. And for 6s 8d similarly charged on account for 1 boat of the same ship with three oars of the same boat. Sum, 36 4d.

Farms of the Ports
The same renders account for 46s 8d from farm of the port of Marazion per year at Easter and Michaelmas equally. And for 12s from the farm of the port of Penzance per year at the same terms. And for 20s from the farm of the port of Newlyn per year at the same terms. And for 100s from the farm of the port of Mousehole per year at the same terms. And for 12d from the farm of the ports of Lamorna and Porthminster. And for 12s from the farm of the ports of Porthgwarra [*Porgorwythau*] and Land's End [*Londeshened*] per year at the same terms. And for 8s from the farm of the port of 'Porthplement' per year at the same terms. And for 40s from the farm of the port of Fowey per year at the same terms. And for 25s from the farm of the port of Porthallow in Kerrier [*Porthalou in Kerr'*] per year at the same terms. And for 20s from the farm of Polruan per year at the same terms. And for 20s from the farm of the ports of Port Isaac, Portgaverne, and Portquin [*Portysek, Pentevoran et Portquyn*] in Trigg per year at the same terms. And for £6 from the farm of the port of St Ives [*Porthyan*] per year at the same terms. And for 6s 8d charged on account for the farm of the port of Porthzennor [*Porthenor*] and Portheras. Sum, £21 11s 4d.

FARM OF MERCHANTS WITH TRANTERY

The same renders account for 6s 1d received from fines of merchants with trantery during the time of the account and no more because ships and boats were in the service of the lord king for the whole summer. Sum, 6s 1d.

PLEAS AND PERQUISITES OF THE COURT

The same renders account for 3s 6d received for pleas and perquisites of marine courts and no more for the aforesaid reason. Sum, 3s 6d.

Sum total of receipts: £120 10s 8d

CARE OF WINES

Then he accounted for payment of 19d for carriage of 19 tuns wine at Plymouth from ship to land. Also 3s 2d for rollage of the same to the cellar, at 2d per tun. Also for 36 gallons of wine in ullage of 18 tuns of the aforesaid from 3 November to 30 December for 8 weeks, priced at 4d per gallon, which is 12s. Also 6s 8d for 21 gallons of wine in ullage of one tun from the aforesaid 19 tuns, and this because by licence [*in lecacionem*] for one night, 20 gallons. Also 13d for the lease of one cellar there for 8 weeks, at 3d per week.

Also 2s 3d for carriage of 13 tuns wine taken at Fowey from ship to land. Also 2s 2d for rollage of the same to the cellar, namely at 2d per tun. Also 57 gallons wine in ullage of the said 13 tuns from 3 November to 1 April on which day the butler [*Pincerna*] of the lord received these wines in the cellar, for 21 weeks and 1 day, priced at 4d per gallon, which is 19s. Also 5s for the lease of one cellar there for 20 weeks, at 3d per week. Also 6d for carriage of 3 tuns wine taken at Falmouth from ship to land, at 2d per tun. Also for rollage of the same to the cellar, 9d, at 3d per tun. Also 6 gallons in ullage of said three tuns from 3 November to 29 December for 8 weeks, which is 2s, priced at 4d per gallon. Also 16d for the lease of one cellar for the said 8 weeks.

Also 4d for carriage of 2 tuns wine taken at Mousehole from ship to land. Also 6d in rollage of the same to cellar. Also 16d for 4 gallons in ullage of the said tuns for 8 weeks, priced at 4d per gallon. 16d for the lease of one cellar for the said 8 weeks, and no more because two tuns wine taken at Padstow were sold there in a ship without cost. Sum, 60s 9d

WAGES AND FEES

Then £6 13s 4d paid to him for his wages. Also 13s 4d to the same for his robe. Sum, £7 6s 8d.

MONEY PAID FOR ASSIZE

He also accounted for payment of £36 for assize of 36 tuns of wine taken from all ships during the time of the account.

Sum, £36.

Sum of all expenses, £46 7s 5d. And he owes £74 3s 2d. Also he owes £61 from the remainder of his account from similar issues of last year. Also he owes £14 16s 4d from the remainder of his account from issues of the cocket, as appears in the back of this roll for this year. Sum of joined debts, £149 19s 6d.

Then he delivered £20 to Sir John de Pyrye, receiver of the lord duke of Cornwall in the counties of Cornwall and Devon, from the profits of his bailiwick by indenture sealed by John de Portes, clerk of the said John, delivered signed on account [*sign' super comp' lib'*]. Also £11 2s to Tydman de Lymbergh, receiver of the said lord duke after the aforesaid John de Pyrye, for the issues of his bailiwick, by indenture sealed by John Conyng, attorney of the said Tydman, delivered signed on account. Sum of said deliveries, £31 2s. And he owes £118 17s 6d.

From which was allowed to him £8 6s 8d from part of £13 6s 8d which was charged in his account of the 16th year [1342] for the price of one ship and 100 quarters of salt arrested at Penryn by the said keeper as much as for waif because it was found by an inquisition taken before John de Mountvyroun according to the order of the said havener that the aforesaid ship and salt would not be valued except for 100s for which the said keeper remains charged.

And £16 18s 4d from part of £29 6s 8d which he was charged in his account of the 15th? year [1341] for the price of 11 tuns of wine taken by fishers of Golant [*Galananta*] as wreck of sea and carried away by them as was then presented before the auditors because it was found by Sir Peter de Guldeburgh, Nicholas Pynnok and their fellows, auditors of account, that 3 tuns of the aforesaid 11 tuns were wholly lost at sea and that the remaining 8 tuns was sold by the aforesaid fishers for £12 8s 4d for which the said keeper remains charged. Sum of said allowances, £25 5s. And he owes £93 12s 6d for which he responds at the foot of his account of customs profits in the following year.

For which he responds to him for £10 which he was charged in his account of the 17th year [1343] for the price of (1) body [*corpor'*] of one ship taken and abducted by Richard de Penworth.

Also £12 6s 8d which he says he spent for carriage of 71 tuns of wine and flour [*farine*] carried by him by water from Cornwall to London in the 19th year [1345] in the ship of John le Parkere of Lostwithiel for household expenses of the lord for which nothing was first allowed [*nulla prius exigb' alloc'*].

And for £7 which was charged in his account from Michaelmas in the 19th year to the same feast in the 20th year [1345/46] for the price of 3 tuns of wine delivered to Sir William Daubeneye, knight, by letters of Sir William de Northwell, keeper of the wardrobe of the lord.

Also 63s 6½d which he says he spent on rollage, *undag'*, towage, and stowage [*remag'*] of 48 tuns of wine and other diverse expenses made for them. Sum total received, £32 10s 2d. And he owes £61 2s 3½d.

(m. 7d)

PLYMOUTH

The same renders account for 19 tuns of red wine taken from ships docking there during the time of the acccount of which:

4 tuns of wine from a ship called *le Redecog* of Plymouth of which Alan Gade is master, on 3 November

2 tuns of wine from a ship called *le James* of Plymouth of which Richard Bole is master, on 4 November

2 tuns of wine from a ship call *le Cogg Johan* of Plymouth of which John Holeman is master, on 6 November

1 tun of wine from a ship called *le Seint Marie* of Fuenterrabia [*Fountarabie*] of which Raymond Arnaund is master, on 11 November

2 tuns of wine from a ship called *le Cogg Seint Savour* of Plymouth of which Simon Carston is master, on 26 February

2 tuns of wine from a ship called *le Cogg Peter* from the same of which Richard Brustax is master, on the same day in February

2 tuns of wine from a ship called *le Katerine* of Bristol of which Walter Galyot is master, on 27 January

2 tuns of wine from a ship called *le Trynite* of Plymouth of which Robert Pole is master, on 22 April

2 tuns of wine from a ship called *le Cogg Edward* of Plymouth of which Adam Coule is master, on 20 April

2 tuns of wine from a ship called *le Cogg Johan* of Plymouth of which John Holeman is master, on 20 April.

Sum, 19 tuns red wine.

FOWEY

The same renders account for 13 tuns of red wine taken from ships docking there during the aforesaid time of which:

2 tuns of wine from a ship called *le Grace Dieu* of Fowey of which *Emeric* Piper is master, on 3 November

1 tun of wine from a ship called *le Rede Cogg* of Ross [*Ros*] of which John Fissher is master, on 4 December

2 tuns of wine from a ship called *le Leonard* of Ravenser [*Ravensore*] of which Richard de Peterflete is master, on 4 December

2 tuns of wine from a ship called *le Faucon Dieu* of Fowey of which John Cogan is master, on the Saturday after the feast of the Conversion of St Paul [28 January]

2 tuns of wine from a ship called *le Katerine* of Bristol of which John Edward is master, on 26 February

2 tuns of wine from a ship called *le Seint Marie Cogg* of Bodinnick [*Boddennek*] of which Henry William is master, on 16 April

2 tuns of wine from a ship called *le Peter* of Fowey of which Thomas Hellelond is master, on 16 April

Sum, 13 tuns red wine.

FALMOUTH

The same renders account for 3 tuns of wine taken from ships docking there during the aforesaid time of which:

2 [tuns of] white 1 tun of red wine from a ship called *le Michel* of Bristol of which Odo de Flete is master, on 17 November

2 tuns of white wine from a ship called *le Seint Marie* of *Gyterne* of which Stephen John is master, on 4 May

Sum, 3 tuns of wine of which 2 tuns white wine.

MOUSEHOLE

The same renders account for 2 tuns of red wine taken there during the aforesaid time, namely from a ship called *le Grace Dieu* of Fowey of which Stephen Alard is master, on 16 April. Sum, 2 tuns of red wine.

PADSTOW

The same renders account for 2 tuns of white wine taken there during the aforesaid time namely from a ship called *le Seint Johan* of Mortrygo [*Mortreigo*] of which Thomas Reole is master, on 1 May. Sum, 2 tuns of white wine.

Sum of all wines: 39 tuns of which 2 tuns of white. From which 10 tuns of red delivered to John Skirbek, butler [*pincerna*] of the lord prince at Plymouth on 24 April per letters of the lord directed to the said keeper dated 22 February in the 19th year [1345] by indenture made between them. 29 tuns sold. And none remain.

Sum as above [*Summa que supra*]

Keeper of the Cocket
Account of Thomas Fil' Henry, keeper of the cocket, from Michaelmas in the 20th regnal year of King Edward III after the conquest until the same feast following in the 21st year for one whole year.

Profits of the seal which is called Cocket
The same renders account for 4s 2¼d received from Walter Stonard for 13 dickers and 3 hides carried in a ship called *le Seint Marie Cogg* of Polruan, of which Michael Cook is master, on 13 November, and no more because 7 dickers were previously customed at Fowey on 12 September in the 19th year [1345]. He also responds for 15¼d received from John Vadlet for 1 dicker and 9 hides, carried in the aforesaid ship of which the same Michael is master, on 14 November. Also for 12½d received from Randolph Marcant for 1 dicker and 6 hides, carried in the same ship under the same date.

Also for 3s 7½d received from John Hille for 5 dickers 3 hides carried in a ship called *le Redcogg*, of which Henry Lauri is master, on 23 January. Also for 3s 2d received from Robert Conyng for 4 dickers 8 hides, carried in the same ship on the aforesaid day.

Also for 3s 2¼d received from John Rokebere for ½ last and 8 hides carried in a ship called *le James* of London [*Londres*], of which Roger Leylond is master. Also for 18s from Robert Coulyng for 1 last and 6 dickers [hides], carried in the same ship. Also for 7s 1½d from John Symon for ½ last and 8 hides, carried in the same ship. Also for 12s received from Roger Monk for 18 dickers of hides, carried in the same ship.

Also for 20s from Roger Dagel for 1½ last of hides carried in a ship called *le Katerine* of Plymouth, of which Robert Pole is master.

Also for 20s received from Alexander Austel for 1½ last of hides, carried in a ship called *le Godyer* of London, of which William Trygon is master. Also for 6s 9½d from John de Guldesburgh for 10 dickers 2 hides, carried in the same ship.

Also for £6 18s 10½d received from Stephen Roger for 6 sacks 50? cloves [*claw'*] of wool and no more by assent of Sir Nicholas Pynnok, John Mountviroun, John Dabernoun and others of the council of the lord in Cornish parts for the profit of the lord as they agreed among themselves [*pro comodo dm' sic se inde concordarunt*]. Sum, £12 3s 3d.

MALTOLT

The same renders account for 22s 6d received from Hugh Martyn of Castrourdiales [*Castro*] merchant of Spain, for the sale of iron at Lostwithiel in the month of October, valued at £90, at 3d per £.

And for 13s 4d received from Michael Pierres, merchant of Spain, for the sale of salt to Philip Joce of Lostwithiel valued at £53 6s 8d, at 3d per £.

And for 5s 9d received from John Vermeu, merchant of Spain, for the sale of salt in the port of Fowey valued at £23, at 3d per £.

And for 11s 6d received from a certain Spaniard buying fish and cheese at Mousehole, valued at £46 in the month of August, namely at 3d per £. Sum, 53s 1d.

Sum total received: £14 16s 4d, which he owes and hence is charged in his account for custody of the ports, as appears in the foot of said account for this year.

(m. 9)

ACCOUNT OF JOHN DE PRYE, RECEIVER GENERAL OF THE DUCHY OF CORNWALL IN CORNWALL AND DEVON [...]

[...]

ISSUES OF THE PORTS

The same renders account for £53 6s 8d received from Thomas Fil' Henry, keeper of the ports, by bill for the issues of his bailiwick during the time of the account.

[...]

1348/49

DCO Minister's Account Roll 4

22–23 Edward III. 12 membranes. Ministers' account of the duchy of Cornwall in Cornwall and Devon (mm. 1–9d); accounts of the havener (mm. 10–10d), keeper of the fees (mm.11–11d), receiver (m.12). Membrane 9 is torn on the right side, so some words are missing or illegible, particularly in the SUMMA section. Membrane 11 is very long and was used as a wrapper for the roll. As a result, much of m. 11d in particular is very faded or defaced by gall, rendering much illegible. The receivers' account (m. 12) only covers the period 10 December 1348 to 1 February 1349, during which the havener and many other bailiffs and ministers reported collecting nothing.

(m. 2)

[...]

TREMATON

[...]

CONVENTIONARY RENTS OR FARMS

The same renders account for £19 8s 7½d received from rent or conventionary farms both free and villein, per year at the aforesaid four terms, namely [...] as assessed before Edmund de Kendale and his fellows for a term of 7 years, this year the second, along with 5s from the fishery in Lynher Water and [...]. And for [...] the market toll with petty customs and the toll of oysters that is worth by estimation 8s per year [...] and custom of barges and ~~arrows~~ (seines) [*sagittarum (sagenarum)*] there with other customs belonging to the said borough that are worth 16s per year, leased to the burgesses of the said town for the aforesaid term of 7 years [...]. More on the other side.

(m. 2d)

[account continued] £10 farm of the passage of Saltash Water at Easter and Michaelmas terms with rents of oars belonging to the same passage and with barges and 4 oars for the said passage. And £10 received from the farm of the Water and Pool of Sutton leased in conventionary tenure [*in convent'*] to Richard de Bremmore for the term of 7 years, this year the 2nd, with all customs and dues belonging to the said Water or pertaining to the honour of the castle of Trematon, except for all chattels in any way forfeit at the suit of the lord, wreck of sea, prisage of wines and fines on felons' chattels made or to be made according to the lord's custom [*ex' omnibus cat' aliq' modo forisfactis ad sect' dm' wrecc' maris*

pris' vinium et cat' felon' fin' cor' cons' dm' factis vel faciendi] [...] and rents of the borough of Trematon including toll of oysters. [...]
[...]

Sum of all expenses, £11 9½d. And he owes [...]. From which is allowed to him £13 18s ½d, namely 2s (^ in decayed) rent of 2 free conventionaries which could not be raised on account of poverty, 18s 8½d in decayed rents of dead villein conventionaries [*nativorum convent' defunctorum*] per ... whose goods the lord has by custom of the manor, and £11 4s from the decayed passage of the conventionary farm of the borough of Saltash there and part of 2 water mills, £28 from the decayed farm per year and 33s 4d from the farm of the Water and Pool of Sutton for part of £10 per year. And he owes £47 3s 10d.

Hence Owing [*Unde Super*]
£4 5s 3d from John Kene bailiff of the Water and Pool of Sutton for the 16th year and first part of the 17th year. £17 10s from John de Haule farmer of the aforesaid Water by commission of the lord prince for the 20th year and three parts of the 21st year. [...]

(m. 3d)
[...]
Lostwithiel
[...]
    Farms
And for £13 6s 8d received from the farm of 3 water mills per year and issues of the fishery of Fowey Water with customs of the same water, pleas and perquisites of the marine courts there, at the terms of Easter and Michaelmas equally, thus leased to the community of the aforesaid town for the term of 10 years, this year the 8th. [...]
[...]

Sum total received, £33 21½d which is owing. [...] From which is allowed to him 66s 8d for the decay of the farm of mills and issues of the fishery of Fowey Water for part of £13 6s per year because the greater part of the tenants who were accustomed to grind at the said mill are dead from the pestilence. And he owes £8 6d.
[...]

(m. 10)

ACCOUNT OF THOMAS FIL' HENRI, KEEPER OF THE PORTS IN THE COUNTY OF
CORNWALL AND PRISAGE OF WINES IN THE SAME COUNTY AND IN SUTTON WATER
IN THE COUNTY OF DEVON, FOR PROFITS OF PORTS IN THE SAME COUNTY OF
CORNWALL AND WRECK OF SEA IN THE SAME COUNTY, NAMELY FROM
MICHAELMAS IN THE 22ND YEAR TO THE SAME FEAST IN THE 23RD YEAR.

SALE OF WINES

The same responds for £10 13s 4d for 2 tuns red wine thus sold this
year, at the price of <u>106s 8d</u> per tun as testified by John de Portes,
controller of the same Thomas, by commission of the lord prince which
is contained in the controlment of the same John. Sum, £10 13s 4d.

WRECK OF SEA

The same responds (^ for 3s 4d) for the body of a certain damaged
fishing boat [*debil' batell piscator*] landed in the port of Porthluney
[*Porthleveny*] thus appraised as is testified by John de Portes, controller
of the same Thomas. Nothing here in pence from one mast [*masto*]
landed in the port of Falmouth not appraised nor sold here for money
because there are no buyers [*quia rem' pro defectu emptor'*]. {Let him
respond in a future year.}[29] And for 10s remaining from certain tuns of
white wine ~~landed in~~ (salty from the sea) occurring from wreck of sea
next to the priory of St Anthony [*Antonini*] thus sold to the same prior.
Sum, 13s 4d.

FARMS OF THE PORTS

The same responds for 46s 8d for the farm of the port of Marazion per
year, paying at Easter and Michaelmas equally. And for 12s for the
farm of the port of Penzance at the same terms equally. And for 20s for
the farm of the port of Newlyn per year at the same terms. And for
100s for the farm of the port of Mousehole per year at the same terms.
And for 12d for the farm of the port of Lamorna per year at the same
terms. And for 12s for the farm of the port of Porthgwarra
[*Porgorwetheu*] per year at the same terms. And for 8s for the farm of
the port of 'Porthplement' per year at the same terms. And for 40s for
the farm of the port of Fowey per year at the same terms. And for 25s
for the farm of the ports of Kerrier per year at the same terms. And for
20s for the farm of the port of Polruan per year at the same terms. And

---

[29.] Scribbled in the left-hand margin.

for 20s for the farm of the ports of Trigg per year at the same terms. And for £6 for the farm of the port of St Ives per year at the same terms. ~~Nothing for the farm of the port~~ (^ and for 6s 8d charged on account) for Porthzennor [*Porcener*] and Portheras, because no boats are there by which farm can be raised. Sum, £21 11s 4d.

Fines of Merchants with Trantery
Nothing this year from fines of merchants with trantery because no foreign fishermen were outside the liberty [*extr' lib'*] this year on account of the pestilence.

The same renders account for 9d for pleas and perquisites of maritime courts. Sum, 9d.

Sum total received, £32 18s 9d.

Wages and Fees
The same accounts for paying himself £6 13s 4d this year for his fee and wages for custody of the ports, prisage of wines, and wreck of sea. ~~And 13s 4d for his robe this year by charter of the lord king for the term of his life~~ (^ because it was ordered by agreement of the lord at Berkhamstead on 25 January in this 23rd year, that no robe to be allowed as is contained) in a certain schedule directed to the auditor under the seal of the lord and by letters of the lord directed to the auditor under the same date. Sum, ~~£10~~ £6 13s 4d.

Money Paid for Assize
The same accounts for £10 paid for assize on 5 tuns of wine taken from diverse merchants, namely at <u>40s</u> per tun. Sum, £10.

Custody of Wines cancelled because the said butler [*pincerna*] accounts for all debts and all customs in the wardrobe.
For leasing diverse cellars for 110 tuns of wine bought from merchants of Spain for the use of the lord, and £6 8s 1½d for laying down in the cellar [*cuband'*] 11 tuns of wine from prisage from 22 January (this year) until 11 May and for rollage, towage, windage, rebatage [*rebatage*], stowage [*rumeag'*] and carriage along with 25½ gallons bought for ullage of 3 tuns of wine from prisage, as appears in an indenture between John de Skirbeck, butler of the lord, and the said Thomas, containing payment of the said wines which is dated 11 May, as copied [*extract'*] and as appears in the particulars [*per parcell'*] shown on account and cancelled on the copy. Sum, £6 8s 1½d.

Sum of all expenses, £23 17½d. And he owes £9 17s 3½. And £50 6s 3d remains from his last account. Sum of common debts, £60 3s 6½d. From which is allowed 13s 4d to the same for the farm of the port of Portheras [*Portherek*] for this year and last year because no boats are hosted in the same [port] so the said farm is decayed as contained in a new extent made by Sir William de Cusance and Hugh de Berwyk.

Also £9 6s 8d is allowed to the same for part of £10 which he was charged in his account from the 17th year (1343) for the price of the body of one ship coming to the lord from wreck at Pentire [*Pentir*], captured and taken by ... [Ralph?] de Pewgra? as was suggested [*suggestum fuit*] to Sir Peter de Gildesburgh and the auditors by a bill exhibited to them on the account of the ministers of the lord prince in Cornish parts; and afterwards it was decided by an inquest before Thomas atte Fenne sheriff of Cornwall and John de Montviroun, by virtue of letters of the lord prince at the suit of said Ralph, that the same Ralph does not have the body of the said ship nor one timber [*lignum*] and 1 empty tun that are appraised at 2s 6d whence the said sheriff has the said timber for sale at the ... [said?] castle of Tintagel appraised at 2s for which appraisal of the timber and tun the said Ralph remains ... [charged?] for 13s 4d for a fine made before the auditor.

Also £12 6s 8d is allowed to him which ... John le Parker of Lostwithiel for carriage of 71 tuns of wine and flour [*ferine*] carried by him by water from Cornwall to London in the 19th year (1345) for expenses of the lord's household in the same year, paid to the said John by letters directed to him on account from Thomas which are dated 1 July in the 21st year (1347) at Westminster.

Also 100s allowed to him for the farm of diverse ports, namely 12s for the farm of the port of Porthgwarra [*Porgorworth*], 8s from the farm of the port of 'Porthplement,' 10s from part of the 20s from the farm of the ports of Trigg, £4 from part of £6 from the farm of St Ives, which can not be raised because fishermen were dead from pestilence and also by war.

Also 63s 6½d is allowed to him which were spent on rollage, towage, windage, and stowage [*remag'*] of 48 tuns of wine and other diverse expenses made by them not allowed in the previous year. Sum of said allowances, £31 2½d. And he owes £39 3s 4d which he is charged at the foot of his account for the custody of the ports for next year.

RESPITED

From which he is respited £7 in his account of the 20th year for the price of 3 tuns of wine delivered to William Daubigny by a lettter of Sir

William de Northwell, keeper of the wardrobe [*Garderob'*] of the lord. And he owes £22 3s 4d.

(m. 10d)

ACCOUNT OF THOMAS FILII HENRI KEEPER OF THE PORTS IN THE 23RD YEAR[30]

PLYMOUTH

The same renders account for 2 tuns of white wine taken for assize [*per ass'*] from a ship called *nau Seint Johan* of Bilbao [*Bilbau*] of which *Garci* Garcias is master, on 16 May.

And for 2 tuns of white wine taken for assize from a ship called *le Nau Seinte Marie* of Castrourdiales [*Castre*] of which Nicholas Runnylon is master, on 16 May. Sum, 4 tuns of white wine.

FOWEY

The same renders account for 2 tuns of white wine taken for assize from a ship called *Nau Seinte Marie* of *Gitaire* of which Peter de Gitaire is master, on 12 November.

And for 2 tuns of of red wine from a ship called *le Seinte Marie cog* of Plymouth of which John Taunton is master, on 23 February.

And for 2 tuns of red wine from a ship called *le Bertholemeu* of Lostwithiel of which John Portland is master, on 19 May. Sum, 6 tuns of wine of which <u>2 white</u>.

FALMOUTH

The same responds for 1 tun of red wine, quit for assize, taken from a ship called *le Rode cog* from Weymouth of which Richard Clerc is master, on 27 February.

PADSTOW [*PADRISTOWE*]

From prisage of wines in the port of Padstow, he renders nothing because no ships docked there this year with wine.

MOUSEHOLE

From prisage of wines in said port, nothing because no ships docked there this year with wines.

Sum of all wines (^ from prisage), 11 tuns of which

[30.] This is written upside down at the bottom of m. 10d.

WINES PURCHASED

~~The same responds for 80 tuns of wine purchased from a certain merchant from Spain by Sir Peter de Gildesburgh for the benefit of the lord's household, which money is paid into the wardrobe of the lord.~~ (Cancelled because ~~Will~~ purchased said wines and paid the money for their price into the wardrobe and John Skirbek, butler of the lord, received from these same wines 68 tuns and 12 tuns to Hugh de Cortenay the son [*filius*] as a gift from the lord, as appears below in a cancelled record of proceedings [*per processum cancellat'*].) ~~Sum, 80 tuns of wine~~.

Sum of all aforesaid wines, ~~91 tuns~~ (11 tuns) of which <u>11 tuns</u> from prisage.

From which are delivered to John Skirbek, butler of the lord prince, ~~77 tuns~~ (9 tuns) (of wine from prisage) ~~of which 10 from prisage (and 68 from ...)~~ by letters of the lord directed to the said Thomas, which are dated 18 March in the 23rd year and an indenture under the seal of the said John dated at Fowey 11 May in this 23rd year (^ in which indenture is contained payment for 68 tuns of wine purchased) enrolled below and similarly delivered on account. ~~And delivered to Sir Hugh de Courtenay the son, as a gift of the lord prince, 12 tuns of wine purchased from the same by letters of the lord directed to him and dated 12 March in the 23rd year, in respect of the same remaining~~ (because not charged? above in purchase of said wines). Sold, as below, 2 tuns of wine. Sum as above. And none remains.

EXPENSES MADE AT FOWEY FOR WINES OF THE LORD PRINCE, NAMELY FOR PURCHASED WINES.[31]

First, <u>36s</u> for diverse cellars leased from 22 January until 11 May. Also 15s 10d for rowage from cellar to ship, namely for 76 tuns of wine, at <u>2½d</u> per tun. Also 6s 4d for towage of the same, at <u>1d</u> per tun. Also 12s 8d for windage of said tuns, at <u>2d</u> per piece. Also 2s 2d for barrel hoops placed on the said tuns in repair [*in rebatying*]. Also 28s 6d for stowage [*runag'*] of said tuns, at <u>4½d</u> per piece. Also 2s for carriage of 1 tun of wine from Falmouth to Fowey, which tun was from prisage. Also 4d for 4 tuns taken from prisage from Spaniards [*Spaynolfs*] at Plymouth for towage of said tuns, at <u>1d</u> per piece. Also 8d for rollage

---

[31.] This entire paragraph has a large X through it.

of said tuns to the cellar, at 2d per piece. Also 4d for one cellar leased for one week for storing [*imponend'*] said tuns. Also 8d for rollage of the tuns from the cellar to the sea, at 2d per piece. Also 4d for towage of them to the boat, at 1d per piece. Also 8d for windage of said tuns into the boat, at 2d per piece. Also 10s for carriage of said tuns from Falmouth to Fowey. Also 6s 8d for 16 gallons of red wine purchased for ullage of 1 tun of wine taken from prisage at Falmouth and carried by water to Fowey for carrying with other wines to London and drawn [*extract'*] by [ ] serjeant-at-arms of the lord king and for carriage. Also 3s 11½d for 9½ gallons of red wine purchased for ullage of 2 tuns of wine laying in the cellar of Fowey for 18 weeks and 5 days before it was delivered to John Skirbeck, butler of the lord, priced at 5d per gallon. Also 4d for towage of 4 tuns of wine from prisage at Fowey, at 1d per piece. Also 8[d] for rollage of said tuns from sea to cellar, at 2d per piece. Sum, £6 8s 1½d, as appears in an indenture between Sir John de Skirbeck and the aforesaid Thomas, as enrolled below. {All this parcel [is] contained in the indenture below.}[32]

This indenture testifies that John de Skirbeck, butler of the honorable lord the prince of Wales, received from Thomas Filz Henri, havener [*havener*] of the said prince in the ports of Cornwall and Devon, 76 tuns of wine of which 9 tuns are from prisage, which wines were purchased from merchants of Spain and the said Thomas then paid £5 cash for their price, £6 8s 1½d for cellarage of the said wines from 1 January in the 22nd year [1349] to 11 May in the 23rd year [1349] and for other costs made for the said wines, that is portage, stowage [*rumage*], towage, windage and cooperage. In witness of this thing, the said butler afixes his seal to this indenture. Given at Fowey on 11 May, in the 23rd regnal year of our lord the king of England [1349] and the 10th year of France.[33]

---

32. This sentence is written in the left-hand margin at about the middle of the paragraph to explain why this section has been cancelled.

33. This indenture is in French. The X through the previous section also includes this paragraph.

1349/50

DCO Minister's Account Roll 5

23–24 Edward III. 12 membranes. Ministers' accounts of the duchy of Cornwall in Cornwall and Devon (mm. 1–11d), with accounts of the havener (mm. 12–12d). Many sections of the accounts are illegible because the bottom part of all the membranes are frayed and torn and because many sections have been defaced by gall.

(m. 2)

[...]

TREMATON

[...]

CONVENTIONARY RENTS OR FARMS

[...] The same responds for £4 7s 7d for ... (m. 2d) ... for the barges and 4 oars for the said passage. And ... [Sutton Water] leased to Richard de Bremmore for the term of 7 years, this year the 3rd, with all customs and dues belonging to the said Water or pertaining to the honor of the castle of Trematon ... [except for][34] forfeitures, wreck of sea, prisage of wines and fines on felons' chattels ... [...]

[...]

Sum of all expenses, 14s 7d. And he owes £71 7s 2½d. And he is charged for £47 3s 10d from the remainder of the account of Geoffrey atte More, reeve of this manor last year. Sum of joined debts, £118 11s ½d. From which £9 19s 7d is delivered to John de Kendale, receiver of the lord duke of Cornwall in the counties of Cornwall and Devon for the arrears of Geoffrey atte More [...]. And he owes £55 4s 6d.

From which 66s 8d is allowed to him from £10 charged above for rents or farms of the Water and Pool of Sutton because it was abandoned [*relict' fuit*] to the hands of the lord by the death of the tenant in the time of the pestilence and is now conceded to John Dabernoun for his whole life by letters patent of the lord to the same John made and dated 5 February this 23rd year. Hence rendering annually ten marks of silver at the usual terms for which the reeve remains charged.

And 100s of £10 charged above for the farm of 2 water mills that were abandoned to the hands of the lord in the time of the pestilence for lack of tenants and afterwards leased for 100s per year by William Daubeney knight and Nicholas Pynnok clerk and their fellows assigned

---

34. See the wording of this section in the previous account.

to lease the lands and tenements in the hands of the lord for these existing causes.

And £4 of £10 charged above for the passage of Saltash in a similar way abandoned to the hands of the lord and afterwards leased by the same assessors for £6 per year for which the said reeve remains charged.

And for 58s charged above for the rent and farm of 9 tenements and Lynher Water abandoned to the hands of the lord in the time of the pestilence and which are not yet leased for lack of tenants and whose acreage and names of those who were recently tenants are contained in a certain schedule attached to this roll. Sum of these allowances, £15 4s 8d. And he owes £39 19s 10d.

HENCE OWING [*UNDE SUPER*]
£4 5s 3d of John Kene bailiff of the Water and Pool of Sutton for the 16th year and the first part of the 17th. £16 of John de Haule farmer of the aforesaid Water by commission of the lord prince for the 20th year and three parts of the 21st. [...]

(m. 3d)
[...]
LOSTWITHIEL
[...]
  FARMS
And for £13 6s 8d received from the farm of 3 water mills per year and issues of the fishery of Fowey Water with customs of the same Water, pleas and perquisites of the marine courts there, at the terms of Easter and Michaelmas equally, thus leased to the community of the aforesaid town for the term of 10 years, this year the 9th. [...]
[...]

Sum of all receipts, £26 9s 7d which is owing. [...] From which is allowed to him 66s 8d in decay of the farm of the mills and issues of the fishery of Fowey Water for part of £13 6s 8d per year because the greater part of the tenants who used to grind at the said mills are dead in the pestilence. [...]

(m. 5)
TEWINGTON
[...]
Sum of receipts [...]. From which is allowed to him 7s 6d of 15s charged above for the rent or farm of the fishery and trantery of this manor

because they were abandoned to the hands of the lord in the time of the pestilence for lack of tenants and afterwards leased for 7s 6d per year for the term of another conventionary by William Daubey knight and Nicholas Pynnok clerk assigned to lease lands and tenements in the hands of the lord for these existing causes. [...]
[...]

(m. 11d)
[ACCOUNT OF THE HUNDREDS OF CORNWALL]
[...]

EAST [HUNDRED]
[...] 2s 3d received from the tithing of Sheviock [*Schevyek*] for the price of 1 boat with all its equipment in which John Hurneway, Walter Damerell and others were drowned, appraised before the coroner. And 6d from the tithing of St Germans [*Sanct' Germani*] for the price of 1 bad boat [*mali batelli*] thus appraised before the coroner. And 3d from the tithing of Calstock [*Calstuke*] for the price of a boat in which John Jobbele was drowned. [...]
[...]

(m. 12)
ACCOUNT OF THOMAS SON OF HENRY, KEEPER OF THE PORTS IN THE COUNTY OF CORNWALL AND PRISAGE OF WINES IN THE SAME COUNTY AND IN SUTTON WATER IN THE COUNTY OF DEVON, OF ISSUES OF PORTS IN THE SAME COUNTY OF CORNWALL AND WRECK OF SEA IN THE SAME COUNTY, NAMELY FROM MICHAELMAS IN THE 23RD REGNAL YEAR OF KING EDWARD III AFTER THE CONQUEST UNTIL THE SAME FEAST IN THE 24TH YEAR OF THE SAME KING FOR ONE WHOLE YEAR.

SALE OF WINES
The same renders account for £124 received from 31 tuns of wine from prisage sold for the household of the lord, priced at £4 per tun. Sum, £124.

WRECK OF SEA
The same renders account for £4 6s 8d received from the profits of 6 tuns and 1 pipe of red wine coming from wreck at '*Porth Gone Hollye*' [*Porthgonely*] in the parish of Sennen [*Sancti Senani*] on Sunday in the feast of St Lucy virgin this year [13 December 1349], priced at 2 marks per tun and no more because half of the aforesaid price of wine is

conceded as common prize for saving the said wine by the controller and keeper of the ports. Nothing here from one mast landed in the port of Falmouth by wreck, not appraised nor sold, because it remains in the custody of the said keeper of the ports for lack of buyers so he is to respond in a future year. Sum, £4 6s 8d. {Let him respond in a future year}[35]

FARMS OF THE PORTS

The same responds for 46s from the farm of the port of Marazion per year at the feasts of Easter and Michaelmas equally. And for 12s from the farm of the port of Penzance at the same terms. And 20s from the farm of the port of Newlyn at the same terms. And for 100s from the farm of the port of Mousehole per year at the same terms. And for 12s from the farm of the port of Lamorna per year at the same terms. Nothing from the 12s farm of the port of Porthgwarra, because no men or boats (^ are hosted) there by which the said farm can be raised. Nothing from the 8s farm of the port of 'Porthplement,' for the aforesaid cause. And 40s from the farm of the port of Fowey per year at the aforesaid terms. And 20s (25s) from the farm of the ports of Kerrier per year at the same terms. And for 20s from the farm of the port of Polruan at the same terms. And for 20s from the farm of the ports of Trigg per year at the same terms. And for 26s 8d from (£6 charged on account) for the farm of 4 boats in the port of St Ives this year at the same terms and no more this year because there are no more boats [*non sunt plur' batell*] in the said port and there used to be 28 boats which rendered £6 per year. And nothing from the 6s 8d farm of the port of Porthzennor and Portheras, because no boats are there by which said farm can be raised, as was found in the extent made by Sir William de Cusance and Hugh de Berwyk. Sum, £20 4s 8d.

FINES OF MERCHANTS WITH TRANTERY

The same responds for 7s 11d from fines of merchants with trantery this year. Sum, 7s 11d.

PERQUISITES OF MARITIME COURTS

The same responds for 5s 4d from pleas and perquisites of maritime courts. Sum, 5s 4d.

[35.] This phrase is written in the left-hand margin at the bottom of this section.

~~The same responds for £28 15s received from John de Kendale, receiver of the lord duke of Cornwall, for payment for prisage of wines and expenses made for them. Sum, £28 15s.~~

Sum total of receipts, ~~£177 19s 7d~~ (£149 4s 7d).

WAGES AND FEES

The same accounts for £6 13s 4d for wages and fees of the same Thomas, keeper of the ports and prisage of wines and wreck of sea for this year. ~~And 13s 4d for his robe by charter of the lord king for the term of his life~~ because it is forbidden by the council of the lord at Berkhamstead on the ... day of January in the 23rd year [1350?], no robe is allowed without special warrant of the lord. Sum, £6 13s 4d.

MONEY PAID FOR ASSIZE

The same accounts for payment of £32 for assize of 16 tuns of wine taken from diverse merchants, at <u>40s</u> per tun and no more because 17 tuns similarly taken [were] quit [*xvii dol similiter? capt' quiet'*]. Sum, £32.

CARE OF WINES

The same accounts for 12d for towage of 12 tuns of wine taken in the port of Plymouth from the ship to land, at <u>1d</u> per tun. For ~~3s~~ (2s) for rollage of the same from the sea to the cellar, at <u>3d</u> (2) per tun. For ~~11s~~ (6s 10d) for 1 cellar leased for the same from John Fissakre from 17 November this year to 7 July next following for 32 weeks, at ~~4d~~ (2½d) per week. For ~~3s~~ (2) for rollage of the same from the cellar to the sea, at ~~3d~~ (2) per tun. For 12d for towage of the same from the sea to the ship, at <u>1d</u> per tun. For ~~3s~~ (2s) for windage of the same from the ship to the boat, at ~~3d~~ (2d) per tun. For 30s (12s) for one boat hired to carry the said 12 tuns from Plymouth to Fowey, at ~~2s 6d~~ (12d) per tun. For 2s for windage of the same at Fowey from the boat to the ship, at <u>2d</u> per tun.

For 5d for towage of 5 tuns of wine taken at Fowey from the ship to land there, at <u>1d</u> per tun. For ~~15d~~ (10d) for rollage of the same from the sea to the cellar, at <u>2d</u> per tun. For ~~7s~~ (4s 3d) for lease of one cellar for the same tuns from 22 ~~November~~ December until 6 July, for 28 weeks, at ~~3d~~ (2d) per week. For ~~15d~~ (10d) for rollage of the same from the cellar to the sea, at ~~3d~~ (2d) per tun. For 5d for towage of the same from the sea to the ship. For 10d for windage of the same into the ship, at <u>2d</u> per tun.

Also for 2s 8d for towage of 16 tuns of wine taken in the port of Falmouth from ship to land, at 2d per tun. For ~~7s~~ (4s) for 1 cellar hired to store the said tuns from 19 January until 6 July for 24 weeks, at ~~3d~~ (2d) per week. For 2s 8d for rollage of the same from cellar to sea, at 2d per tun. For 2s 8d for towage of the same from the sea to the boat, at 2d per tun. For 2s 8d for windage of the same into the boat, at 2d per tun. For ~~32s~~ (19s) hire of said boat for carrying the said wines from Falmouth to Fowey, at ~~2s~~ (10d) per tun. For 2s 8d for windage of the same from the boat into the ship, at 2d per tun. For 8s 5d for 101 barrel hoops purchased to bind the said 32 tuns, at ... per hoop band. ... [36] ~~... Also to John Mark, lord of a certain ship called *la Katerine* of Fowey? and to Henry Edm... of the ship in full payment of £18 for the aforesaid, £18 for freightage of the aforesaid wine ... by letters of the lord ... sealed with the seals of the aforesaid John and Henry delivered on account. And 102s 10d residue ... for paying into the wardrobe of the lord as apears by the aforesaid letters of the lord. Sum, £4 19s 6d.~~

Sum of all expenses, £43 12s 10d. And he owes 105 ... And he is charged for ...

(m. 12d)

ACCOUNT OF THOMAS ...

PLYMOUTH

The same responds for 2 tuns of red wine taken for assize on 18 November from a ship called *le James* of ... of which ... de Raile is the master.

And for 2 [tuns] of red wine taken for assize on 25 November from a ship called ... of Dartmouth of which Gervase Whytyng is master.

And for 2 tuns of red wine taken for assize on ... from a ship called *le Katerine* of Bayonne of which *Domyng'* de Raile is master.

And for ... for assize on 4 December from a ship called *Edward* of Plymouth of which Walter ... is master.

And for 2 tuns of red wine taken for assize on 7 December from a ship called *le Cok* ... of which Richard Sampson? is master.

And for 2 tuns of wine taken for assize on 2 December ... from a ship called *la Trinite* ...

Sum, 12 tuns of red wine.

[36.] Here follows about nine lines which are illegible because of a large tear in the manuscript. They seem to list expenses for storing wine and carrying it to the prince's household.

FOWEY

... [first two lines are illegible] of which Peter Tyr is master.

And for 1 tun of red wine taken for assize on ... January from a ship called *la Seinte Marie cogg* of which Nicholas Cok is master, and he does not respond for another tun because the said ship did not land within the port but took 1 tun out of the port with the assent of the controller. Sum, 5 tuns of red wine.

FALMOUTH

[blank space left]

ACCOUNT OF THOMAS FILZ HENRI, KEEPER OF THE NEW CUSTOM AND COCKET IN THE COUNTIES OF CORNWALL AND DEVON, FROM MICHAELMAS IN THE 23RD REGNAL YEAR OF KING EDWARD III AFTER THE CONQUEST TO THE TO THE SAME FEAST OF MICHAELMAS IN THE 24TH YEAR FOR ONE WHOLE YEAR.

COCKET

The same renders account for 2s received from William Botringan for 3 dickers of hides carried to parts overseas on the last day of October.

And for 7s 1¼d received from Stephen Comyng for 10 dickers and 7 hides in *la Trinyte* of Fowey whose master is Robert Trusse, on 10 April.

And for 13s 4d received from Ralph Marcant for 20 dickers of hides carried on *le Bartholomeu* of Lostwithiel whose master is Peter Tyr, on 7 May.

Sum of all receipts, 22s 5d, which is owing and for which he responds in his account as keeper of the ports this year the 24th as appears there at the foot.

Sum of all receipts, 22s 5d, which he owes and for which he responds in his acount for guardianship [*custod'*] of the ports for this year, the 24th, as appears there at the foot.

1350/51

PRO, SC6/817/1

24–25 Edward III. 20 membranes. Ministers' account of the duchy of Cornwall in Cornwall and Devon (mm. 1–15d); accounts of the havener (mm. 16–17d), keeper of the fees (mm.18–18d), and receiver (mm.

18–20). PRO, E119/1, an account of all the estates of the duchy, contains the accounts of Thomas de Ocham, receiver for the duke in Cornwall for the same year (mm. 22–25), including returns for individual manors in Cornwall that add further details to this account.

(m. 2d)

[...]

TREMATON

[...]

CONVENTIONARY RENTS OR FARMS

He responds for [...] £8 rent or farm of fixed rents of the borough of Saltash, which is 64s 2½d as is said, for toll of mills which are worth 5s per year, and market tolls with petty custom and toll of oysters,[37] which are estimated to be worth 8s per year [...] and custom of barges and seine nets with other customs belonging to the borough which are worth 16s per year, are leased to the burgesses of the town for the said term of 7 years, reserving to the lord fines of arrests or seizures of any hues there and any pleas and perquisites? [*fin' arestat' seu arestand' que hutes ibidem, que placita et perq'et presentar' debunt in cur' dom' coram sen' et etiam reservat dno escaet' cum acciderint vid ad f. Pasch et Mich'*] and ought to be presented in the court of the lord before the steward and also reserving to the lord escheats when they occur, namely at the feasts of Easter and Michaelmas. And for £10 for the farm of the pasage of Saltash Water at the feasts of Easter and Michaelmas with rents of the oars at the same passage (^belonging to [it] and the barge and 4 oars of the passage). Nothing rendered from a conventionary lease of the farm of the Water and Pool of Sutton to Richard de Brounmore for a term of 7 years, this year the 4th, for £10 per year with all customs and dues belonging to the said Water or to the honour of Trematon castle except for all chattels which may be forfeited in any way to the exchequer of the lord as wreck of sea, prisage of wines, chattels of felons and fines made before the lord's council [*fin' cor' consil' dm' factis seu faciend'*] because conceded to John Dabernon for the term of his life for £6 13s 4d as rendered below. [...]

---

[37]. PRO, E119/1, m. 22d, notes the following issues in Trematon this year: 3d from custom of oysters, 4s from seines, and 11s 4d from barges. The figure for the issues of the Pool of Sutton is obscured by an ink blob, but it looks to be £10 9s.

FARMS FOR THE TERM OF LIVES

He responds for [...]. And for £6 13s 4d received from the farm of the
Water and Pool of Sutton conceded and leased to John Dabernoun
(^ by the lord) for the term of his life by letters patent of the same lord
duke, dated as appears at the foot of the account in the preceding year
(^ ... which was accustomed to be leased before the pestilence at £10
per year) on 5 February in the 24th year [1350]. [...]
[...]

(m. 3)

DECAYED RENTS

[...] For 3s 4d for decay of the farm of the fishery of Lynher Water
which Richard Jeul, Nicholas Penour, Auger Walter recently held, which
was accustomed to rent at 5s, and the fishery of the whole Water is
leased to John Beneyt for next year for 2s 6d. [...]
[...]

CARE OF THE MILLS AND BOAT

For 66s 8d for 1 boat purchased for the passage of Saltash Water because
the boat there was worn out, as viewed and testified by the steward.
For 5s for looking for [*quer'*] the same in Looe Water and bringing [it]
[*ducend'*] to Saltash, by testimony of the same steward. [...]
[...]

SUM

And he received £4 5s 3d by the same from the remainder of the said
account by the hand of John Kene, bailiff of Sutton Water for the 16th
year [1342]. [...]

HENCE OWING [*UNDE SUPER*]

Nothing paid to the receiver by John Kene, bailiff of the Pool and
Water of Sutton in the 16th year [1342] and the first part of the 17th
year [1343] as above in the foot [of the account]. For £17 10s of John
de Haule, farmer of the aforesaid Water by commission of the said lord
prince for the last part of the 18th year and the 19th, 20th, and first
part of the 21st year [1344/5–1347/8]. [...]

(m. 4d)

LOSTWITHIEL

[...]

FARMS

The same responds for £13 6s 8d for the farm of 3 water mills per year and the issues of the fishery of Fowey Water with the customs of the same Water, pleas, and perquisites of the marine court there at Easter and Michaelmas terms equally as leased to the community of the aforesaid town for a term of 10 years, this year the 10th.[38] [...]

[...]

(m. 16)

ACCOUNT OF THOMAS FITZ HENRI, KEEPER OF THE PORTS IN THE COUNTY OF CORNWALL AND PRISAGE OF WINES IN THE SAME COUNTY AND IN SUTTON WATER IN THE COUNTY OF DEVON, FOR ISSUES OF THE PORTS IN THE SAME COUNTY OF CORNWALL AND WRECK OF SEA IN THE SAME COUNTY FROM MICHAELMAS IN THE 24TH REGNAL YEAR OF KING EDWARD III AFTER THE CONQUEST UNTIL MICHAELMAS IN THE 25TH YEAR.

SALE OF WINES

The same responds for £102 10s from 20 tuns and 1 pipe of wine in the household of the lord, at 100s per tun as appraised in the same household, as contained in 1 quittance of Peter de Lacy, general receiver, made to John de Kendal, receiver this year. And for £4 from 2 tuns of scrapped [*de refus'*] and insufficient red wine (from) the allowance? for the household of the lord [*de car' pro hospic' dom'*] and left in the custody of the said keeper, so sold. And for 20s similarly paid on account for the price of 3 tuns of wine sold on account of the said keeper in the 20th year of the present king [1346] for £7 which wine was delivered to Sir William Daubene, knight, by letters of Sir William de Northwell, then wardrober [*Garderobar'*] of the lord, and which was appraised by the same wardrober at £8 of which he has quittance versus the ~~executors~~ (receiver) during delivery for this year. Sum, £107 10s. (He receives nothing for custom of taking 2s from each tun of wine imported by Gascon merchants because none of these merchants imported any wine within his bailiwick this year.)[39]

---

[38]. PRO, E119/1, m. 23 notes that 4s 4d was rendered for customs of ships in Fowey Water this year.

[39]. This last sentence is written in the margin underneath the marginal heading.

WRECK OF SEA

The same responds for 5s from the sale of 1 semi-filled tun of white wine coming from wreck of sea at Pentire [*Pentyr*] on 4 October. Nothing from 1 mast coming from wreck in the port of Falmouth not appraised nor sold for lack (and he responds) of buyers. Sum, 5s. (He responds [*r'*].)[40]

FARMS OF PORTS

The same responds for 46s 8d from the farm of the port of Marazion per year paid at the feasts of Easter and Michaelmas equally. And for 12s from the farm of the port of Penzance per year at the same terms. And for 20s from the farm of the port of Newlyn per year at the same terms. And for 100s from the farm of the port of Mousehole per year at the same terms. And for 12d from the farm of the port of Lamorna per year at the same terms. Nothing from the 12s from the farm of the port of Porthgwarra [*Portgorwychent*] because no men or boats are there by which the said farm can be raised. And nothing from the 8s farm of the port of 'Porthplement' for the same reason. And for 40s from the farm of the port of Fowey per year at the same terms. And for ~~20s~~ (25s) from the farm of the ports of Kerrier [*Kirier*] per year at the same terms. And for 20s from the farm of the port of Polruan per year at the same terms. And for 20s from the farm of the ports of Triggshire per year at the same terms. And for ~~26s~~ (£6 charged on account) from the farm of ~~4 boats~~ in the port of St Ives ~~this year~~ at the same terms ~~and no more because there are not many boats in the same port and they are accustomed to be 28 boats who render per year £6~~. Nothing from 6s 8d from the farm of the port of Porthzennor [*Portener*] (and Portheras) because there are no boats there during the same time by which the farm could be raised as was accounted by extent made before Sir William de Cusance and Hugh de Berwyk. Sum, £20 4s 8d.

FINES OF MERCHANTS WITH TRANTERY

The same responds for 6s 10d from the ~~farm~~ (fines) of merchants with trantery this year. Sum, 6s 10d.

PERQUISITES OF THE COURT OF MARINERS

The same responds for 7s 3d from pleas and perquisites of the court of mariners this year.

[40.] This last sentence is written in the margin underneath the marginal heading. PRO E119/1, m. 23d notes under MEMORANDUM that 2 great cords and 2 anchors came from wreck this year that will be responded for next year.

FORFEITED GOODS

The same responds for £46 13s 7½d received from 140 quarters of salt from the goods of Thomas Vrsiwyk forfeited and arrested in the port of Fowey, sold, by letters of the lord directed to John Dabernon, steward, and John Kendal, receiver, dated 10 July in the 24th year [1350], priced at 7s a quarter, then deducting 6 quarters 5 bushels, namely 21 quarters for 20 and he does not respond for more quarters because they were decreased in measure by 10 quarters on account of damage in the granary through long delay. Sum, £46 13s 7½d.

Sum of all receipts, £175 7s 4½d.

WAGES AND FEES

The same accounts for £6 13s 4d in wages and fees of the same Thomas, keeper of the ports, prisage of wines and wreck of sea this year. ~~And 13s 4d for his robe by charter of the lord king for the term of his life~~ (because it is ordered by council at Berkhamstead on 25 January in the 23rd year that no robe is allowed as contained in a certain schedule directed under seal to the lord's auditors). Sum, £6 13s 4d.

MONEYS PAID FOR ASSIZE OF WINE

The same accounts for payment of £20 for assize on 10 tuns of wine taken from diverse merchants, at 40s for a tun and no more because 14 tuns similarly taken for quittance of prisage [*capt' de pris' quiet'*]. Sum, £20.

Sum of all expenses, £26 13s 4d.[41] And he owes £148 14s ½d. He also owes £33 8s 10½d from reminder of his account (for) similar issues last year. And he is charged for £11 7s 9¾d from the remainder of his account as keeper of new custom and cocket in the county of Cornwall this year. Sum of the aforesaid debts and charges, £193 10s 8¾d. Then he delivered £175 3s 7½d to John de Kendale, receiver of monies of the lord duke in the county of Cornwall and Devon assigned per indenture sealed by the said receiver, delivered on account. And he

---

41. It is unclear why this account does not include the usual expenses on the custody of wines (for transport from the quay to cellars or the prince's household, for lease of cellars, for ullage, and other charges) that appear in the other accounts. It may be that he immediately disposed of the wine (see below, under 'Sum of the aforesaid wines').

owes £18 7s 1¼d. From which £4 18s 4d is allowed to him, namely 5s from part of 25s from the farm of the ports of Kerrier and £4 13s 4d from part of the £6 farm of the port of St Ives for lack of fishers dead from the pestilence. And he owes £13 8s 9¼d. ~~He responds.~~[42]

(m. 16d)

PLYMOUTH

The same responds for 8 tuns of red wine taken for assize from 6 ships landing in the port there, namely:

2 tuns of red wine from the ship *La Katerine* of Youghal [*la Youghel*], of which Reginald Goudfelawe is master, on the last day of February [28 February 1351].

2 tuns of red wine from a ship called *la Trinite* of Plymouth, of which William Lake is master, on the last day of February.

1 tun of red wine from a ship called ~~Petyr~~ (*Peter*) (^ of Dartmouth), of which Robert Notore is master, on 26 February.

1 tun of red wine from a ship called *Seint Mare Cog* of Ipswich, of which Thomas Gaunt is master, on 23 March.

1 tun of red wine from a ship called *Cog Johan* of Exmouth, of which Robert de Exston is master, on 23 March.

1 tun of red wine from a ship called *Garlaund* of Yarmouth, of which Geoffrey Fund is master, on 23 March.

Sum, 8 tuns of red wine.

FOWEY

The same responds for 16 tuns of red wine taken for assize from 7 [sic] ships landing in the port there, (namely):

2 tuns of red wine from a ship called *la Redecog* of Dartmouth, of which Adam Brian is master, on 24 February.

2 tuns red win from a ship called *Nicholas* of Sidmouth, of which Robert Hoke is master, on the aforesaid day.

2 tuns red wine from a ship called *Constans* of Dartmouth, of which William Buleman is master, on the aforesaid day.

2 tuns red wine from a ship called *Seint Savoures cog* of Plymouth, of which Richard Stonhous is master on the aforesaid day.

2 tuns of red win from a ship called *la Plente* of Hook [*Houke*], of which Richard Olak is master, on 24 February.

2 tuns of red wine form a ship called *la Savoye* of Fowey, of which Nicholas Sok is master, on 26 February.

[42.] Written in the left margin near the bottom of this section.

2 <u>tuns</u> of red wine from a ship called *la Katerine* of Fowey, of which William Boswin is master, on the aforesaid day.

2 <u>tuns</u> of red wine from a ship called *Seint Marie cog* of Bayonne, of which Peter de la Huhet is master and William Drynenhill is merchant, on 15 June.

Sum, 16 tuns of red wine.

FALMOUTH

Nothing from prisage of wines because no ships landed with wines this year.

PADSTOW

Nothing from prisage of wines in the port this year for the aforesaid reason.

MOUSEHOLE

Nothing from prisage of wines in the port this year for the aforesaid reason.

Sum of all the aforesaid wines, 24 tuns of red wine.

From which he delivers 1 tun of red wine to Sir William Daubene, knight, by gift of the lord prince, by virtue of letters from the said lord prince, delivered on account, which is handed over [at] London on 6 May in the 25th year [1351]. He also delivered 1 pipe of red wine to Sir Nicholas Pynnok [and] Thomas de Hockele, auditors of John Dabernon, steward, and John de Kendal, receiver, for their expenses on the account of the auditors, ministers of the lord in parts of Cornwall, by gift of the lord prince, by virtue of letters from the said lord prince directed to the said keeper which are dated [ ]. For 22 tuns 1 pipe of red wine sold [ ]. Sum, 24 tuns. And none remain.

(m. 17)

ACCOUNT OF THOMAS FITZ HENRI KEEPER OF NEW CUSTOM AND COCKET IN THE COUNTY OF CORNWALL AND DEVON FROM MICHAELMAS IN THE 24TH REGNAL YEAR OF KING EDWARD III AFTER THE CONQUEST UNTIL MICHAELMAS NEXT FOLLOWING IN THE 25TH YEAR

ISSUES OF THE COCKET

The same responds for 6s 10¼d received from Benedict Chikston of Millbrook [*Millebrok*] for ½ last and 3 hides carried in a ship called *Seynt Marie cog* of Millbrook, on 2 February, of which William Alas is master. And for 8s received from Richard de Partham for two last and 2 dickers of kips[43] [*kippes*] carried in the aforesaid ship. And for 6s 8d received from John Chambernoun for ½ last of hides carried in the aforesaid ship. And for 22s received from Joel Knoulyngus of Ashburton [*Asshperton*] for 1½ last and 3 dickers of kips, namely 2 hides for 1 kip, carried in the aforesaid ship on the aforesaid day. And for 14s 8d received from John Sparkewell for 1 last and 2 dickers carried in the aforesaid ship on the aforesaid day.

And for 2s 3d received from Richard Page of Lostwithiel for 3 dickers and 4 hides carried in a ship called *le Bartholomew* of Polruan of which Peter Tyr is master, on 10 December.

And for 19s 5½d received from John Page for 1 last 9 dickers and 2 hides carried in a ship called *cog Johan* of Looe of which the aforesaid John is master, on 1 October. And for 19s 4d received from Richard Kyn for 1 last and 9 dickers composed of kips and hides [*inter kyppes et hydes*] carried in the aforesaid ship on the aforesaid day.

And for 16s 4d received from Matthew Tyrel of Galway of Ireland [*la Galue de Yrland*] merchant for 1 last and 4 dickers and ½ hide carried in the aforesaid ship on the last day of December [31 December] of which Thomas Russel is master.

And for £4 11s 3d received of Richard Mareschal and John Peron for 6½ lasts 7 dickers and 9 hides carried in a ship called *le Rede cog* of Dartmouth on 25 March, of which Adam Brian is master. And for 11s received from John Fol of Bodmin for 16 [dickers] ½ hide carried in the aforesaid ship on the aforesaid day. And for 8s received from Roger Antrot of Bodmin for 13 dickers carried in the said ship. And for 2s received from John Symond for 3 dickers of hides carried in the said ship on the aforesaid ship.

Sum total received, £11 7s 9¾d which is charged in the foot of his account of keeper of the ports for this year. And so he is quit here.

(m. 19d)

Edward eldest son of the noble king of England and France, prince of Wales etc..., greetings to all of our faithful and subjects of our duchy of Cornwall and others who will see these letters. Know that as our respected lord and father the king by his charter has given and granted to us all the customs of wools, hides and wool fells that come to be

---

43. Hide of a young animal.

loaded at the ports [*anendrent estre chargez en les ports*] within our duchy of Cornwall, we, pledged by loyalty and agreement, have ordered and assigned and given full power to our dear valet John de Kendal to weigh all the wools that will be brought into our said ports and by you found? [*per vue trove*], examined and approved at London and whatever market in the same city; and to collect and receive at the named prise [*et a coiller et receyvre en prise nou'*] all the said customs provided that he makes a return to us in pennies and shillings as pledged, to have this office as long as it pleases us. By this we order you to be helpful, attentive, and respectful as right requires in whatever may concern the same John touching the said office. And however it may be seeing that our said lord and father has so generously granted to us the aforesaid customs, we, nevertheless, having regard to the great and substantive needs [*les grandes et contenouses bosoignes*] that are currently afoot affecting him and all his realm, would not see that his customs should be diminished [*amenuses*] by others outside our said county on our account, command to all that no one carry to the said ports any manner of wools from other foreign countries but from our said county; and as you have heard this directed, and we have charged the said John Kendal that he should not suffer any other wool in any way to be weighed or customed in the aforesaid ports until he has another command from us. In witness of these things we have made [*fait farre*] these our letters patent sealed with our privy seal. Given at London on 16 December in the 24th regnal year of our very dear seigneur and father the king of England and 11th [regnal year] of France [1350][44]

(m. 20)

THE ACCOUNT OF JOHN DE KENDAL, COLLECTOR AND RECEIVER OF MONIES COMING FROM CUSTOMS OF WOOL, HIDES AND FELLS APPERTAINING TO AND ARISING WITHIN THE PORTS OF THE DUCHY OF CORNWALL FROM 16 OCTOBER IN THE 24TH YEAR. ON WHICH DAY THE DUKE COMMISSIONED HIM TO THE THE AFORESAID OFFICE BY HIS LETTERS PATENT AS APPEARS IN THE BACK OF THIS ROLL ENROLLED UNDER THE SAME DATE, TO HAVE AS LONG AS IT PLEASES THE DUKE. ON CONDITION THAT HE RESPOND TO THE DUKE FOR MONIES COMING FROM THEM, AS IS APPROPRIATE, NAMELY, FOR MONIES RECEIVED BY HIM AND DELIVERED BY REASON OF THE AFORESAID OFFICE FROM THE SAID 16 OCTOBER IN THE 24TH YEAR TO MICHAELMAS IN THE 25TH YEAR.
[...]

[44.] The above is in French.

CUSTOMS OF WOOLS

The same responds for £7 received from Richard Cereseaux, knight, for custom on 7 sacks of wool, priced at 20s per sack this first year by commission of the lord as above.

And for 35s received from William Odum [*Odu'*] and John Page of Looe for similar custom for 1¾ sack.

And for 40s 2d received from William Odum for similar custom for 2 sacks.

Sum total of receipts, £10 15s 2d which was delivered to him the same receiver of monies of the lord for this year. So he is quit here.

He responds [*r'*]

The same responds for 1 balance called tron [*ancell' voc' trona*] bought at London by the said receiver. And 1 tron remains.

[...]

ISSUES OF PORTS AND COCKET

The same responds for £175 3s 7½d received from Thomas Fitz Henri keeper of the ports there for the said time. Sum, £175 3s ½d.

WOOL CUSTOM

And for £10 15s 2d received from John de Kendal now accounting for the keeper and receiver of the wool customs by commission of the lord prince during the time of the account. Sum, £10 15s 2d.

[...]

FINES MADE FOR WRECK OF SEA before William Daubeneye and Nicholas Pynnok, auditors of John Moniron and others

The same responds for 6s 8d received from Richard son of Henry Trewynnard and Benedict Bren in full payment of 13s 4d from fines made before the same as appears in the account of the preceding year. And for 3s 4d received from a fine of William Tremwy for fine made before the same as appears in the same place. And for 12s received from Henry Bray, William Bosistou, David William of Treworgans [*Treworghans*], William Treuref and David Nanskynmon, manucaptors of William Lauri, John Yedene, John Woluel, David Nought', Roger Meleder in part payment of 16s 4d from the same fines before the same. And no more because no more can be raised this year so let him respond for the rest in a future year (let him responds in a future year)[45].

[45.] Scribbled in the margin next to this entry.

And for 2s received from William Treuref for fine made before the same as appears in the same place. He responds for nothing from 73s 4d arrears existing from £20 for fines of the men of Treslothan [*Tresolwethen*] that he made with the council of the lord as contained in the account of the receiver for the 18th year [1344] because nothing could hence be raised during the time of the account so to be levied in the next account. Sum, 24s.

1351/52

DCO Ministers' Account Roll 6

25–26 Edward III. 20 membranes. Minsters' accounts of the duchy of Cornwall in Cornwall and Devon (mm. 1–15d); accounts of the havener (mm. 16–17d), keeper of fees (mm. 18–18d) and receiver (mm. 20–20d).

(m. 3)

TREMATON

[...]

CONVENTIONARY RENTS OR FARMS

The same responds for [...]. For £10 from the farm of the passage of Saltash Water at Easter and Michaelmas with rents of oars belonging to the same (^ passage) as contained in the preceding account and [...] toll of oysters that is worth 3d each year [...]. Nothing from the farm of the Water and Pool of Sutton that was accustomed to a conventionary lease for £10 because it is leased to John Dabernoun for the term of his life as is rendered below. [...]

FARMS FOR TERMS OF LIVES

The same responds for £6 13s 4d received for the farm of the Water and Pool of Sutton as leased and conceded to John Dabernoun for the duration of the term of his life by letters patent of the lord duke, dated 5 February in the 24th year [1350] as appears in the foot of the account of the 23rd year [1349] which before the pestilence was accustomed to rent for £10 per year. [...]

[...]

(m. 3d)

Sum of all debts [...]. And he owes £29 8s 9d. From which he is exonerated for 66s 8d for part of £18 which he was charged last year for the farm of the borough and passage of Saltash which was abandoned into the hands of the lord after the pestilence and leased by the steward for £14 13s 4d, for which he did not at first have an allowance. And he owes £ 26 2s 1d.

Hence Owing [*Unde Super*]

£17 10s from John Haule farmer of the Water of Sutton by commission of the lord prince for the last part of the 18th year and for the 19th, 20th, and the third part of the 21st years [1344–47]. [...]

Saltash and Trematon boroughs

[...]

Farms

The same responds for [...] customs of the barge and seines with all customs belonging to the said borough, which are valued at 16s per year, leased to the burgesses of the town there before [*coram*] the same Edmund de Kendal and his fellows for the term of 7 years, this year the 5th, reserving to the lord fines of arrests [...] And for £10 from the farm of the passage of Saltash Water thus leased to the sad burgeses for the aforesaid terms and rent of the oars belonging to the aforesaid passage for the aforesaid two terms equally. [...]

Decay of Farms

For 100s in decay of rents or farms of 2 water mills, rents of the *sensar'*[46] of the borough of Trematon, pleas and perquisites of the court of the same borough, toll of oysters and herbage of the castle ditch there, abandoned into the hands of the lord after the pestilence and leased by the auditors and steward until the next assession for 100s per year and first leased ~~with the aforesaid profits~~ for £10. Also 66s 8d in decay of the farm of the borough of Saltash which was farmed out before the pestilence for £8 and farm of the passage which was farmed out before

---

[46.] This was a tax paid by some or all tenants in the borough that was noted as worth 12d per year in 1337; see P. L. Hull, ed., *The Caption of Seisin of the Duchy of Cornwall (1337)*, DCRS, n.s., vol. 17, 1971, p. 119. This tax could also be the same as the *censaria pro libertatem eiusdem manerii habendo*, paid at the rate of 1d per year by persons who livied on Duchy manors without leasing land; see John Hatcher, *Rural Economy and Society in the Duchy of Cornwall 1300–1500* (Cambridge, 1970), p. 219.

the pestilence for £10 as charged above and now leased (for this year) for £14 13s 4d. [...]

[...]

(m. 6)

LOSTWITHIEL

[...]

ISSUES OF THE PORT AND WATER OF FOWEY

And for 9s 6d from the fishery of Fowey Water as contained in the aforesaid indenture against [*contra*] John de Kendal, receiver. And for 5s 4d for 1 quarter of salt coming from the custom of the water of a ship (of strangers) landing in the port of Fowey from which the lord should have 1 bushel from each ship having 20 quarters of salt, and [if] exceeding [20 quarters], 2 bushels by the aforesaid indenture. And for 2s 8d received from keelage of 2 barges belonging to strangers that landed in the said port with salt, by the aforesaid indenture, namely 16d per barge. And for 2s 4d for pleas of the marine court this year by the aforesaid indenture. Sum, 19s 10d.

[...]

(m. 16)

ACCOUNT OF THOMAS FITZ HENRY, KEEPER OF CUSTOMS WHICH ARE CALLED MALTOLT AND COCKET, IN THE COUNTY OF CORNWALL, FROM MICHAELMAS IN THE 25TH REGNAL YEAR OF KING EDWARD III AFTER THE CONQUEST TO THE SAME FEAST IN THE NEXT FOLLOWING, NAMELY THE 26TH.

ISSUES OF COCKET

The same responds for 2s ¾d received from William Kent for 3 dickers and 1 hide carried in a ship called *Gudbeat* of Fowey, of which Hugh Tudy is master, on 12 October. A dicker contains 10 hides whence 20 dickers make a last, 13s 4d taken per last.

And for 15¼d received from William Hor for 1 dicker and 9 hides carried in a ship called *Coghere* of H̶o̶ (Looe) of which Adam Clerk is master, on 7 November.

And for 2s 6½d received from Ralph de Truru for 3 dickers and 8 hides carried in a ship called *Coghere* of which Adam Clerc is master, on 1 November.

And for 9s 3¾d received from John Breton for 14 dickers and 1 hide carried in ship called *Bartholomeu* of Plymouth [*Plemuth*] of which William Lake is master, on 18 N̶o̶v̶e̶m̶b̶e̶r̶ January.

And for 16s from William Caperon for 1 last and 4 dickers carried in a

ship called *la Katerine* of Looe of which William Posman is master,
on 8 December. Sum, 31s 3¼d.

ISSUES OF MALTOLT

The same responds for 21s 1d received from Martin Sankadye, alien,
of Bermeo [*Vermeu*], for custom on £84 8s of salt sold at Falmouth,
namely at 3d per £.

And for 30s received from Peter Jon of Mortrygo [*Mectrigo*], alien, for
custom on £120 of salt sold at Fowey, namely per £ as above.

And for 20s received from Peter Macatre of Bermeo, alien, for custom
on £80 of salt sold at Mousehole, per £ as above.

And for 16s received from *Jonell* Mabile of Guérande [*Garant*] alien
for custom on £64 of salt sold at Falmouth.

And for 15s from John ~~Martines~~ (Matynes) of Bermeo, alien, for custom
on £60 of salt sold at Falmouth.

And for 8s received from *Gracion* Piers of Bilbao [*Bilbau*], alien, for
custom on £32 of salt sold at Mousehole.

And for 2s 6d received from John Piers of Lequeitio [*Laketif*], alien,
for custom on £10 of salt sold there.

And for 6s 3d received from John Otys, alien, for custom on £25 of
salt sold in the same place.

And for 8s 3d received from Peter Skanalus of San Sebastian [*Sebastian*],
alien, for custom on £33 of salt sold in the same place.

And for 16s from John [*Joun*] Flaggard of Bermeo? [*Herneo*] for custom
of £64 of salt sold in the same place.

And for 7s received from Peter Bowygas of Guérande, alien, for custom
on £28 of salt sold in the same place.

And for 6s received from Peter Skanalus of San Sebastian, alien, for
custom of £24 of salt sold in the same place.[47]

Sum, £7 16s 1d.

CUSTOM OF WOOL

Nothing here from the custom on wool because John de Kendale,
receiver, should respond for it by commission of lord made to him
[*inde deb' respond per commiss' domini inde sibi fac'*].

[47.] An X, with dots in each triangle section and a perpendicular line connecting the
top and bottom of the X on the left side, is written in the left-hand margin next
to the bottom line. It is obviously meant as a kind of footnote for the reader to
look below where a similar mark occurs at the marginal heading for FURTHER
ISSUES OF MALTOT.

Sum total received, £9 7s 4¼d, which is charged at the foot of his account for custody of the ports this year. And so he is quit. (He responds.)[48]

(EXTRA [*Ex'*]) FURTHER [*ADHUC*] ISSUES OF MALTOLT
For 20s 11¼d owed to the lord for £83 16s 5d from the price of 19,576 pounds of stamped [*cunat'*] tin [exported] by John Syngham, alien, this year, at the price per thousandweight of tin of £4 6s 8d beyond coinage [*ultra cunag'*] besides [*seu*] 35s 2½d from £140 18s as the price of 32,516 pounds of stamped tin of the same John in the last year, of which the lord should have 3d from each £, he responds for nothing here because the said John says he is a burgess of the lord of Liskeard [*Liskirt*] and Bodmin [*Bodmyn*] and for this reason claims to be quit of this custom, for which he has day to proceed against the custom of the lord before the next account or then to pay custom [*per quod habet diem ad pros' versus cons' domini citra prox' comp' vel solvere tunc custum'*], by pledge of Thomas Goldsmyth, Stephen Trewynt, Stephen Rogg' and John Symond.

(m. 16d)
[blank]

(m. 17)[49]
ACCOUNT OF THOMAS FITZ HENRI, KEEPER OF THE PORTS IN THE COUNTY OF CORNWALL AND PRISAGE OF WINES IN THE SAME COUNTY AND IN SUTTON WATER IN THE COUNTY OF DEVON, AND PROFITS OF THE SAME PORTS IN THE SAME COUNTY OF CORNWALL, AND OF WRECK OF SEA IN THE SAME COUNTY, FROM MICHAELMAS IN THE 25TH REGNAL YEAR OF KING EDWARD III AFTER THE CONQUEST TO THE SAME FEAST IN THE FOLLOWING 26TH YEAR OF THE SAME KING.

FARMS OF PORTS
The same responds for 46s 8d from the farm of the port of Marazion to be paid each year at the feasts of Easter and Michaelmas equally. And for 12s from the farm of the port of Penzance at the same terms. And (for) 20s from the farm of the port of Newlyn each year at the same terms. And for 100s from the farm of the port (of) Mousehole

---

[48.] "r" for "he responds" is written in the left-hand margin.
[49.] *Dupl'* is written in the top left-hand margin.

each year at the same terms. And for 12d from the farm of the port of
Lamorna each year at the same terms. And for 2s from the farm of the
port of Porthgwarra each year at the same terms, which is accustomed
to rent each year for 12s, and no more this year for lack of men and
boats because of the pestilence. And for 2s from the farm of the port of
'Porthplement' at the same terms, and it is accustomed to pay each
year 8s, and no more for the aforesaid cause. And for 40s from the
farm of the port of Fowey each year at the same terms. And for 25s
from the farm of the ports of Kerrier each year at the same terms. And
for 20s from the farm of the port of Polruan each year at the same
terms. And for 20s from the farm of the ports of Trigg at the same
terms. And for 60s from the farm of the port of St Ives at the same
terms, which is accustomed to pay £6, and no more this year for the
aforesaid cause. Nothing this year from the farm of the port of
Porthzennor and Portheras for the aforesaid cause, and they are
accustomed to pay (^ each year) 6s 8d. Sum, £17 8s 8d.

Sale of Wines

The same responds for £163 6s 8d received from 35 tuns of red wine
sold, at £4 13s 4d per tun. And for £21 6s 8d received from 4 tuns of
which, of which 2 tuns are red Gascon wine and 2 tuns are wine of
Spain, namely 1 tun white and the other red, at the price of 106s 8d for
each tun. And for £4 from the price of 2 tuns of wine conceded to
Peter de Gildesburgh by the lord, at the same price that the lord pays
for wines from prisage, as contained in letters of the lord directed to
the same keeper, as subtracted in the wines given to the same Peter.
Sum, £188 13s 4d.

Wreck of Sea

The same responds for 3s 4d arising from 1 mast, retained a long time
for lack of buyers, which came from a wreck in the port of Falmouth,
and no more because it will be sold [*vendebatur*] for 6s 8d, from which
was delivered 3s 4d to diverse men for salvage of the said mast. Nothing
from 1 boat arising from a wreck at Gwendra [*Wyndreth*] because
plundered [*dirupt'*] and taken away by tenants of John Lercedekne. So
to be distrained to make fine before the next account. Nothing from 5
chasubles with 5 pairs of parures of bordelisaundre[50] [*v inful' cum v*

---

50. Parures were a type of ecclesiastical vestment, and bordilsaundre was a type of
striped silk, named after its supposed affiliation with Alexandria.

paribus parur' de Bourdealisaundr'] and 1 coffer arising from a wreck in the parish of St Goran [*Sancti Goroni*] because they remain to be sold for lack of buyers. Sum, 3s 4d.

FINES OF MERCHANTS WITH TRANTERY
The same responds for 13s 4d received from fines of merchants with trantery this year. Sum, 13s 4d.

PERQUISITES OF MARITIME COURTS
And for 16s 3d from pleas and perquisites of maritime courts this year. Nothing from forfeited chattels because nothing arose this year. Sum, 16s 3d.

Sum total received, £207 15s 3d.

WAGES AND FEES
The same accounts for wages of the same Thomas Fitz Henri from Michaelmas in the 25th year until the same feast in the next following 26th year for one whole year, £6 13s 4d. And for his 1 robe conceded to him by charter of the lord king for the term of his life, for 13s 4d. (Cancelled because it was ordered at Berkhamstead on 25 January in the 23rd year 1349] that there was no allowance for a robe for anyone as contained in a certain schedule under seal of the lord directed to the auditor. {allowed in the previous account} Sum, £6 13s 4d.

MONEY PAID FOR ASSIZE OF WINE
The same accounts for payment of £38 for assize on 19 tuns of wine taken from diverse merchants, at 40s per tun, and no more because 24 tuns similiarly from prisage are quit. Sum, £38.

The same accounts for 2s (12d) for towage of 12 tuns of wine taken at Plymouth from ships to land, at 2d (1d) per tun. And 3s (2s) for rollage of said tuns from the sea to the cellar, at 3d (2d) per tun. Also 9s (5s 7½d) in hire of a certain cellar for placing said wines in from 4 October to 13 April for 27 weeks, at 4d (2½d) per week.
Also 14d for towage of 14 tuns at Fowey, at 1d per tun. Also 3s 6d (2s 4d) for rollage of said tuns from the sea to the cellar, at 3d (2d) per tun. Also 9s (5s 7½d) for hire of 1 cellar for placing said wines in from 4 October to 12 April for 27 weeks, at 4d (2d) per week.
2d for towage of 2 tuns at Looe from ship to land, at 1d per tun. For 12d (6d) rollage of said tuns from sea to the cellar, at 6d (3d for bad

carriage) [*pro male portu*] per tun. Also ~~12d~~ (6d) for hire of one cellar for placing said wines in from 29 March to 19 April for 3 weeks, at ~~4d~~ (2d) per week.

Also ~~16s 3d~~ (2s 6d) for towage of 15 tuns taken at Falmouth from a ship to land, at ~~13d~~ (2d) per tun. Also ~~5s~~ (2s 8d) for rollage of said tuns from the sea to the cellar, at ~~5d~~ (3d) per tun, as in the aforesaid account. Also ~~14s 4d~~ (7s 2d) for hire of 1 cellar for placing said wines in from 7 October to 5 August for 43 weeks, at ~~4d~~ (2d) per week, as in the aforesaid account.

Also 9s for 18 gallons of wine for ullage of 4 tuns from the first seizure [*de' prima capt'*] at Plymouth kept in the cellar from 4 October to 6 December, when they were sold, for 9 weeks, priced at <u>6d</u> per gallon. And 6s for 12 gallons of wine for ullage of another 8 tuns from 6 December to 13 April, for 18 weeks, priced at <u>6d</u> per gallon.

Also for 2d for 2 gallons of wine for ullage of 2 tuns at Looe, priced at 6d per gallon.

Also 7s 6d for 15 gallons of wine for ullage of 3 tuns at Fowey from the first seizure, from 4 October to 13 December, for 10 weeks, when they were sold, priced at <u>6d</u> per gallon. Also 7s for 14 gallons of wine for ullage of another 11 tuns there (from) 13 December to 12 April, for 17 weeks, priced at <u>6d</u> per gallon.

Also 2s for 4 gallons for ullage of 1 tun from first seizure at Falmouth, from 7 October to 2 December, when they were sold, for 8 weeks, priced at <u>6d</u> per gallon. And 20s for 40 gallons of wine for ullage of another 14 tuns there from 2 December to 5 August, for 36 weeks, before which last day they were sold, priced at <u>6d</u> per gallon.

Sum, £4 3s 9d.

Sum of all expenses, £48 17s 1d. And he owes £158 18s 2d. And £13 8s 9¼ remains from his account of his office of customer from last year [*de rem' compi' sui sui cons' de offo' de anno ulterio praeter'*]. And £9 7s 4¼d remains from his account for custody of the cocket in Cornwall for this year. Sum of common debts, £181 14s 3½d. From which he delivers £179 5s 4d to John de Kendale, receiver of the lord prince of Wales in the county of Cornwall and Devon, by sealed indenture under the seal of the said receiver delivered on account. And he owes 48s 9½d.

RESPITED

From which are respited to him, 34s 1d from diverse particulars disallowed above for custom of wines, because the steward is one of the justices in Cornwall and Devon for punishing the excesses of artisans, he indicated he would remit the said excess if the said keeper wanted to be discharged [*pro excesus artific' puniend' pretendit dictum excessum resolvere si dictus custos exequi voluerit*]. And he still owes 14s 10½d.

(m. 17d)[51]

PLYMOUTH

The same responds for 12 tuns of red wine taken from a ship landing there, of which 10 for assize and 2 quit, as contained in the controlment of Henry de Totham, attorney of William Baccoun, controller of prisage of wines [and] cocket, delivered on account containing all particulars written below, testified by oath of said the Henry, namely:

From a ship called *Seint Maribot* of Dartmouth, of which Richard Matheu is master, 2 tuns of red wine, on 4 October.

From 2 ships of Hull whose masters' names and copies of charters and their dates are lost [*amisit*] by the attorney of the same keeper, 2 tuns of red wine, quit, taken from beyond the port at the Island of Saint Nicholas [*Insula Sct' Nichi'*], where ships are not required to pay, by virtue of an agreement made between the keeper and merchants.

From a ship called *cog Johan* of Plymouth, of which Richard Brustakes is master, 2 tuns of red wine, on 19 December.

From a ship called *Edward* of Plymouth of which Robert Pole is master, 2 tuns of red wine, on the same day.

From a ship called *Edward* of Plymouth of which Robert Pole is master, 2 tuns of red wine, on 29 March.

From a ship called *Holman* of Plymouth of which Richard Brustakes is master, 2 tuns red wine, on the same day.

Sum, 12 tuns of wine. (The keeper is ordered to sell all wines coming from prisage from Michaelmas until the feast of St Martin [11 November]).[52]

[FOWEY]

The same responds for 14 tuns of wine taken from a ship docking there of which 12 for assize and 2 quit, namely:

A ship called *le Pedrok* of Dartmouth of which John Boys is master, 1 tun of red wine, quit, taken beyond the port by agreement between the keeper and merchants, on 4 October.

[51.] The writing on this dorse reads from the bottom of membrane to the top.
[52.] This sentence is written in the left-hand margin at the end of this section.

From a ship called *cog John* of Dartmouth of which John Wyndstowe is master, 2 tuns of red wine, on the same day.

From a ship called *Seintespirit* of Bordeaux [*Burdens*] of which William Kunc is master, 1 tun red wine, on 16 December, taken within [*infra*] the port from 16 tuns existing in the same ship, from a merchant of Haverfordwest [*Hareford*] for the lord's custom of assize.

From a ship called *Seintsavorescok* of Fowey, of which Richard Mighelstowe is master, 2 tuns of red wine, on 31 December.

From a ship called *Seint Mariecog* of Fowey of which James Taxcinon (^ is master), 2 tuns of wine, on 24 December.

From a ship called *le Katerine* of Polruan of which William Botsweyn is master, 2 tuns of red wine, on 28 December.

From a ship called *Nicholas* of Polruan of which Hamelin Jacob is master, 2 tuns of red wine, on 4 January.

From a ship called *Seint Maricog* of Fowey of which Nicholas Cok is master, on 29 March, 2 tuns of red wine.

Sum, 14 tuns of wine.

LOOE

The same responds for 2 tuns of red wine taken from a ship called *cog Thomas* of Looe docking there, of which Adam Clerc is master, on 29 March. Sum, 2 tuns of red wine.

FALMOUTH

The same responds for 15 tuns of wine taken from ships landing there, of which 14 tuns for assize and 1 tun of red wine quit. Namely:

From a ship called *Seintespirit* of Bayonne [*Baone*], of which Arnulph Ganderas is master, on 7 October, 1 tun red wine taken outside [*extra*] the port. For 12 tuns taken, kept in the same ship, from the chattels of a certain English merchant and the rest of the wine of the same ship from a Gascon merchant who pays nothing but for each tun, 2s, whether they were unloaded or not unloaded in Cornwall [*De 12 dol' capt' exist' in eadem navi de cat' mercator' Anglic' et resid' vini eiusdem navis de mercator' vascon' qui null' solv' set de quolibet dol' 2s ubi discarcantur et non discarat' fuer' in Cornub'*].

From a ship called *Seintmaricog* of Dartmouth of which Henry de la Suerie is master, 2 tuns of red wine, on 20 December.

From a ship called *Nicholas* of Teignmouth [*Tegmuth*], of which John Gras is master, 2 tuns of red wine, on 23 December.

From a ship called *cog Johan* of Endleford [*Endelforth*][53] of which John Gerles is master, 2 tuns of red wine, on the same day.

From a ship called *cog Johan* of the Forest of Dean? [*Forest*],[54] of which Thomas Cook is master, 2 tuns of red wine, on 30 December.

From a ship called *la Trinite* of Bristol, of which Roger Langele is master, 2 tuns of red wine, on 31 December.

From a ship called *le James* of Tenby [*Tynbugh*], of which William Huchon is master, 2 tuns of red wine, on the same day.

From a ship called *Seintanton* of Castrourdiales [*Castr'*] of which Simon Dys is master, 2 tuns of Spanish wine of which 1 white and the other red, on 12 April.

Sum, 15 tuns of wine of which 1 white from Spain and 14 red of which 1 from Spain.

PADSTOW

Nothing this year from prisage of wines in the port there because no ships docked with wine there this year.

MOUSEHOLE

Nothing this year from prisage of wines in the port there, for the aforesaid reason.

Sum of all wines, 43 tuns of which 1 white and 42 red.

From which is delivered to Peter de Gildesburgh as a gift from the lord, 2 tuns of red wine, priced at 106s 8d per tun, by letters of the lord directed to the same Thomas le Havener which are dated 18 April in the 26th year (which letters remain between the middle [of the account?] of this year [*que lettera rem' inter med' de hoc anno*], and, by these same letters, he has the tuns for the sale price that the lord pays for prisage. In sale of 41 tuns of wine of which 1 white and 40 red, of which 1 from Spain. Sum, 43 tuns. And none remains.

(m. 19)

ACCOUNT OF JOHN DE KENDALE, RECEIVER OF THE LORD EDWARD, PRINCE OF WALES, DUKE OF CORNWALL AND EARL OF CHESTER [...]
[...]

---

53. Two ships from Endleford visited Bristol in 1378–9; see E. M. Carus-Wilson, *The Overseas Trade of Bristol* (Bristol Record Society, 1937), pp. 181, 188.

54. A ship from Forest visited Bristol in 1378; see Carus-Wilson, *Bristol*, p. 184.

ISSUES OF THE PORTS AND WRECK

The same responds for £179 5s 4d received from Thomas filz Henri, keeper of the ports during the said time. Sum, £179 5s 4d.

[...]

CUSTOMS ...

The same responds for ~~75s 9d~~ (77s 1d) received from John de Kendale now accounting for the keeper and receiver of customs of wool and fells by commission of the lord prince during the time of the account. Customs ... overseas ~~this year~~ taking 20s per sack (^this year) by ordinance of the council of the lord as contained in letters patent. John de Kendale, receiver, hence made enrollment in his account for the same custom last year, namely, 33s 1d from William Caperoun for 1½ sack and 8 cloves of wool. And 13s 4d from William Northill for ½ sack 8 cloves of wool. 30s 11d from William Odom for 1½ sacks 17 pounds of wool as contained in the controlment of William Baccon, delivered on account. Sum, 77s 1d.

[...]

1352/53

PRO, SC6/817/3

26–27 Edward III. 19 membranes. Ministers' accounts of the duchy of Cornwall in Cornwall and Devon (mm. 1–16); accounts of the havener (mm. 17–19d). The receiver's account for this year is in PRO, SC6/ 812/6.

(m. 2d)

TREMATON

FARMS AT TERMS OF LIVES

[...] And for £6 13s 4d received from the farm of the Water and Pool of Sutton as conceded and leased to John Dabernoun by the lord for the term of his life by virtue of letters patent of the same lord duke dated 5 February in the 24th year [1350] as appears in the foot of the account of the 23rd year [1349] which before the pestilence was accustomed to lease for £10 per year. [...]

[...]

DECAYED RENTS

For 2s 6d in decay of the farm of the fishery of Lynher Water that

Richard Jeul, Nicholas Priour and Aunger Walter recently held in conventionary tenure, relinquished into the hands of the lord because of the pestilence because it was leased and is accustomed to render 5s. Sum, 2s 6d.

HENCE OWING [*UNDE SUPER*]

£17 10s from John Haule, farmer of Sutton Water by commission of the lord prince for the last part of the 18th year and the 19th, 20th years and the third part of the 21st year [1344–7]. [...]
[...]

SALTASH AND TREMATON BOROUGH

RECEIPTS

[...] £8 received from the rent of farm of the borough, which [includes] 16s rent of the barge, seines with other customs belonging to the said burgesses for 7 years, this year the 6th [...] and £10 for the farm of the passage of Saltash Water leased to the burgesses for the said terms, with rent of 4 oars [...].
[...]

DECAY OF RENTS

For 100s in decay of rents or farms for 2 water mills, pleas and perquisites of the court of the same borough, toll of oysters, and herbage of the castle ditch remain in the the hands of the lord after the pestilence and are leased by the auditors and steward until the next assession for 100s per year, and earlier they were leased with other profits as above for £10. And 60s in decay of the farm of the borough of Saltash which was farmed out before the pestilence for £8 and farm of the passage which was farmed out before the pestilence for £10 as charged above and now leased this year for £15. [...]
[...]

(m. 6)

LOSTWITHIEL

ISSUES OF THE PORT AND WATER OF FOWEY

And for 8s 3d from 2 quarters 6 bushels of salt coming from custom on 11 ships landing in the port of Fowey this year, taking 4 bushels from each ship, priced at 4½d per bushel. Nothing from wheat or other corn or any bushellage measure [*mensurand' cum bz*] arising from similar customs, namely from each ship as above, because none landed. And for 53s 4d received from the fishery of Fowey Water from Michaelmas to the feast of Easter by tally of John Hora, mayor of the aforesaid town. And for 13d from the same fishery from the same feast of Easter to Michaelmas as contained in an indenture against [*contra*] John de Kendale, receiver. And for 4s from keelage of 3 foreign barges [*barbiag' extranearum*] landing in the said port with diverse merchandise from Michaelmas to Easter as contained in the aforesaid indenture agianst John Hora, at 16d from each barge. And for 9s 4d from keelage of 7 foreign barges landing in the said port from the said feast of Easter to Michaelmas as contained in an indenture of John de Kendal, amount per barge as above. And for 8d from pleas and perquisites of the maritime court this year as contained in the said indenture. Sum, 76s 8d.

(m. 17)

ACCOUNT OF THOMAS FITZ HENRI, KEEPER OF THE PORTS IN THE COUNTY OF CORNWALL AND PRISAGE OF WINES IN THE SAME COUNTY AND IN SUTTON WATER IN THE COUNTY OF DEVON AND ISSUES OF THE PORTS IN THE SAME COUNTY OF CORNWALL AND WRECK OF SEA IN THE SAME COUNTY, FROM MICHAELMAS IN THE 16TH REGNAL YEAR OF KING EDWARD TO THE SAME FEAST FOLLOWING IN THE 27TH YEAR OF THE SAME KING.

FARMS OF PORTS

The same responds for 46s 8d for the farm of the port of Marazion per year at the feasts of Easter and Michaelmas equally. And for 12s from the farm of the port of Penzance per year at the same terms. And for 20s for the farm of the port of Newlyn per year at the same terms. And for 100s from the farm of the port of Mousehole per year at the same terms. And for 12d from the farm of the port of Lamorna per year at the same terms. And for 2s from the farm of the port of Porthgwarra [*Porgorwetheu*] per year at the same terms which is accustomed to render per year 12s and no more this year because of lack of men and boats because of the pestilence. And for 2s from the farm of the port of 'Porthplement' per year at the same terms, which was accustomed to rent per year at 8s, and no more this year for the aforesaid reason. And for 40s from the farm of the port of Fowey per year at the same terms. And for 25s from the farm of the ports of Kerrier per year at the same terms. And for 20s from the farm of the port of Polruan per year at the same terms. And for 20s from the farm of the ports of Trigg per year at the same terms. And for £4 from the farm of the port of St Ives per year at the same terms, which was accustomed to render per year £6 and no more this year for the aforesaid reason. Nothing from the 6s 8d for the farm of the ports of Portzennor [*Portcenear*] and Portheras this year because of the pestilence. Sum, £18 8s 8d.

CUSTOM OF WINES

The s ame responds for 6s received from strangers [*extran'*] for customs on 3 tuns of wine sold in the port of Padstow. And for 66s 8d received from a fine on a certain shipmaster of a ship of Tenby [*Tynby*] called *la Trinite* of Tenby made before the steward for breaking arrest made by him in the port of Falmouth with a ship loaded with wines from the victuals of the earl of Stafford [*carcat' cum vinis de victual' com' Stafford*]. Sum, 72s 8d.

SALE OF WINES

The same responds for £188 received from 47 tuns of wine of which 43 tuns [are] red Gascon wine and 4 tuns Spanish white, priced at £4 per tun. And for £37 6s 8d received from 8 tuns of red Gascon wine priced at £4 13s 4d per tun. And for £18 received from 3 tuns of red Gascon wine sold at the price of £6 per tun. And for 66s 8d from 1 tun of Gascon wine sold because it lost color and wine because of shaking? [*tonutr'*]. And for £6 13s 4d for 2 tuns of *borect'* wine sold at 66s 8d per tun. And for 43s 4d from 1 tun of Spanish wine. And for ~~100s~~ (£10) from 5 tuns of wine of prisage conceded to Peter de Gillesbourg for the price that a merchant is held to pay as contained in letters of the lord directed to the same keeper enrolled on the back of this account in the possession of the same keeper, who responds because said Peter claims to have the same tuns for 100s. Sum, £265 10s.

WRECK OF SEA

The same responds for 22s coming from 1 partly-filled tun of white wine from wreck in Mount's Bay [*le Mountesbaie*] and no more because it was sold for 44s from which 22s will be delivered to diverse men for salvage of the same tun. And for 26s 8d coming from 1 partly-filled tun of red wine arising from a wreck in the port of Padstow and no more because it was sold for 53s 4d from which 26s 8d was delivered to diverse men for salvage of the same tun. And for 6s 8d coming from 1 partly-filled hogshead arising from a wreck in the lordship of Sir William de Bodrigan and no more because it was sold for 14s 4d from which 6s 8d will be delivered to diverse men for salvage of the same. And for 9d coming from 1 broken-down boat arising from a wreck at Trerose? [*Treuros*] and no value except as firewood? [*nullus prec' pret' focal'*] which sold for 18d from which 9d was delivered as above. And for 9s from one-half of the sale price of 9 chasubles of bordelisaundre silk with parures, maniples, and stoles cut from them? [*casularum de brodalisaundr' cum parur' maniculis et stol' de eadem secca*] arising from a wreck discovered in a certain coffer in the sea of the parish of St Goran in Powder [*Sancti Geran' in Poudr'*] and the other one-half given for salvage. Sum, 65s 1d.[55]

FINES OF MERCHANTS WITH TRANTERY

And for 37s 2d from fines of two merchants of Waterford of Ireland for a certain rescue [*recursu*] made by them on the ministers of the lord in the port of Mousehole and no more because John Darundel, bailiff of that hundred[56] had 2s 2d from them as part of 40d for an amercement he had levied on them. And for 28s 4d received from fines of merchants with trantery this year. Sum, 65s 2d.

PERQUISITES OF MARITIME COURTS

The same responds for 39s 4d from perquisites of the maritime court this year. Sum, 39s 4d.

Sum total of receipts, £196 23d.[57] Thence [*Inde*]

WAGES AND FEES

The same accounts for £6 13s 4d paid to him for his wages and fee from Michaelmas in the 26th year to the same feast in the 27th year for one whole year. ~~And for 13s 4d for his robe conceded to him by charter of the lord king for the term of his life~~ (cancelled because it is was forbidden by the council of the lord at Berkhamstead on 25 January in the 23rd year that nothing was to be allowed for any robe as contained in a certain schedule under the seal of the lord directed to the auditors as alleged in the preceding account). Sum, £6 13s 4d.

---

55. Wreck profits are also noted elsewhere in this account. For the manor of Tintagel, 7d from wreck of sea is recorded under PERQUISITES OF COURT (m. 13). In the account for the hundred of Lesnewth, 12d from wreck of sea is noted under RECEIPTS (m. 15).
56. The receiver's account in SC6/812/6 (m. 1) notes that 'And for 37s 10d received from the same keeper for fines of 2 merchants of Waterford of Ireland and no more because John Darundell, bailiff of Penwith [*Pen'*] hundred has 2s 2d from the same as part of a 40d amercement of the same for hue [*hutes*] raised on them by the hand of Benedict Vyuyan'.
57. The receiver's account in PRO, SC6/812/6 (m. 1) notes total receipts from the ports and cocket as £219 3d.

CUSTOM OF WINES

The same pays £50 to diverse merchants for 25 tuns of wine taken from them for assize, at 40s per tun.

CARE OF WINES

In 2s 8d for towage of 8 tuns at Plymouth carried from St Nicholas Island beyond the port for the space of one league by sea to land, <u>at 4d</u> per tun, and he used to give 2d. Also for16d for towage of 8 tuns of wine from the sea port to land, at <u>2d</u> per tun, and he used to give 1d. Also 4s for rollage of the same from the sea to the cellar, and he used to give <u>2d</u> per tun. Also 8s for the lease of a cellar for storing the said wines from 30 October to 16 April for 24 weeks and ... days, at <u>4d</u> per week, and he used to give <u>2½d</u>.

Also 16d in towage of 16 tuns taken for prisage in the port of Fowey from the sea to land for <u>1d</u> per tun.

Also 8d for towage of 8 tuns at Fowey coming from Plymouth, at <u>1d</u> per tun. Also 6s for rollage of said 24 tuns from the sea to the cellar, at <u>3d</u> per tun, and he used to give 2d. Also 7s 8d for lease of a cellar for storing said wine from 7 November to 16 April for 23 weeks and 2 days, at <u>4d</u> per week, and he used to give <u>2d</u>.

Also 19s for towage of 19 tuns at Falmouth from the sea to land for the space of 2 leagues, at 12d per tun, and he used to give <u>2d</u>. Also 4s 10d for rollage of the same from the sea to the cellar, at 3d per tun. Also 7s 8d for lease of a cellar for storing the said wine from 5 November to 16 April for 23 weeks, at <u>4d</u> per week, and he used to give <u>2d</u>.

Also 4s for towage of 4 tuns at Padstow towed by 3 boats breaking free from their towage by destruction of a tempest and ...? from the sea to land [*towat' per iii batell' corumpant' eord' towag' distrie' tempest' et ...fer predict' de mar' usque terram*], at <u>12d</u> per tun. Also 10d for rollage of the same from the sea to the cellar, at 2½d per tun.

Also 12d for towage of 1 tun from Newlyn to Mousehole and 4d for rollage of the same. And 9d for lease of a cellar for the same for three weeks, at <u>3d</u> per week.

Also 4s for rollage of 11 tuns at Plymouth and leakage [*lecag'*] of the same from 1 September to ... when sold. And delivery of 90 gallons of wine, at <u>6d</u> per gallon, because 2 tuns lacking [*lecat'*] and ... tuns which were delivered to Sir Peter de Gildesbourgh from the same wine existing in the custody of the keeper until 13 ....

Also 18s for 36 gallons of wine in ullage of 9 tuns at Fowey during the said time, at <u>6d</u> per gallon. Also 12d for 2 staves placed into one defective tun. Also 6d for 6 barrel hoops for the same and 4s for 6 gallons of wine for ullage of the same tuns of wine, priced at <u>6d</u> per gallon. And 2d for carriage for a porter for lifting the said tun for repair. Also 2s 6d for 5 gallons for leakage [*lecage*] of another tun defective in 1 stave, priced at <u>6d</u> per gallon. Also 2s for 6 barrel hoops [*circulis*] for the same tun and for a porter to lift the same tun for repair.

Also 22s 6d for 45 gallons of wine for ullage of 15 tuns of wine at Falmouth, priced at <u>6d</u> per gallon. Also 4s 4d for 8½ gallons for leakage [*locage*] of 1 tun there, priced at <u>6d</u> per gallon. And 8d? for 8 barrel hoops for the same and 2d for a porter to lift the same for repair.

Also ... for ullage of 5 tuns at Plymouth from 25 March to 10 June. Also 13s 9d for 27½ gallons for 11 weeks more when not sold [*pro 11 sept' ultra non vend'*], just short of [*citra*] the view of account, priced at <u>6d</u> per gallon. Also 2s 4d for hire of a cellar from 18 April for 7 weeks and 4 days for storing the said tuns, at <u>4d</u> per week.

Also 28s 3d for 56½ gallons for ullage and leakage of 5 tuns at Fowey from the seizure of remaining vintage wines [*de captione vendage' remanent'*], unsold because of lack of buyers, on the other side [*ultra*] of the view of account, namely from 6 November before sold, for 22 weeks and for 25 weeks, priced at <u>6d</u> per gallon. Also 15s for 30 gallons for ullage of 8 tuns from wine of La Rochelle [*Roich'*], there from 7 March before sold, for 7 weeks, priced at <u>6d</u> per gallon. Also 8d for hire of a cellar for storing said wine from 18 April until the day it was sold, for 2 weeks, at 4d per week.

Also 7s 6d for 15 gallons of wine for ullage and leakage of 2 tuns at Falmouth from 5 March to 19 June, piced at <u>6d</u> per gallon. Also 6d for repair [*ad r'batend'*] of the same and 4s 6d for 9 gallons for ullage and leakage of the same, priced at <u>6d</u> per gallon. Also 3s for leasing a cellar for 9 weeks for storing the said wine, at <u>4d</u> per week.

Also 5s for 14 gallons of wine for ullage of 4 tuns at Padstow from 2 April to 21 May for 7 weeks, priced at <u>6d</u> per gallon and 21d in hire of a cellar for the same per the same account, at <u>4d</u> per week.

Also 12d for 1 gallon for ullage of 8 tuns at Mousehole, priced at 4d per gallon. Sum, £12 15s 4d.

Sum of all expenses, £69 8s 8d. And he owes £226 13s 3d. And 48s 11½d remains on his account from last year. And £14 20¼d remaining from his account for customs of cocket and maltolt in Cornwall for this year. Sum owed together, £243 3s 10¾d. From which he delivers £217 2s 5d to John de Kendal, receiver of monies of the lord prince in the counties of Cornwall and Devon for issues of his bailiwick for this year, by recognizance of said receiver and by indenture sealed with his seal and delivered on account. And 14s 10½d to the same reciever from the remainder of his account of last year to the same receiver by bill. And he owes £25 6s 7¼d. From which 34s 1d is allowed to him from diverse particulars of customs of wines he affixed with a seal last year and there disallowed because he could not make less expenses and care than he accounted for as he asserts by his oath [*quia minis facere expen' et custus non potuit quam computauit ut asserit per sacrum suum*]. And he owes £23 12s 6¼d. From which he delivers 37s 10d to the receiver for fines of 2 merchants of Waterford in Ireland by the hand of Benedict Fyman. And he owes £21 14s 8d.

100s of the aforesaid arrears are respited to the same keeper until the next assession for part of £10 which is charged above in the title for the sale of wines for the price of 5 tuns of wine granted to Peter de Gildesburgh by letters of the lord directed to the same keeper, until the council of the lord decides whether or not to pay 40s per tun [*quousque scrutiatur per consilum dom' ut solvere pro dol' 40s necne?*]. And he owes £16 14s 8¼d, for which he demonstrates ability to pay, so etc... [*ad quos ostend' debitor' suffic' ideo etc...*].

(m. 17d)

RECEIPTS OF WINES

PLYMOUTH

The same responds for 27 tuns of wine of which 25 red Gascon and 2 tuns white, taken from ships landing there, of which 8 for assize and 19 tuns quit as contained in the counter-roll of Henry de Tottham, attorney of William de Batte, controller of prisage of wines and cocket delivered on account containing all the particulars written below, certified by the oath of the same H., namely:

2 tuns of red wine on 29 October, from a ship called *la Nicholas* of Lympstone? [*Lunucton*] of which Robert Toterich is master.

1 tun of red wine on 2 November from a ship called *la Seintanton* of Santander [*Seintandreu*] of which Martin Gosseles is master, taken outside the port in the St Nicholas Island because ships there are not obliged to pay by agreement made between the keeper and merchants.

1 tun of red wine on the same day from a ship called *Blithe* of Hull of which Robert de Jernemouthe is master, taken in the same place for the same reason.

2 tuns of red wine taken at Looe (on the same day) from a ship called *Laurens* of Hull of which William Kelyng is master for the aforesaid reason.

2 tuns of red wine taken on the same day in the same place for the same reason from a ship called *la Constance* of Dartmouth, of which William Brilemere is master.

1 tun of red wine taken on the same day in the same place and for the same reason from a ship called *le Gaynepain* of Harwich of which Richard Prior is master.

1 tun of red wine on the same day in the same place and for the same reason from a ship called *la Katerine* of Ipswich of which Robert Warner is master.

1 tun of red wine on the same day in the same place and for the same reason from a ship called *Seint Marie cog* of Dartmouth of which Henry Sueweri is master.

1 tun of red wine on 6 November in the aforesaid place and for the aforesaid reason from a ship called *Cog John* of Exmouth of which John Saundre is master.

1 tun of red wine on the same day in the aforesaid place for the aforesaid reason from a ship called *Magdalene* of Ipswich of which Thomas Gaunt is master.

1 tun of red wine on 9 November taken in the aforesaid place and for the aforesaid reason from a ship called *Seint Anton* of Bermeo of which Peter Martyn is master.

1 tun of red wine on 21 November taken in the aforesaid place for the aforesaid reason from a ship called *Cog John* of Maldon of which Robert Kendale is master.

2 tuns of red wine on 2 November from a ship called *le Bartholemeu* of Plymouth of which Robert Pole is master.

1 tun of red wine on the same day from a ship called *le Nicholas* of Plymouth of which Hugh Bourgois is master.

2 tuns of red wine on 20 November from a ship called *le Katerine* of Youghal [*Yeachel*] of which William Godok is master.

2 tuns of white wine on 24 December from a ship called *Seint Martin* of Mortrygo [*Mortrike*] of which John Mendar is master.

2 tuns of red wine on 25 March from a ship called *la Nicholas* of Lymington of which John Vour is master.

2 tuns of red wine on 26 March from a ship called *Edward* of Plymouth of which Richard Stonhous is master.

2 tuns of red wine on 28 March from a ship called *Cog Johan* of Plymouth of which Richard Crop is master.

FOWEY

The same responds for 16 tuns of red Gascon wine taken from ships landing there of which <u>7 tuns</u> for assize and <u>9 tuns</u> quit, namely:

<u>2 tuns</u> of red wine on 7 November from a ship called *Seintmariecog* of Fowey of which James Taxmon is master.

<u>2 tuns</u> of red wine on the same day from a ship called *Seintmariecog* of Polruan of which John Loveck is master.

<u>2 tuns</u> of red wine on 26 November from a ship called *Savoie* of Polruan of which Thomas John is master.

1 tun of red wine on 28 November from a ship called *le Gudbeat* of Fowey of which William Bodier is master.

<u>1 tun</u> of red wine taken on 8 March from <u>16 tuns</u> in *le Jonete* of Dartmouth of which Thomas Chernemouth is master, for consideration [*cons'*] of the auditors and the steward of the lord.

<u>2 tuns</u> of red wine on 29 March from a ship called *la Savoie* of Polruan of which Thomas John is master.

<u>2 tuns</u> of red wine on the same day from a ship called *Seintmariecog* of Fowey of which William Bodier is master.

<u>1 tun</u> of red wine on 20 March from a ship called *Seintmariecog* of Polruan of which Richard Wymark is master.

<u>1 tun</u> of red wine taken on the same day from 10 tuns and 4 pipes in ship called *James* of Fowey of which John Withia is master for consideration of the auditors and steward of the lord.

LOOE

Nothing presented of wines there because no wines landed this year.

FALMOUTH

The same responds for 19 tuns of wine of which <u>17 tuns</u> of red wine of which <u>2 tuns</u> of *borect'* wine (^ of Bayonne) and <u>15 tuns</u> Gascon and <u>2 tuns</u> Spanish white wine of which <u>7 tuns</u> for assize and <u>11 tuns</u> quit, taken there from diverse ships, namely:

<u>2 tuns</u> of white Spanish wine on 2 November from a ship called *le Vessel Seintmarie* of Bermeo of which John Pers is master.

2 tuns of red *de borect'* wine on 16 January from a ship called *le Neif Seintmarie* of Bayonne of which Martin Saar? [Daar?] is master.

2 tuns of red wine on 16 January from a ship called *Seintcespiru'* of Bayonne of which John de la Haneat is master.

1 tun of red wine on 4 March taken by agreement between the merchant and the keeper so that they will not hinder one another [*pro convent'*

inter mercator' et custod' ne impederent alius de eorum] from a ship called *Peter billing* of Yarmouth of which Nicholas Thorp is master.

2 tuns of red wine on the same day from a ship called *le Margarete* of Shoreham of which William Conyng is master.

2 tuns of red wine on the same day from a ship called *Cog Thomas* of Dartmouth of which Henry Randolf is master.

1 tun of red wine on 6 March for the same reason from a ship called *le Nicholas* of Plymouth of which Hugh Bourgeis is master.

1 tun of red wine on 5 March for the same reason from a ship called *le Mighel* of Maidstone of which Denis Stephen is master.

1 tun of red wine on the same day from a ship called *la Rose* of Yarmouth of which Robert Hakmon is master.

2 tuns of red wine on the same day from a ship called *le Gerland* of Yarmouth of which Walter Southfeld is master.

2 tuns of red wine on the same day from a ship called *le Bartholomeu* of Plymouth of which Robert Joole is master.

PADSTOW

The same responds for 4 tuns of red Gascon wine taken there from 2 ships landing there of which 2 tuns for assize and 2 tuns quit, namely:

2 tuns of red wine on 2 April from a ship called *Cog Johan* of Dartmouth of which John de Milton is master.

2 tuns of red wine on the same day from a ship called *Cog Johan* of Dublin [*Develyn*] of which John Weymouth is master.

MOUSEHOLE

The same responds for 1 tun of red Spanish wine quit and no more because a second tun not valued for assize because of the weakness of the wine coming there on the last day of August from a certain ship called *Seintemariecog* of Castrourdiales [*Castr'*] of which John Kybon is master.

Sum of all wines, 67 tuns of which 60 tuns Gascon red, 1 tun Spanish red, 2 tuns *Borect'* red, 4 tuns Spanish white.

And he accounts for the sale and the aforesaid 67 tuns of wine as appears below. And nothing remains.

LETTER OF PETER DE GILDESBOURG

Greetings from Edward eldest son, etc., to our dear clerk, Thomas Filz Henry, our havener of Cornwall. Since we have granted to our dear clerk, Peter de Gildesbourg, five tuns of our wines of prisage in Cornwall, provided he pays the merchants for them as much as we would have to pay for them [*sique il paie pour iciaux as marchauns tant come nous en deverions paier*], we order you to deliver these five tuns of wine from our prisage wines to him in this manner And this letter will be your guarantee? [*Et ceste letre vous eut? s'ra garant'*]. Given under seal of the prince the 8th day of November in the 26th regnal year [1352] of our very dear lord and father the king of England and the 13th as king of France. [58]

The letter remains with the said keeper because of an inquiry into the custody of the wines.

(m. 19)

ACCOUNT OF THOMAS FILZ HENRI, KEEPER OF CUSTOMS WHICH ARE CALLED MALTOLT AND COCKET IN THE COUNTY OF CORNWALL, FROM MICHAELMAS IN THE 26TH REGNAL YEAR OF KING EDWARD III AFTER THE CONQUEST UNTIL THE SAME FEAST IN THE FOLLOWING YEAR, THE 27TH OF THE SAME KING.

ISSUES OF COCKET

The same renders account for 18d received from John Simond for 2 dickers and 3 hides loaded in a ship called *Cog Thomas* of Looe of which John Selman is master, on 18 December.

And 13s 4d received from Richard Marcsch for one last of hides carried in a ship called *Le Bartholomeu* of Plymouth of which Henry Trewef is master, on 24 May. Sum, 14s 10d.

ISSUES OF MALTOLT OF FOWEY

The same responds for 8s received from *Jonell* Mabilo of Guérande [*Garant*], alien, for custom on £32 of salt sold at Falmouth, namely 3d per £.

And for 18d received from Bartholomew Joun of Guérande, alien, for £7 of salt sold at Lostwithiel.

And for 4s received from Peter Bastart (alien) for custom of £16 of salt sold in the aforesaid place.

And for 8s received from John Flaggard, alien, for custom on £32 of salt sold at the aforesaid place.

And for 9s received from Peter Belug' of Guérande for custom on £36 salt sold at Fowey.

[58.] In French. See also *BPR*, II, p. 38.

And for 7s received from Peter Belewe for custom on £28 of salt sold
in the aforesaid place.

And for 10s 4d received from Peter Belug' of Guérande for custom on
£42 3s 4d of salt sold at Fowey.

And for 6s received from the same for custom of £24 of the price of a
certain ship bought by him in the water of (^ Fowey).

And for 40s received from William de la Roch, attorney of Francis
[*Ffranc'*] Spinoles for custom on 20 M [*millenar'*] of tin bought a
Lostwithiel, at £8 per M.

And for 8s 10d received from *Gillen* Dir of Guérande for custom on
£35 5s of salt at the aforesaid place.

And for 5s 8¼d received from *Yvon* Maler, alien, for custom on £22
15s of salt sold at the aforesaid place.

And for 4s 6d received of *Garcy* Arnandel, alien, for custom on £18 of
salt sold at the aforesaid place.

And for 18s received of William Compnan, alien, for custom on 9 M
of tin, priced at £8 per M bought at Lostwithiel.

And for 5s 4½d from John Gudfelawe of Guernsey for custom on 2 M
of tin, priced at £8 13s 4d per M, and ½ M, priced at £4 5s.

Sum, £6 16s 2¾d.

FALMOUTH

The same responds for 15d received from William Dowar of Conquet
for custom on £5 of salt sold there.

And for 15d received from John Peliter of the same for custom on £5
of salt sold there.

And for 2s 6d received from Bernard de Garant for custom on £10 of
salt sold there.

And for 2s 6d received from John Jagewey of Guérande for custom on
£10 of salt sold there.

And for 3s received from Henry Rous for custom on £12 of salt sold
there.

And for 5s received from William Dir for custom on £20 of salt sold
there.

And for 4s 9d received from *Assedancesone* de Sclus for custom on £19
of tables and onions sold there. And for 21d received from Henry
Tribel for custom on £7 of salt sold there.

And for 15d received from John Prat for custom on £5 of salt sold
there.

And for 5s received from Henry Meneward for custom on £20 of salt
sold there.

And for 6d received from Peron Hermoun for custom on £2 of salt
sold there.
Sum, 28s 9d.

MOUSEHOLE

The same responds for 11¼d received from *Yonet* de Estounet for
custom on 75s received from salt sold at Marazion.

And for 18d received from John Joce of St Malo for custom on £6 of
salt sold there.

And for 6s received from John Larg of Guérande for custom on £24 of
salt sold there.

And for 9s received from *Yvet* Flaggard, alien, for custom on £35 of
salt sold at Mousehole.

And for 8s received from Gelemot de la Sparr for custom on £27 for
hake [*hakes*] exposed for sale at Mousehole.

And for 14¼d received from *Yvonet* de Boys, alien, for custom on £4
15s of salt sold at Newlyn.

And for 9d received from John Gloyrek for custom on £3 of salt sold
at Mousehole.

And for 2s 6d received from *Tangi* de la Cunket for custom on £8 of
salt sold at Mousehole.

And for 2s 6d received from *Morise* Kermeu for custom on £10 for
wine and honey sold at Mousehole.
Sum, 31s 10½d.

(m. 19d)

CONTINUATION FROM FOWEY

And for 56s 4¾d (^ received from) John Syngham, alien, for petty
custom, namely for £225 14s 7d for price of 32,516 pounds of stamped
[*cunat'*] tin in the coinage roll for the 25th year and for 19,576 pounds
of stamped tin in the coinage roll from the 26th year, priced at £4 6s
7d per thousandweight [*M*] beyond coinage, taking 3d per £. And for
13s 7¼d from the same John for the same custom for £54 11s 2d from
the price of 6,820 pounds of stamped tin for the coinage roll of this
year, priced at £8 per thousandweight beyond coinage, per £ as above.
Sum, 70s.

WOOL CUSTOM

Nothing here from wool custom called cocket because the receiver of Cornwall responds for it in his account.[59]

Sum total received, £14 20¼d which is charged at the foot of his account as keeper of the ports for this year. And thus he is quit here.

1353/54

PRO, SC6/817/4

27–28 Edward III. 15 membranes. Ministers' accounts of the duchy of Cornwall in Cornwall and Devon (mm. 1–10); accounts of the havener (mm. 11–11d), and receiver (mm. 12–14), which consists of three pieces sewn end to end to form the wrapper for the entire roll).

(m. 2)

TREMATON

[...]

CONVENTIONARY RENTS OR FARMS

The same responds for [...]. Nothing from the farm of the Water and Pool of Sutton which are accustomed to lease for £10 per year because (^ here leased to) John Dabernon for the term of his life for which he responds below. [...]

[...]

FARMS AT TERMS OF LIVES

The same responds for £6 13s 4d for the farm of the Water and Pool of Sutton as conceded and leased to John Dabernon by the lord for the term of his life by letters patent from the same duke dated 5 February in the 24th year [1350] as appears in the foot of the account of the

---

59. In PRO, SC6/812/6 (m. 1), the receiver accounts for customs of wool: "the same responds for £12 4s 8¼d received from customs of wool carried from Cornwall this year, taking 13s 4d per sack by order of the council of the lord, namely, from Adam (Clerk) £45 13s 4d for 7 sacks. From Robert Langmon, 18s ¼d for sack and 18 cloves. From the prior of St Germans, 100s for 7½ sacks. From William att Weie, 33s 4d for 2½ sacks, as contained in the roll of Henry Totham, lieutenant of William de Bacoun, controller of the cocket and prisage of wine. Sum, £12 4s 8¼d". Under WAGES AND FEES (m. 3), William Bacoune, controller of the havener, cocket, and wreck of sea this year receives £4 11s 3d.

23rd year which since the pestilence is accustomed to lease for £10 per year. [...]
[...]

HENCE OWING [*UNDE SUPER*]
But the major sum, £18 10s, from John de Haule, once farmer of the Water of Sutton by commission of the lord prince for the last part of the 18th year, for the 19th, 20th and third part of the 21st year [1344–7]. [...]
[...]

(m. 3)
BOROUGH OF SALTASH
RECEIPTS
[...] And for £10 from the farm of the passage of Saltash Water as leased to the said burgesses for the aforesaid term with rent of oars belonging to the same passage, barge, 4 oars of the aforesaid passage, at the said two terms equally [...].
[...]

DECAY OF FARMS
[...] And 60s in decay of the farm of the borough of Saltash which was farmed out before the pestilence for £8 and the farm of the passage which was farmed out before the pestilence for £10 as charged above and now leased for this year for £15. [...]
[...]

(m. 5)
LOSTWITHIEL
ISSUES OF THE PORT AND WATER OF FOWEY
And for 32s½d received from the fishery of the Fowey Water this year as contained in the said indenture against John de Kendale. And for 15d from the pleas and perquisites of the maritime court held there by the mayor of the town this year as contained in the said indenture. And for 7s 3d from keelage of 5 foreign barges landing in the said port with diverse merchandise this year as contained in the said indenture, taking 16d from each barge. And for 7s 8d received from 3 quarters 3 bushels of salt arising from customs on 11 ships landing in the port of Fowey this year, taking 2 bushels from each ship at the price of 3½d per bushel. And nothing from wheat or other corn or any other bushel measures arising from customs, namely from each ship as above, because none landed. Sum, 48s 2½d.

CUSTODY OF THE FISHERY
10s for one new net with cords [*cordis*] and all rigging [*apparatu*] of
the same net, namely 7s for the net, 2s for the cords, and 12d for the
repair of the same net. And they remain. {For which the bailiff to
respond in a future year}. Sum, 10s.
[...]

(m. 11)

ACCOUNT OF THOMAS FILII HENRI, KEEPER OF THE PORTS DURING THE ABOVESAID
TIME

FARMS OF THE PORTS
The same responds for 46s 8d for the farm of the port of Marazion per
year at the feasts of Easter and Michaelmas equally. And for 12s for the
farm of the port of Penzance per year at the same terms. And for 20s
from the farm of the port of Newlyn per year at the same terms. And
for 100s for the farm of the port of Mousehole per year at the same
terms. And for 12d from the farm of the port of Lamorna. And for 2s
from the farm of the port of Porthgwarra per year at the same terms
which is accustomed to render per year 12s and no more because of
lack of men and boats. And for 2s from the farm of the port of
'Porthplement' [*Porthplenynt*] per year at the same terms, which is
accustomed to render per year 8s and no more this year for the aforesaid
reason. And for 40s from the farm of the port of Fowey per year at the
same terms. And for 25s from the farm of the ports of Kerrier per year
at the same terms. And for 20s from the farm of the port of Polruan
per year at the same terms. And for 20s from the farm of the ports of
Trigg per year at the same terms. And for £4 from the farm of the port
of St Ives per year at the same terms, and it is accustomed to render per
year £6, and no more for the aforesaid reason. For 6s 8d from the farm
of the ports of Porthzennor and Portheras, nothing this year because of
the pestilence. Sum, £18 8s 8d.

CUSTOMS OF WINES
He does not respond for the custom of alien wines from which the
duke should have 2s from each tun for custom because no aliens
unloaded within his bailiwick this year. Sum, nothing.

SALE OF WINES
The same responds for £34 13s 4d received from 8 tuns of red Gascon
wine priced a £4 6s 8d per tun. And for £80 received from 20 tuns of

red Gascon wine priced at £4 per tun as sold in ships. And for £116 received from 29 tuns of red Gascon wine, at £4 per tun. And for £36 received from 9 tuns of wine of which 7 tuns red Gascon wine and 2 tuns white Gascon, sold for the household of the lord, priced at £4 per tun. And for £38 6s 8d received from 10 tuns of red Gascon wine sold at sea, priced at 76s 8d per tun. And for £23 received from 6 tuns of red Gascon wine priced at (^£4) and another tun of white Gascon priced at £4 3s 4d per tun. And for 73s 4d received from one tun of red wine *de Borect*. And for 53s 4d from one tun of weak red Gascon wine because it was taken from wines collected from diverse wines lost at sea. And for 40s from the price of one tun conceded to Nicholas Pynnok by the lord at the same prise as the lord paid for prisage wines as contained in letters directed to the same keeper as below in wines given to the same Nicholas. Sum, £359 16s 8d.

WRECK OF SEA

He does not respond here for one little whale [*cet'iculo*] taken in Mount's Bay [*Montisbay*] because it was delivered to Sir William de Northwell, keeper of the wardrobe of the lord for expenses of the household by an indenture under the seal of the same William without price, by letters of the lord dated 10 September in the 28th year [1354], delivered on account. The same responds for 50s received from 1 tun and 2 pipes of red wine coming from a wreck at Connerton [*Coner*], both full, and not more because they were sold to Sir John Darundel for 100s from which 50s was delivered to the same Sir John for their salvage. And for 50s received from 1 tun and 2 pipes coming from wreck of sea at *Treueneck*, not full, and no more because they were sold to Alan Kernek for 100s from which 50s was delivered to him for their salvage. And for 66s 8d received from 1 tun of red wine coming from wreck of sea at 'Scawen' [*Skawen*][60] in the parish of Perranzabuloe [*Sancti Pirani*] thus sold and because another tun of wine coming from wreck of sea there and 1 pipe with a certain remainder of wine was extracted and placed in these two tuns and then were not full from which one full and one hardly-full [*peins*] tun was handed over [*dimiss' fuit*] to John Tresausan and his fellows for another salvage. And for 11s received from one mast coming from a wreck at Treloyan? [*Trelowan*] and no more because it was sold for 22s from which 11s was delivered to the bailiff of Sir Henry de la Pomeray for its salvage. Sum, £8 17s 8d.

[60.] A now-lost place in Tywarnhaile manor; see *Caption of Seisin*, pp. 80–82, 174.

FINES OF MERCHANTS WITH TRANTERY
The same responds for 18s (4d) from fines of merchants with trantery [*Tranentur'*] this year. Sum, 18s 4d.

PERQUISITES OF THE MARITIME COURT
The same responds for 32s 3d from perquisites of the maritime (court) this year. Sum, 32s 3d.

Sum total received, £389 13s 7d.

WAGES AND FEES
The same accounts for (payment) of £6 13s 4d to himself for his wages and fees from Michaelmas in the 27th year (1353) until the same feast in the 28th year following for one whole year. ~~And 13s 4d for his robe for the term of his life as conceded by charter of the lord king~~ (cancelled because it was forbidden by the council of the lord at Berkhamsted [*Berkampstede*] that this was not to be henceforth allowed, but he should take the robe from the wardrobe of the lord. Sum, £6 13s 4d.

CUSTOM OF WINES OF PRISAGE
The same pays £90 to diverse merchants for 44 tuns of wine and 1 pipe of Cretan wine [*crete*] from the same taken for assize, at 40s per tun and 40s for the pipe of Cretan wine. Sum, £90.

CARE OF WINES
For 22d for towage of 10 tuns at Plymouth from the sea to land, of which 2d per tun for 9 tuns and 4d for the other tun towed from St Nicholas Island for the space of two leagues to land. And 2s 6d for rollage of them, at 3d per tun, and he used to give 2d. And 8d for lease of a cellar for storing 2 tuns from the first seizure [*de prima capt'*] from 15 January to 12 February for 4 weeks, at 4d per week, and he used to give 2½ d. And 3s for lease of a cellar for storing wines from the last seizure from 1 March to 2 May for 9 weeks, at 4d per week. And 20s 3d for 40½ gallons of wine for leakage and ullage of the same 10 tuns from the day of seizure to the day of sale, priced at 6d per gallon.

Also 4d in rollage of 1 tun at Looe. And 6d for lease of a cellar for the same for 3 weeks, at 2d per week. Also 2s for 4 gallons for ullage of the same, at 6d per gallon.

Also 2s 1d for towage of 25 tuns at Fowey from the sea to land, at 1d per tun. And 6s 3d for rollage of the same from the sea to the cellar, at 3d per tun, and he used to give .... And 8s for lease of a cellar for storing the said wines from 28 November to 26 July for 25 weeks, at 4d per week. And 6s for 16 gallons of wine for ullage of 6 tuns here, priced at 6d per gallon. And 33s for 66 gallons of wine for ullage of 17 tuns, priced at 6d per gallon. And 12d for 2 staves put in 2 defective tuns, priced at 6d per stave. And 4d for a porter to lift the same tuns, at 2d per tun. And for 2s 4d for 28 great barrel hoops for repairing defects in these tuns, priced at 1d per hoop band. And 8s for 16 gallons for leakage [*leicage*] and ullage of said two tuns, priced at 6d per gallon.

And 19s for towage of 19 tuns at Falmouth from the sea to land for the space of 2 leagues, for 12d per tun, and he used to give 2d. And 6s for hire of a certain boat for serving the keeper at the time of sale and taking of prisage for 6 days, at 12d per day (allowed first in this year? [*alloc' hoc anno primo*]). And 4s 9d for rollage of the same 19 tuns from the sea to the cellar, at 3d per tun. And 4s for hire of a cellar for storing the said wines from 21 November to 14 February for 12 weeks, at 4d per week, and he used to give 2d. 11s for 22 (^ ½) gallons for ullage of 9 tuns, priced at 6d per gallon. And 12s 3d for 24½ gallons of wine for ullage and leakage of 7 tuns, priced at 6d per gallon. And 18d for 3 staves placed in 3 defective tuns, priced at 6d per stave. And 6d for lifting by porters [*sublevdend in porct'*], at 2d per tun. And 18d for 18 barrel hoops for binding and repairing the same, priced at 2d per hoop band. And 7s 6d for 15 gallons of wine for ullage and leakage of the same, priced at 6d per gallon. And 16d for towage of 2 pipes of Cretan wine from the sea to land, priced at 8d per pipe. And 4d for rollage of the same from the sea to the cellar, priced at 2d per pipe. And 6s 8d for hire of 1 boat for carrying the same from Falmouth to Fowey by sea. And 4d for rollage of the same from the cellar to the boat, at 2d per pipe. And 2d for towage of the same at Fowey from the sea to land, priced at 1d per pipe. And 4d for rollage of the same from the sea to ~~land~~ (cellar), at 2d per pipe.

Also 2s for ~~carriage~~ (towage) of 4 tuns at Padstow from the sea to land, at 6d per tun. And 10d for rollage of the same from the sea to the cellar, at 2½d per tun. And 6d for lease of a cellar for storing 2 tuns taken there from prisage from 2 January to the 22nd of the same month for 3 weeks, at 2d per week. And 10d for lease of the same cellar from 14 April to ~~29~~ (19) May for 5 weeks, at 2d per week. And 4s 6d for 9 gallons of wine for ullage of the same during the same time, priced at 6d per gallon. Sum, £9 5s 2d.

Sum of all expenses, £105 18s 6d. And he owes £84 15s 2¾d. And £21 14s 8¼d from remainder of his account of last year. And 33s 2¾d from remainder of his account of custody of custom called maltolt this year, as appears in the foot of his account on the back of this roll. Sum of all joined debts, £307 3s. From which he is exonerated for 100s from part of £10 that he was charged in his account from last year for 5 tuns of wine from prisage that, by letters of the lord, Sir Peter de ~~Larg~~ Gyldesburgh was allowed to pay for as the lord prince paid to merchants for these same wines because the lord prince ordered by letters directed to his auditors of the account of the same Thomas, dated 10 September in the 28th year, that they should exonerate the said Thomas for the same 100s that he was charged; he was then charged for another 100s that the same Peter paid to the same Thomas for the same wines.

And 20s is allowed to him that he paid to Thomas Kempe and his fellows for assize of custom [*assens'cons'*] of the lord for seizure of one little whale [*corticuli*] taken by him in Mount's Bay [*Mountysbay*] in the month of September this year and retained [*retent'*] and delivered to William de Northwell, keeper of the wardrobe of the lord, for the expenses of the household, by letters of the lord.

And he owes £301 3s. From which he delivered £16 14s 8¼d on the remainder of his account to John de Kendale, receiver of the lord duke in part of Cornwall and Devon by indenture delivered on account. And he delivered to the same receiver £283 3s 5¾d for issues of his bailiwick by indenture on his account. And he owes 24s 10d.

(m. 11d)

RECEIPT OF WINES

PLYMOUTH
The same responds for 13 tuns of wine taken from diverse ships landing there of which 6 tuns assize and 7 quit of which 12 tuns [are] red Gascon and the remaining tuns [are] white, namely:
From a ship called *Redecog* of Plymouth of which William Lake is master, on 15 January, 2 tuns of wine (red [*R'*]).
From a ship called *Edward* of Plymouth of which Richard Stonhous is master, on 2 January, 2 tuns of wine (red).
From a ship called *Cog John* of Plymouth of which Robert Pole is master, on the same day, 2 tuns of wine (red).
From a ship called *Constance* of Dartmouth of which William Bulman is master, on 1 March, 1 tun (red) taken in St Nicholas Island where ships are obliged to pay nothing by agreement made between the keeper and merchants.

From a ship called *Cog John* of Plymouth of which Robert Pole is master, on 18 March, 2 tuns of wine (red).

From a ship called *Edward* of Plymouth of which Richard Stonhous is master, on the same day, 2 tuns of wine (red) one white and the other red.

From a ship called *le Neif Seint John* of Bayonne [*Baone*] of which John Luck is master, on 3 May, 2 tuns of wine (red).

LOOE

The same responds for 1 tun of red Gascon wine, taken in the port of Looe from a certain scaff [*calfa*] called *Dieu le Gard* of Portsall [*Portsal*] of which Hervy Tremesyn is master, on 9 January, which scaff carried 12 tuns, collected from the aforesaid diverse wines in a certain ship in parts of Brittany [*Bretann'*].

FOWEY

The same responds for 25 tuns of wine taken from diverse ships landing there of which 22 tuns [are] red Gascon and 2 tuns white. And 1 tun of red Bayonne *borect'* wine from which 12 for assize and 13 quit, namely:

From a ship called *le Savoye* of Polruan of which Thomas Johan is master, on 28 November, 2 tuns of wine (red).

From a ship called *le Godbeate* of Fowey of which Simon Pichermaker is master, on the same day, 2 tuns (of wine red).

From a ship called *le Seintemariecog* of Polruan of which Nicholas Cok is master, on the same day, 2 tuns of wine (red).

From a ship called *le Elianor* of Dartmouth of which Nicholas Piers is master, on 30 December, 2 tuns of wine (red).

From a ship called *Cog John* of Dartmouth of which John Milton is master, on the same day, 2 tuns of wine (red).

From a ship called *le Margaret* of Weymouth of which John atte See is master, on the same day, 2 tuns of wine (red).

From a ship called *le Walfare* of Manningtree [*Manitrue*] of which John Estman is master, on the same day, 2 tuns of wine (red).

From a ship called *le Margaret* of Colchester of which John Wille is master, on the same day, 2 tuns of wine (red [*Rub'*]).

From a ship called *Nicholas* of Polruan of which John Dandie is master, on 27 March, 2 tuns of wine (red).

From a ship called *le Savoie* of Polruan of which Thomas Johan is master, on 27 January, 1 tun *borect*.

From a ship called *Cog John* of Fowey of which John Tegan is master, on the same day, 2 tuns of white wine.

From a ship called *le Gudbeat* of Fowey of which Simon Pichermaker is master, on the same day, 2 tuns of wine (red).

From a ship called *Seintmaricog* of Polruan of which Nicholas Cok is master, on 12 March, 2 tuns of wine (red).

FALMOUTH

The same responds for 49 tuns of red Gascon wine and 2 pipes of crete wine from diverse ships landing there of which 24 tun for assize and 26 tuns quit. And 1 pipe for assize and the other quit.

From a ship called *le Neif Seintanten* of Castrourdiales [*Castr'*] of which John Martines is master, on 19 November, 2 pipes of Cretan wine.

From a ship called *le Margaret* of Hook [*Hoke*] of which John Olak is master, on 21 November, 2 tuns of wine (red).

From a ship called *le Peter* of Exmouth of which Walter Prous is master, on 1 January, 2 tuns of wine (red).

From a ship called *le Laurens* of Hull of which William Kelyng is master, on the same day, 2 tuns of wine (red).

From a ship called *Seintemaricog* of Lyme of which John att See is master, on the same day, 2 tuns of wine (red).

From a ship called *le Maudeleyne* of Ipswich [*Chippeswichh*] of which Thomas Gaunt is master, on 2 January, 2 tuns of wine (red).

From a ship called *le Nicholas* of Teignmouth [*Theymuth*] of which William Knyght is master, on the same day, 2 tuns of wine (red).

From a ship called *le James* of Fowey of which *Everyn* Brewere is master, on the same day, 1 tun of wine (red) taken from the portage of 12 sailors [*xii portag' nautarum*] who are not obliged to pay because the ship was freighted with wines of merchants of London [*quia navis frectebatur vinis mercatorum sunt London*].

From a ship called *le James* of Gloucester [*Glocestr'*] of which John Lucas is master, on the same day, 2 tuns of wine (red).

From a ship called *le Mighel* of Dartmouth of which Roger Beaumund is master, on the same day, 2 tuns of wine (red).

From a ship called *le Gudyer* of Boston [*Botulston*] of which Thomas Ruberal? is master, on the same day, 2 tuns of wine (red).

From a ship called *le Molote* of Gosford Haven [*Goseforth*] of which Hugh Taillour is master, on 1 January, 2 tuns of wine (red).

From a ship called *le Marie* of Gloucester of which William Bacorin is master, on 2 January, 2 tuns of wine (red).

From a ship called *le Rose* of Gloucester, of which Richard Esmaur is master, on the same day, 2 tuns of wine (red).

From a ship called *Waynepayn* of Harwich [*Herewych*] of which Robert

~~Kendal~~ (Richard Priour) is master, on the same day, 2 tuns of wine (red).

From a ship called *le Katerine* of Ipswich [*Gippeswych*] of which Robert Kendale is master, on the same day, 2 tuns of wine (red).

From a ship called *le James* of Gosford Haven [*Gosforth*] of which Hugh Holford is master, on the same day, 2 tuns of wine (red).

From a ship called *le Jorge* of Boston of which Adam Parman is master, on 3 January, 2 tuns of wine (red).

From a ship called *Seintemaribot* of Ipswich [*Chippeswych*] of which Robert Sheward is master, on the same day, 2 tuns of wine (red).

From a ship called *le Portour* of Weymouth of which John Rolf is master, on 4 January, 2 tuns of wine (red).

From a ship called *Seintmaricog* of Yarmouth of which Richard Symonet is master, on 28 December, 2 tuns of wine (red).

From a ship called *le Nicholas* of Sidmouth of which Robert Hake is master, on the same day, 2 tuns of wine (red).

From a ship called *Seintemariship* of Hull of which James de Goseforth is master, on the same day, 2 tuns of wine.

From a ship called *Cogioun* of Maldon of which Robert Ver is master, on 28 December, 2 tuns of wine (red).

From a ship called *Seintemaribot* of Dartmouth of which Richard Gill is master, on 2 January, 2 tuns of wine (red).

PADSTOW [*Padirstouwe*]

The same responds for 4 tuns of red Gascon wine from ships landing here, namely, from a ship called *Seintesavourescog* of Fowey of which Richard Mighelstowe is master on 2 January, 2 tuns of wine (red). From the same ship of which the same is master, on 14 April, 2 tuns of wine (red).

MOUSEHOLE

Nothing there from prisage of wines there because no ships landed there this year.

Sum total received from all wines of prisage, 92 tuns and 2 pipes.

EXPENSES OF WINES

From which he delivered 1 tun of red wine to Sir Nicholas Pynnok as a gift of lord, priced at £4 as appears by letters of the lord directed to the same keeper which are dated 25 October in the 26th year [1352].

Account of Thomas fil' Henr' keeper of customs which are called maltolt and cocket in the county of Cornwall, from Michaelmas in the 27th regnal year of King Edward III after the conquest of England until the same feast following in the 28th year.

Issues of Maltolt

The same responds for 5s received from William Denys alien for custom of £20 [worth] of salt (^ sold) in the port of Fowey, at 3d per £.

And for 2s received from Thomas Stephene alien for custom of £8 of salt and honey sold in the aforesaid port for £ as above.

And for 20¾d received from *Yem* Tresour alien for custom of £6 15s of salt sold in the aforesaid port for £ as above.

And for 18d received from *Rauf* Nauter alien in the port of Falmouth for custom on £6 of salt sold there.

And for 12d received from Daniel Jop alien for custom on £4 of salt sold in the aforesaid port for £ as above.

And for 2s received from William Loweys alien for custom on £48 of salt sold there.

And for 2s 6d received from *Everin* Ferand alien for custom on £10 of salt sold there.

And for 5s received from William von Englys alien for custom of £20 of salt sold there.

He does not respond this year for customs of cocket for carriage of wool fells and hides carried from England [*Anglia*] overseas because it was ordained by ~~year~~ (a new) statute made in Parliament that no denizen [*intrinsec'*] may carry any merchandise overseas but to do so through an ordained staple in England, so William de la Roke alien carried overseas 4 sacks and 21 cloves of wool for which he paid for custom of 58s 10d to John de Kendale receiver. For which the same John de Kendale charged himself in his account for this year under the title [*in titulo*] of issues of customs of wool as stated to the auditor, by inspection of the rolls of the account of the same receiver for this year. Sum total received, 33s 2½d which he owes, for which he responds in the foot of his account for customs of the ports for this year. And so he is quit.

(m. 14)

Account of the Receiver [...]

[...]

Issues of the Ports and Cocket

And for £283 3s 5¾d received from Thomas Filtz Henr', keeper of the ports, for the same time.

ISSUES OF WOOL CUSTOM

And for 58s 10d received from William de le Rode, alien, for custom on 4 sacks and 22 cloves of wool, taking 13s 4d per sack.

1354/55

DCO Ministers' Account Roll 7

28–29 Edward III. 14 membranes. Ministers' accounts of the duchy of Cornwall in Cornwall and Devon (mm. 1–9); accounts of the stannaries (m. 10), hundreds (mm. 10d–11), havener (m. 12), keeper of the fees (m. 13), and receiver (m. 14).

(m. 2d)

[...]

TREMATON

[...]

CONVENTIONARY RENTS OR FARMS

The same responds for [...]. Nothing here for the £10 farm of the passage of Saltash Water at Easter and Michaelmas with rent of oars belonging to the same passage as contained in the preceding account because the bailiff of the borough of Saltash has those profits. And for £10 for the rent or farm of 2 water mills, rents of the *censar* of the borough [*redd' cens' burg'*]of Trematon which are 12d each year, pleas and perquisites of the courts of the same borough which are estimated at 40s, toll of oysters which is worth 3d each year, and herbage of the castle ditch which used to sell for 8d, as contained there. Nothing from the farm of the Water and Pool of Sutton which used to lease for £10 per year because is is leased to John Dabernoun for the term of his life for which he responds below. [...]

RENTS OR FARMS AT TERM OF LIVES

The same responds for £6 13s 4d for the farm of the Water and Pool of Sutton as granted and leased to John Dabernoun by the lord for the term of his life by letters patent of the same lord duke dated 5 February in the 23rd year, as appeared at the foot of the account of the 23rd year, which before the pestilence used to lease for £10 per year. [...]

[...]

BUT A GREATER TOTAL ABOVE? [*SET MAIOR SUMMA SUPER*]
£18 10s from John Haule once farmer of the Water of Sutton by commission of the lord prince for the last part of the 28th[61] year and for the 19th and 20th and third part of the 21st year. [...]

(m. 3d)

SALTASH BOROUGH

FARMS

The same responds for [...]. And for £10 for the farm of the passage of Saltash Water as leased to the said burgesses for the aforesaid terms equally with rent of oars belonging to the same passage, barge, 4 oars for the aforesaid passage. [...]

DECAY OF FARMS

For 60s for the decay of the farm of the borough of Saltash which was farmed out before the pestilence for £8 and the farm of the passage of Water which was farmed out before the pestilence for £10, as charged above, and now leased this year for ~~£15~~ 60s. Sum, 60s.

CARE OF THE PASSAGE BOAT

For 4s ¾d for 4 master carpenters felling timber in the wood of Calstock and 5 men hired for carrying the said timber from the wood to the water for one and one-half day, at 3d per carpenter per day, and 1½d for carriage and 2s 1½d for their victuals and meals [*mensa*]. For carrying the said timber to Saltash from the said wood, 3s at task. 9s 3d for 27 boards purchased for repair and fixing the boat, each (^ board) is 7 feet long, purchased wholesale [*in gross*]. 4s for 6 boards purchased of 12 feet, priced at 8d each. 2s for 12 *sheverbord* purchased for the same, priced at 2d per board. For 2 barells of pitch purchased for the same, priced at 4s 6d for one and 4s 2d for the other. 16d for 2 gallons of bitumen. 10s for 4 master carpenters making the said boat for 1 week for which 3d for their salary per day for each, and 2d for their meals. 3s 6d for 2 carpenters for the same time to clinch [*clinchator*][62] the said boat for which (^ 2d) per day for each of them and 1½d for their meals. 2s for 2 carpenters holding against [*tenent versus*] the aforesaid clincher [*clinchator*] for the same time, for which 1d per day for each of them. 8s 5d for hire of the aforesaid 4 master carpenters for

---

61. This is a mistake for 18th.
62. To rivet nails; a clincher is the name of the person who does this job.

another week for the said boat, each of them as above with meals for 5 days. 2s 11d for clinching [*clinchiand'*] the aforesaid 2 carpenters for the said week, each as above. 20d for the aforesaid 2 carpenters holding for the same time, each as above. 4s 2d for the aforesdaid 4 master carpenters for 2½ days in Pentecost week, each as above. 17½d for the aforesaid 2 clinchers for the same time, each as above. 10d for the aforesaid 2 holders for the same time, each as above. 6d for 2 carpenters hired for throwing down [*prosternuent'*] a certain keel [*kilam*] to the said boat and repairing and making it for one day. 6d for carriage of the same from the castle to the water. 4d for carriage of the same by water to Saltash. 6d for carriage of the aforesaid boards from Plymouth to [*apud*] Saltash by land [*per landam*]. 4d for carriage of the barrels of the aforesaid pitch from Plymouth ~~Water~~ to Saltash. 6s 8d for 4C clinch-nails [*clinchnail*] purchased, priced at <u>20d</u> per C. 2s for 1½C great spikenails purchased, priced at <u>16d</u> per C. 12d for 1C smaller spike-nails [*minor spiknail*] purchased. 8d for 1C small [*parvis*] spiknail purchased. 15d for 3C hachnail for the same. Sum, £4 11¼d.

Sum of all expenses, £7 11d. And he owes [...].

Saltash borough, 60s in decay, by pestilence,(^ for) <u>£4 11¼d</u> for making 1 boat, value £10 19s 3¾d.[63]
[...]

(m. 6)

ACCOUNT OF LOSTWITHIEL CONTINUED
ISSUES OF THE PORT OF FOWEY WATER

And for 24s 8d received from the fishery of Fowey Water this year. And for 3s received from 1 quarter of salt arising from the customs of 4 foreign ships landing in the port of Fowey this year, by view of the said John[64] and the aforesaid indenture, namely, after the feast of St Peter's Chains [1 August] this year. And for 16d received from keelage of one foreign barge landing in the same port with diverse merchandise after the said feast this year, as contained in the aforesaid indenture. And for 3d from the profits of the maritime courts held by the mayor of the said town after the said feast this year, as contained in the aforesaid

---

[63.] This is written in the far right-hand margin, squeezed to the side of the short section summarizing all the expenses.

[64.] John de Kendale, receiver of the duchy in Cornwall.

intendure. And for 13s 4d received from John Curteys mayor of this town for this year as well as for perquisites of the courts of the mariners held by the same mayor, keelage of foreign barges in the said port with customs on merchandise of ships landing with salt and corn until the feast of St Peter's Chains this year and whose particulars are not shown at present because the same mayor after the said feast withdrew part of the writ? so let action be taken against the same mayor for accounting thereof for the particulars [*eo quod idem maior post dictam festum recess' part' writanu' ideo fiet exec' versus eundem maiorem ad computand' inde per parcell'*] {afterwards he then delivered the particulars}. Sum, 42s 7d.

[...]

EXPENSES

The same accounts for 11s for one net purchased for the fishery. [...]

[...]

(m. 12)

ACCOUNT OF THOMAS FILZ HENRY, KEEPER OF THE PORTS IN THE COUNTY OF CONWALL AND PRISAGE OF WINES IN THE SAME COUNTY AND IN SUTTON WATER IN THE COUNTY OF DEVON, AND ISSUES OF THE PORTS IN THE SAME COUNTY OF CORNWALL, AND WRECK OF SEA IN THE SAME COUNTY, FROM MICHAELMAS IN THE 28TH REGNAL YEAR OF KING EDWARD AFTER THE CONQUEST UNTIL THE SAME FEAST IN THE NEXT FOLLOWING.

FARMS OF THE PORTS

The same responds for 46s 8d from the farm of the port of Marazion each year at the feasts of Easter and Michaelmas equally. And for 12s from the farm of the port of Penzance each year at the same terms. And for 20s from the farm of the port of Newlyn each year at the same terms. And for 100s from the farm of the port of Mousehole each year at the same terms. And for 12d from the farm of the port of Lamorna for this year there. And for 2s from the farm of the port of Porthgwarra [*Portgorwetheu*] each year, which usually renders 12s each year, and no more for lack of men and boats. And for 2s from the farm of the port of 'Porthplement' each year, which usually (^ renders) 8s, and no more this year for the aforesaid cause. And for 40s from the port of Fowey each year at the same terms. And for 25s from the farm of the ports of Kerrier each year at the same terms. And for 20s from the farm of the port of Polruan each year at the same terms. And for 20s from the farm of the ports of Trigg each year at the same terms. And for 100s from the farm of the port of St Ives, which usually renders £6, and no more this year because of the aforesaid cause, but he will pay the whole farm next year. And for 6s 8d from the farm of the ports of Porthzennor and Portheras [*Porthherest*], nothing because of the aforesaid cause. Sum, £19 8s 8d.

Custom of Wines

The same responds for 12s received from customs on 6 tuns of wines of aliens landing in the port of Plymouth and sold, namely 2s from each tun for custom, and no more because more aliens' wine did not land in his bailiwick this year. Sum, 12s.

Sale of wines

The same responds for £11 (received) from 2 tuns of wine sold at Plymouth, at 110s per tun of red Gascon wine. And for £10 16s 8d from 2 tuns of red Gascon wine sold at Fowey, at 108s 8d per tun. And 100s from 1 tun of red Gascon wine. And 100s 8d from 1 tun of red Gascon wine sold there. And for £10 from 2 tuns of red Gascon wine sold at Falmouth, priced at 100s per tun. And (for £21 from 4 tuns of red Gascon wine sold at Falmouth, priced at 105s per tun). And for £17 6s 8d from 4 tuns of red Gascon wine sold at Plymouth, priced at £4 6s 8d. And for £8 13s 4d from 2 tuns of white Spanish wine sold at Falmouth, priced at £4 6s 8d per tun. And for £9 from 2 tuns of white Spanish wine sold at Fowey, priced at £4 10s per tun. And for £17 6s 8d from 4 tuns of red Gascon wine sold for the household of the lord, priced at £4 6s 8d per tun. And for £10 13s 4d from 2 tuns of red wine sold at St Nicholas Island in Plymouth. And for £6 13s 4d from 2 pipes of Cretan wine [*cret'*] remaining in the hands of the keeper for lack of buyers last year, and no more because 8 measures? are destroyed on account of the long storage time [*quia devastabantur inde 8 pollices propter diurnam conservationem*]. Sum, £150 3s 4d.

Chattels arrested

And for £22 10s from a certain ship arrested in the port of Plymouth taken from the Normans by English mariners during the time of truce then [*sic*] sold to John le Bakere of Plymouth by the steward and keeper. He does not respond for a certain ship, called *Seint Eustace* of Dieppe loaded with herring *de Caka*, taken by Lawrence Porcher at sea and led to Plymouth and arrested there by the bailiffs of the same town, because the lord prince by his letters directed to the steward and keeper, dated 24 April in the 29th year [1355], that the force [*vis*] of the aforesaid letters ordered delivery of the said ship with tackle and all merchandise to Vincent de Castell of Dieppe, which letters are enrolled at the back [*tergo*] of this account and the rest remains with the said keeper. Sum, £22 10s.

Wreck of sea

And for 13s 4d from 1 tun, not full, of salty red wine coming from a wreck of sea at 'Porth Gone Hollye' [*Portgoneli*] and no more because it was sold to Sir John Beaupre for 26s 8d, from which 13s 4d was delivered to diverse men for salvage of the same. And for 15s from 1 tun of white Spanish wine, and not full, coming from a wreck of sea at St Ives, and no more because sold to a fisherman for 30s from which 15s was delivered to the men who salvaged the same. Sum, 28s 4d.

Fines of merchants with Trantery

The same responds for 13s 4d received from fines of merchants with trantery this year at Mousehole and no more this year because the fishermen were coerced to fish for the household of the lord [*quia piscatores conarti fuer' piscare pro Hospic' domini*]. Sum, 13s 4d.

Perquisites of the court

The same responds for 47s received from the perquisites of the maritime courts this year as appears in the court roll held by the said keeper. Sum, 47s.

Sum total received, £197 2s 8d.

Wages and fees

The same accounts for payment to himself for his wages and fees from Michaelmas in the 28th year to the same feast following for one whole year, £6 18s 4d. ~~And 13s 4d for his robe, conceded to him by charter of the lord king for the term of his life.~~ (cancelled because forbidden by the council of the lord at Berkhamstead ...) but taken from Robert of the wardrobe of the lord [*Rob' de Gardrob' dom'*]. Sum, £6 13s 4d.

Custody of wines

The same pays £28 to diverse merchants for 14 tuns of wine taken from them for assize. Sum, £28.

Care of Wines

For 2s for carriage of 2 tuns at Plymouth, carried [*carcat'*] from Tamar [*Tamere*] to Plymouth. And 4d for towage of them from the boat. And

2d [sic] for windage of 6 tuns there from sea to land, at 12d per tun. And 2s for rollage of the said 8 tuns to the cellar, at 3d per tun. And 10s 8d for hire of a cellar there for storing the said wines from 3 November to 15 June, for 32 weeks, at 4d per week. And for 8 gallons of wine for the price of 5s 4d for ullage of 2 tuns retained there in the cellar for a month, priced at 8d per gallon. And for 32 gallons of wine for the price of 16s for leakage of 1 tun there, priced at 6d per gallon. And for 60 gallons of wine for the price of 30s for ullage of 5 tuns there, priced at 6d per gallon, staying in the cellar for the whole time of the cellar's lease.

For 11d for towage of 11 tuns at Fowey, priced at 1d per tun. For 22d for rollage of the same from the sea to the cellar, priced at 2d per tun. For 10s for lease of a cellar to store the said wines in from 16 November until 14 June, for 30 weeks, at 4d per week. And for 4 gallons for the price of 2s 8d for ullage of 2 tuns there from the first sale, priced at 8d per gallon. And for 12 gallons for the price of 8s for ullage of 3 tuns of wine laying in the cellar for 5 weeks, priced at 8d per gallon. And for 50 gallons of wine for the price of 25s for ullage of 5 tuns laying there in the cellar for 35 weeks before sale, priced at 6d per gallon. And for 12 gallons of wine for the price of 6s for ullage of 1 tun there retained in the cellar for 30 weeks, priced at 6d per gallon. And for 3s for 36 barrel hoops for binding and repairing the said tuns, at the price of 1d per hoop band. And for 12d for 2 staves put on 2 tuns, for the price of 6d per stave.

And for 10s for towage of 10 tuns at Falmouth, towed for the space of two leagues, at 12d per tun, and used to give 2d. And for 2s 6d for rollage of them from the sea to the cellar, at 3d per tun. And 2s 4d for the lease of a cellar from 13 November until 9 January for 7 weeks, for the wines from the first seizure [*de prima capt'*], at 4d per week. And for 6s 4d for the hire of another cellar there from 11 February until 15 June for 16 weeks and 5 days, at 4d per week. And for 24 gallons of wine for the price of 16s for ullage of 6 tuns lying there in the cellar for 7 weeks, priced at 8d per gallon. And for 22 gallons of wine priced at 11s for leakage of 1 tun of white, priced at 6d per gallon. And 8d for 8 barrel hoops [*circulis*] for binding and repairing the same [tun], priced at 1d per band. And 6d for a stave placed in the same. And for 27 gallons of wine for the price of 13s 6d for ullage of 3 tuns lying there for 17 weeks and 5 days, priced at 6d per gallon. And for 11d for 11 barrel hoops for binding and repairing the same, priced at 1d per hoop. Sum, £9 9s 6d.

CARE AND EXPENSES INCURRED FOR ARREST OF A CERTAIN SHIP CAPTURED FROM
    NORMANDY [*CAPT' DE NORMAN'*]

For 40d for the expenses of men arresting a certain ship by the order of
Robert Elford, steward, and the said keeper. For 7s for 3 valets hired
for 14 days to safeguard the same ship [*super salva custod'*], each of
them took 2d per day. And 13s 4d paid to John Swet for leading
[*conducend'*] the said ship into the said port of Plymouth. And 40d
paid to diverse men carrying the sail [*ducent' velum*], cables, anchors
and other equipment [*instrumenta*] pertaining to the said ship in a
certain boat to land. And 3s 4d for lease of a certain house to store the
said equipment. And 20d paid to diverse men hired to carry the said
equipment at different times for drying out [*diversis locat' ad portand'
dicta instrumenta ad diversos vices ad siccand'*]. And 12d for 3 men
hired to remove water from the said ship [*conduct' pro aqua de dicta
navi ex^a ponend'*]. And 2s paid to diverse men hired to change [*ad
mutend'*] the said cables and move the said anchor twice. And 15s
given to the water bailiffs [*ballivis aque*] of Plymouth and other men
making the arrest of the said ship, by order of the said steward. Sum,
50s.

Sum of all expenses, £46 12s 10d. And he owes £150 9s 10d, And 38s
2½d remains from his account of customs called maltolt and cocket of
this year. And 24s 10d remains from his account from last year. Sum of
common debts, £153 12s 10½d. From which he delivers £115 10s
4½d to John de Kendale, receiver of the lord duke in the county of
Cornwall and Devon, by one indenture delivered on this account and
recognized by this same receiver [*recogn' ipsius Rec'*]. And he owes £38
2s 6d. From which he pays £24 to the said receiver on 14 February on
this account, without a bill by recognizance of the same receiver. And
he owes £14 2s 6d. {For which he responds in the great roll of debts
for this year, the 29th.} The issues of ports and maltolt with £20 from
one forfeited ship valued at £152 8s ½d.[65]

{HENCE OWING [*UNDE SUPER*]
Sir Nicholas Pynnok, recently an auditor (of the ministers' accounts)
of the lord prince, for the price of one tun of wine delivered to him
from the aforesaid wines by his own recognizance, owes £4 for this
and for other things. For which [debt] and for other monies owed by

---

[65.] This last sentence is written in the right-hand margin at the end of this section.

him and received by him from John de Kendale, receiver, as appears at the foot of the account of the same receiver for this year, all the goods of this Nicholas before his death? [*ante finem istius defuncti*] at his church of Lanteglos [*Lantegles*] within the lordship of the lord were seized into the hands of the lord. So the said Thomas was asked to pursue raising the money for the aforesaid [debts] in order to hasten discharging himself. And for him [*super ipsum*]Thomas delivered £10 2s 6d to the same John de Kendale, receiver, at the end of this account, by a bill containing the major sum by recognizance of the same receiver.}[66]

(m. 12d)

CRETAN WINES

The same responds for 2 pipes of Cretan wine remaining from his account of last year. Sum, 2 pipes of Cretan wine. {And they are added later below. And clear of debt.}

PLYMOUTH [*PLUMPMUTHE*]

The same renders account for 10 tuns of wine taken there from diverse ships docking there, of which 4 tuns for assize and 6 tuns quit and all [are] red Gascon wines, namely:

From a ship called *Edward* of Plymouth of which Robert Pole is master, on 3 November, 2 tuns of red wine.

From a ship called *le Nicholas* of Plymouth of which William Lake is master, on 12 November, 2 tuns red.

From a ship called *Cogion* of Plymouth of which Walter Crop is master (on the same day), 2 tuns red.

From a ship called *le Godale* of Gosford of which Stephen Jook is master, on 7 December, 2 tuns red.

From a ship called *la Rose* of Colchester [*Colcestr'*] of which Richard Estmar is master, on 7 December, 1 tun (red) taken at St Nicholas Island where ships are not held to pay custom because of an agreement made between merchants and the keeper.

[66.] The style of handwriting and colour of the ink suggests that this section was inserted after the body of the account had been written. Sir Nicholas Pynnok was still alive in December 1355; see *The Register of John Grandisson, Bishop of Exeter, 1327–69*, ed. F. C. Hingeston-Randolph, 3 vols (1894–9), II, p. 124. The Lanteglos here was probably that by Camelford, which was a duchy living. I thank Oliver Padel for pointing this connection out to me.

From a ship called *Cog Anne* of Yarmouth of which Geoffrey Frend is
master, on 8 December, <u>1 tun</u> red taken in the same Island under
the same agreement. Sum, 10 tuns of red wine.

LOOE

In the port there, nothing this year because no ships landed there this
year.

FOWEY

The same responds for 11 tuns of wine taken in the same port from
diverse ships, of which 9 tuns [are] red Gascon wine and 2 tuns white
Spanish wine and 5 tuns for assize and 6 tuns quit, namely:

From a ship called *Seintsaverescog* of Fowey of which Richard
Migelestawe is master, on 16 ~~December~~ November, <u>2 tuns</u> red.

From a ship called *la Maudeleygne* of Fowey of which Walter Hore is
master, on the same day, <u>2 tuns</u> red.

From a ship called *le Savoye* of Polruan of which Thomas Jean is master,
on the same (day), <u>2 tuns</u> red.

From a ship called *le Nicholas* of Polruan of which John Dandye is
master, on the same day, <u>2 tuns</u> red.

From a ship called *le ~~Nichol~~ Mighel* of Bodinnick [*Bodynnak*] of which
William Grek is master, on 8 November, <u>1 tun</u> red taken from the
same ship of 16 tuns by consent [*cons'*] of Robert Elford, steward.

From a ship called *le Neef Seintemarie* of *Mundak* of which John Pierres
of Rouen? [*Rane*] is master, on 25 October, 2 tuns of Spanish white.
Sum, 11 tuns of wine, 9 tuns red, 2 tuns Spanish white.

FALMOUTH

The same responds for 10 tuns of wine taken from diverse ships in the
same port of which <u>5 tuns</u> for assize and <u>5 tuns</u> quit. From which 8
tuns red Gascon wine and 2 tuns white Spanish wine, namely:

From a ship called *Cog Thomas* of Dartmouth of which John Wille is
master, on 13 November, <u>2 tuns</u> red.

From a ship called *le Elianor* of Dartmouth of which Nicholas Pierres[67]
is master, on the same day, <u>2 tuns</u> red.

From a ship called *le Mighel* of Dartmouth of which Roger Beamund is
master, on the same day, <u>2 tuns</u> red.

[67.] This name is written over an erasure.

From a ship called *Seintemarie Maudeleine* of Castrourdiales [*Cestr'*] of which Senchu Seys is master, on 11 February, 2 tuns of Spanish white.

From a ship called *le Nief Seint Nicholas* of the Ile de Batz [*del Isle de bas*] of which *Ruddyng* le Veillont is master, on the last day of February, 2 tuns red. Sum, 10 tuns wine of which 8 red, 2 white.

MOUSEHOLE AND PADSTOW

In the ports there, nothing this year because no ships landed there this year.

Sum of all tuns, 31 tuns and 2 pipes of which 2 pipes Cretan wine, 27 tuns red wine, 4 tuns Spanish wine.

From which he delivered to Sir Robert Pil, rector of the church of Crewkerne [*Crokerne*], from the gift of the lord, 1 tun of red wine, priced at 106s 8d, as appears in the letters of the lord directed to the same keeper, dated 13 September in the 28th year, remaining in the memoranda of this year.

Sold, as below, 2 pipes of Cretan wine, 26 tuns of red Gascon wine and 4 tuns of white Spanish wine.

And none remains.

ACCOUNT OF THOMAS FILZ HENRY, KEEPER OF THE CUSTOMS WHICH ARE CALLED MALTOLT AND COCKET IN THE COUNTY OF CORNWALL IN THE TIME WRITTEN BELOW.

ISSUES OF MALTOLT

The same responds for 4s 2d from Oliver Leys of Guérande, alien, for custom on £16 16s 4d [worth] of salt sold in the port of Fowey.

And for 2s 3d from *Adon* Lukyn, alien, for custom on £8 18s of salt sold in the aforesaid port.

And for 4s 1d from Oliver Bisen, alien, for custom on £16 4s 4d of salt sold in the aforesaid port.

And for 6s from *Furteyn* Eveneis, alien, for custom on £24 of salt sold in the aforesaid port.

And for 3s from *Guillelm* Sandroun, alien, for custom on £12 of salt sold in the aforesaid port.

And for 4s 1d from *Guillelm* Eder, alien, for custom on £16 of salt sold in the aforesaid port.

And for 2s 7½d from Stephen Godare, alien, for £10 12s 6d of salt sold in the aforesaid port.

And for 2s 6d from John Gader, alien, for custom on £10 of salt sold in the aforesaid port.

And for 4s 6d from William Berad, alien, for custom on £18 of salt sold in the aforesaid port.

And for 18d from Robert Burges, alien, for custom on £6 of salt sold in the port of Mousehole.

And for 18d from Roger Haukyn, alien, for custom on £6 of salt sold in the aforesaid port.

And for 6d from *Wyo* Uschent, alien, for custom on 40s of salt sold in the aforesaid place.

And for 18d from Daniel Cunket, alien, for custom ~~of salt~~ on £6 of salt sold in the aforesaid place.

He does not respond this year for custom of cocket for carriage of wool, skins, and hides carried from England overseas, because it was ordered by a new statute made in Parliament that no denizens should carry this merchandise overseas except to staples ordered in England [*set ad stapulum ordinatum in Angl'*] .

Sum, 38s 2½d. For which he responds below at the foot of his account for custody of the ports this year. And he is quit here.

LETTER ON THE DELIVERY OF A CERTAIN ALIEN SHIP CALLED *LE ESTACE* OF DIEPPE [*DEPE*][68]

Edward etc., greetings to our dear servants, Robert de Elleford, our steward and sheriff of Cornwall, and to Thomas Fitz Henry, our havener there. Because it was witnessed to our beloved lord and father the king and his council by our beloved cousin, the duke of Lancaster, and the earl of Arundel that the ships and merchandise contained in them that were taken and arrested at sea during the last truce [*puis le darreyn trewe ount estez? sur miere*] from English merchants by foreign enemies [*des parties de laa*] should be entirely restored to them as they were when taken and arrested, it was thus ordered by our said lord and his council that the ships and merchandise taken by us at sea from foreign [*de delaa*] merchants should also be entirely restored to them. And we have heard that a ship called *la neof de Seynt Eustace* of Dieppe, loaded with *caka* herring [*harrang Caka*], was taken while sailing at sea by one Lawrence Porcher and taken to Plymouth and there arrested by the bailiffs of the same. And the said Lawrence was ordered by the said bailiffs to give his warranty for one year and one day [*de faire venir son*

---

68. The following is in French.

garrant deuz un an et un jour] and he guaranteed [*il wayna*] the said ship and its merchandise were forfeited to us. And then one Vincent Chastell of Dieppe came to us contesting the said ship and the merchandise because they were taken during the truce and praying they should be restored as our merchandise was restored to us by foreigners [*delaa*]. Thus we order you that you should soon deliver to the said Vincent [*P' quei vos mandons q' tantost vous cestes fatez deliver' au dit Vincent*] the said ship and said merchandise together also with all the equipment [*laparaill'*] of the same ship as they were when arrested. And in case the said ship should be sold or nothing of the said merchandise remains, do this hastily and without delay. Given at London, 24 April, in the 29th year.

1355/56

PRO, 30/26/258 [69]

29–30 Edward III. 11 membranes. Ministers' accounts of the duchy of Cornwall in Cornwall and Devon (mm. 1–9d), with accounts of the keeper of fees (m. 9d), havener (mm. 10–10d), and sheriff (mm. 11–11d). The havener's account, which is on m. 10, consists of three shorter membranes sewn end-to-end.

(m. 2)

TREMATON

[...]

RENTS OR CONVENTIONARY FARMS

[...] 5s from fishery of Lynher Water [...] He responds for nothing from the £10 from the farm of the passage of Saltash Water at Easter and Michaelmas with rent of oars belonging to the same passage as contained in the preceding account, because leased to Ric Juyl and others with

---

[69]. This roll was originally listed as Ministers' Account Roll 9 in the nineteenth-century catalogue in the Duchy of Cornwall Office. By the 1960s, however, it was missing since Stella Campbell did not include it in her list of havener's accounts (Campbell, p. 144). In August 1997 it was brought into the Devon Record Office, where it was marked 'Temporary Deposit 382'. It was transferred to the Public Record Office in Kew in November 1997. It is likely that the roll was separated from the other duchy documents when they were stored on Dartmoor during World War II.

the mills and other profits written below for the term of 7 years this
year being the first, for 22 marks per year, for which the bailiff of
Saltash in his account for this year [...] and he responds for nothing
from the toll of oysters that is commonly worth 3d, for the same reason.
And he responds for nothing from the farm of the Water and Pool of
Sutton that is accustomed to lease for £10 per year, because leased to
John Dabernoun for the term of his life as he responds below. [...]

RENTS OR FARMS FOR THE TERM OF LIVES
He responds for £6 13s 4d from the farm of the Water and Pool of
Sutton as conceded and leased to John Dabernon for the term of his
life by letters patent of the lord duke, dated 5 February in the 24th
year [1350], as appears at the foot of the account for the 23rd year,
which before the pestilence rented for £10 per year. [...]

(m. 2d)

[...]

HENCE OWING [*UNDE SUPER*]
£18 10s of John de Haule, once farmer of Sutton Water by commission
of the lord prince for the last part of the 18th year and the 19th and
20th and the third part of the 21st year. From diverse fishers tenants of
John de Monte Acuto for fish sold against the statute and outside the
lordship who were amerced 40s; for which he was charged above, to
respond to him next Michaelmas, because the same John says that his
tenants do not owe amercements for these sales. So that meanwhile he
should follow the custom with a view to better clarifying his right? [*Ita
quod interim sequatur cons' cm' pro iure suo melius inde declarand*].[...]
[...]

SALTASH BOROUGH
    FARMS
The same accounts for [...] the tolls of the fair, estimated worth 5s, and
market tolls and petty custom and toll of oysters, estimated worth per
year 8s, the barges and seines and other customs belonging to the said
borough are worth 16s per year, as in the preceding account, all leased
to the burgesses of Saltash for 7 years, as in the preceding account. [...]
And £14 13s 4d from the rent and farm of Saltash Water with the rent
of oars belonging to the same passage, which rents for £10 per year
and the farm of the water mills, rent of the *cens'* of the borough of
Trematon, which is worth 12d per year, and the pleas and perquisites

of the same borough, estimated worth is 40s, the toll of oysters, worth 3d per year, and the herbage of the castle ditch [...] leased to Richard Juyl and his fellows from Michaelmas in the 29th year of Edward III [1355] for 8 years, this year being the first.

[...]

(m. 4)

LOSTWITHIEL

[...]

PROFITS OF THE FISHERY OF FOWEY WATER AND OTHER PROFITS OF THE SAME WATER

And for 11s 6½d from profits of the fishery of Fowey Water during the time of this account as contained in the same indenture delivered on this account. And for 15s 6d arising from keelage of ships of foreigners during the time of the account, whence 16d from each ship having a boat and 8d from each ship not having a boat, except 1 ship of Guernsey whence 2 *tum?* by its liberty as contained in a certain roll of names of these ships delivered on this account.

And for 2s 6d received from the pleas and perquisites of maritime courts during the same time as contained there.

And for 10s 2d from the price of 1 quarter 1 bushel of wheat arising from the custom of measures [*modii*] of the lord, priced at 13½d per bushel, ½d more in total [*plus in toto ob'*] as contained there.

And for 14d from the price of 2 bushels of barley arising from the same custom as contained in the same place.

And for 3s 4d from the price of 4 bushels of rye arising from the same custom at 10d per bushel as contained there.

And for 2s 4d from the price of 2 bushels of wheat arising from the same custom as contained there.

And for 2s 2d from 2 bushels of beans arising from the same custom as contained there.

And for 6d from the price of 2 bushels of *stoncol* arising from the same custom as contained there.

And for 8d from the price of 2 bushels of *stoncol* arising from the same custom as contained there.

And for 7s 6d from the price of 2½ quarters of salt from 10 ships landing in the port of Fowey for having measurage [*modio*] of the lord, priced at 3½d per bushel as contained there. Sum, 57s 4½d.

[...]

Care of the Mill and Other Necessaries

He renders account for [...] 2s for 12 men repairing the mill pool for one day and 9s for the purchase of 1 new net and all equipment [*appar'*] of the same. And 8s 6d for collecting all the aforesaid customs and carrying them from Fowey to Lostwithiel along with doing the measures [*factura modiorum*] during the same time, as appears in the roll of particulars. [...]

[...]

(m. 10)

Account of Thomas Filz Henry keeper, of the ports in the county of Cornwall and prisage of wines in the same county and in Sutton Water in the county of Devon, and issues of ports in the same county of Cornwall and wreck of sea in the same county from Michaelmas in the 29th regnal year of king Edward III after the conquest until the same feast next following in the 30th year for one whole year.

Farms of the Ports

The same responds for 46s 8d from the farm of the port of Marazion per year at the feasts of Easter and Michaelmas equally. And for 12s from the farm of the port of Penzance per year at the same terms. And for 20s from the farm of the port of Newlyn [*Newlyn*] per year at the same terms. And for 100s from the farm of the port of Mousehole per year at the same terms. And nothing of the 12d from the farm of the port of Lamorna this year because boats cannot be found there for lack of men because of the pestilence. And for 2s from the farm of the port of Porthgwarra per year which used to render 12s per year and no more for lack of men and boats because of the pestilence. And for 2s from the farm of the port of 'Porthplement' [*Porthplenenum*] per year which used to render 8s per year and no more for the aforesaid cause. And for 40s from the farm of the port of Fowey per year at the same terms. And for 25s from the farm of the ports of Kerrier per year at the same terms. And for 20s from the farm of the port of Polruan per year at the same terms. And for 20s from the farm of the ports of Trigg per year at the same terms. And for £6 from the farm of the port of St Ives which used to render per year £6. Nothing from the 6s 8d from the farm of the ports of Porthzennor and Portheras for the aforesaid cause. Sum, £20 7s 8d.

SALE OF WINES

The same responds for £18 13s 4d for 4 tuns of white Spanish wine sold at Plymouth, priced at £4 13s 4d per tun. And for £16 6s 8d for 3 tuns and 1 pipe of red Gascon wine sold there, priced at £4 13s 4d per tun. And for £10 for 2 tuns of red Gascon wine sold there, priced at 100s per tun. And for £10 6s 8d for 2 tuns of red Gascon wine sold there, priced at 103s 4d per tun. And for £13 6s 8d for 2 tuns and 2 pipes of red Gascon wine sold there, priced at 106s 8d per tun. And for £10 for 2 tuns of white Spanish muscadine [*musto*] sold there, priced at 100s per tun.

And for £23 6s 8d for 5 tuns of red Gascon wine sold at Fowey, priced at £4 13s 4d per tun. And for £10 6s 8d for 2 tuns of red Gascon wine sold there, priced at 103s 4d per tun. And for £9 6s 8d for 2 tuns of red Gascon wine sold there, priced at £4 13s 4d per tun.

And for £9 6s 8d for 2 tuns of red Gascon wine sold at Falmouth, priced at £4 13s 4d per tun. And for £41 6s 8d for 8 tuns of red Gascon wine sold there, priced at 103s 4d per tun. And for £18 13s 4d for 4 tuns of red Gascon wine sold there, priced at £4 13s 4d per tun. And for £10 13s 4d for 2 tuns of red Gascon wine sold there in a ship, priced at 106s 8d per tun. And for £10 6s 8d for 2 tuns of red Gascon wine sold there, priced at 103s 4d per tun. And for £9 6s 8d for 2 tuns of red Gascon wine sold there, priced at £4 13s 4d per tun. And for 40s from the price of 1 tun of wine granted to Richard de Wolueston by the lord, at the same price that the lord pays for wine of prisage, as contained in letters of the lord directed to the same keeper, as wine drawn to give to the same Richard.

Sum, £223 6s 8d from 45 tuns of wine of which 4 tuns white Spanish, 2 tuns Spanish muscadine, 39 tuns red Gascon.

CUSTOM OF WINES OF ALIENS

Nothing this year from the customs of wines of aliens landing at the ports of Cornwall which is accustomed to have 2s from each tun for custom because no foreigners landed this year. Sum, nothing.

WRECK OF SEA WITH FORFEITURES

The same responds for 3s from 1 mast of a certain boat arising from wreck at Porthoustock [*Porthustek*] and no more because it was sold for 6s. From which 3s was delivered to men for salvage of the same. And for 30s for one scaff [*chaffa*] found sunk at sea and towed to land at Looe and no more because sold for 60s for which 30s was delivered to the men for their labor salvaging the same. And for 13s 4d for a

~~certain cock-boat [coketta]~~ (for the price of 1 boat of Walter Holman)[70] forfeited to the lord because of the death of a certain man falling from it and drowning in the sea at Padstow. ~~He does not respond for a certain mast arising from wreck at the River Allen [Leygne][71] within the lordship of Penrose [Penros] this year because it was not proclaimed during the time of this account but in the next following year. The same is to respond in a future year for a certain boat arising from wreck at Porthoustock [Porthusteck] for the aforesaid reason.~~ So he is to respond in a future year. {~~let him respond in a future year~~ cancelled here because below}[72]

FINES OF MERCHANTS WITH TRANTERY
The same responds for 34s received from fines of merchants with trantery at Mousehole this year. Sum, 34s.

PERQUISITES OF MARITIME COURTS
The same responds for 63s received from perquisites of the martime courts this year. Sum, 63s.

WRECK
He does not respond here for a certain mast arising from wreck at the River Allen [Lengne] within the lordship of Penrose this year because it was not proclaimed to the lord during the time of this account but in the next following year. So he is to respond in a future year. Nor for a certain boat arising from a wreck at Porthoustock for the aforesaid reason. So he is to respond in a future year. Sum, nothing. {let him respond in a future year}[73]

Sum total received, £250 17s 8d. From which:

WAGES AND FEES
The same accounts for payment of stipend of £6 13s 4d for his wages

---

70. This boat of Walter Holman's is also noted under the section of this account for the hundred of Pyder (m. 8), where 13s 4d collected from the price of the boat, appraised by Robert de Elleford, sheriff and steward. In the SUMMA of that account, the bailiff of the hundred is exonerated for this amount because Thomas Havener, keeper of the ports was charged for it in his account.

71. The River Allen was called the *Layne* in the middle ages (O.J. Padel, *A Popular Dictionary of Cornish Place-Names* (Penzance, 1988), p. 50).

72. This last is written in the right-hand margin.

73. This last is written twice in the right-hand margin, once for each entry.

and fees from Michaelmas in the 29th year until the same feast following for one whole year to the 30th year. And 13s 4d for his robe for the term of his life as conceded by charter of the lord (cancelled because forbidden by council of the lord at Berkhamstead that this should not be allowed but he can take a robe from the wardrobe of the lord). Sum, £6 13s 4d.

CUSTOM OF WINES

The same pays £42 to diverse merchants for 21 tuns of wine taken from them for assize, at <u>40s</u> per tun and no more because 1 tun of wine recently taken for assize from a ship called *Seyntemaribot* of Dartmouth was restored to Richard C..., master of the ship, by letters of the lord as in the dorse of this roll. Sum, £42.

CARE OF WINES

For 20d for towage of 10 tuns at Plymouth from the sea to land, at <u>2d</u> per tun. And 2s 6d for rollage of them to the cellar, at <u>3d</u> per tun. Also 8d for hire of a cellar for storing 3 tuns of wine from the second seizure from 29 December to 12 January for 2 weeks, at <u>4d</u> per week. Also 4s for 8 gallons of wine for ullage of the same, at <u>6d</u> per gallon. Also 4d for hire of the same cellar in the high street for storing 2 tuns of wine from 15 March to the 22nd day of the same month for one week. Also 2s 6d for 5 gallons of wine for ullage of them and 2 other tuns in the cellar for 3 days, priced at <u>6d</u> per gallon. Also 2s for towage of 2 tuns towed there from St Nicholas Island, for <u>12d</u> per tun. Also 8d for towage of another 4 tuns in the port there from the sea to land, at <u>2d</u> per tun. Also 18d for rollage of 6 tuns to the cellar, at <u>3d</u> per tun. Also 2s for hire of a cellar for storing the said wines from 29 April to 11 June for 6 weeks, at <u>4d</u> per week. Also 6s for 12 gallons of wine for ullage of the same during the same time, priced at <u>6d</u> per gallon. Also 18d for the price of 3 gallons for ullage for 2 tuns of muscadine from the aforesaid 6 tuns, priced at <u>6d</u> per gallon.

And 9d for towage of 9 tuns at Fowey, at <u>1d</u> per tun. Also 2s 3d for rollage of the same to the cellar, at <u>3d</u> per tun. Also 4d for the hire of a cellar for storing 4 tuns from 13 December to the 20th day of the same month for one week. Also 3s 6d for price of 7 gallons of wine for ullage of the same with one tun from the first seizure in the cellar for 3 days, priced at <u>6d</u> per gallon. Also 16d for the price of 2 gallons for ullage of another 2 tuns there, priced at <u>8d</u> per gallon. Also 3s for the price of 6 gallons of wine for ullage of 2 tuns there from the last seizure, laying in the cellar for 4 weeks, priced at <u>6d</u> per gallon.

Also 10s for towage of 10 tuns at Falmouth towed for the space of 2 leagues, at 12d per tun. Also 2s 6d for rollage of the same to the cellar, at 3d per tun. Also 2s 6d for the price of 5 gallons of wine for ullage of 2 tuns from the first seizure from the first of December to the 15th day of the same month, priced at 6d per gallon. Also 12d for the price of 2 gallons for ullage of another 2 tuns, priced at 6d per gallon. Also 8d for cellarage of the same for 2 weeks, at 4d per week. Also for 2s 8d for cellarage of 6 tuns from the last seizure from 21 March to 20 June for 8 weeks, at 4d per week. Also 12s for the price of 24 gallons of wine for ullage of the same during the same time, priced at 6d per gallon. And for 15d for 15 barrel hoops for binding and repairing the same tuns, priced at 1d per hoop band. Also 2s for one boat hired to serve the keeper in a ship with five men for 2 days, taking 12d per day. Also 12d for another boat hired by the sheriff to serve the same keeper for 1 day. Sum, 72s 1d.

Sum of all expenses, £52 5s 5d. And he owes £198 12s 3d. And £4 13s 4d from the remainder of the account of customs called maltolt from this year as enrolled on this dorse. And £14 2s 6d from the remainder of his account of prisage of wines for last year. Sum of common debts, £217 8s 5d. From which he delivered to John de Kendal, receiver, the aforesaid £14 2s 6d from the arrears by one indenture delivered on this account and acknowledged by this same receiver. And £122 10d to the same receiver from the issues of this year by one indenture delivered on this account and acknowledged by this same receiver. And £77 16s 8d to this same receiver on this account on 11 March in the 31st year [1357] from the issues of this 30th year without indenture by recognizance of the same receiver. And 68s 5d to the same receiver on the same 11th day for issues of the aforesaid without indenture by recognizance of the same receiver. Sum of moneys delivered, £217 8s 5d. And he is quit. {prisage of wines (^ with other petty customs) worth £298 12s 3d}[74]

(m. 10d)

Plymouth

The same responds for 14 tuns of wine and 2 tuns of muscadine taken from diverse ships landing there from which 10 tuns of red Gascon wine and 6 tuns of white Spanish wine and muscadine of which 7 tuns for assize and 9 tuns quit, namely:

[74.] This last is written in the right-hand margin.

From a ship called *le Edward* of Plymouth of which Robert Pole is master, on 15 December, 2 tuns of red without charter of the butler [*sine cart' Butiller'*] (it unloaded in port).

From a ship called *le Nicholas* of Plasencia [*Plesance*] of which Martin Fanus is master, on 29 December, 2 tuns of white with charter of the butler because freighted [*frecta*] (outside the duchy).

From a ship called *le Neif Seintmarie* of Lisbon [*Lussebon*] of which Peter Seyntmartyn is master, on the same day, 2 tuns of wine with charter of the butler for the aforesaid reason.

From a ship called *le Jorge* of Plymouth of which Richard Coke is master, on 15th day of the same month, 2 tuns of red without charter for the aforesaid reason.

From a ship called *le Nau Seyntanton* of Bayonne of which Martin Lode is master, on 29 March, 2 tuns of white with charter for the aforesaid reason.

From a ship called *le Gudberad* of Zierikzee [*Cirice*] of which Peter Clayssone is master, on 29 April, 1 tun of red taken in St Nicholas Island where ships are not obliged to pay except [*nisi*] by agreement of the keeper and merchants, with charter for the aforesaid reason.

From a ship called *le Andreu* of Yarmouth of which Thomas Box is master, on the same day, 1 tun of red taken in St Nicholas Island where ships are not obliged to pay except by agreement of the keeper and merchants, with charter for the aforesaid reason.

From a ship called *le Edward* of Plymouth of which Robert Pole is master, on 3 May, 2 tuns of red without charter because it unloaded in port.

Sum, 14 tuns of wine of which 10 tuns red wine, 4 tuns white wine; and 2 tuns of white muscadine. Of which <u>7 tuns</u> from assize, 9 tuns quit of prisage.

FOWEY

The same responds for 9 tuns of red Gascon wine taken from diverse ships landing there, of which <u>4 tuns</u> for assize and <u>5 tuns</u> quit, namely:

From a ship called *le Savoye* of Polruan of which Thoams John is master, 1 tun red taken on 23 November outside the port by order and council of Robert de Elleford, steward, with charter of the butlery [*Botillerie*] because they were not unloaded in the duchy.

From a ship called *Cog Johan* of Fowey of which John Tegan is master, on 13 December, 2 tuns of red without charter because unloaded in port.

From a ship called *le James* of Fowey of which *Everyn* Crouwe is master, on the same day, 2 tuns of red without charter for the aforesaid reason.

From a ship called *le Trinite* of Plymouth of which Walter Hereward is master, on 15 May, 2 tuns of red without charter for the aforesaid reason.

From a ship called *le Maudeleigne* of Fowey of which Walter Hor' is master, on the last day of April, 2 tuns of red without charter for the aforesaid reason.

Sum, 9 tuns of red Gascon wine of which 4 for assize, 5 quit.

FALMOUTH

The same responds for 23 tuns of red Gascon wine taken from diverse ships landing there of which 11 tuns for assize and 12 tuns quit, namely:

From a ship called *le Cog de Tousseyns* of Dartmouth of which William Fisher is master, on 1 December, 2 tuns of red with charter of the butler because it was freighted outside the liberty of the duchy.

From a ship called *le Grace Dieux* of Yarmouth of which John Wilcatyn is master, on 20 March, 2 tuns of red with charter for the aforesaid reason.

From a ship called *le Grace Dieu* of Hook of which John Weryn is master, on the same day, 2 tuns of red with charter for the aforesaid reason.

From a ship called *Clement* of Dartmouth of which William Combe is master, on the same day, 2 tuns of red, with charter for the aforesaid reason.

From a ship called *Seintmaribot* of Dartmouth of which Richard Gille is master, on the same day, 2 tuns of red, with charter for the aforesaid reason.

From a ship called *le Naudieu* of Bayonne [*Baone*] of which Martin de Hubeage is master, on the same day, 2 tuns of red with charter for the aforesaid reason.

From a ship called *le Gabriel* of Dartmouth of which John Knol is master, on 21 March, 2 tuns of red with charter for the aforesaid reason.

From a ship called *le Welfare* of Shoreham of which Nicholas Blake is master, on 5 April, 2 tuns of red with charter for the aforesaid reason.

From a ship called *le Nau Seintespirit* of Bayonne of which John Ranefe is master, on the same day, 2 tuns of red with charter for the aforesaid reason.

From a ship called *la Jonete* of Lynn [*Lynne*] of which John Pounfrect is master, on 20 March, 2 tuns of red with charter for the aforesaid reason.

From a ship called *la Custance* of Dartmouth of which Robert Belman is master, on 18 March, 1 tun of red taken outside the port of Falmouth by agreement of the keeper and merchants becuase freighted in Flanders with charter.

From a ship called *Seintmaribot* of Dartmouth of which Richard Gille is master, on 19 June, 2 tuns of red with charter for the aforesaid reason.

The same responds for 1 tun of red wine taken at Land's End in the high seas [*Londeshend in summo mar'*] by agreement of the keeper and merchants of a ship called *le Nau Tousseyne* of Bayonne of which *Arnald* Dalysdourt is master, on 10 April with charter for the aforesaid reason.

Sum, 24 tuns of red Gascon wine of which 11 tuns for assize, 13 tuns quit.

Padstow

Nothing from prisage of wines in the port there this year because no ships land with wine this year. Sum, nothing.

Mousehole, Looe

Nothing from prisage of wines in the ports there this year for the aforesaid reason. Sum, nothing.

Sum total, 49 tuns of wine of which 2 tuns muscadine, of which 22 tuns from assize, 27 tuns quit. And from which:

From which 1 tun of wine was delivered to Richard de Wolveston from the first vintage wines as a gift of the lord from the ship called *le Cog de Touz Seyntz* of Dartmouth, landing in the port of Falmouth on 1 December, as above, as appears in letters of the lord directed to the same keeper which are dated 6 December[75] in the 29th regnal year of king Edward III [1355] after the conquest. And he has 1 tun for 40s from the same ship, as in the sale of wines below, as enrolled in the same letters below, delivered on this account; the said keeper by these orders should make delivery to the same Richard of the said two tuns of wine from the first wines coming from the prisage of the lord, receiving from him the money that merchants paid for the same wines.

[75.] This is a mistake for September. See below, and n. 78, for the letter.

And also he delivered from the said wines to Richard Gille, master
of the ship called *Seyntmaribot* of Dartmouth as a gift of the lord, 2
tuns of wine taken from prisage of the same ship landing in the port of
Falmouth on 19 June this year, as above, conceded to him by the lord
for his voyage from Gascony in England with *Dagenet*, messenger of
the lord, as appears in letters of the lord directed to the same keeper
which are dated 4 November in the 30th regnal year of king Edward
III after the conquest, namely from the year of the lord 1356, enrolled
after the end of this account.

For sale, as below, 45 tuns. And none remain.[76]

ACCOUNT OF THOMAS FITZ HENR', KEEPER OF CUSTOMS WHICH ARE CALLED
MALTOLT AND COCKET, IN THE COUNTY OF CORNWALL FROM MICHAELMAS IN
THE 29TH REGNAL YEAR OF KING EDWARD III AFTER THE CONQUEST TO THE
SAME FEAST FOLLOWING IN THE 30TH YEAR OF THE SAME KING.

ISSUES OF MALTOLT

The same responds for 7s 9d received from William Plomer alien for
custom on £31 for wine purchased at Fowey, that is, 3d on the £.

And for 5s 3d received from *Evoun* Pascal alien for customs on £21 for
salt sold in the aforesaid place.

And for 3s 5d received from William Gille alien for custom on £13 13s
for salt sold in the aforesaid place.

And for 3s 11d received from *Morice* Raulyn alien for custom on £15
13s for salt sold in the aforesaid place.

And for 2s 1d received from *Focard* Merchant alien for custom on £8
6s 8d for salt sold in the aforesaid place.

And for 5s received from *Even* Tannon alien for custom on £20 for
corn sold at Falmouth.

And for 4s received from *Prygent'* Cardynat alien for custom on £16
for corn sold in the aforesaid place.

And for 3s 9d received from *Hervy* Juncour alien for custom on £19
for corn sold in the aforesaid place.

And for 5s recevied from *Hervy* Tydolet for custom on £20 for salt
sold in the aforesaid place.

And for 6s received from *Tangy* Bretoun alien for custom on £24 for
salt sold in the aforesaid place.

And for 5s received from John Kerneketh alien for custom on £20 for
corn sold at Newlyn in Mount's Bay [*Lulyn en le Mountesbaye*].

---

[76] There are several illegible lines scribbled in the right-hand margin.

And for 4s (^ 6d) received from William Engleys alien for custom on
£18 for salt sold at Mousehole.

And for 9s received from William Parcel alien for custom on £26 for
corn sold at Marazion.

And for 5s received from Martin Tangy alien for custom on £20 for
salt sold at Mousehole.

And for 5s received from Robert Brachel alien for custom on £20 for
corn sold at Marazion.

And for 8s received from Richard Garant alien for custom on £32 for
corn sold at Newlyn.

Sum, £4 13s 8d. For which the same keeper responds at the foot of the
account of prisage of wines as below. And he is quit here.

He does not respond for the custom of cocket for carriage of wool fells
and hides carried from England to parts overseas this year because it
was ordered by a new statute made in Parliament that no denizens
should carry this merchandise to parts overseas but to the designated
staple in England.

LETTERS FOR RICHARD GILLE[77]

Edward etc., greetings to our dear valet Thomas (^ filz) Henry, our
havener in parts of Cornwall and Devonshire. Because of certain pressing
needs affecting us on the way to England [*devers England*] from the
feast of St John the Baptist last, we send our messenger *Dagenet* de
Baione to your parts in a ship called *Sent Marie Bot* of Dartmouth for
which passage we excuse the master of the said ship the prise that he
must pay to us when he comes to your parts [*perdonismes a meistre du
dit nefe les prises qil nous devoit paier a sa venue en vos dites parties*].
And we command that if you have taken any prise from the said master
for this passage that you repay it according to our aforesaid grant. And
this letter will be your warrant. Given at Bordeaux the 4th of November
in the year of grace 1356.

LETTERS FOR RICHARD DE WOLVESTON[78]

Edward, etc., greetings to our dear valet Thomas fitz Henri, our havener
of Cornwall. Because [*Pur ceo q'*] we have given to our dear clerk

---

77. The following is in French. This letter is not noted in the BPR.
78. The following is in French. This letter is noted in BPR, II, p. 87, where it is
   dated 7 September 1355 and written at Plymouth.

Richard de Wolveston, keeper of our privy seal, two tuns of wine from the first wines that will come to us from prise in your bailiwick, we order you to make delivery of the same wine to him, receiving from him the money that you have paid to merchants for the said wine. And by this letter you will be warranted. Dated at Plymouth on 6 September in the 29th regnal year of our beloved father the king of England and the 16th of France [1355].

Receipt of Charters [*Rec' cart'*]

The same keeper renders account for 25 blank charters [*cart' alb'*] received from John de Hale, recently keeper of the privy seal of the said lord prince, on 14 September in the 28th year [1354] by the hand of Nicholas Pynnok by 1 indenture between this John and the aforesaid keeper. And for 30 blank charters received from John de Kendal, receiver of monies of the lord prince in Cornwall, on 5 September, by 1 indenture between him ~~keeper~~ John de Kendal and the aforesaid keeper. Sum, 60 blank charters.

Delivery of Charters

The same accounts for delivery of 8 blank charters to diverse sailors [*naut'*] paying prise and not unloading within the duchy between Michaelmas in the 28th year to the same feast in the 29th, as appears in his account for the same year. And for delivery of 30 blank charters to diverse sailors paying prise and not unloading within the duchy between Michaelmas in the 29th year to the same feast in the 30th year, as appears in his account for the same time. Sum, 29 and 30 remain.

Part III

Customs Accounts for the
Earldom of Cornwall

1284–87

PRO, E122/39/3

13–15 Edward I. 1 thin membrane, indented on the left side. Account of John Coulying and Walter la Byry of Bodmin of 'new' custom[1] collected for the king in Cornwall. The handwriting is small, cramped and sometimes faded.

Receipt of collection of new custom of the lord king of England by the hand of John Coulyng and Walter la Byry of Bodmin, collectors of the aforesaid custom in Cornwall in the 13th regnal year of King Edward [1284–85].

The same collectors received from Roger Karudov? of Looe for ½ last of hides
From Roger de Templo for 12 dickers and 1 hide
From Robert de Sancto Genesio for 13 dickers and 9 hides
From William Parvo for 11 dickers and 7 hides
From Edward de la Byry for 16 dickers and 1 hide
From Roger Ylg' for 1 last and 4 dickers
From John Coulyng for 1 last and 3 dickers and 5 hides
From John Coulyng junior for 2 dickers and 1 hide
From Stephen le Bera for 15 dickers
From *Draco* de la Byry for 15 dickers and 5 hides
From *Ancret* Hynton? for 9 dickers and 1 hide
From Richard Vatecoln? for 5 dickers
From Walter de Sancta Margareta for 1 last and 4 dickers
From John Mollyng for 8 dickers
From Ralph Reda for 2 lasts.
From William Habram for 8 hides
From Roger Lowys for 2 dickers and 7 hides

[1.] After 1303, this was called 'ancient custom,' the name by which it is more commonly known.

From William de Camileford for 1 dicker and 8 hides
From Hugh Ivo for 4 dickers and 5 hides
From Thomas Minor? of Truro for ½ last and 2 hides
From Hervey Bally for 1 last and 15 dickers and 3 hides
From John de Nansaluys for 9 hides
From Roger Martyn for 1 last
From John Coulyng for 9 ½ dickers
Sum, 16 lasts 3 dickers and 8 hides.

ALSO IN THE 14ᵀᴴ REGNAL YEAR OF KING EDWARD [1285–86]

From William de Camileford for 18 dickers and 2 hides
From Walter Cliber of Looe for 14 dickers and 3 hides. Also from the
    same, 13 hides
From David de Truru for 1 last and 13 hides
From Gervase de Talgarret for 1½ lasts and 1 dicker and 6 hides
From John Lernnar for 8 dickers
From Hervey le Bally for 16 dickers
From Robert Herson for 9 dickers
From Stephen le Rous for 2½ lasts and 2 hides
From Walter de Sancta Margareta for 18 dickers and 1 hides
From Stephen le Bera for 8 dickers and 3 hides
From John Mollyng for ½ last and 2 hides
From Peter de Canteville for 16 hides
From Osmund Fellard for 3 dickers
From William Brun for 1 dicker
From Sarra widow of Roger Ylg' for 26 dickers and 5 hides
From John Coulyng junior for 13 dickers and 9 hides
From Walter de Sancta Margaret for 3 dickers and 5 hides
From Walter Parvo for 13 dickers
From William de Polifont for 16 dickers and 3 hides
From William de Esse for 6 dickers
From Roger de Templo for 2 dickers
From John le Pref of Helston [*Helliston*] and John le Croyl? From the
    same for 2½ lasts and 25 hides
Form Edward de la Byr for 16 dickers and 1 hide
From John Coulyng senior for 1½ lasts and 4 dickers
From John Coulyng junior for 3 lasts and ½.
From Droco de la Byry for 17 dickers and 2 hides
From Godfrey le Mercer for 16 dickers
Sum, 24 lasts, 19 dickers and 1 hide.

ALSO IN THE 15TH REGNAL YEAR OF KING EDWARD [1286–87]

From William de Wis? of Truro and Gervase de Talgarr for 4 lasts
From Roger de Trelurnis for 8 dickers and 3 hides
From John de Penhal for 7 dickers and 2 hides
From Gregory Luca of Looe for 8 hides
From Walter Parvo for 10 dickers
From Michael Carballa, 6 dickers and 2 hides
From Roger Waspedor, 2 hides
From Walter de Rupe for 5 dickers
From Richard Fatta junior for 17 dickers
From William de Esse for 9 dickers and 5 hides
From Walter de Esse for 9 dickers
From William de Polafont for 1 last and 3 hides
From Osmund Feland for 3 dickers
From Richard Vatacoln?, ½ last 1 dicker and 1 hide
From Stephen le Rous for 2 lasts 1 dicker 3 hides
From Walter de Sancta Margaret for 1 last 2 dickers 3 hides
From Sarra widow of Roger Ylg' for 18 dickers 7 hides
From William (^ Parte) for 17 dickers 3 hides
From John le Pref of Helston [*Helliston*] and John Sleyton?, from the
    same for 2 lasts and 1 dicker and 5 hides
From John le Bari for 14 dickers and 1 hide
From John Coulyng senior for 1 last 13 dickers
From John Coulyng junior for 1 last.
From Roger de Templo for 7 dickers
From Richard Vatecok for 10 dickers
From *Droco* de la Byry for 8 dickers
Sum, 21 lasts 7 dickers and 9 hides.

Sum of sums, 62½ lasts and 7 hides
Sum of money, £41 13s 9¼d.

1289–93

PRO, E122/39/4

17–21 Edward I. One short piece of parchment indented on the top.
Account of John Culling and Walter de la Byry, collectors for the king

of 'new' custom in the ports of Cornwall from 10 April 1289 to March 1293. The sections are written in run-on paragraphs.

ACCOUNT OF JOHN CULLING AND WALTER DE LA BYR' COLLECTORS OF NEW CUSTOM OF THE LORD KING IN THE PORTS OF CORNWALL FROM EASTER IN THE 17TH REGNAL YEAR OF KING EDWARD UNTIL EASTER IN THE 21ST YEAR OF THE SAME AS IS CONTAINED BELOW IN PARTICULARS

The same renders account from Easter in the 17th year [10 April, 1289] until Easter in the 18th year [2 April, 1290], namely:
From Stephen le Rous for 15 dickers of hides
From Richard Carburra for 6 dickers of hides
From Edward de la Byr for 10 hides
From Hugh Glade for 11 hides
From Gerard de Vilers for 1 last 13 dickers
From Hervey Balli for 1 last 4 hides. From Stephen le Rous for 18 dickers
From Michael de Talglighi for 5 dickers 8 hides
From Roger de Templo for 2 dickers 5 hides
From *Bonachius* de Lark' for 4 sacks of wool and 3 dickers of hides
From Robert de Sancto Gennasio for 5 dickers
From Stephen Perci for 6 dickers
From Walter de Rupe, 1 dicker 9 hides
From Richard de Caburra for 2 dickers 5 hides
Sum of hides, 6 lasts 1 dicker 8 hides
Sum of money [*argenti*] £4 14¼d
Sum of wool, 4 sacks. Sum of money, 26s 8d. Sum total, 107s 10¼d.

The same renders account from Easter in the 18th year [2 April 1290] to Easter in the 19th year [22 April 1291], namely:
From Gerard de Vilers, 3 lasts 11 dickers
From William Bron for 6 hides
From John Popa, 1 dicker.
From Michael Cissore for 1 last 5 hides
From Richard Richeman for 9 dickers
From Roger le Trentrut for 5 dickers 2 hides
From Geoffrey de Monet for 5 dickers 5 hides
From Peter de Lesgre for 1 last 1 dicker 5 hides
From John Malamper, 12 dickers 4 hides
From John Colling, 7 dickers
From Godfrey de Aqua for 2 dickers 6 hides

From Gerard de Vilers for 1 lst 3 dickers
From Richard Rede for 3 dickers
Sum of hides, 9 lasts 3 dickers 3 hides. Sum of money, £6 2s 2¼d.
{These two preceding years are entered at the end of the account for the 21st year.}[2]

The same renders account from Easter in the 19th year [22 April 1291] to Easter in the 20th year [6 April 1292], namely:
From Gerard de le Villers for 16 dickers 7 hides
From Gregory le Soper for 5 dickers 3 hides
From Roger de Templo for 1 last for 8 dickers
From Walter de la Byr for 3 dickers
From Michael de Talglighy for 4 dickers 7 hides
From David de Treuereu for 1 last.
From Richard de Sancta Margareta for 3 lasts 19 dickers 9 hides
From John de Arbore for 14 dickers
Sum of hides, 8 lasts 11 dickers and 6 hides. Sum of money, 114s 3¾d.
{Entered in the account of that year.}[3]

The same renders account from Easter in the 20th year [6 April 1292] to Easter in the 21st year [129 March 1293], namely:
From John Pref and his fellows for 15 dickers 1 hide
From Robert de Sancto Ginnasio and his fellows for 6 lasts 3 dickers 5 hides
From Michael de Trofeu and his fellows for 2 lasts 2 dickers 3 hides
From Michael de Talglighy for 6 dickers
From Roger de Templo for 7 dickers
From John Ingelot for 1 dicker
Sum of hides, 9 lasts 15 dickers. Sum of money, £6 10s.
{Entered in the account of that year.}[4]
Sum of sum of moneys [*denar'*], £23 5¼d.

De f' Dunwich Winchelsea Exeter[5]

[2.] A line is drawn from this phrase and up and around the right-hand margin, encompassing the above two paragraphs.
[3.] A line is drawn from this phrase up and around the right-hand margin to encompass this paragraph.
[4.] A line is drawn from this phrase up and around the right-hand margin to encompass this paragraph.
[5.] Scribbled at the bottom right-hand corner of the parchment

1308–1317

PRO, E122/39/5

2–11 Edward II. 1 membrane. Account of John Coulying and Richard le Taillur of Bodmin for receipts of cocket in Cornwall, from 29 September 1308 to 26 July 1317. Repaired and much faded, with holes in some places.

ACCOUNT OF JOHN COULYNG AND RICHARD LE TAILLUR OF BODMIN, RECENTLY DECEASED, FOR RECEIPT OF MONEYS FROM COCKET OF THE KING IN CORNWALL, RECEIVED BY THEM IN EQUAL PORTIONS FROM MICHAELMAS IN THE 2ND REGNAL YEAR OF KING EDWARD SON OF KING EDWARD UNTIL 26 JULY IN THE 11TH YEAR OF THE SAME KING

[1308–09]

From Thomas Clerk for 3 dickers of hides	Sum of money, 2s
From John Ingelot for 4 dickers of hides	Sum of money, 2s 8d
From William Carbura for [8 hides]	Sum of money, 7½d
From Walter Churlebrok for [1 dicker 5 hides]	Sum of money, 12d
From Richard de Eglosmerher for 7 hides	Sum of money, 5d ...
From John Petit of Truro for 3 dickers of hides	Sum of money, 2s
From William Borani of Helston for 2 dickers of hides	Sum of money, 16d
From Robert le Potter of Looe for 2 dickers	Sum of money, 16d
Sum of hides, [ ] lasts 7 dickers and 1 hide, 17 dickers 1 hide	Sum of money, 11s 5¼d
From issues of the seal that is called cocket, 16d.	

[1309–10]

From Adam Scarlet for 4 dickers of hides	Sum of money, 2s 8d
From Henry Bayly of Truro for 3 dickers of hides	Sum of money, 2s
From *Amedas* de Bodmina for 4 dickers of hides	Sum of money, 2s 8d
From Gervase le Bray and Robert Tolon for 6 dickers of hides	Sum of money, 4s
From William Medewyn for 2 dickers of hides	Sum of money, 16d

From Philip de Karleghayn for 3 dickers
of hides   Sum of money, 2s

From William Wylder for 3 dickers of
hides   Sum of money, 2s

From Robert le Potter of Looe for 4
dickers of hides   Sum of money, 2s 8d

From John Picard of Truro for 3 dickers
and 4 hides   Sum of money, 2s 3¼d

Sum of hides, 3 lasts and 2 dickers (1 last
12 dickers) and 4 hides

Sum of money,. ....

From issues of the seal that is called cocket, 18d.

ACCOUNT OF THE SAME FOR COCKET IN THE AFORESAID COUNTY IN THE 4TH
REGNAL YEAR OF KING EDWARD SON OF KING EDWARD [1310–11]

From Stephen de Trewent for 8 dickers
and 1 hide   Sum of money, 5s 5d

From John Ingelot for 3 dickers   Sum of money, [ ]

From William Fraunceys for 2 dickers   Sum of money, 16d

From William de Pengersek for 3 dickers   Sum of money, 2s

From William Refet of Helston for 3
dickers and 1 hide   Sum of money, 2s 1d

From John Tuc of Lostwithiel for 6
dickers   Sum of money, 4s

From Osbert Ospy for 4 dickers of hides   Sum of money, 2s 8d

From Stephen Treglethy for 6 dickers
of hides   Sum of money, 4s

Sum of hides, 3 last 15 dickers 2 hides

Sum of money, 23s 6d

From issues of the seal that is called cocket, 16d.

ACCOUNT OF THE SAME FOR COCKET IN THE AFORESAID COUNTY IN THE 5TH
REGNAL YEAR OF KING EDWARD SON OF KING EDWARD [1311–12]

From Walter Tlyn for 3 dickers of hides   Sum of money, 2s

From John Cristian for 1 dicker 4 hides   Sum of money, 11d

From Walter Pentek for 2 dickers 3 hides   Sum of money, 18½d

From John de la Pole for 2 dickers of hides   Sum of money, 16d

From Robert Berson for 5 dickers 4 hides   Sum of money, 3s 7¼d

From Richard Carburra for 5 dickers 4
    hides   Sum of money, 3s 7¼d
Sum of hides, 19 dickers 5 hides
Sum of money, 13s
~~From issues of the seal that is called cocket, 12d.~~

ACCOUNT OF THE SAME FOR COCKET IN THE AFORESAID COUNTY IN THE 6TH
REGNAL YEAR OF KING EDWARD SON OF KING EDWARD [1312–13]

From Robert le Dycher for 2 dickers of
    hides   Sum of money, 16d
From John Ponna of Truro for 3 dickers of
    hides   Sum of money, 2s
From John Antret of Bodmin for 4 dickers
    of hides   Sum of money, 2s 8d
From Walter Maynhyr of Tregony for 6
    dickers of hides   Sum of money, 4s
From Richard de Carburra for 3 dickers
    and 5 hides   Sum of money, 2s 4d
From Robert Capon *de la Bore*[6] for 6
    dickers of hides   Sum of money, 4s
From John Martyn for 5 dickers of hides   Sum of money, 3s 4d
From William de Tregudyn and William
    Burdoun for 6 dickers   Sum of money, 4s
Sum of hides, 1 last 15 dickers 5 hides
Sum of money, 23s 8d
~~From issues of the seal that is called cocket, 16d.~~

ACCOUNT OF THE SAME FOR COCKET IN THE AFORESAID COUNTY IN THE 7TH
REGNAL YEAR OF KING EDWARD SON OF KING EDWARD [1313–14]

From Robert Parys for 3 dickers of hides   Sum of money, 2s
From Nicholas Lovputa for 5 dickers of
    hides   Sum of money, 3s 8d
From Roger Founteyn for 2 dickers of
    hides   Sum of money, 16d
From Adam Vaym [Haym?] for 1 dicker
    of hides   Sum of money, 8d

[6.] Oliver Padel suggests (pers. communication) that this may refer to present-day
Bore Street in Bodmin.

From Walter Maynon for 2 dickers of
hides   Sum of money, 16d

From John Candy for 5 dickers of hides   Sum of money, 3s 4d

From William Pengersyek for 4 dickers of
hides   Sum of money, 2s 8d

From James de Tregemynion for 6 dickers
of hides   Sum of money, 2s 8d

From John Pychard for 3 dickers of hides   Sum of money, 2s

From Bernard Cosyn for 4 dickers of hides   Sum of money, 2s

From Oliver Breton for 5 dickers of hides   Sum of money, 3s 5d

From Michael de Coysgaran for 3 dickers
of hides   Sum of money, 2s

Sum of hides, 2 lasts 3 dickers 1 hide

Sum of money, 28s 9d

~~From issues of the seal that is called cocket, 2s.~~

(m. 1d)

ACCOUNT OF THE SAME FOR COCKET IN THE AFORESAID COUNTY IN THE 8TH
REGNAL YEAR OF KING EDWARD SON OF KING EDWARD [1314–15]

From John Sumond of Liskeard for 1
dicker of hides   Sum of money, 8d

From John Candy for 2 dickers of hides   Sum of money, 16d

From William Cary for 3 dickers of hides   Sum of money, 2s

From William Maynhyr for 1 dicker of
hides   Sum of money, 8d

From John Margh' and Stephen le Gros
for 2 dickers of hides   Sum of money, 16d

From Robert Cronan for 1 dicker of hides   Sum of money, 8d

From Godfrey le Mercher for 1 dicker
and 2 hides   Sum of money, 9¾d

From Nicholas Antret? for 2 dickers of
hides   Sum of money, 16d

From John Tut of Lostwithiel for 1 dicker
5 hides   Sum of money, 12d

From John Ingelot for 2 dickers of hides   Sum of money, 16d

From Henry de Lym of Looe for 1 dicker
of hides   Sum of money, 8d

From Roger de Penceyd for 2 dickers of
hides   Sum of money, 16d

Sum of hides, 18 dickers 7 hides

Sum of money, 13s 1¾d

~~From issues of the seal that is called cocket, 2s.~~

ACCOUNT OF THE SAME FOR COCKET IN THE AFORESAID COUNTY IN THE 9TH
REGNAL YEAR OF KING EDWARD SON OF KING EDWARD [1315–16]

From Richard Carburra for 3 dickers of hides	Sum of money, 2s
From William Fraunceys for 2 dickers of hides	Sum of money, 16d
From William Pengersyek for 5 dickers of hides	Sum of money, 3s 4d
From William Bordon for 3 dickers of hides	Sum of money, 2s
From William Caruballa for 2 dickers of hides	Sum of money, 16d
From Roger Lowys for 4 dickers of hides	Sum of money, 2s 8d
From Bernard Petit for 5 dickers of hides	Sum of money, 3s 4d
From John Herungard for 4 dickers of hides	Sum of money, 2s 8d
From Thomas Petit of Truro for 5 dickers of hides	Sum of money, 3s 4d

Sum of hides, 3 lasts and 3 dickers

Sum of money, 22s

~~From issues of the seal that is called cocket, 18d.~~

ACCOUNT OF THE SAME FOR COCKET IN THE AFORESAID COUNTY IN THE 10TH
REGNAL YEAR OF KING EDWARD SON OF KING EDWARD [1316–17]

From Hugh de Launeueton for 6 dickers of hides	Sum of money, 4s
From Hugh le Rede for 5 dickers of hides	Sum of money, 3s 4d
From John Antret for 4 dickers of hides	Sum of money, 2s 8d
From Richard Scotbrigg for 5 dickers 2 hides	Sum of money, 3s 5¾d

Sum of hides, 1 last 2 hides

Sum of money, 13s 5¾d

~~From issues of the seal that is called cocket, 8d.~~

ACCOUNT OF THE SAME FOR COCKET IN THE AFORESAID COUNTY FROM
MICHAELMAS IN THE 11TH REGNAL YEAR OF KING EDWARD SON OF KING EDWARD
TO 26 JULY FOLLOWING. [1317–18]

From Robert Ingellot for 3 dickers of hides Sum of money, 2s

From William Carburra for 4 dickers of hides Sum of money, 2s 8d

From Robert Coulyngh for 2 dickers of hides Sum of money, 16d

From Stephen Parti for 2 dickers of hides Sum of money, 16d

From John Ingellot for 1 dicker of hides Sum of money, 8d

From John Tuc of Lostwithiel for 3 dickers of hides Sum of money, 2s

Sum of hides, 15 dickers

Sum of money, 10s

~~From issues of the seal that is called cocket, 12d.~~

1322–24

PRO, E122/39/6

16–18 Edward II. 1 membrane. Account of William de Milleburn and Richard de [Holland] of wine customs and new custom in Cornwall from 20 July 1322 to 26 July 1324. Torn, very worn, and repaired.

ACCOUNT OF WILLIAM DE MILLEBURN AND RICHARD DE ... [HOLLAND] COLLECTORS OF CUSTOMS OF WINES IN EACH PORT IN THE COUNTY OF CORNWALL FOR ISSUES OF THE SAME CUSTOM FROM 20 JULY IN THE 16TH REGNAL YEAR OF KING EDWARD SON OF KING EDWARD BY LETTERS PATENT OF THE KING DATED THE SAME 20 JULY ... [TO 26 JULY IN THE 18TH YEAR WHEN] JOHN NAUNTYN OF TRURO AND JOHN COK OF ...[PADSTOW] ... [WERE ASSIGNED TO RECEIVE THE SAME CUSTOMS THERE][7]

FROM 20 JULY IN THE 16TH YEAR TO MICHAELMAS AT THE BEGINNING OF THE 17TH YEAR

PORT OF ... [FOWEY?] [1322–23]

From Raymond Willam of *Cleron?* and from Hugh Keynack for 11 tuns of wine, 24s

From *Jerard* de Idravre? and *Arnald* de Rey for 16 tuns of wine, 32s

From Peter Trurel of Bordeaux and his fellows for 50 tuns of wine, 100s

(approved [*pb'*]. Sum of wines, ... [77] tuns, hence custom, £7 16s

---

[7.] The wine account is very blurred from damp. Items in square brackets have been supplied from the information in the account for new custom, below

FROM MICHAELMAS IN THE 17ᵀᴴ YEAR TO 26 NOVEMBER IN THE 17ᵀᴴ YEAR
PORTS OF FOWEY AND LOSTWITHEL ... [1323]
[nothing][8]

From 26 November in the 17th year the wine noted below was imported:
From Bernard de Bayon for 9 tuns of wine, 18s
From Peter de Burdeaux for 20 tuns of wine, 38s
Sum of tuns, 28 [sic] tuns, hence customs 66s, approved

They do not respond for the same custom in the ports of Falmouth, ...
[Mousehole, Padstow, and Lelant [*Lanaunta*] because there were no
wines landing in these ports during the aforesaid time.

ACCOUNT OF THE AFORESAID WILLIAM (^ DE MILLEBURN) AND RICHARD
(^ HOLLAND) COLLECTORS OF NEW CUSTOM ON WHATEVER GOODS AND
MERCHANDISE IN EACH PORT IN THE COUNTY OF CORNWALL FROM ISSUES OF
CUSTOM FROM 20 JULY IN THE 16ᵀᴴ REGNAL YEAR OF KING EDWARD SON OF
KING EDWARD BY LETTERS PATENT OF THE KING DATED 20 JULY TO 26
NOVEMBER IN THE 18ᵀᴴ YEAR WHEN JOHN NAUNTYAN OF TRURO AND JOHN
COK OF PADSTOW [*YALDESTOWE*] WERE ASSIGNED TO RECEIVE THE SAME CUSTOMS
THERE [1322–24]

NEW CUSTOM
FROM 20 JULY IN THE 16ᵀᴴ YEAR TO MICHAELMAS AT THE BEGINNING OF THE
17ᵀᴴ YEAR [1322–23]

PORT OF FOWEY
From Raymond Willam for 2250 pounds of tin, priced at £10, 3s 9d
From *Arnald* le Roy and Hugh Keynak for tin, cod [*merlus*], cloth, and
    horses [*caball'*] which are estimated at £56, 14s 1d.
    From the same for 1325 pounds of tin, priced at £8 16s 8d, 2s 2½d
From Peter Berueys of Spain for figs and raisins which are estimated at
    60s, 9¼d
From John Bosas of *Alsoson* for salt appraised at £63 10s, 15s 10½d
From Peter Truel for 2100 cod fish [*mᶦmᶦ c pisc' de merlus*], priced at
    £8 8s, 2s 1d
From *Arnald* Pry for garlic and onions priced at £14 ½ mark, 3s 8d
Estimated sum of aforesaid merchandise, £169 15s 4d, hence custom,
    42s 5¼d, proved.

---

8. Since there is space for only one word.

They do not respond for the same customs in the ports of Falmouth, Mousehole [*Mushole*], Padstow and Lelant because no merchandise landed there during the said time.

FROM MICHAELMAS IN THE 17TH YEAR TO 26 NOVEMBER IN THE 18TH YEAR [1323–24]

FOWEY

From William Vilers for (^ fish called) hakes [*hakes*], priced at £100, 25s

From Henry le Faukener for 30 M of tin, priced at £177 16s 8d, 44s 5½d

From John le Veske of *Alevyle* for corn called maslin [*mixtilione*], priced at £40, 10s

From John Noun of Guernsey [*Grenesie*] for salt, priced at £6 17s, 20½d

FALEMOUTH [*FALEMEWE*]

From *Jakes* Mornel of Amiens [*Amyas*] for wheat, priced at £20 5s, 5s 1½d

From the same for tin, priced at £20, 5s

FOWEY

From John Gros of St Valery [*Seint Wallery*] for 20 quarters of maslin [*mixtil*], priced at 10 marks, 20d[9]

From the same for 1700 [pounds] of tin, £10, 2s 6d

FALMOUTH

From John Noun of Guernsey for barley and wheat, priced at £10 5s, 2s 8d

From the same for tin, priced at £11, 2s 9d

From the same for horses [*equis*] and cheese, priced at 100s, 15d

[FOWEY][10]

From Ives de Sancto Paulo for corn, priced at £12, 3s

From the same for tin, priced at 60s, 9d

[9.] Because of the way that the port names are written in the margin, it is possible that this entry belongs to Falmouth.

[10.] Although these entries are not explicitly associated with a port, the arrangement of the marginal headings suggests they belong to the port of Fowey.

From Nicholas Adyn for corn, priced at £6, 18d
From Robert Ageneys for garlic and onions, priced at 40s, 6d

FALMOUTH
From Nicholas Adyn for corn, priced at £10, 2s 6d

Sum (^ of the value) of the aforesaid merchandise: £446 (^ [£440] 17s) (^ hence custom, 110s 8½d, proved.

1323–24

PRO, E122/40/7A

16–17 Edward II. 3 membranes. Account of Thomas Fartheyn and Henry Lovecok, collectors of new custom and increments on the imports and exports of aliens in Exeter and the ports of Devon, from 3 February 1323 to 30 April 1324. The part of this account containing ancient custom is printed in Gras, *English Customs*, pp. 250–54. A similar account for new custom is also printed there (pp. 394–8) for the period beginning April 1324, but it does not include the entries for Plymouth.

m. 3

ACCOUNT OF THOMAS FARTHEYN AND HENRY LOVECOK, COLLECTORS OF NEW CUSTOM IN EXETER AND THE DEVON PORTS ON GOODS THAT STRANGERS AND ALIENS EXPORT OR IMPORT, NAMELY AN INCREMENT OF 40D PER SACK OF WOOL BEYOND ANCIENT CUSTOM, AN INCREMENT OF ½ MARK PER LAST OF HIDES, AN INCREMENT OF 40D FOR EVERY 300 WOOL-FELLS BEYOND ANCIENT CUSTOM, AND 2S FROM EVERY SCARLET AND CLOTH DYED IN GRAIN, 18D FROM EACH CLOTH PARTLY DYED IN GRAIN, 12D FROM FROM EACH CLOTH WITHOUT GRAIN, 12D FROM EACH QUINTAL OF WAX, 3D ON EACH £ OF AVOIRDUPOIDS AND ALL OTHER MERCERIES IMPORTED OR EXPORTED BY THEM FROM THE 3RD OF FEBRUARY IN THE 16TH YEAR OF KING EDWARD [II] TO THE 30TH OF APRIL IN THE 17TH YEAR OF THE SAME KING

[... Imports at Exeter, exports from Exeter, imports at Dartmouth, and imports at Teignmouth are listed first]

PLYMOUTH. GOODS IMPORTED:
Astoricus de Cergynhole, alien, imported on 9 December tin and dried fish to the value of £50.

William Burnard of Outre Mer, alien, imported on the same day dried
 fish to the value of £20.
Peter Borry, alien, imported on the same day cloth and dried fish to the
 value of £12.

The sum value of the goods of aliens is £82 on which the custom is 20s
6d.
[...]

Appendices

Other Surveys of the Maritime Revenues of the Earldom and Duchy of Cornwall

Information about Cornish maritime revenues and their management by the earldom and duchy of Cornwall is available in several sources besides the havener's and ministers' accounts for this estate. Three sources in particular stand out. The first is the Assession Rolls, which record the leases made by conventionary tenants at the courts of assession held every seven years from the early fourteenth century on.[1] Conventionary tenure, which encompassed the largest group of tenants on the Cornish manors of the duchy, was a leasehold tenure in which the duchy as landlord agreed to demise a particular holding in exchange for an annual rent and specified services, as well as an assession fine, which reflected changes in demand. Most leases ran for seven years, from Michaelmas to Michaelmas, hence the need to re-negotiate them a few months before the seven years was up. The system was originally imposed around 1333 as a way to increase revenues by taking advantage of the demand for land at the time. The Assession Rolls completely ignore the chief maritime revenues, such as those arising from the port farms, wreck, prisage, and the maritime courts, probably because they were always retained in the hands of the lord, a policy that directly fostered the practice of keeping separate havener's accounts. But maritime profits associated with particular manors, such as Sutton Pool (the port of Plymouth) and Saltash ferry, both pertaining to the honour of Trematon, or individual fisheries or rights to trantery at coastal

---

[1.] For a full discussion of assessions and conventionary tenure, see John Hatcher, *Rural Economy and Society in the Duchy of Cornwall 1300–1500* (Cambridge, 1970), esp. pp. 52–8, 71–9.

manors, could appear in the Assession Rolls.[2] The Assession Rolls are also valuable for the details they add on who leased the maritime properties and on the changing market value of the properties. Details regarding maritime revenues from the Assession Rolls of 1333, 1347, and 1356 are summarized below. Besides the usual entries on the maritime properties in Trematon and Lostwithiel, the transcriptions also include selected details on the Calstock weirs and fisheries in other duchy manors.

The second source is the Caption of Seisin, a survey ordered by the ducal chancery within two months of the formation of the Duchy of Cornwall in 1337.[3] Completed during May 1337 by James de Wodestoke, steward of the lands of the duke, and William de Monden, clerk of Prince Edward and past clerk and secretary of John de Eltham, the last earl of Cornwall, the estate portions of the Caption were modelled after the Assession of 1333.[4] Since the Assession Rolls did not contain a section covering the ports, however, the Caption's format seem to have followed that found in the early havener's accounts. The Caption is available in a fine edition by P. L. Hull, but since the passages relating to maritime matters are scattered throughout his edition, and since Hull provides only a cursory discussion of these revenues and on occasion offers flawed translations of several relevant passages, it was considered useful to provide summaries of these sections here for purposes of comparison with the material in the havener's accounts and other records.

The third source is another extent of the duchy's estates taken in 1345 by William de Cusancia and Hugh de Berwyk. The reason for a new survey only eight years after the Caption is unclear, but it did provide revised estimates of the value of several properties that future reeves had to compare their revenues with and explain any discrepancies. This survey has not been published, probably because only later fragments of copies and transcriptions survive. The copy closest in date to the original extent survives in several fragments written in a sixteenth-century hand. The largest part of this sixteenth-century copy,

---

[2.] The Assession Rolls are in the PRO, generally under SC6, and in the Duchy of Cornwall Office, where Ministers' Accounts Rolls 471–486 cover the period from 7 Edward III to 23 Henry VII. There is also an early contemporary copy of the Assession of 1340, for a few manors only, in PRO, SC11/153.

[3.] PRO, E120/1. A full edition and commentary is in P. L. Hull, ed., *The Caption of Seisin of the Duchy of Cornwall (1337)* (Devon and Cornwall Record Society, n.s., v. 17, 1971).

[4.] Hull, "Introduction," *Caption*, p. x.

which also contains the section on the revenues of the sea ports, is bound with several late eighteenth-century copies of the entire extent and deposited in the Duchy of Cornwall Office.[5]

The DCO fragment starts in the middle of the section on Helstone-in-Trigg, and is followed by entries for Penmayne; Camelford borough; Tintagel; Launceston manor, borough, castle and honour; coinage and stannaries; the sea ports; advowsons; and wages and fees of ministers. Another fragment of this same sixteenth-century copy may be found in the Public Record Office, bound up in a volume with several intro-ductory pages in a nineteenth-century hand.[6] It contains the sections on Tybesta, Grampound borough, Talskiddy, Moresk, Helston-in-Kerrier, and Tywarnhaile. The binding, size of the paper folios, style of arrangement, and handwriting are all identical to the copy in the Duchy of Cornwall Office. A third fragment of this sixteenth-century copy is deposited in the Cornwall Record Office, but it contains only part of the extent of Trematon.[7] The section containing the beginning of the extent, along with the manors of Calstock, the rest of Trematon (including the castle and honour, as well as the boroughs of Trematon and Saltash), Rillaton, Climsland, Liskeard, Restormel, Penlyne, Penkneth, and Tewington is missing.[8] The section on sea ports that is

---

5. There is no press mark, but the volume is entitled *An Abridgement of the Extent Taken by Cusancia and Berwick 1345 and Fragment of the Extent*. The title pages also notes that the copy was made by Robert Gray in 1793 and that "the fragment was found by Richard Gray amongst rubbish of decayed and condemned records in a dark garret over the Exchequer chamber in the year 1790". The heading on the first transcript of the whole extent is "Extent of the manor of lord Edward, illustrious king of England and France, made before William de Cusancia and Hugh de Berwyke assigned by a new commission to survey all lands and tenements of the said lord prince etc.., in the month of March, in the 19th regnal year of King Edward III after the conquest." This copy is followed by two additional transcripts in a much later hand, and then by the 16th-century copy on which the translation below is based.

6. PRO, LR2/247. The volume is titled *Surveys of Helleston, Moresk, Tybest, Tywarnil*. The first page, on modern paper, lists the contents of the volume and notes "Though there are no dates to the surveys they are from the character of the writing evidently of the reign of Henry the Eighth. They were repaired and bound anno 1837. T. T. Tearnside".

7. CRO, ME 1676. This group also contains a stray folio listing free tenants, a copy of two folios recording free tenants in Devon, a much later transcript that also covers free tenants and some conventionary tenants. Unfortunately, the section on Trematon is incomplete and contains nothing on Sutton Pool in Plymouth.

8. The missing sections can be found in a 17th-century copy in CUL, MS Dd. ix–36, ff. 1-79.

in the earliest surviving copy of the extent, from the early sixteenth century, is here transcribed in full because of the details it provides about the port revenues, as well as for its comparative value.

The Assession Rolls of 1333, 1347, and 1356

The following provides an abbreviated transcription of the references to maritime revenues in the Assession Rolls. The major headings under which the sub-headings fall are underlined.

1. Assession Roll of 1333

DCO Ministers' Account Roll 471

7 Edward III. 14 membranes. Assession Roll of the duchy of Cornwall.

TINTAGEL
[There is no mention of the customs on boats that normally appear in the manor's accounts.] (m. 3)

TYBESTA
William de Milborn, parson of the church of Creed [*Sanct' Crede*] took the fishery of the manor of Tybesta that Thomas de Trevell held up to now in conventionary tenure, from next Michaelmas to the end of 7 years, for 6d per year and a fine of 6s 8d. (m. 5)

TEWINGTON
The fishery that was surveyed [*extendit*] at 4s per year was not leased because no profit can be found there nor could trantery be leased. (m. 6)

CALSTOCK
FISHERY AND WEIR. {The abbot of Tavistock took the tenement from Michaelmas in the 13th year [1339] to the same feast next and from that feast to the end of 7 years for £10 per year, as in a certain memoranda.}[9] There is nothing new here from the weir with the fishery

---

[9.] This note starts in the margin and runs over as a superscript above the beginning of the main text, which follows.

in Tamar Water pertaining to this manor because Sir William de Reseyvene, rector of Calstock church, and three of his fellows, held it from Michaelmas next for the following five years for 20 marks per year, payable at the terms of Easter and Michaelmas equally; except it is complained that the fishery of the pool of the manor belongs to the demesne and the said farmer does not want it removed. (m. 12)

PASSAGE. William att Hacch, bondman, took the passage of Tamar Water next to the weir of Calstock (with one boat attached to it) to hold in conventionary tenure for the time of the said farm, for 4s 6d per year and a new increment of 4d and a fine of 12s. (m. 12d)

TREMATON

SUTTON WATER. Thomas de Spekenton [who also leased two grain mills] took the Water and Pool of Sutton with all the customs belonging to the said Water or pertaining to the honour of the castle of Trematon except for all chattels forfeited in any way at the suit of the lord, wreck of sea, prisage of wine, and chattels of felons, etc.. To hold in conventionary tenure for the said time for £17 10s per year at Easter and Michaelmas terms, with an increment of 30s. And he gave to the lord a fine of 110s. And he did fealty, etc., by the pledges noted above (^ for the mills). And by the aforesaid bond prepared since then in the possession of the steward, remains for the aforesaid reason [*Et per predictum script' obligator' inde confect' penes sen' rem' causa predicta*]. (m. 13d)

SALTASH BOROUGH: John Dirwyn, Matthew de Donestaple, and William Michell, burgesses of Saltash, took the rents of assize, fairs, markets, rents with pleas and perquisites of the court, the assize of bread and ale, Saltash passage with the rent belonging to the common passage with the barge and 4 oars for the passage, customs of the barges and seines in Tamar Water with all things belonging to the said borough except for fines from arrests or things that ought to be pleaded in the court of Trematon before the steward of the lord, and any escheats that may occur; to hold in conventionary tenure for £18 per year at Easter and Michaelmas terms, with a new increment of 5s 9½d, and a fine of 40s.[10] Pledges, William atte Hamme, Reginald Batecok of *Erich*, John atte Torre. (m. 13d)

[10.] This passage is almost identical to that in the *Caption*, pp. 118–19.

2. Assession Roll of 1347

DCO Ministers' Account Roll 472

21 Edward III. 18 membranes. Assession roll of the duchy of Cornwall.

CALSTOCK
[FISHERY]
John de Montvyroun took the fishery of Calstock weir which is called *hacches*, to hold in conventionary tenure, with works pertaining to the weir extending to 12 7d per year, for £10 per year and no fine. (m. 5)

TAMAR PASSAGE. William atte Hacche took the passage of Tamar Water next to the Calstock weir, for 4s 6d per year and a 12s fine. (m. 5d)

TREMATON
LYNHER WATER. Richard Juyl, Nicholas Priour, and Auger Walter, bondman [*nati'*],[11] took it for 5s per year and a fine of 12d. (m. 7)

SALTASH BOROUGH. Roger Burgh', John Halgane, John Geffray, William Michel, Geoffrey atte Doune, Robert Torry, Thomas Bakere, Richard de Wadesworth and (Walter Payn) take the borough of Saltash (64s 2½d), with fair tolls (value estimated at 5s), market toll with petty custom and toll on oysters (8s), rents of the *censar'* (10s), pleas and assizes of bread and ale and fines (40s), custom on barges and seines (16s) for 7 years for £8s per year and a fine of 6s 8d. (m. 7)

SALTASH PASSAGE. William Pode takes the passage of Saltash Water with rent of oars and barges and 4 oars for passage, for £10 per year and a fine of 40s. Pledges are Ralph Burell and Geoffrey atte Doune. (m. 7)

SUTTON WATER. Richard de Brounmore takes Sutton Water for £10 per year and no fine. Pledges, Maurice Sprigga and Edmund de Northcote. (m. 7d)

---

11. It is unclear whether all the men or just Walter were bondmen. In 1357, Thomas, Richard and Joan Walter of the prince's manor of Helston-in-Kerrier, and Richard Juyl of Trematon and others, petitioned for an inquisition to defend themselves against accusations they were not free, but bondmen. Both the Walters and Juyl were found to be free men. See *BPR*, II, pp. 119–20, 139–40.

T<small>YBESTA</small>
F<small>REE CONVENTIONARIES</small>. Henry Trenellek took Fal Water [*aquam de Fala*] that William de Meldeburn recently rector of the church of Creed held and which remained in the hand of the lord at the last assize, for 6d per year and a fine of 3d. (m. 12)

3. The Assession Roll of 1356

DCO Ministers' Account Roll 472a

30 Edward III. 22 membranes. Assession roll of the duchy of Cornwall. There is a duplicate in PRO, E306/2/1, but it is badly defaced by gall.

C<small>ALSTOCK</small>
[W<small>EIRS</small>]
The abbot and convent of Tavistock take *Golyaworekihacche* weir in the upper part and *Toklyngstorr'* etc [there follows a long section with the names of different weirs and orders for keeping them in good repair] for £10 per year; they can distrain for the sum in their manor of Hurdwick. (m. 6)

T<small>AMAR</small> P<small>ASSAGE</small>
The passage of Tamar Water next to Calstock weir that William atte Hacche took, etc., for the rent of 4s 6d per year, etc.. And 12s fine for the seven years. (m. 6d)

T<small>REMATON</small>
S<small>UTTON</small> W<small>ATER</small>. Leased for the term of life. John Dabernon holds Sutton Water for his whole life as appears in the foot of the account of the reeve of Trematon for the 29th year [1355/6], rendering £6 13s 4d per year at the said terms and leased to the same John by letters patent of the lord prince dated 5 February 1350 and enrolled at the foot of the account of the reeve of Trematon in the 24th year [1350/1]. Before the pestilence it was accustomed to pay £10 per year. (m. 8)

S<small>ALTASH</small> P<small>ASSAGE</small>. John Halgane, Richard Juyl, and John Beneyt took the passage of Saltash Water with rent of oars and 2 water mills, rents of the *censar'* of the borough of Trematon, pleas and perquisites, etc, to hold in conventionary tenure, etc., rendering £14 13s 4d per year at the said terms.

Lʏɴʜᴇʀ Wᴀᴛᴇʀ. The water there that Richard Juyl, Nicholas Priour, and Auger Walter took for the rent of 5s per year and a fine of 12d for seven years is now in the hand of the lord for lack of tenants. (m. 8)

Tᴇᴡɪɴɢᴛᴏɴ
Fʀᴇᴇ ᴄᴏɴᴠᴇɴᴛɪᴏɴᴀʀɪᴇꜱ
Fɪꜱʜᴇʀʏ ᴀɴᴅ Tʀᴀɴᴛᴇʀʏ. Roger de Castelgothou Pasc' of the same and Richard de Porton together took the fishery there which is accustomed to rent for 7s per year and trantery pertaining to the manor of Tewington which was accustomed to be leased for 4s per year, rendering 10s per year at the said terms by pledge of each other. Fine, no increment, rendering [*r'*] 5s.[12] (m. 15)

The Caption of Seisin of 1337

Because the Caption is available in a fine edition by P. L. Hull, only a summary of the revenues in the sections on the Ports, and those on Trematon and Lostwithiel dealing with maritime revenues, are included here. All page citations are to Hull's edition of the Caption. The major headings under which the sub-headings fall are underlined.

Cᴀꜱᴛʟᴇ, Mᴀɴᴏʀ, ᴀɴᴅ Bᴏʀᴏᴜɢʜ ᴏꜰ Tʏɴᴛᴀɢᴇʟ
Each boat in the port of Bossinney [*Boscyni*] renders 2s per year. And this is usually worth ½ mark per year. (p. 32)

Vɪʟʟ ᴏꜰ Lᴏꜱᴛᴡɪᴛʜɪᴇʟ
Cʟᴀɪᴍ: The burgesses of the borough of Lostwithiel claim to have a mayor and sergeants [*servientes*], custody of Fowey Water as well as the fishery, the pleas and perquisites of the maritime court of the Water, and the court of pie-powder. They also claim to receive by their hands for the use of the lord a custom, called keelage, that is 4d from every vessel mooring in the port of Fowey and being unloaded (and not having a boat), 8d from ships having boats and being within 40 tuns, and 16d from ships carrying 40 tuns or more that unload. And boats and ships give a similar custom if they fully load within the said port. The mayor and commonalty also claim a fief pertaining to the office of the mayor by which all ships below 40 tuns unloading a cargo of salt or corn

---

12. This last sentence is written in the left-hand margin.

within the port owe one bushel of corn or salt; ships over 40 tuns unloading such cargoes owe 2 bushels of corn or salt. They were accustomed to do this as far back as the time of Earl Richard, king of Germany, until the time of Earl John [de Eltham], brother of the current king, when his servants took this fee into his hand. Questioned if they have a special deed from the lord king or his progenitors of premises, they show nothing. Therefore speak with the council. (pp. 39–40)

MANOR OF TREMATON
BOROUGHS OF SALTASH AND TREMATON. There is a passage there worth £10 per year, paid at Easter and Michaelmas terms, for which the lord shall find a boat. There is also a certain custom of 12d per year from every barge carrying sand, worth 8s per year. There is also a certain custom of 12d per year from each seine net of the sea [*sagena maris*] worth 8s per year. [The lease of the passage of Saltash, customs on barges and seines, and other revenues leased by the three burgesses of Saltash in the Caption of Seisin in 1337 (see above) is also noted here.] (p. 118)

BOROUGH OF TREMATON. Among the obligations tenants owe to the lord is an annual toll of 1½d at Michaelmas for oysters. In time of war they are also required to carry two boat-loads [*batellas*] of stone as far as *Clyve* for the fortification of the castle, and then do homage as far as the castle. They are also required to sell 1 gallon of unshelled oysters [*hostrium extra scalam*] to the constable of the castle for 1d, as well as 100 in their shell for ½d. (p. 119)

CASTLE AND MANOR OF TREMATON. FREE TENANTS. John de Ferar' holds a third part of the honour of Trematon from the lord duke for 21 knights' fees. Among his obligations are payment of 22d at Saltash passage and four oars for the boat at Michaelmas, although he and his household and carts are quit of toll when they cross the rest of the year. And John can be the first to drag his net [*trahere recia sua*] and to fish everywhere throughout Tamar Water whenever and as often as he wishes for the year. And his barges and seines [*bargie et sagene*] and those of his bondmen may always cross quietly throughout the said Water without paying custom. John de Alneto holds four knights' fees, crosses the passage at the rate of John de Ferar', and does similar services; his barges and seines may also cross freely. John Lercedekne holds 1 knight's fee, pays 2s rent at Michaelmas at the passage, and has similar services and perquisites as John de Ferar'.

TAMAR WATER. The Water of Tamar with its members is held by the lord duke as of the honour for 1½ fees, which are in the hand of the lord duke. The boundaries begin from the Tamar as far as Penlee Point? [*Penleigh subter Makre*] and from there as far as Sheepstor [*Shiteristorre*] [in Devon] and then as far as Sutton Pool and from there up to Worston [in Yealmpton, Devon] [*Beliston' in Plym'*]. The duke as lord of the castle has regalian rights there, namely wreck of sea, maritime pleas, and prisage of wines, forfeited chattels of felons in the said Pool, and all other regalian rights pertaining to the said castle and honour which cannot be enumerated here. (p. 124)

SUTTON WATER. Thomas de Spekynton holds the Water and Pool of Sutton for £17 per year, with all customs and dues pertaining to the said Water or to the honour of the castle of Trematon, except for all chattels forfeited in any way at the suit of the lord, wreck of sea, prisage of wines, and chattels of felons, etc...[13] Rendering £17 for these yearly for the term aforesaid by equal portions at the feasts of Easter and Michaelmas, by the aforesaid surety. And because Thomas has failed to make payment for a long time, and neither he nor his pledges has the means to pay, Richard de Bakhampton is ordered to take back all the customs and dues of the Water and Pool into the lord duke's hand, and to answer for the revenues. (p. 131)

There is a certain fishery in Lynher Water for which all the conventionaries and bondmen shall pay 5s each year at Michaelmas. (p. 133)

CAPTION OF SEISIN OF THE PORTS OF THE SEA, OF PRISAGE OF WINES AND WRECKS OF SEA IN THE COUNTY OF CORNWALL
PORTS OF THE SEA IN THE COUNTY OF CORNWALL

A certain rent of 40s pertaining to the port of Fowey is to be paid by the hands of various tenants there yearly at Michaelmas. Similar wording is given for the annual rents due at:
Mousehole, 100s at the feast of St James.

---

13. Here Hull appears to have mis-translated *ex^tis* as *exitibus*, when it should be *exceptis*, meaning these latter privileges were excepted from the grant. This seems to be the meaning of similar entries in the Assession Roll of 1333 (above), the accounts for Trematon in the ministers' accounts (above, Part II), and in another part of the Caption relating to Tamar Water (p. 124). The duke clearly never gave up the prisage of wines, as Hull's translation implies.

Land's End [*Londeseynde*], 12s at the feast of St James and Michaelmas.

Portminster [*Portmynster*], 2s.

Newlyn, 10s.

Penzance, 12s.

St Ives, £6 at Michaelmas and the feast of St James.

Porthallow [*Portalou in Kirr'*], 22s.

Port Isaac, Portgaverne, and Portquin in Trigg [*Portusek, Porcaveran et Porthquyn in Trygs'*], 20s at Michaelmas.

Polruan, 20s at Michaelmas.

Marazion, 60s at the feast of St James and Michaelmas.

Let inquiry be made concerning the ports of Sutton, Plymouth, Saltash, St Germans, Truro, Penryn, Merthen, Lelant and Padstow [*Sotton' Plimmouth' Saltassh' Seynt Germeyn Tgruru Peryn Mortaion Lanant et Oldestowe*] [where] there are not any yearly rents pertaining as far as can be ascertained at present. (pp.136–7)

PROFITS OF THE PORTS

There is a certain profit arising from the farm of foreign merchants and fishers which is commonly worth 30s per year.

There is a certain profit arising from the fines of certain tranters [*trauentariorum*] which is commonly worth 6s 8d per year.

PERQUISITES OF THE COURTS OF THE PORTS

The pleas and perquisites of the courts of all the said ports are commonly worth 40s per year. (p. 137)

PRISAGE OF WINES

The yearly value of the prisage of wines is not yet known because ships with wines have not yet moored because of the war between the kings of England and France. But when peace is restored, there should be an inquiry about the annual value of the prisage. (p. 138)

WRECK

The annual value of wreck of the sea cannot be estimated because the profits fall fortuitously by chance, sometimes more, sometimes less... (p. 138)

THE KEEPER [CUSTOS] OF THE PORTS

Thomas fitz Henry, keeper of the said ports, produces a charter from King Edward III, which grants him for life, for good service to John [de Eltham], earl of Cornwall, the king's brother, and in fulfillment of the earl's promise, the bailiwick of keeping the ports of Cornwall, receiving prisage of wines brought to the port of Sutton in Devon, and other ports in Cornwall, and of keeping wreck there. He is to receive 10 marks per year for his fee and a robe worth 1 mark. (pp. 138–9)

PRESENTMENT

The same Thomas presents that the bishop of Exeter has usurped to himself the pleas and perquisites and custom in the port of Falmouth which belong to the lord duke. He also presents that Lord William de Boterell usurps the pleas and perquisites and customs on the port of Lelant which belong to the duke. Therefore this must be discussed in Council. (pp. 139–40)

DEVON

The sum of the value of the Water of Dartmouth is £4 13s 4d.[14] (p. 140)

CONSTABLES

Thomas fitz Henry, keeper of the ports for term of life by charter of the king, takes 10 marks yearly for his fee and for his robe yearly, 13s 4d. (p. 142)

UTENSILS AND OTHER NECESSARIES FOUND IN CERTAIN CASTLES AND MANORS IN CORNWALL

TREMATON: In the castle and manor of Trematon there is one barge worth 20s and four oars worth 4d for the passage at Saltash. (pp. 143–4)

The Extent of 1345

Fragment (38 folios) of a copy of an extent of 19 Edward III, probably made in the sixteenth century and bound up with later copies in the DCO volume (n. 5, above). The other parts of the copy are in PRO, LR 2/247 and Cornwall Record Office, ME 1676. A complete copy made in the seventeenth century is in CUL, Dd. ix–36, ff. 1–79.

[14.] Gall stain obscures the amount, but a transcription of the Caption made *c.* 1800 by G. Vanderzee provides the amount; see Hull, ed., *Caption*, pp. viii, 140, 148.

(f. 22)

<u>Tintagel</u>

Profits of Boats. And each boat of fishers mooring in the port of Tintagel renders per year 2s. And it is usually worth 10s per year.[15]

(f. 34)

<u>Ports of the Sea</u>. The port of Fowey is accustomed to render 40s per year at the feasts of Easter and Michaelmas equally.

The port of Mousehole is accustomed to render 100s per year at the same terms.

The port of Land's End [*Londesende*] port of Porthgwarra [*Porwytheu*] is accustomed to render 12s per year at the same terms.

The ports of Porthminster [*Portmenstr'*] and Lamorna [*Nansmorna*] are accustomed to render 12d per year at the same terms.

The port of Newlyn is accustomed to render 20s per year.

The port of Penzance is accustomed to render 12s per year.

The port of St Ives [*Porthiau*] is accustomed to render £6 per year.

The port of Porthallow in Kerrier [*Portaleu in Kerr'*] is accustomed to render 25s per year.

The ports of Port Isaac, Portgaverne, and Portquin in Trigg [*Portusek, Porteueran et Portequyn in Trygg*] is accustomed to render 20s per year at the same terms.

The port of Polruan is accustomed to render 20s per year.

The port of Marazion is accustomed to render 46s 8d per year.

The port of Sutton

The port of Plymouth

The port of Saltash [*Saltassh*]

The port of St Germans

The port of Truro [*Truru*]

The port of Penryn

The port of Merthen [*Mortayon*]

In these ports there is no other rent or fine arising as far as can be ascertained in any way at the present, etc...

The port of Padstow

The ports of Porthzennor and Portheras [*Porthsenar et Portherest*] are accustomed to render 6s 8d per year at the same terms.

---

15. The CUL copy (f. 5) only notes 'profits of certain boats mooring there'.

Afterwards it is found by the aforesaid jurors that no ships moored at this port [*isto portu*] during the whole time, nor for a long time before, nor are there any tenants who could pay the farm.[16]

The port of 'Porthplement' is accustomed to render 8s per year at the same terms.

Sum total, £20 11s 3d.

(f. 34v)

PRISAGE OF WINES AND WRECK OF SEA

The prisage of wines in the aforesaid ports, namely that the keeper of the ports of the lord there should take 1 tun of wine from each ship landing with wines in the aforesaid ports for custom, paying nothing for it, [or two tuns of wine to be paid for the same assize, that is, 40s for the other tun].[17] And profits of wreck of sea occurring in the aforesaid ports or at every port on the sea coast in parts of Cornwall cannot be certain because they depend on fortune. The value of prisage and wreck, as rendered per year in the four preceding years, is £70.[18]

PLEAS AND PERQUISITES OF COURT THERE

Pleas and perquisites of the court with fines of trantery [*tabernar'*][19] there, foreign merchants and fishermen, are worth 13s 4d per year. Sum, £70 13s 4d.

---

16. This section is barely legible in the original copy, so much of the wording was taken from the 17th-century transcript in CUL, Dd. ix–36, f. 35 and the 18th-century copy in the DCO volume, *An Abridgement*. Note also that *isto porto* probably refers to 'Porthplement'.

17. The phrase in brackets is in the 18th-century transcript, but not in the earlier copy transcribed here.

18. The last two sentences are barely legible, so they are taken from the CUL copy, f. 35.

19. This is probably a mistake by the 16th-century transcriber; the original term was probably *traventar'*.

CUSTOMS FOR MERCHANDISING [*Custuma marcand'*] [20]

There is there a certain custom arising from merchants and their merchandise, namely that each merchant who is denizen [*indigenia*] or alien exporting hides beyond the parts of Cornwall overseas [*ad partes extras*] should pay 8d for each dicker. And each alien merchant exporting tin overseas should pay 12d for each 1000 pounds of tin thus exported. And alien merchants should pay 12d for each 20s worth of merchandise that they export from these parts or import to these parts to sell. And this custom is worth £6 13s 4d per year. And all who merchandize by exporting from these parts to parts overseas should have letters recording the aforesaid custom, sealed with a seal called *le Coket*. Sum, £6 13s 4d.

[20.] Parts of this section are very faded or torn so missing sections were on occasion supplied from the 17th-century transcript except for the heading which appears only in the 18th-century transcript in the DCO volume, *An Abridgement*.

Appendix II

The Haveners and Port Officials
up to 1356

Although Stella Campbell, the chief authority on the haveners of the duchy of Cornwall, identified two grants of the custody of the ports of Cornwall in the early fourteenth-century earldom, she believed that 'the appointment was more that of a water bailiff' than a true havener.[1] The list below, however, indicates that during the earldom there were other men, specifically called 'havener,' who clearly had responsibilities similar to those of the havener under the duchy.[2] They were employed by the lord of Cornwall to manage—in person—the maritime resources of the Cornish ports, whether the lord was the earl of Cornwall, the king when the earldom was in the hands of the crown, or the queen when she held Cornish lands in dower. They levied customs, ensured the lord received the profits due to him from wreck, and administered justice in maritime disputes. They include such thirteenth-century haveners as John Lambrun, Benedict de Moelwre, Elias de Bray, William Waldeshef, and William Talcarn, most of whom had strong Cornish connections. This reliance on local men to supervise the earldom's maritime properties appears to have changed during the early fourteenth century when most of the men appointed as 'havener' or 'keeper of the waters of the ports of Cornwall' had connections to the royal court and served at the king's pleasure. The two appointments that Campbell identified belong to this category. Thomas Algar (valet of the chamber of the king), Thomas Leygrave, Henry de Guldeford (valet of Queen

---

[1] Stella M. Campbell, 'The Haveners of the Mediaeval Dukes of Cornwall and the Organisation of the Duchy Ports', *JRIC*, n.s., IV (1962), p. 113.

[2] Unless noted otherwise, the information in the table below comes from the accounts in Part I, above. For a list of the duchy's haveners and a description of their duties from 1337 to 1483, see Campbell, 'Haveners'.

Isabella), Richard Calwar (king's yeoman, sergeant of the buttery), and William de London (king's sergeant and tailor of Queen Philippa) were among this group, along with Richard de Hewish and Henry de Wylington, sheriffs and stewards of Cornwall who also received custody of the ports for short periods. Some of these men were still termed 'havener' in the extant records, and two—Alan Wolwayn and Wynand Tyrel—may have been Cornish men.

On one hand, this perceived difference between the thirteenth-century and early fourteenth-century haveners may stem in part from the nature of the surviving documentation. We know about the thirteenth-century haveners not from their appointments, but from descriptions of their actual activities as recorded in inquisitions and court rolls. In contrast, the early fourteenth-century haveners come to our attention only through official appointments. These fourteenth-century haveners had the right to collect revenues, but almost certainly committed the actual work of supervision to bailiffs in their employ. We know of one such bailiff, the 'sergeant' who received an annual stipend to collect the farms and issues of the ports in northern Cornwall, from c. 1287 to 1334. There were almost certainly others contracted to do this work, men who were probably similar to the fifteenth-century 'deputies' of the havener whose accounts for their activities and revenues in specific ports occasionally survive.[3] On the other hand, this distinction between the thirteenth- and early fourteenth-century haveners could be real and reflect the earls' and kings' growing recognition of the value of the maritime revenues of Cornwall and their concomitant interest in exploiting these revenues by selling the office of havener to the highest bidder, or by rewarding a loyal servant with the revenues for a brief period.[4] Because of the rapid turnover in both the lords and administrators of these revenues in the early fourteenth century, however, the names of the deputy haveners doing the actual work do not happen to survive. With the creation of the duchy, the man appointed havener, Thomas Fitz Henry, sometimes called Thomas le Havener, both carried out the duties in person, as the thirteenth-century haveners did, and accounted for the maritime revenues, as the early fourteenth-century haveners did.

Another group of officials were the men appointed by the dukes as controllers of prisage, wreck and customs, whose duties consisted of

---

[3.] For example, PRO SC6/819/13, 14; 823/16, 20; PRO E122/180/2, 3; DCO Ministers' Account Roll 36 (1405/6).

[4.] See the Introduction, above, for a more extended argument on this point.

checking the accounts of the havener to ensure he followed orders and proper procedure. Most of these men were professional administrators whose supervision of the haveners' accounts was but one part of their job.[5]

Name and Appellation	Date(s) of Service	Activities
John de Baiocis 'keeper of the coast'	1224	Appointed by king (when Cornwall under his control) to administer all things pertaining to sea-shore of Cornwall and Devon (*CPR 1216–1225*, p. 468). Accompanied sheriff to investigate wreck taken illegally in Cornwall (*Rotuli Litterarum Clausarum*, II, p. 12).
John de Lambrun[6] and Benedict de Moelwre 'havenatores'	In time of Earl Richard (1225–72)	Levied customs for drying fish on shore and also took custom from fish sellers arriving with boats (PRO, JUST1/112, m. 2d). Lambrun took part of profits of wreck (*ibid.*, m. 1).
Elias de Bray,[7] 'recently *hafneator* of Cornwall' & 'havener' & 'havenator'	Before 1275–6	Took herring from wrecks before valued by coroners and disposed of it at his pleasure (*Rotuli Hundredorum*, p. 56; JUST1/112, m. 2d).

---

5. John de Portes was controller in 1347 (*BPR*, I, p. 45). In 1349, William de Baketon, yeoman of the prince's buttery, was appointed controller of prisage, wreck, and cocket by Prince Edward for good service during the prince's pleasure, along with the office of bailiff of Blackmore stannary taking 3d per day for wages. In 1357, he was later granted these offices for life (*BPR*, II, pp. 111, 187). For an account of the controller of the havener in the fifteenth century, see PRO E122/180/31.

6. Perhaps from Lambourne in Perranzabuloe. A John Lambrun owned land in St Winnow in 1271(*CFF*, pp. 129–30). A John Lambrun 'knight' also held rights of the chief lords in Moresk around this time (*CCR 1268–1272*, p. 101). He was also described as a 'knight' (*A Descriptive Catalogue of Ancient Deeds in the Public Record Office* (London, 1906), I, p. 24; *Parliamentary Writs and Writs of Military Summons*, ed. F. Palgrave, 4 vols. (London, 1827–34), I, p. 655. I have been able to find no references to Benedict de Moelwre.

7. Many Brays held land in Fowey, but not an Elias (*CFF*, passim).

Name and Appellation	Date(s) of Service	Activities
William Waldeshef,[8] 'havenator,' 'bailiff of the earl' and 'keeper of the sea-coast'	In time of Earl Edmund (1272–1300)	Collected profits of wreck for Earl Edmund (JUST1/118, mm. 56d, 68). Arrested men accused of killing Breton sailors and took them to Launceston castle (m. 68d). As *custodes maris per costeram* with Thomas de Pridias attempted to arrest a ship at Truro (PRO, E163/2/4).
Name Unknown, 'Serjeant' [*servient*'] or 'bailiff to keep [*custod*'] the sea-shore'[9]	1287–1334	Kept the sea-shore and manors of Tybesta, Moresk, Tewington [all in north Cornwall] 'and other neighbouring manors'. Usually entered as an expense under 'Tybesta', but noted under 'Marine Account' in some years; the account of 1333–34 notes his duties were 'collecting farms and issues of said ports'. In 1307, he was noted as 'one of the bailiffs of the marine warden'.
WilliamTalcarn,[10] 'bailiff of the ports' & 'havenator'	*c.* 1302	Levied new custom from tranters and forestallers seeking fish on shore (JUST1/118, m. 53). Collected profits from wreck (m. 69).
Alan Wolwayn,[11] 'havener'	1308–09	Granted issues of the ports by the king by charter at Michaelmas (above, p. 107).

---

8. Waldeshef farmed the profits of Stratton hundred in 1296/7 and also served as keeper of Restormel castle for the earl for about two months. For these references and his landholdings in Tintagel and Helston in Kerrier, see Midgley, ed., *Ministers' Accounts*, II, pp. 223, 231, 247, 250, 252. William Waldechief was also presented in the eyre of 1302 for selling 3 tuns of wine against the assize in Kirkhampton [in Stratton hundred] (PRO JUST1/118, m. 46). In 1315, John son of William Waldeshef settled his dispute with the prior and convent of Tywardreath, whom he claimed owed him £40 from arrears of an annual rent of 40s; *CCR 1313–1318*, p. 338.

9. He received a stipend and wage of 13s 4d per quarterly term.

10. Possibly from Tolcarne in St Just-in-Roseland. Sometime before 1310, a William de Talcarn was accused, with 31 others, including Thomas de la Hide, who served as steward and sheriff of Cornwall from *c.* 1297–1312 (above, Part I), of illegally plundering a wreck off the Cornish coast (*CPR, 1307–1313*, pp. 255–6).

11. This was probably the same Alan Wolwayn who had received maintenance from the prior and convent of Mount St Michael before 1316, when he was said to be deceased; *CCR 1313–1318*, p. 437.

Name and Appellation	Date(s) of Service	Activities
Thomas Algar,[12] 'havenar' & 'keeper of the waters of the king's ports in Cornwall'	April 1313– Sept. 1314	Received custody of the waters and issues of the ports of Cornwall, appointed at the king's pleasure (*CPR, 1313-1317*, p. 34; *CFR 1307-1319*, p. 167), at the usual rent. Collected ship customs and profits of wreck; also received custom of ships at Lostwithiel (above, p. 113).
Wynand Tyrel jr[13]	Mar. 1315– May 1316	Received custody of the issues of the ports of Cornwall, appointed at the king's pleasure, for as much as custodians of the ports accustomed to render, plus 30s per year (*CFR 1307–19*, pp. 238, 278, and above, p. 114, n. 34).
Richard de Hewish	Sept. 1315– May 1316	Appointed keeper of the lands of Peter de Gaveston in Cornwall; served as sheriff and steward of Cornwall (*CFR 1307–1319*, p. 262). Custody of the ports mentioned only in the order that he deliver the lands, etc... in his keeping to Henry de Wylington (*ibid*, pp. 278–9). His account of the ports (above, p. 114, n. 34) is very summary because they were being farmed to Wynand Tyrel, jr.

[12.] Called 'valet' or 'yeoman' of the chamber of the king. He may have been the same Thomas Algar who in 1305, with his brother John and about 100 others, plundered a ship near Portland, Dorset (*CPR 1301–07*, p. 350). He may have come from Algar in Lincolnshire, where the prior and convent of Spalding illegally acquired lands in mortmain from a Thomas Algar (among others) without licence (*CPR 1317–21*, p. 211).

[13.] In 1302, Wynon, son of Wanan Tyrel was pardoned at the instance of Robert Hastang, for the death of Robert de Treureu and for robberies, etc., in the realm and any consequent outlawry (*CPR 1301–1307*, p. 42). In 1306, Wynan Tyrel and his wife, Sarah, granted rents in Penquite and Roscraddock in St Cleer to Thomas de la Hyde (*CFF*, pp. 226–7), who was steward and sheriff of Cornwall from *c.* 1297–1312 (above, Part I). It may be significant that John Hastang held land in Cornwall around this time (*CFF*, p. 418) and that he was probably the same man who served as steward in the household of Margaret, the second wife of Edward I (*CPR 1301–07*, p. 460). In 1322, a Wynan Tyrel received a safe-conduct for accompanying Thomas Hastang who was going on the king's service with Edmund, earl of Arundel (*CPR 1321–4*, p. 200).

Name and Appellation	Date(s) of Service	Activities
Henry de Wylington	May 1316– July 1317	Received custody of all castles, lands, manors, and the ports of Cornwall, including Trematon with Sutton Water; appointed at the king's pleasure (*CFR 1307–1319*, pp. 278–9, and above, pp. 116, 117). Supervised collection of huge sums from a wreck off Lizard (*Ancient Deeds*, V, p. 49).
Thomas Leygrave[14]	May 1317– March 1324	Received custody of the keeping of the king's seaports in Cornwall, appointed at king's pleasure, for as much as other keepers of the ports accustomed to render (*CFR 1307–1319*, p. 329).
Henry de Guldeford,[15] 'keeper of havens in Cornwall'	March 1324	Appointed by Queen Isabella, who held Cornwall in dower.[16]
Richard Calwar, 'office of havener'	Jan. 9, 1331	Appointed to the bailiwick of the office of havener of the ports of Cornwall, during pleasure. Called 'king's yeoman, sergeant of the buttery' (*CPR 1330–34*, p. 43).
William de London, 'office of havener'	Jan. 16, 1331	Appointed to the bailiwick of the office of havener of the ports of Cornwall, during good behaviour. Called 'king's sergeant and tailor of Queen Philippa,' so possibly nominated by her (*CPR 1330–34*, p. 40). He seems to have farmed the office to John Croth'.
John Croth', 'sub-farmer of the farmer of the ports'	Sep.–Oct. 1331	Collected issues of the ports of Cornwall (above, p. 122). He appears to have farmed the office of havener from William de London.

[14.] No reference to Leygrave survives in the accounts. He may have been related to Alice de Leygrave, the nurse of Edward II, who rewarded her richly with several wardships around this time (*CFR 1307–1319*, pp. 72, 241, 380). He is mentioned in the lone surviving account from the tenure of Queen Isabella; see the account of 1322/3 in Part I, above.

[15.] He was termed 'valet of Queen Isabella'.

[16.] For his letter of appointment, see the account of 1322/3, above, Part I.

Name and Appellation	Date(s) of Service	Activities
Thomas Fitz Henry, 'havener'	Feb. 1337–73	Appointed 'for good service to John, earl of Cornwall, the king's brother, and in fulfillment of the said earl's promise' (*CFR 1337–1347*, p. 4). Accounted for the issues of the ports, including prise of wines in Cornish ports and Plymouth in Devon, and wreck of sea. Received a fee of 10 marks a year plus a robe worth 1 mark (above, Part II). In 1361, granted income from the offices of weigher of tin and keeper of the tinners' gaol at Lostwithiel (*BPR*, II, pp. 186–7). Probably lived at Fowey; also served as a customs collector for the king, and traded in his own right (Campbell, pp. 114–15).

Appendix III

Glossary

Aliens in a medieval context refers to foreigners, those not born in England. Some aliens purchased the right to become 'denizens' and thus avoided paying the higher customs duties owed by foreign merchants.

Ancient custom was authorized in Parliament in 1275 (when it was known as the 'new custom') as a customs duty of 6s 8d on exports of a sack of wool, ½ mark on wool-fells, and 1 mark on a last of hides. It was paid by both foreign and denizen merchants. In these accounts, ancient custom is usually contained in the 'cocket' accounts.

Assize of wine as used in these accounts refers to the second tun of wine owed to the duke as prisage, for which the havener paid 40s.

Barrel-hoops [*circulis*] were bands of metal or wood placed around wooden staves of a barrel or wine tun to make them stronger. They usually cost about ½ d each.

Boat-hire [*batellagium*] was a payment for carrying goods to or from a ship in a small boat. In these accounts, the term always referred to the carriage of tuns of wine. The payment was usually 1d–3d per tun, depending on the distance traveled.

Buret [*borect*] wines may have been wines of a deep red, almost purple color [from OF *buret*]. They must have been cheaper wines since two tuns cost only £6 13s 4d in 1353/4 when one tun of vintage or reek wine cost over £5.

Butlerage was the new custom on wine paid, at the rate of 2s per tun, by alien merchants to the crown per the agreement recorded in the Carta Mercatoria of 1303. Butlerage replaced the prisage previously owed by alien merchants. The earls and dukes' right to collect butlerage in their ports was part of their right to collect prisage.

C refers to a measure of a hundredweight.

Cabrotyns were cured skins to be used for apparel. It probably refers to kid skins (from OF *cabron*), but it may also be related to the type of squirrel skins known as 'calabre' which originally came from Calabria in southern Italy.

Caka herring refers to *kaakherring*, *kaak* being a barrel. This type of herring was packed and cured in barrels at sea and then re-packed in barrels on shore before being shipped out.

Clove [*clawe*] was a measure of wool that usually contained 7 pounds.

Cocket [*cokettus*] in these documents usually refers to the certificate that merchants received acknowledging their payment of national port customs (in these accounts, 'ancient custom') on the wool or hides they were exporting, but it can also refer to the seal on this document, or to the custom paid.

Cretan wine was any (usually sweet) wine from Greece.

Denizens were native-born residents of England; see also **Aliens**, above.

Dicker is a measure containing 10 hides. Twenty dickers equal one last of hides.

Freightage was the payment charged by the ship owner for carrying merchants' goods. It varied according to the amount of the cargo shipped, as well as the distance traveled and risks undertaken.

Keelage [*cullag'*, *killage*] was a toll on boats (literally, a toll on boats with keels) for mooring at a particular port.

Kips were hides of young animals (usually cattle). Two kips were equivalent to one hide of an adult animal.

Last was a measure of capacity for a variety of goods. One last of hides equaled 20 dickers.

Leakage [*lecage, locage, leicage*] refers to the loss of wine because of leaking or evaporation, usually due to holes in the wooden tuns or barrels. The cost of replacing the wine lost was called '**ullage**'.

M refers to a measure of a thousandweight.

Maltot [*maltote*] (which means 'evil tax') was an arbitrary tax normally imposed without sanction from Parliament. In these documents, maltot seems to refer to new custom on the imports and exports of alien merchants and was an *ad valorem* duty charged at the rate of 3d for every £ of value.

New custom [*nova custuma*] was a tax on all imports and exports that was first levied in 1303 on aliens (foreign merchants), who agreed to pay the extra custom in exchange for increased privileges. The custom raised the amounts paid by these merchants to 10s on each sack of wool and 20s per last of hides and also included the first duties on cloth exports and imports; for wine, see **butlerage**, above. New custom was temporarily suspended in 1309–22 because it was imposed without the consent of Parliament, but thereafter it became a permanent duty paid by foreign merchants. In these accounts, the term **maltot** seems to have replaced new custom by 1346.

Prisage was a custom, dating from at least the twelfth century, imposed on ships importing wine into England by which the king had the right to collect one tun of wine before and one tun behind the mast as long as he paid 20s for each tun. In 1302, Gascons were exempted from prisage by agreeing to pay 2s on every tun of wine they imported; the following year this payment was extended to all alien wine importers, a custom known as **butlerage**. Individual lords, such as the earl and duke of Cornwall, could receive the right to collect prisage and butlerage from the king in specific ports. The king or these lords used wine collected from prisage in their own households, or sent them as gifts to allies, or made a profit by selling them at the higher market price.

Quinzaine or quindene, was the 15th day after any feast, the date of the feast being included in the 15 days.

Rebatage [*rebatage*] was a payment for repairing barrels of wine, probably by placing new hoops around them to strengthen the barrel.

Reek or racked wine [*vinis reckis, de rec, recca*] was Gascon wine drawn off the lees (the dregs) in January and February and normally exported to England in the spring. It was more expensive than vintage wine, which was usually shipped to England before Christmas, because it was more mature and clearer.

Rollage [*rollagium*] was a payment for rolling casks of wine from their landing place on shore to the cellar for storage, or from the cellar back to a boat or ship for further transport, normally at the rate of 1–4d, probably depending on the distance rolled. The payment also seems to include the task of laying down [*cuband'*] the tun in the cellar.

Rundlet was a measure of wine equal to 1/14 of a tun, or a bit over 18 gallons.

Sack was the standard weight of wool exports; one sack of wool was reckoned to contain about 364 pounds of wool from an estimated 260 sheep.

Salvage in these records is a customary payment awarded to those who first found a wreck. It was usually half the value of the item(s) found and served to encourage local residents to report wreck to the lord holding the foreshore rights.

Scaff [*caffa*, *calfa*] was a type of small sea-going boat probably used largely in coastal trade.

Sheverbord probably refers to wood boards that had been split since 'shever' [ME] refers to a piece, splinter, or fragment while 'sheiveres' [ME] means 'to break into bits'.

Staple was an officially designated depot, both in England and abroad, where merchants were required to trade their wares, especially wool. The staple system made it easier for the Crown to collect customs revenues and enforce quality, but it also became a diplomatic tool as different foreign ports vied to be designated the official staple for English exports. Ordinances of 1297, 1326, and 1353 set up home staples through which wool exports were supposed to pass, while ordinances in 1313 and 1325 attempted to make exports to specific foreign staples compulsory.

Stone-coal [*stoncol*] was coal dug out of the earth.

Towage [*towagium*] was a payment for towing a boat into or out of the harbour.

Trantery [*tranentria*] was a toll levied on those who came, with a horse or cart, to purchase fish for re-sale elsewhere.

Trone is a type of balance used to weigh heavy goods (particularly wool) for the purpose of assessing port customs.

Tun is a measure of capacity in the form of a cask or barrel used for wine and other liquids. One tun contained 252 gallons, or two pipes, or four hogsheads.

Tun staves are the wooden slats that form the sides of a barrel or cask.

Ullage [*ullagium*] referred to the wine needed to replace the amount (usually measured in gallons) lost through leakage or absorption while the cask of wine was being stored.

Unloading charge [*discarcagium*] was paid for unloading casks of wine from the ship onto a smaller boat to take to shore, normally at the rate of 2d per tun.

Vintage wines were the early wines that arrived in the late fall.

Waif [*weif, wayf*] was the right of the lord to confiscate goods abandoned by thieves or otherwise forfeited.

Windage [*wyndagium*] was a payment for hoisting casks into or out of boats, probably with the aid of a windlass, normally at the rate of 2d per tun. Seems to be the same as 'haulage' [*tractatione*] of tuns from a boat to the shore.

Wool-fells were sheep-skins with the wool still attached. Up to 1368, 300 fells were charged ancient custom at the same rate as one sack of wool; thereafter the rate was 240 fells to one sack of wool.

Index

Surnames, forenames, place names and ship names are alphabetized in their standardized form (usually the modern or most common spelling of the name), although unusual forenames have been left in their original form. Spelling variations of surnames and ship names have been placed in round brackets after the standardized names and cross-referenced if sufficiently different from the standardized form; spelling variations of place names are noted in the text. The parishes of Cornish locations, the counties of other English locations, and regions or countries of places on the continent are given in round brackets. A * designates a person who worked for the central administration of the earldom or duchy (but not local or manorial officials). References to the location of particular wrecks, fisheries, and prisage at individual ports are noted under the place name.

Abbeville (Picardy), ship of, 178
Abbey de Vyre (Picardy?), ship of, 178
Achym, Thomas, 120
admiral, 43 & n., 137
Adyn, Nicholas, 294
Ageneys, Robert, 294
Alard, Stephen, 189
Alas, William, 213
Albon, John, 168
Alevyle (France?), merchant of, 293
Algar (Lincolnshire), 319 n.
Algar (Alger. Algor), John , brother of
    Thomas, 319; *Thomas, 9 & n.,
    111, 112, 113 & n., 114, 315, 319
    & n.
aliens, 136, 173, 294, 323
Alneto, John de, 307
Alsoson (France?), merchant of, 292
Amiens (Picardy), merchant of, 293
Ance (Normandy?), ship of, 73 n., 178

anchor, 260; from wreck, 84, 90, 95,
    210 n.
anchorage, near Bristol, 140 n.
Antret (Antrot), John, 290; John, of
    Bodmin, 288; Nicholas, 289; Roger,
    of Bodmin, 214
Aqua, Godfrey de, 284
Aragon (Spain), skins of, 142, 143
Arbore, John de, 285
armour, 37
Arnandel, Garcy, 240
Arnaund, Raymond, 188
arrows, 16
Arundel, earl of, 264, 319
Arundell (Darundel), 24; Sir John, 25
    n., 173, 232, 245
assession, fine, 296; leases at, 218, 229;
    of 1333, 10 & n.,11, 47 n., 51, 57,
    300, 302, 303 & n., 308 n.; of 1347,
    47 n., 52, 57, 58, 300, 302, 304–5;

DEVON & CORNWALL RECORD SOCIETY PUBLICATIONS

ISSN/ISBN 0 901853

Obtainable from the Administrator, Devon and Cornwall Record Society, 7 The Close, Exeter EX1 1EZ

§ No longer available.   * Restricted availability: please enquire

New Series

1§   *Devon Monastic Lands: Calendar of Particulars for Grants, 1536–1558*, ed. Joyce Youings, 1955   **04 6**

2   *Exeter in the Seventeenth Century: Tax and Rate Assessments, 1602–1699*, ed. W. G. Hoskins, 1957   **05 4**

3§   *The Diocese of Exeter in 1821: Bishop Carey's Replies to Queries before Visitation*, vol. I, Cornwall, ed. Michael Cook, 1958   **06 2**

4*   *The Diocese of Exeter in 1821: Bishop Carey's Replies to Queries before Visitation*, vol. II, Devon, ed. Michael Cook, 1960   **07 0**

5§   *The Cartulary of St Michael's Mount*, ed. P. L. Hull, 1962   **08 9**

6   *The Exeter Assembly: The Minutes of the Assemblies of the United Brethren of Devon and Cornwall, 1691–1717*, as Transcribed by the Reverend Isaac Gilling, ed. Allan Brockett, 1963   **09 7**

7*,10*, 13*, 16*, 18* *The Register of Edmund Lacy, Bishop of Exeter, 1420–1455*. Five volumes, ed. G. R. Dunstan, 1963–1972   **10 0**   **12 7**   **15 1**   **02 X**   **17 8**

8§   *The Cartulary of Canonsleigh Abbey*, calendared & ed. Vera London, 1965   **16 X**

9§   *Benjamin Donn's Map of Devon, 1765*. Introduction by W. L. D. Ravenhill, 1965   **11 9**

11§   *Devon Inventories of the Sixteenth and Seventeenth Centuries*, ed. Margaret Cash, 1966   **13 5**

12   *Plymouth Building Accounts of the Sixteenth and Seventeenth Centuries*, ed. Edwin Welch, 1967 **14 3**

14   *The Devonshire Lay Subsidy of 1332*, ed. Audrey M. Erskine, 1969   **00 3**

15   *Churchwardens' Accounts of Ashburton, 1479–1580*, ed. Alison Hanham, 1970   **01 1**

17§   *The Caption of Seisin of the Duchy of Cornwall (1377)*, ed. P. L. Hull, 1971   **03 8**

19   *A Calendar of Cornish Glebe Terriers, 1673–1735*, ed. Richard Potts, 1974 **19 4**

20   *John Lydford's Book: the Fourteenth Century Formulary of the Archdeacon of Totnes*, ed. Dorothy M. Owen, 1975 (with Historical Manuscripts Commission) **011 440046 6**

21   *A Calendar of Early Chancery Proceedings relating to West Country Shipping, 1388–1493*, ed. Dorothy A. Gardiner, 1976   **20 8**

22   *Tudor Exeter: Tax Assessments 1489–1595*, ed. Margery M. Rowe, 1977   **21 6**

23   *The Devon Cloth Industry in the Eighteenth Century: Sun Fire Office Inventories, 1726–1770*, ed. Stanley D. Chapman, 1978   **22 4**

24, 26   *The Accounts of the Fabric of Exeter Cathedral, 1279–1353*, Parts I & II, ed. Audrey M. Erskine, 1981 & 1983   **24 0**   **26 7**